Dr. Thomaz de Aquino has given us a fine study of the neglected theme of land justice in Luke-Acts, a theme with considerable modern relevance. His work is located carefully within the social settings of the Roman empire, where land injustice was common, and the contemporary world of Israel, drawing particularly on the jubilee laws in Scripture. He goes on to illuminate key passages in Luke-Acts by looking at them through the lens of land justice (or injustice), particularly through observing that God is the ultimate landowner. He identifies numerous places where the Roman and Jewish social settings "color" the reading of key passages, and thus helps us read Luke-Acts in fresh ways. Warmly recommended!

Steve Walton, PhD
Senior Research Fellow in New Testament,
Trinity College, Bristol, UK

While many have explored Lukan wealth ethics, Thomaz de Aquino makes a powerful argument that the land is central to Jesus's vision of discipleship. Given that God is the ultimate owner of the land, Jesus's disciples are called to find creative ways to enact the Old Testament's jubilee legislation. Readers of this work will not only find careful analysis of the Lukan writings but will also be able to situate Jesus's teachings within the historical and social realities of the Roman Empire.

Joshua Jipp, PhD
Director of the Henry Center for Theological Understanding,
Professor of New Testament, Trinity Evangelical Divinity School, Illinois, USA

The Earth is the Lord's

Land Justice in Luke-Acts

João Paulo Thomaz de Aquino

ACADEMIC

© 2025 João Paulo Thomaz de Aquino

Published 2025 by Langham Academic
An imprint of Langham Publishing
www.langhampublishing.org

Langham Publishing and its imprints are a ministry of Langham Partnership

Langham Partnership
PO Box 296, Carlisle, Cumbria, CA3 9WZ, UK
www.langham.org

ISBNs:
978-1-83973-934-7 Print
978-1-78641-128-0 ePub
978-1-78641-129-7 PDF
DOI: https://doi.org/10.69811/9781839739347

João Paulo Thomaz de Aquino has asserted his right under the Copyright, Designs and Patents Act, 1988 to be identified as the Author of this work.

All rights reserved. No part of this publication may be reproduced, stored in a retrieval system or transmitted, in any form or by any means, electronic, mechanical, photocopying, recording or otherwise, without the prior written permission of the publisher or the Copyright Licensing Agency.

Requests to reuse content from Langham Publishing are processed through PLSclear. Please visit www.plsclear.com to complete your request.

Scripture quotations marked (ESV) are taken from The Holy Bible, English Standard Version® (ESV®), copyright © 2001 by Crossway, a publishing ministry of Good News Publishers. Used by permission. All rights reserved.

Scripture quotations marked (NIV) are taken from the Holy Bible, New International Version®, NIV®. Copyright © 1973, 1978, 1984, 2011 by Biblica, Inc.™ Used by permission of Zondervan.

Scripture quotations marked (NRSV) are taken from the New Revised Standard Version Bible, copyright © 1989 National Council of the Churches of Christ in the United States of America. Used by permission. All rights reserved.

Scripture quotations marked (NKJV) are taken from the New King James Version. Copyright © 1982 by Thomas Nelson, Inc. Used by permission. All rights reserved.

British Library Cataloguing-in-Publication Data
A catalogue record for this book is available from the British Library

ISBN: 978-1-83973-934-7

Cover & Book Design: projectluz.com

Langham Partnership actively supports theological dialogue and an author's right to publish but does not necessarily endorse the views and opinions set forth here or in works referenced within this publication, nor can we guarantee technical and grammatical correctness. Langham Partnership does not accept any responsibility or liability to persons or property as a consequence of the reading, use or interpretation of its published content.

My beloved wife and friend, Juliana.
You are the most compelling
earthly argument of God´s
love and care for me.
Thank you for
your love and
support.

Contents

Abstract ix

Acknowledgements xi

Abbreviations xiii

Chapter 1 1
Introduction
    1.1 God as the Ultimate Owner of Land 3
    1.2 Literature Review: Chronicle of an Absence 8
        1.2.1 Jubilee Theology in Luke-Acts and the Absence of
            the Land Subject 8
        1.2.2 Studies on Possessions in Luke and the Absence of
            the Land Theme 13
    1.3 Methodology 14

Chapter 2 17
Land Injustice in the Roman Empire
    2.1 Social Stratification in the Roman Empire 20
    2.2 Land Conflicts from the Republic to the Rise of the Empire 27
    2.3 The Agrarian Economy and Economic Exploitation in the
        Roman Empire 35
        2.3.1 Exploitation by the Empire 35
        2.3.2 Exploitation by the Ruling Classes 41
    2.4 Final Remarks 58

Chapter 3 59
Land Injustice in Israel
    3.1 Land Exploitation from the Return from Exile to
        Hasmoneans Rule 60
    3.2 Land Exploitation in Palestine during Roman Empire 73
        3.2.1 Land and Tax Under Herod the Great 73
        3.2.2 Land and Tax After Herod the Great 80
    3.3 Final Remarks 86

Chapter 4 89
Land Justice and Injustice in the Hebrew Bible: Principles of a
Jubilee Informed Ethics
    4.1 From Creation to the Promised Land: The Centrality of Land 90

    4.2 The Jubilee Laws 93
        4.2.1 The Jubilee Laws in the Pentateuch..94
        4.2.2 Jubilee-Like Laws in the ANE...108
        4.2.3 The Jubilee Laws in the Prophets..110
        4.2.4 The Jubilee Laws in Second Temple Judaism.......................116
    4.3 From the Promised Land to the Babylonian Exile: The
        Jubilee Ethics Despised and Its Consequences............................121
    4.4 Prophecy and Reality: Life After the Return from Babylon 126
    4.5 Final Remarks 131

Chapter 5 133
Land Justice in Luke-Acts
    5.1 The Centrality of the Jubilee in Luke 135
        5.1.1 The Programmatic Character of Luke 4:16–30 135
        5.1.2 The Fundamental Importance of the Jubilee in
        Luke 4 and throughout Luke-Acts 142
    5.2 God as the Ultimate Landowner in Luke.....................................150
    5.3 Blessings and Curses Related to Land Administration 160
        5.3.1 The Parable of the Rich Man and Lazarus
        (Luke 16:19–31)...161
        5.3.2 The Conversion of Zacchaeus (Luke 19:1–10) 165
    5.4 Jesus Identifies with the Landless 168
    5.5 Land Giving in Acts of the Apostles 171
        5.5.1 The Community of Goods of Acts 171
        5.5.2 The Community of Goods in Acts of the Apostles
        and Land..178
        5.5.3 Land Jubilee Ethics and Christian Hospitality....................183
    5.6 The Expansion of the Holy Land 185
    5.7 Final Remarks 190

Chapter 6 193
Luke 12:13–21: The Parable of the Rich Fool

Chapter 7 207
Luke 20:9–19: The Parable of the Wicked Tenants
    7.1 History of the Interpretation: An Introduction..........................208
    7.2 Interpretation of the Parable..214
    7.3 Does this Parable Teach about Land?...223

Chapter 8 227
Conclusion: Summary and Significance

Bibliography 235

Abstract

Land was the most important economic resource in the Roman Empire and was concentrated in the hands of a small percentage of the wealthy. This was also the situation for those living in Israel under the Roman Empire and throughout Israel's story. Luke draws upon the ethics of the Old Testament, especially that of the jubilee legislation in order to propose that Jesus presents God as the ultimate owner of land. Based on this, Luke teaches that those who follow Jesus Christ have the obligation of dealing with land in light of God´s ownership of it for God punishes those who ignore this fact by only using land for their own well-being. On the other hand, God blesses those who divest themselves of land because of him on behalf of the neighbor or who use their own property to the common good.

Acknowledgements

There is a sense in which a dissertation is a teamwork effort. There was an army of many good people who helped me in many ways to accomplish this herculean but humbling task. I want to start by expressing my deep gratitude to my *doktorvater* Dr. Joshua Jipp, who has guided, encouraged, and criticized me in a very amicable and prompt way. Also, to Dr. Constantine Campbell and Dr. Richard Averbeck, my sincere gratitude for helping this work become better than it would be without you.

I am grateful to some institutions that supported me in prayers and financially: the Presbyterian Church of Brazil in the person of its president, Dr. Roberto Brasileiro Silva; the Board of Education of the Presbyterian Church of Brazil in the person of its president, Dr. Augustus Nicodemus Lopes; Andrew Jumper Graduate Center in the person of its president, Dr. Mauro Meister and of all my colleagues professors; Mackenzie Presbyterian Institute in the person of its Chancellor, Dr. David Charles Gomes; Langham Partnership in the persons of its international director for the Scholars Program, Dr. Riad Kassis and its US Scholar Care Coordinator, Dr. Fred Gale; Scholar Leaders International in the person of its vice-president, Dr. Evan Hunter. I am grateful also for Trinity International University for the quality of the training, scholarship and mostly for the environment of piety and respect for the Bible as the word of God.

Nobody has been more important to me in the pursuit of this PhD than the members of my family. I would like to thank my parents who chose me, invested their love and instilled in me love for Christ and for the most precious word of God. My children, Joao Paulo Jr., Maria Eduarda and Gabriel have been a constant source of joy and encouragement even amidst all changes my academic life meant to them. Most importantly, I wish to express my profound gratitude towards my wife, Juliana, who helps me every day to be a better man, believer, gospel minister, and scholar. I am grateful for her more than I will ever be able to express and thank with justice. What a strength you have! You are such a blessing of God to me and to you I dedicate this dissertation.

Finally, to the One who made me and led my steps throughout my whole life, my deepest gratitude, the fruits of my labor and my life. "Now to him who is able to do far more abundantly than all that we ask or think, according to the power at work within us, to him be glory in the church and in Christ Jesus throughout all generations, forever and ever. Amen." (Eph 3:20–21).

Abbreviations

11QMelch	The Melchizedek Document (11Q13)
11QpHab	Pesher of Habakkuk found in Cave 11 of Qumran
1QM	War Scroll
ANE	Ancient Near Eastern
Ant.	*Antiquitates Judaicae*
Apocol.	*Apocolocyntosis*
B Civ.	*Bella civilia*
BDAG	Bauer, Danker, Arndt, and Gingrich, *Greek English Lexicon of the New Testament*
BJ	*Bellum Judaicum*
CD	Damascus Document of Qumran
Controv.	*Controversiae*
De prof. virt.	*De profectu in virtute*
Dio Cass.	*Dio Cassius*
Dio Chrys. Or.	*Dio Chrysostomus Orationes*
Disc.	*Epicteti dissertationes*
DJD	Discoveries in the Judeaean Desert
EDNT	*Exegetical Dictionary of the New Testament*
Ep.	*Epistulae*
Epict. diss.	*Epicteti dissertationes*
Eth. Eud.	*Ethica Eudemia*
Flor.	*L. Annaeus Florus*
Fragm. Cult.	*Fragmentos de Cultura*
Gk	Greek
GThom	Gospel of Thomas

HN	*Naturalis Historia*
ILS	*Inscriptiones Latinae Selectae*
In Verr.	*In Verrem*
iu.	*Iugera (land measure)*
JBL.	*Journal of Biblical Literature*
JSJ	*Journal for the Study of Judaism in the Persian, Hellenistic, and Roman Period*
Jian Dao	*Jian Dao: A Journal of Bible and Theology*
LCL	Loeb Classical LIbrary
Leg. agr.	*De Agraria Lege*
Liv.	*Livy*
Low-Nida	*Greek-English Lexicon of the New Testament*
Mor.	*Moralia*
Nov. Vetera	*Nova et Vetera*
Oec.	*Oeconomica*
Or.	*Orationes*
P. Col.	Papiry of the University of Cologne
P. Oxy	Oxyrhynchus Papyri
P.Cair.Zen.	Zenon Papiry, Catalogue général de antiquités égyptiennes du Musée du Caire, Ed. C. C. Edgar, Cairo
P.Lond.	Greek Papiry in the British Museum of London
P.Mich.	Papiry of the University of Michigan
P.Par	Papiry of the Museum of Louvre
P.S.I. 903. (AD 47)	Papyrus of the Italian Society
P.Sel.Warga	Select Papiry ed. R. G. Varga, Jr. Diss. University of Illinois Urbana-Champaign 1988
Phil.	*Orationes Philippicae*
PssSol	Psalms of Solomon
QS	Community Rule of Qumran
Qumran Chron.	The Qumran Chronicle

Rust.	*De Re Rustica*
Sci. Esprit	*Science et Espirit*
Symp. Filos.	*Symposium de Filosofia*
T.Levi	The Testament of Levi
Ti. Gracch.	*Tiberius Gracchus*
Vit. Cat. Mai. Min.	*Vita Cato Maior, Minor*
Way	The Way
ZPE	*Zeitschrift für Papyrologie und Epigraphik*

CHAPTER 1

Introduction

"Land is a central, if not *the central theme* of biblical faith."[1] Walter Brueggemann's assessment makes sense when one focuses on the studies of the Old Testament on land, which include studies on covenant, the promised land, eschatology, post colonialism, immigration, archaeology, and land reform.[2] While land has been a very important topic in Old Testament studies, the same cannot be said for the study of land in the New Testament. So Lilburne states: "The problem appears to be that while the Hebrew Scriptures speak centrally of the land, its preservation and proper use, this concern is entirely lost in the New Testament. By universalizing the scope of God's reign, the New Testament appears to trivialize the concern with place and locality and to move its spirituality beyond issues of the land."[3] Is that so? Is it possible that such a central subject, fundamental to life, economy, culture, politics, and relationships is spiritualized in the New Testament to the point of virtually disappearing?

Searching for studies on land in the NT academia suggests that this is the case. Even with regards to the Gospel of Luke, the book of the New Testament that most frequently deals with subjects of social standing, there are very few

---

1. Brueggemann, *The Land*, 3 (emphasis in original). Another scholar said: "The history of the biblical people is practically confused with the struggle for the conquest of land." Da Silva, "Direito à Terra," 596.

2. Besides the importance of the subject in the Old Testament, land has a central role in life: "The land is the major factor of production and as such it is both property and capital. Early in human society it became evident that political power and privilege were linked to the control of land. Land is still one of the most important aspects of the economy, but in the pre-industrial age it was certainly the pre-eminent source of wealth and prestige." Pastor, *Land and Economy*. 1.

3. Lilburne, *A Sense of Place*, 10.

academic studies focusing on land. The exceptions are studies devoted to the Lukan Jesus's appropriation of the jubilee theology applied to the quest for land reform. These studies include church and social organization documents, mainly from South America and Africa, but no academic treatment of the subject has yet been offered.[4]

I suggest, therefore, that NT scholars have not adequately reckoned with the important theme of land present in the Gospel of Luke nor the way in which Luke connects this theme to the land aspect of the Levitical jubilee and the general Old Testament concern with land justice.[5] It is important to note that when I speak of land in this dissertation, I am not directly interested in "the land" of Israel, but I am rather interested in studying land as a socio-economic factor, as productive property, and a generator of social status.[6]

Most Lukan scholars agree that when Jesus draws upon Isaiah 61 and 58 to announce the beginning of his public ministry (Luke 4:18–19), he is drawing upon Israel's scriptural tradition of jubilee.[7] Isaiah 61 is interpreted in relation to the jubilee by the Qumran community in 11QMelch and by many OT scholars who are specialists in Isaiah.[8] However, although many recognize the presence of the jubilee theme in Luke, oddly enough, scholars have not

---

4. Miller, *Jesus Goes to Washington*, 92; Jakonda and Rural Development Counselors for Christian Churches in Africa, *Your Kingdom Come*, 161; Wright, "Land and Land Reform," 535–37; Vengeyi, "A Luta Continua Biblical Hermeneutics," 367 et seq.

5. Justice is understood as defined by Walter Brueggemann, "the maintenance of a viable socioeconomic, political order that makes neighborly solidarity possible and available to all members of the community." Brueggemann, *God, Neighbor, Empire*, 13.

6. "Land means different things to different people. Land embraces the atmosphere, the soil and the underlying geology, the hydrology, and the plants on, above and below a specific area of the earth's surface. It also includes the results of past and present human activities as well as the animals within this area, in so far as they exert a significant influence on the present and future uses of the land by man. Other more limited and overlapping concepts of land can be identified: land as *space*, three-dimensional, unchangeable and fixed in quantity; land as *nature*, defined in terms of natural or man-made ecosystems influenced by natural processes; land as a *gene resource;* land as a *production factor*, together with labour and capital; land as a *consumer good* or *commodity* as a support for highways, buildings, etc.; land as a source os *pleasure* and *recreation*; land as *location*, in modern economy and politics; land as *property*, exerting so powerful upon man's attitudes and actions; and finally, the related legal and economic connotation of land as *capital.*" Whyte, *Land and Land Appraisal*, 1–2. (italics original)

7. The list of these scholars include Calvin, *Commentary on a Harmony*, 229; Godet, *Commentary on the Gospel of St. Luke*, 150–51; Marshall, *Gospel of Luke* 184; Green, *Theology of the Gospel of Luke* 78; Bock, *Luke 1:1–9:50*, 406; Ringe, *Luke*, 68; Thielman, *Theology of the New Testament*, 124. The monographs that deal specifically with this subject will be referred to ahead.

8. Among the OT scholars who interpret Isaiah 61:1–2 as referring to the jubilee one finds Alexander, *Commentary on the Prophecies of Isaiah*, 397; Young, *Book of Isaiah*, 459; Hanson,

asked whether Luke's appropriation of the jubilee theme has influenced how he speaks of land in his work. Thus, there is a syllogistic reasoning behind this research: since the jubilee is fundamental to Luke and land is central to the jubilee, then it is just to expect land to play an important role in the Gospel of Luke. This dissertation aims to confirm this syllogistic reasoning.

Thus, in this dissertation, I remedy this scholarly silence by investigating land ownership in Luke. Specifically, I aim to answer the question: what is Luke's view on land ownership and justice in Luke-Acts? To answer this question, it is necessary to examine the teaching and ethics of land ownership rights both in the Old Testament and in the historical-cultural context in which Jesus preached and Luke wrote. My intention here is to examine in what ways Israel's Scriptures and other factors have influenced Luke's depiction of the appropriate and inappropriate use of land. This dissertation, therefore, is about land as an economic and ethical factor in Luke-Acts. It shows how land was portrayed and used in a radically different fashion by Jesus and his followers when contrasted to the background of the Roman Empire and even Israel in particular. Thus, I am not interested in geographical and territorial discussions related to the promised land of Israel, instead, my focus is mainly economic and ethical. The thesis I defend is that Luke, influenced by a jubilee ethics, presents God as the supreme landowner and, consequently, the one who defines how land should be used. He does that by cursing those who use the soil wrongly and blessing those who use it correctly, to the benefit of one's fellow humans.

1.1 God as the Ultimate Owner of Land

The work of Norman Habel is useful for the contextual examination of land rights in the Old Testament. He proposes that there are six different biblical land ideologies in the Old Testament: royal, Deuteronomic, ancestral, prophetic, agrarian, and immigrant ideology.[9] The constant factor in all these ideologies is that God is the proprietor of land. Christopher Wright concurs, affirming that there are two aspects in the dealings of God with land and

---

Isaiah 40–66, 205; Brueggemann, *Isaiah: 40–66*, 214; Oswalt, *Book of Isaiah*, 297; Childs, *Isaiah*, 505; Paul, *Isaiah 40–66*, 538.

9. Habel, *The Land Is Mine*.

people: God is the owner of the land and he is also the giver of it, both to humanity and to Israel.[10] He also says that with the fall of humanity into sin, Israel becomes a paradigm of the way God intends to deal in the future with the whole redeemed humanity.[11] Since God is the owner of the land (Gen 14:19–20; Lev 25:23; Psa 24:1), he gives land and defines how it is to be divided and used (Num 32: Deut 6:18; Josh 5:6; 13–14). He also defines that his people are expected to use land with justice. This last aspect is evident in many texts throughout the OT, in which the claims of injustice are made against landowners who oppress the poor. That is the case, for example of 1 Kings 21 (Ahab and Jezebel and Naboth's Vineyard), Deuteronomy 5:21; Isaiah 58:5–10, Amos 3:15; 4:9; 5:11; 8:4–6, Micah 2:1–4; Zephaniah 1:12–13, among other texts.

According to the OT, therefore, God is the ultimate landowner and the one who defines how his land is to be used. He rewards those who use land with justice and punishes those who do not. I defend that the central assertion that the land belongs to the Lord and these ancillary teachings are consciously propagated by Luke in Luke-Acts.

This idea, however, was highly countercultural in the contexts where Jesus and Luke lived. For those living in the Roman Empire in the first century, land ownership patterns depended on whether one lived in Italy or in the provinces.[12] The affluent families of Rome owned large quantities of land throughout Italy, where they were excused from paying property taxes. It was common for these rich and powerful families to lease their land and live sumptuously in Rome as a result of the arduous work of peasants and slaves that worked their lands. In Italy, therefore, both the land and the properties in Rome were owned mainly by people belonging to the upper class.

In the provinces, the situation was somewhat different. The Roman Empire collected heavy taxes from the land owners and reserved the right to compel specific cultures to sustain the army or to provide for Rome.[13] The collection of agricultural taxes served as the primary source of revenue to sustain the empire's structure and ensure the provision of grain to the inhabitants of

---

10. Wright, *God's People in God's Land*.
11. Wright, *God's People in God's Land*.
12. Toutain, *Economic Life*, 272–73; Temin, *Roman Market Economy*, 147.
13. Garnsey and Saller, *Roman Empire*, 82–83.

Rome. In the provinces, land was owned mostly by the State, by the emperor himself and by those in his favor, and tenancy was a very common institution.[14]

Another common situation, both in Italy as well as in the provinces, was that the rich accumulated more and more land due to increasing prices and heavy taxes.[15] Thus, in the mid-first century AD, Seneca, Pliny and Columella deplored the existence of latifundia, i.e. large properties of land with slaves and/or free citizens in a state of complete dependency.[16] In today's rates, the largest fortune in the empire would amount to an estimated 20 billion American dollars, from which seventeen billion were invested in land.[17] As Temin concludes, "Wealth in this context was land."[18]

Against the harsh reality of dispossession of the masses, works were written proposing utopian egalitarian societies. Some of these works, such as *The Holy Story* of Euhemerus, *The Cimmerian State* of Hecateus and *Sun Polis* of Iambulus portray utopian societies in which the land and all means of production were held collectively.[19] The realities of land ownership and use were harsh for most of the population, both in the Empire and particularly in Palestine. Luke's writings address these harsh realities. Chapter 2 will present this agrarian situation of Rome in detail.

During the Herodian era, Palestine reflected the same economic organization as the Roman Empire, although on a smaller scale, with rulers owning sizable portions of land taken care of by tenants. Priests and other rich people also owned lands throughout the region, which were also cared for by renters or slaves, while the owners lived in important cities.[20] In addition, many farmsteads would be owned by non-Jews who lived in the cities of Palestine.[21]

---

14. Temin, *Roman Market Economy*, 148.

15. "There is substantial evidence of debt causing the loss of land among peasants in the first century." Malina and Rohrbaugh, *Social-Science*, 281.

16. Garnsey and Saller, *The Roman Empire*, 93.

17. Jeffers, *Greco-Roman World*, 183. This calculus uses US$ 50,00 as the value paid for a day of work, a denarius.

18. Temin, *Roman Market Economy*, 145. Moxnes adds that in such a culture: "Power meant control of land and of agricultural production." Moxnes, *Economy of the Kingdom*, 28.

19. Baloglou, "Hellenistic Economic Thought," 109–10.

20. Pastor, *Land and Economy*, 98–135.

21. Safrai, *Economy of Roman Palestine*, 85. Ahead, Safrai affirms that land in Palestine was commonly owned by the government, wealthy people and those close to the government, independent farmers who owned small tracts of land and the cities (322).

After thirty-five years of Herodian domination, in AD 6, the emperor Augustus appointed a Roman governor from the equestrian order to govern Judea. This added a heavy load of additional taxes, and the corruption of the prefects and the ruling classes alike made the situation worse for the people in general, who often had to succumb to debt.[22] "A major cause of poverty was the pressure put on labour through contractual tenancy arrangements and indebtedness."[23] Both the government and the rich would benefit from the hard work of poor people who had no opportunity to enjoy their own production. This acute social inequality was a major cause of social tensions in the region, resulting in resistance to and eventual war against Rome.[24] Many of Luke's parables and teachings presuppose this context of tenancy, slavery, indebtedness and generalized poverty. The situation of land ownership and oppression in Israel are further explained in chapter 3.

Against the background presented in the last paragraph, Luke sets forth an alternative economy that criticizes the way people were dealing with land ownership in the Roman Empire. This alternative land economy has the core belief that God is indeed the ultimate owner of all land and, therefore, the one who has the right to determine land laws. Luke is more concerned with divine rights than human rights.[25]

Thus, Luke is proposing that a jubilee ethic is enacted in the ministry of Jesus and should be lived by his followers. Understanding this enables the reader of Luke-Acts to better grasp the social and economic contexts of Luke's world, and even more importantly, sheds significant light upon Jesus's social and economic teaching in the Gospel of Luke. Thus, a variety of Lukan texts become clearer when we situate them within both the social and economic realities of life in the Roman Empire *and* within the Old Testament context of divine land ownership. The fourth chapter focusses on this last aspect.

For example, although the position of the rich land owner was ethically objectionable, God and/or Jesus in Luke are frequently represented in parables as farmers (Luke 3:8–9, 17; 10:2; 13:6–9; 20:9–18), masters of the house (Luke 12:35–38, 39–40, 41–48; 13:22–30; 14:15–24; 16:1–13; 19:11–27), or as a father

---

22. Pastor, *Land and Economy*, 139–50.
23. Hamel, "Poverty and Charity," 312.
24. Safrai, *Economy of Roman Palestine*, 330.
25. This idea of divine rights is developed in Strieder, "A Bíblia E A Fundamentação," 11–17.

who divides his properties (Luke 15:11–32). That happens, I contend, because Luke wants to convince his readers that God is the real owner of all land. Luke also makes clear that God rebukes those who use their land or house only for their own good (Luke 12:13–21; 16:19–31; 20:9–18, 47), but blesses those who use their lands to benefit others (14:12–14; 18:28–30; 19:1–10). The Lukan Jesus even declares plainly that God is the Lord of the earth (Luke 10:21). Also, in the beginning of Acts, what one does with his or her own land is an important symbol of one's standing with God (Acts 2:45; 4:36–37; 5:1–11).

Although these aspects will be dealt with in chapters 5 to 7, it is interesting by way of introduction to show this here in more details. A specific example is in the parable of the rich fool (Luke 12:13–21). This parable was prompted by a question related to someone's inheritance and, according to the economy of that time, the bulk of an inheritance was land. It makes more sense, then, that Jesus told a parable saying, "The *land* of a rich man produced plentifully" (Ἀνθρώπου τινὸς πλουσίου εὐφόρησεν ἡ χώρα, Luke 12:16). Being rich, this man was not the one who worked in the land himself, he had slaves and/or hired people and/or tenants to do that for him. Also, such a special harvest was due mainly to the weather, a condition that the human owner could not produce by himself. In Lukan theology, land is God's property to be shared with those in need, but the man of the parable decided to keep all the blessings of the land to himself alone. It is even possible to affirm that he was planning on keeping the land unproductive for years to come because he already had enough for himself. That man was rebuked for not being rich toward God. In sum, he should have reckoned that God is the rich one and the real owner of the land and, therefore, both the land itself and its surplus should serve other children of God, not just himself.

This kind of reading is informed by my research and brings forth some Lukan values and contextual information that are currently not well known to many interpreters. Bringing those values and contexts to the surface is the main contribution of this dissertation. In summary, although land plays an important role in Luke-Acts, and despite possessions in general being a much-studied subject in Luke, the same cannot be said about land.

1.2 Literature Review: Chronicle of an Absence

Land is an important theme in the Old Testament and in the Gospel of Luke, both theologically and exegetically. Luke depicts Jesus's ministry in terms of a jubilee and presents Jesus continuing in the prophetic tradition of denouncing, among other aspects of injustice, those related to land. From an exegetical perspective, land is crucial in the historical-cultural context of the gospel and appears both directly and indirectly, especially in the parables.

Despite this, scholars have often failed to examine the importance of land in Luke, even when dealing with subjects intimately related to it. After dealing with scholars who approach the jubilee in Luke, I will show that those who address the subject of possessions in Luke-Acts rarely explore the importance and substance of land either. Thus, in what follows I present two areas of study in Lukan scholarship, one related to jubilee and one to possessions. Despite dealing with related subjects, in none of these studies does one finds a deeper treatment of the agrarian perspective of Luke.

1.2.1 Jubilee Theology in Luke-Acts and the Absence of the Land Subject

The first trend in Lukan studies which relates intimately to land is the jubilee theology. There are two important consensuses in the study of Lukan theology that relate to this subject. First, Luke 4:16–21, the so-called Nazareth Manifesto, is a programmatic text in the sense that it introduces the main themes of the Gospel of Luke.[26] Second, Jesus in this text defines his ministry in terms of the jubilee of Isaiah 61. If jubilee, therefore, is central in the gospel of Luke and if one of the most important aspects of the jubilee was that God is the proprietor of the land (Lev 25:23) together with the resulting ethical responsibilities relating to the land, how do these aspects surface in

---

26. Garland, *Luke*; John Nolland, *Luke*, 195; "This inaugural episode is laced with theological concerns that bear great import in Luke's narrative. Jesus' messianic vocation is developed with the aid of several significance associations: empowerment by the Spirit of God; fulfillment of Scripture; the prophetic role; a mission of deliverance for the marginalized, the needy, and outsiders; and resulting rejection by well-placed insiders." Carroll, *Luke*, 108; "Jesus' word, which announces God's message and the intermediary role of the Messiah, is programmatic. Equally programmatic is the soteriological content and also, unfortunately, the human rejection." Bovon and Koester, *Luke*, 157; "The passage is made into a programmatic prophecy which guides the reader's understanding of the subsequent narrative." Johnson, *Gospel of Luke*, 81.

Luke-Acts? The answer depends on how each scholar interprets the jubilee in Luke, that is to say, whether in a historic, eschatological, or symbolic fashion.

Some scholars affirm that Jesus announced a *historic, literal jubilee* in Luke 4. André Trocmé, for example, argues that it was the proclamation of a literal jubilee by Jesus in Nazareth in September, AD 26 that prompted the people from the city to kill him.[27] Defining the jubilee as revolutionary, he explains its importance in the gospels using the words ἄφεσις and ἀποκατάστασις, this last one because Philo uses it in relation to the jubilee.[28] He affirms that the jubilee had two main principles: first, God is the owner of the land of Israel, and second, God is the liberator of his people.[29] Furthermore, Trocmé suggests that there were four provisions of jubilee: (1) letting the land lie fallow; (2) canceling of debts; (3) liberation of slaves; and (4) return of patrimony – and all of them are fulfilled in the gospels.

The last provision relates intimately to our proposal. Trocmé affirms that the return of patrimony is fulfilled mainly in the Lukan texts where Jesus asks his hearers to sell everything and give alms (Luke 11:41; 12:30–33; 18:22). One sees it also in the negative examples of the rich ruler (Luke 18:18–23) and the rich man of Luke 16:19–31 on one hand, and on the positive examples of the poor widow (Luke 21:1–4), the apostles (Luke 18:28–30), and Zacchaeus (Luke 19:1–10) on another. Although the jubilee provision had provisions specifically related to the land, Trocmé's explanation relates more broadly to money and possessions.[30] Based on his interpretation of the Lukan jubilee, Trocmé affirms that from time to time the church should proclaim a jubilee as led by the Spirit, as well as support social revolutions and dedicate itself to social justice.[31]

---

27. André Trocmé, *Jesus and the Nonviolent Revolution*, 29.
28. *The Decalogue*, 164.
29. Trocmé, *Jesus and the Nonviolent Revolution*, 34–35.
30. Trocmé, *Jesus and the Nonviolent Revolution*, 52.
31. "If it is put into practice by the church whenever the Spirit blows, the Jubilee that announces the kingdom of God will propose practical solutions to the problems of ownership, exploitation of man by man, freedom of the oppressed, and capital sharing. The Jubilee will once again give the church its place in the modern world." Trocmé, *Jesus and the Nonviolent Revolution*, 75–76. John Howard Yoder presents a mirrored version of Trocmé's interpretation. See John Howard Yoder, *The Politics of Jesus*, 29. Against this kind of reading, Willoughby says: "What Yoder and Blosser seem unable to accept is that, certainly in the context of Luke's gospel, Jesus' use of the Jubilee motif by way of Isaiah, is metaphorical. Such 'concrete expectation' is not expected." Willoughby, "The Concept of Jubilee," 51.

Also from a more historic approach, at the same time in which he affirms that the New Testament spiritualizes the concerns of land in the concepts of rest and kingdom of God, Roy May also argues that Jesus announced a literal jubilee, denouncing oppression and fomenting the cancellation of debts and protection for the poor.[32] May draws the reader to the problem of land in Latin America and proposes practical solutions to it. The biblical basis provided for this, though, is very thin. In the same manner, May's OT rationale is insufficient and does not do justice to the reality of the text.

Also defending a more literal reading of the jubilee in Jesus's ministry, Wes Howard-Brook names the Lukan resistance to the Roman Empire as a proclamation of jubilee. He affirms that the sermon of Nazareth (Luke 4:18–21) is the "mission statement" of Jesus, in which he announces relief against "disease, debt, demons and death". In his assessment, "The fulfillment of jubilee flows through Luke-Acts from beginning to end".[33] While he speaks clearly about the jubilee message of liberation from the oppression of the economic system enacted by the empire, he is silent about the land problem even when dealing with the account of Ananias and Sapphira.[34]

Although the efforts of the above-mentioned scholars are commendable, their treatments of the subject lack proof from the texts of the NT. Furthermore, they read some aspects of New Testament texts that are themselves presented as also having spiritual fulfillment as if they were only historic. These interpreters therefore reduce the jubilee to a literal and leftist way of promoting social justice.

In contrast to the above-mentioned scholars who emphasize a literal reading of the text, there are researchers who contend for an *eschatological reading* of the jubilee in Luke-Acts. One of the most quoted books on the jubilee in Luke is Robert Sloan's thesis. He begins by showing the provisions and eschatological themes on the jubilee legislation. The first provision is the return of all property, which had as a primary theological motivation the fact that Yahweh is the owner of the land.[35] The eschatological themes Sloan finds in the

---

32. May, *The Poor of the Land*.
33. Howard-Brook, *"Come out, My People,"* 422–23.
34. Howard-Brook, *"Come out, My People,"* 431.
35. Sloan, *Favorable Year of the Lord*, 5.

jubilee legislation are the social emphasis, the restoration of all things,³⁶ certain cultic features, and the importance of faith. Sloan shows how the jubilee themes appear in the beatitudes and woes (Luke 6:20–26), in the injunction to love one's own enemies (Luke 6:27–38), and in the Lord's prayer (Luke 11:2–4), mainly in the use of the words εὐαγγελίζω and ἄφεσις. He concludes that "Luke has purposefully employed the picture of jubilee – consistent with its historical application by Jewish legislators, prophets, apocalyptists, and priestly sectarians – as a metaphorical expression of the *eschatological salvation of God*."³⁷

Sloan clarifies that this eschatological perspective is both present, as inaugurated by Jesus, and future, in the consummated kingdom of Jesus Christ. He disagrees with Trocmé, affirming that the jubilee proclaimed by Jesus was neither a literal one, nor only a social entity, but mainly eschatological and related to the cultic-religious structure of the people of God. Sloan also draws practical ethical implications of his thesis for the people of God.³⁸

There has not been much development on this subject since Sloan wrote. His arguments and proof texts were copied but hardly expanded and his seasoned judgement on the eschatological perspective of the jubilee did not easily find a match. As I will demonstrate in chapter 5, Sloan's findings have been deeply influential on subsequent scholarship so that the presence and influence of the jubilee legislation in Luke became a field of research of its own. The present dissertation will build upon Sloan's work in order to present its implications for the specific area of land ownership and use.

Also defending an eschatological reading of the jubilee in Luke, Razouselie Lasetso contends that the jubilee theology can be found throughout Luke-Acts especially in the use of the word ἄφεσις. This eschatological restoration/liberation finds its fulfillment in Jesus and does not have only the Jews in view, but also the gentiles together with all other marginalized people.³⁹ Lasetso claims that the liberation proclaimed and embodied by Jesus was both physical (from economic duress, sickness, social taboos, and demonic oppression) and spiritual (from sins). Following also the concepts of poor (πτωχός) in

---

36. "Man and nature are to be restored to the idyllic dignity and social equality which existed at the time of the tribal federation." Sloan, *Favorable Year of the Lord*, 14.
37. Sloan, *Favorable Year of the Lord*, 162–63.
38. Sloan, *Favorable Year of the Lord*, 176.
39. Razouselie Lasetso, *The Nazareth Manifesto*, 223.

Luke, κοινωνία in Acts, and ἐλεημοσύνη (alms) in Luke-Acts, he proposes that the jubilee theme of sharing possessions is clearly present in the Lukan writings. However, Lasetso overlooks the important topic of God as the owner of the land and its consequences throughout the gospel of Luke and towards social action of the Asiatic church in the much-needed area of land reform.[40]

Besides the historic and the eschatological interpretations of the jubilee in Luke Acts, there is also the *symbolic interpretation* of Sharon Ringe. For her, the only important and unnegotiable thing is seeing Jesus as the model of liberator for the community of faith. Ringe is careful in her tracking of jubilee images in the New Testament. She notes that "there is not distinctive Greek vocabulary associated with jubilee traditions" and therefore, "one ought to be very cautious about claiming to find references in the Synoptic Gospels to jubilee traditions not actually quoted or paraphrased, such as Leviticus 25."[41] Although also recognizing an eschatological aspect of the jubilee images in the New Testament, the book concludes with a call to church engagement.[42] Ringe presents a good exposition of themes related to Lukan jubilee theology, but does not refer once to the important subject of land nor to the fact that God is presented as owner of the land in Scripture.

On another completely different spectrum from the historic, eschatological and symbolic readings of the jubilee in Luke-Acts, Art Lindsley writes an article that goes against the idea that the jubilee was concerned with land reform and argues against an interpretation of Acts used to justify socialism. Based on a close reading of Leviticus 25, Lindsley contends that there are five myths about the jubilee from which people mistakenly defend the state redistribution of wealth: (1) jubilee meant a forgiveness of debt; (2) jubilee involved a redistribution of wealth (land); (3) jubilee shows the relative nature of private property; (4) jubilee leads to income equality and (5) jubilee is a universally applicable principle.[43] Finally, he argues that interpretations that

---

40. Holden, Otsuka, and Deininger, *Land Tenure Reform in Asia and Africa*.

41. Ringe, *Jesus, Liberation, and the Biblical Jubilee*, 34–35. Even so, she finds jubilee images in the question from John the Baptist (Luke 7:18–23), the Beatitudes (Luke 6:20–22), the banquet parable (Luke 14:12–24), the rich young man (Luke 18:18–23), the history of Zacchaeus (Luke 19:1–10), the sinful woman forgiven (Luke 7:36–50), the healing of a paralytic (Luke 5:17–26); the saying about forgiveness (Luke 11:4), the Lord's Prayer (Luke 11:2–4) together with its parallels and a few other texts in the other Synoptics.

42. Ringe, *Jesus, Liberation, and the Biblical Jubilee*, 98.

43. Lindslay, "Does God Require the State to Redistribute Wealth?," 79–93.

see socialism in Acts 2–5 are wrong. Thus, he disagrees with all three readings that affirm the social aspect of the jubilee as being important to Luke.

While there are different forms in which NT scholars have dealt with the jubilee in Luke and in the ministry of Jesus – historic, eschatological, and symbolic – the constant in all those studies is that the jubilee injunctions related specifically with land are not properly explored. The present dissertation aims on moving this discussion forward by presenting that Luke's land ethics is influenced by the central tenet of jubilee legislation that God is the definitive owner of all land.

1.2.2 Studies on Possessions in Luke and the Absence of the Land Theme

A second trend in Lukan scholarly studies that is important to our research is found among those who research poverty and possessions in the gospel of Luke. In these studies, one finds no or only generic comments about land. Halvor Moxnes, for example, while stressing the importance of land and houses in the economy and social structures in the context and in the gospel of Luke, besides speaking about hospitality, does not develop how the evangelist views the role of land in the kingdom.[44] Christopher Hays shows consciousness of the subject but does not develop it.[45] Philip Esler and Luke Timothy Johnson mainly ignore the specific subject of land.[46] James Metzger does not specifically develop the economic importance of land, but makes an assertion that is at the center of our proposal: "Material possessions do not really belong to them anyhow. As creator, God ultimately owns all of the land and its resources, and human beings are but stewards – who one day will also have their stewardship taken away."[47]

Thus, after researching land in Lukan studies and in the NT academia in general, one finds that, despite being central in the Old Testament and for subsistence, social relations and economy, land has not been properly dealt with in academic treatments of Luke-Acts. Possession and dispossession of land is, therefore, an absent, ignored or underdeveloped subject in Lukan

---

44. Moxnes, *Economy of the Kingdom*, esp. 28–41 and 85.

45. Hays, *Luke's Wealth Ethics*.

46. Esler, *Community and Gospel in Luke-Acts*; Johnson, *Sharing Possessions*; Johnson, *Prophetic Jesus, Prophetic Church*.

47. Metzger, *Consumption and Wealth*, 129.

studies. This dissertation gives a small contribution to remediate this great gap, by defending the claim and exploring some of the ethical implications that one essential aspect of the jubilee theology of Luke is that God is the real owner of all land.

1.3 Methodology

Among a plethora of methods of studying and applying the biblical texts, the method of reading the biblical texts chosen for their analysis in this dissertation is best described in Jonathan Pennington's *Reading the Gospels Wisely*. He acknowledges that the gospels are ancient biographies intended, among other things, to incentivize people to imitate its main character, Jesus.[48] The interpreter must take the initiative of not only describing what he or she reads, but also the responsibility to speak into his context.[49] Pennington's method can be called hybrid or eclectic – he calls it multilayered or multi-avenued – because it draws from perspectives behind the text, in the text and in front of the text at the same time and acknowledges a supernatural action of God himself in the process of interpretation.[50] It is a method that benefits both from the precritical ways of approaching the text as well as of current trends in hermeneutics.

The gospel of Luke will also be dealt with as Scripture, not in the sense of Brevard Childs or Francis Watson, but in the manner developed by Michael Kruger.[51] On the use of the Old Testament in Luke, which has a very important role in this dissertation, it is important to clarify that the Scriptures of the Old and New Testament will be treated here in their final forms, as God's Word and as comprising a revelation which is progressive, historic, organic

---

48. Cf. Burridge, *What Are the Gospels?* Burridge, *Imitating Jesus*.

49. "part of the responsibility of a Christian interpreter of Scripture today is to try to understand out contemporary context and to explore the Bible's relevance to it in ways that reflect serious critical engagement with that context." Bauckham, *Bible in the Contemporary World*, 7.

50. Pennington, *Reading the Gospels Wisely*, 108 et seq.

51. Watson, *Gospel Writing*, 411 et seq. Childs, *Biblical Theology in Crisis*; Childs, *Introduction to the Old Testament as Scripture*. Kruger presents a multilayered perspective of the concept of canon, acknowledging extrinsic (historic and communitarian) and intrinsic (divine) qualities that result in an authoritative divine-human document. Kruger, *Canon Revisited*; Kruger, *The Question of Canon*.

and adaptable, as Geerhardus Vos explains it.[52] One last explicit aspect of the methodology employed here is that it is integrative. Although this is a thesis on a very specific subject and New Testament exegesis and biblical theology are the main areas of interest, this thesis will also deal directly with Old Testament studies, history, sociology, economics, and Christian ethics; and, indirectly, also with Systematic Theology.

With the methodology and aims expressed above, this dissertation is organized in the following way:

In the next chapter I will deal with land use and property rights in the first century Roman Empire. The chapter presents Roman society's stratification, laws and taxes on land, benefits of the wealthy, and the struggles of small landowners and land workers. I also present some of the reactions and resistance that the Roman land ownership rights were facing. The reader will get a sense of how a first century person would hear some of the agrarian images and teachings presented in Luke and understand how countercultural the third evangelist was in the defense of a land ethic based in the fact that God is the owner of all land.

In the third chapter, I focus on the situation of land exploitation in Israel. The chapter shows that since the return of the Babylonian exile the Judean society organized itself in a way that benefitted the foreign powers and its clients as well as Israelite religious and economic leaders that worked for the betterment of such foreign powers. The result is a spread of poverty and land dispossession for the masses and concentration of land and money for a few. In doing so, this chapter also provides the historical context related to which Luke writes and presents his proposal of an ethic that produces land justice, at least amidst those who decide to follow Jesus Christ.

With the aim of providing part of the theological and ethical contexts in which Luke writes, chapter 4 presents a brief analysis of the theme of land justice in the Old Testament, especially in the prophets, showing how these texts spring from the concept that God is both the owner of the soil and the one who establishes how it is to be used. The chapter shows how the monarchy perverted the land ethics established by God in the law and the prophets vociferate against this situation. Most of the teaching Luke develops on land is already present in the pages of the Old Testament.

---

52. Vos, *Biblical Theology*, 14–17.

Chapter 5 is the central part of the present dissertation. It presents an aerial view of the subject of land ownership in Luke-Acts, focusing mainly on the ways God is presented as the supreme land proprietor and the one who blesses the land givers and punishes the pretense of human landowners. Before doing that, however, the chapter deals with the importance that jubilee has in Luke. The chapter also shows that Luke presents Jesus as someone destitute of land and finishes showing the importance of the community of goods in Acts for the message Luke wants to convey about land justice.

Chapters 6 and 7 present the exegesis of two specific parables which have land as a central theme, respectively the parable of the rich fool (Luke 12:13–21) and the parable of the wicked tenants (Luke 20:9–18). Both parables present condemnations because someone did not use the land the way they were supposed to. In the second parable, God is clearly represented as the wealthy owner of land, who punishes those who unjustly arrogate the right to take land for themselves. Although these chapters do not use the parabolic texts according to their main purpose, it is warranted to use them to prove this dissertation's point since following Craig Blomberg, I defend that parables carry more than just one point.

Thus, while chapters 2 to 4 are of a contextual nature, chapters 5 to 7 develop Luke´s proposal on land justice, i.e., that God is the main proprietor of land and the one who has the right to define how humans should use land. He also imposes sanctions or injunctions on people, according to the way they deal with the soil. Finally, in the conclusion I expect to draw broad and specific ethical implications of this study to the way the people of God could deal with the questions of land ownership.

CHAPTER 2

Land Injustice in the Roman Empire

Land was the most important asset in Roman economy and belonged almost entirely to the emperor and the Roman *élites*. Thus, when Luke proposes that God is the proprietor of all land and the one who has the right to establish the way land is to be used, he is going against his contemporary status quo.

Thus, this chapter envisages presenting the context of injustice in which and against which Luke writes. Luke's proposal of land ethics informed by the jubilee was completely antagonistic to the concentration of land by a privileged few, the rampant indebtedness, and the abuses of people through enslavement that characterized Roman society. By presenting these realities this chapter presents the need of Luke's proposal as well as the risks he exposed himself by defending a radically different way of life based in a radically different worldview.

It is impossible to exaggerate the economic and social importance of land in the ancient Roman context. Its importance is evident in that the empire depended heavily on land conquest and production as well as in the fact that the urban elite received their main income from their farms that were spread throughout the empire. Most of the workers, slaves and freeman, worked the land to produce the food consumed by the Roman aristocracy and given to the poor in the form of the imperial *annona* (donation of grains financed by the emperor). It is not without reason, therefore, that Garnsey and Saller affirm that "agriculture was the creator of the bulk of the empire's wealth."[1]

---

1. Garnsey and Saller, *The Roman Empire*, 82. McGeough highlights both the importance and the difficulty of the subject: "Ownership and control of land are central issues in understanding agricultural economy. Who owns the land and who has rights to it are important, but also usually very complicated, issues." McGeough, *The Romans*, 97.

Kehoe illustrates this affirmation well, showing that the Roman elite depended deeply on land production to maintain their status:

> Agricultural wealth played a crucial role in the social and political structure of the Roman Empire. The elite classes that ruled the empire, including the emperor and the imperial family, the senatorial and equestrian orders, and the curial classes in the empire's many cities, depended on the production of their estates for the revenues that maintained their social and political privileges.[2]

Besides the production of wealth per se, owning land was the most prestigious way of enriching one's assets. Manufacturing, commerce and especially money lending were not seen as fitting commercial activities for citizens of high status. Columella, for example, confirms this after speaking about the risks of international trade by ships, he concludes: "If good men are to shun these pursuits and their kind, there remains, as I have said, one method of increasing one's substance that befits a man who is a gentleman and free-born, and this is found in agriculture." (*Rust.* 1.0.11).[3] Thus, being of elevated social

---

2. Kehoe, "Landlords and Tenants," 298. In another work, Kehoe relates the situation as such: "In a predominantly agrarian economy, the financial well-being of Roman landowners was inextricably linked to the fortunes of agricultural laborers and small farmers. Agriculture employed the vast majority of the empire's population, and it played a crucial role in the Roman government's efforts to govern this empire. Agriculture constituted the basis for the wealth of the Roman upper classes, who dominated the government both in Rome and in the cities of the empire, and whose social and political privileges it was the imperial government's policy to foster. Many upper-class Romans derived their fortunes from estates cultivated by small-scale tenants. More generally, the economic situation of large landowners was affected by their relationships with small-scale farmers, who worked as laborers on large estates, received credit from landowners, and, in some circumstances, competed with them for land, resources such as water, and even access to markets." Kehoe, *Law and Rural Economy*, 1–2. Weber presents the situation as: "The extent of a citizen's property – as determined by periodic censuses – now became the key to his political and military rights and duties." Weber, *The Agrarian Sociology of Ancient Civilizations*, 309.

3. Cato, The Elder, expresses a similar opinion: "It is true that to obtain money by trade is sometimes more profitable, were it not so hazardous; and likewise money lending, if it were as honorable. . . . On the other hand, it is from the farming class that the bravest men and the sturdiest soldiers come, their calling is most highly respected, their livelihood is most assured and is looked on with the least hostility, and those who are engaged in that pursuit are least inclined to be disaffected" (Cato, *Agr* 1.0.1). Also, Pliny: "Bad husbandry was judged an offense within the jurisdiction of the censors, and, as Cato tells us, to praise a man by saying he was a good farmer and a good husbandman was thought to be the highest form of commendation. That is the source of the word *locuples*, meaning 'wealthy', 'full of room', i.e. of land. Our word for money itself was derived from *pecus*, 'cattle', and even now in the censor's accounts all the

class in the Roman Empire depended mainly on one's access to land and, consequently, no access to land meant being poor and dependent upon others.[4]

It is important to study the message of Luke in the light of the practices of the Roman Empire for Luke settles his work in the context of the whole empire, not just Palestine. He speaks about the birth of Jesus in the context of a decree of Caesar Augustus (Luke 2:1) and relates the beginning of John the Baptist's ministry during the ἡγεμονίας Τιβερίου Καίσαρος (Luke 3:1). Luke also shows that Jesus spoke about Caesar (Luke 20:25) and was unjustly accused of forbidding people of paying taxes to Caesar (Luke 23:2). This imperial amplitude is yet clearer in Acts. In his second volume Luke shows the message of Jesus reaching many parts of the empire. He also shows that the believers were accused of sedition against Caesar, by proclaiming another king, Jesus (Acts 17:1). He refers to a decree of the emperor Claudius expelling Jews from Rome (Acts 18:2). The book concludes with the journey Paul, a Roman citizen (Acts 16:37; 22:25–29), makes to Rome in order to defend his cause before the emperor (Acts 25:11; 27:24) and with his proclamation of the gospel there (Acts 23:11; 28:30–31). All these references make largely clear that Luke as a writer is very much interested in set his work in the context of Rome.

Therefore, having briefly introduced the fundamental importance of land in the Roman society and the Roman ambience of it, this chapter aims, first, to present a portrait of the social stratification of the Roman society during the empire in order to determine who were the fortunate ones with access to land. Second, this chapter will present a short account of the land conflicts and laws during the Roman Republic culminating in the empire. Third and last, the chapter will conclude with a description of the practices of exploitation employed both by the Empire itself and by the Roman aristocracy. The aim is that by the end of this chapter the reader is convinced that the empire and the very wealthy dominated the access to land and used that to perpetuate their power and exploit the rest of the world including first century Israel/Palestine.

---

sources of national revenue are termed 'pastures', because rent of pasture-land was for a long time the only source of public income" (Pliny, *Nat.* 18.3).

4. "Poverty in this pre-industrial world was largely determined by access to land." Osborne, "Introduction: Roman Poverty in Context," 4.

2.1 Social Stratification in the Roman Empire

Because of the exiguity of hard data and the fact that literary documents represent the opinions of the social elite, it is not an easy task to present the social stratification of the Roman Empire. One needs, therefore, to be aware that all academic reconstructions have a significant margin for error and are tentative. The population of the empire in the beginning of the Christian era was approximately 50–60 million.[5] Rome itself had about 1 million inhabitants. All these people were organized in a very hierarchical fashion, through a web of honor and shame, with extreme wealth and poverty balanced by a very developed system of patronage.

The first social division one finds in Roman law is between *honestiores* and *humiliores*.[6] The *honestiores* were those born into an honored family, who had "property, power and prestige".[7] This group included the orders of senators, equestrians, decurions (members of town councils), and some people from the military and religious offices.[8]

---

5. Finley, *The Ancient Economy*, 30. This is only an educated guess. See what Scheidel says on these numbers: "Our ignorance of the size of ancient populations is one of the biggest obstacles to our understanding or Roman history. After generations of prolific scholarship, we still do not know how many people inhabited Roman Italy and the Mediterranean at any given time . . . What I mean is that even the appropriate order of magnitude remains a matter of intense dispute." Walter Scheidel, "Roman Population Size: The Logic of the Debate," 17. Kehoe affirms that the population increased from 45 million in Augustus' time to 55–65 million in the Antonine period. Kehoe, *Law and Rural Economy in the Roman Empire*, 5.

6. "The distinction between *humiliores* and *honestiores* had particular importance in the field of criminal law and procedure. Some kinds of punishments (capital punishment by crucifixion, by being thrown to wild beasts, torture, bodily punishment) were applicable only to *humiliores*. In certain cases where the *humiliores* were punished by death, the *honestiores* were merely sent into exile." Berger, *Encyclopedic Dictionary of Roman Law*, 489–90.

7. Michael Vickers, *The Ancient Romans*, 31. "The system of acquisition and transmission of property was the basis of the Roman framework of social and economic inequality. This was an agrarian society, in which wealth was essentially in land and acquired by inheritance through family." Garnsey and Saller, *The Roman Empire: Economy, Society and Culture*, 133 (see also p. 72).

8. "What do we know about the distribution of resources within the Roman empire in general? If the conventional imperial nomenclature is anything to go by, a small elite lorded over a vast and formally undifferentiated plebeian populace. Imperial legislation bestowed special prominence on the three orders (*ordines*) of senators, knights and municipal decurions, and subsequently distinguished between *honestiores*, comprised of the three orders plus army veterans, and *humiliores*, pretty much everybody else (or at least all other Roman citizens)." Walter Scheidel, "Stratification, Deprivation and Quality of Life," 40–41. Orders are "those social categories defined by the state through statutory or customary rules." Garnsey and Saller, *The Roman Empire*, 136. Finley's definition is as follows: "An order or estate is a juridically defined group within a population possessing formalized privileges and disabilities in one or more

The *humiliores* were the rest of the people, mostly impoverished free born citizens, non-citizens, freedmen, and slaves. Different from Roman citizenship, and eventually replacing it, there was not a title or an official document to prove that someone was part of the *honestionres* or *humiliores*. One's position in society was something evident both by the public presentation and by the census.[9] Sheidel tries to quantify the numbers of these classes:

> The total numbers of *honestiores* were relatively small: the three *ordines* consisted of at least 350,000 but probably not more than 500,000 individuals (including family members), and there cannot have been many more than 100,000 veterans. Together, these groups accounted for approximately 1 per cent of the population of the empire. In the eyes of the government the other 99 per cent of the population may have been 'humble', but they can hardly all have been of modest means.[10]

As seen, the main people comprising the *honestiores* class were those in the orders of *senators*, *equestrians* and *decurions*. They formed the aristocracy of the empire. The qualifications needed to participate in these positions were money, birth, and mainly politics, since the approval of the emperor was central in the nomination process.[11]

The design of Roman social strata changed drastically when Julius Caesar and then his adopted son Gaius Octavius rose to power. After years of civil war, in 27 BC Octavius was named emperor Augustus, marking the end of the Roman Republic. In this process, the Senate of the People of Rome became more of a garnish than a ruling body.[12] Augustus augmented the qualification

---

fields of activity, governmental, military, legal, economic, religious, marital, and *standing in a hierarchical relation to other orders*." Finley, *The Ancient Economy*, 45.

9. On this subject see also Kehoe, "Law and Social Formation in the Roman Empire," 153–54; Grubbs, *Women and the Law in the Roman Empire*, 12.

10. Scheidel, "Stratification, Deprivation and Quality of Life," 41–42. Also, Longenecker states: "But binary rhetorical constructs of this sort are not to be taken as economic descriptors of the Graeco-Roman world." Longenecker, "Exposing the Economic Middle," 247.

11. "Society was run by great men, and great men were defined by the reputation of their families and the public offices that they held. How they made their money was not much talked about, as long as they still owned land and their (often substantial) commercial activities were not too scandalous." Mayer, *The Ancient Middle Classes*, 9.

12. For an explanation of these facts in the view of an American Senator, see Byrd, *The Senate of the Roman Republic*.

of required wealth for becoming a senator to one million sesterces, reduced the number of senators by half, to around 600 men, and asserted that the emperor was the one who made the nominations.[13]

Being a *senator* was a position of enormous prestige and honor. Senators would dress in a belted bleached white tunic with a broad purple stripe and fine jewelry.[14] They would also have special seats in the theatre. The clothes, the special seats in the theatre, the number of slaves and clients, and the properties had the fundamental goal of showing off how powerful the person was and in so doing keeping and augmenting the power and network of influence.

The *equestrian* order had the same requirements of the senatorial, although in a lesser scale. The property should amount to 400,000 sesterces and noble ascendance and moral excellence were also required. There were thousands of equestrians and some of them had more than the necessary amount of money to become senators. Among the *equites* there were the publicans, since the senators were barred from working as tax collectors. Alone or in companies, the publicans purchased five-year contracts from Rome to collect (heavy) taxes from specific rich provinces. They also participated in auctions for many services the empire needed, such as building, deliveries to the army, buying slaves and mining concessions.[15] For the collection of taxes they would use "exploitation rather than cultivation" as their method of choice.[16] While exclusively the emperor and his family could use completely purple tunics, the equestrians would dress in a belted bleached white tunic with a narrow purple string in order to publicize their status.[17]

The last aristocratic order was that of the *decurions*. They were counselors of towns throughout the empire. In some cities, the census qualification to be a decurion was 100,000 sesterces, a quarter of the equestrian census.[18] As

---

13. Garnsey and Saller, *The Roman Empire*, 136 et seq.

14. Croom, *Roman Clothing and Fashion*, 33.

15. Cf. Bang, "Predation," 203. "The Roman companies of publicans were the largest capitalist enterprises in Antiquity. Participation in these enterprises was limited to men with vast capital holdings in salves and cash. They also needed to have extensive landed possessions, preferably with Italic status (which was privileged and therefore at an economic advantage), since they had to offer land as security when bidding for contracts."

16. Roberts, *The Origins of Business, Money, and Markets*, 160.

17. Croom, *Roman Clothing and Fashion*, 26, 33.

18. Saller, *The Roman Empire: Economy, Society and Culture*, 137. Later, they comment: "Wealth was permitted to override the other criteria of social acceptability for strictly practical reasons. Not only were councilors and magistrates unpaid; they were actually required to

a local aristocracy they were respected by the people and would answer with their own property if the city could not pay the taxes to the emperor. They used to wear a belted bleached white toga that could have colored details. The clothes of those pertaining to the *honestiores* class was made of better wool or linen, would be bleached and could have details in colors. Together with the army, they would use togas with a belt, differing from lower classes who used unbelted tunics. The more wealth one had, the more clothes and of better quality one would also have.[19] The self-peacocking had a very important social function in Rome and both well-to-do men and women would exhibit their opulence and be admired and envied for it.

This part of the population, the *honestiores*, living far above the subsistence level, comprised a maximum of 1 to 5% of the total of the empire.[20] On how to portray the other 95% of the population there is much discussion. Because of the binary division used in the Roman law and literature, it became common to transpose that to the subsistence level, affirming both the non-existence of a middle class and the generalization of poverty. Garnsey and Saller, for example, have the opinion that "[t]here was no genuine 'middle class' in the sense of an intermediate group with independent economic resources or social standing."[21]

More recently, however, some scholars are contending for the existence of a middle class in the Roman Empire. Emanuel Mayer, for example, presents a compelling defense of the existence of a Roman middle class in the beginning of first century AD:

> So was there a social class in antiquity that we may call a "middle class"? Clearly, there were a large number of artisans and merchants in the Roman Empire who lived and worked under very

---

contribute fees to the public treasure on entry into the council or into an office or priesthood. Their wealth was used in addition to other, voluntary expenditures to justify their privileged status in the community, and was the ultimate surety for the tax payments due to the imperial treasury." (p. 138)

19. "The prices for clothes range from 55,000 denarii for a woman's shawl (*mafortia*) decorated with vertical stripes using one pound of purple dye, to 500 denarii for a third quality slave's coarse linen tunic or mantle, and 200 denarii for a third quality slave's loin cloth." Croom, *Roman Clothing and Fashion*, 29.

20. Scheidel, "Stratification, Deprivation and Quality of Life," 54; Longenecker, "Exposing the Economic Middle," 252.

21. Saller, *The Roman Empire*, 139.

similar conditions. As they stood between the rich and the poor, we may call them a middle class, by analogy to later historical circumstances, ancient, more recent and even modern middle cases share important and salient features: first, the importance of work in their public self-definition; second, the celebration of love and affection within the nuclear family; and, third, a desire for a comfortable and joyful life.[22]

For Mayer, one of the pieces of evidence for the existence of a middle class in Roman imperial society is that groups of people with the same professional activity were organizing themselves in *collegia*. "At least from the epigraphic record, *collegia* primarily emerge as an odd mixture between religious, dining, and burial clubs."[23] Mayer conjectures that these *collegia* were contacted by authorities when they needed major services in the specific professional specialization of that *collegium*.

Another piece of evidence for the existence of a middle class is that the archaeological data shows a steady increase in the quality of the city houses in the last centuries BC, pointing to a class of people whose quality of life was becoming better to the point of spending money on decorations for their houses.[24]

The people who formed the Roman middle class were those born free, freedman or even slaves of high rank, who were connected to some form of

---

22. Mayer, *The Ancient Middle Classes*, 3. The case of the archaeologist Mayer for the existence of a middle class in Rome is related to the fact that the tombs and the house panels in the house of artisans and business people shown they had a fair amount of money that allowed them to have expensive marble tombs and panels and their houses, as well as the values this group of people shared among themselves and with contemporary middle class. The author admits however, that he is using a useable and justifiable anachronism. Ahead, he defines again the middle class: "Robinson's survey of Pompeii shows that 60 percent of all bakeries and textile workshops were attached to houses of lesser size. They were owned by a social stratum between the landholding political elites and persons who worked and lived in the *tabernae* that they rented from the well-off. In a straightforward economic sense, these people were a middle class." Mayer, 52.

23. Mayer, 86.

24. "As this chapter argues the size of commercial classes increased in the last three centuries B.C.E. Not only were there more artisans and merchants; the new structure of ancient cities also points to high social mobility among these commercial classes. This translated into a broad spectrum of domestic wealth. In the last century B.C.E. house sizes can be mapped on an almost continuous scale, and the same applies to domestic comfort: elegant wall painting, well-made furniture, and high-quality household items were a feature of almost all houses." Mayer, *The Ancient Middle Classes*, 22–23.

production, commerce, or service. They were bakers, bleachers, bath and tavern owners, money lenders, vendors of meat or imported items, and people who owned properties in the cities of the empire and profited from their renting.[25] There were also *pater familias*, owners of land who used to live in the country and possessed one or more properties and a small number of slaves. Those people lived in amicable conditions but not to the point of being part of the *honestiores*.

Friesen estimates "that economically 'middling' non-*élite* groups accounted for a modest share of the population (around 10 per cent)"[26] Mayer expresses how difficult it is to estimate these numbers while at the same time reporting an approximate idea:

> As any classicist knows, it is very difficult, or perhaps impossible, to quantify anything with certainty when it comes to studying the ancient world. This is why I make no attempt to quantify the Roman middle classes. The most recent - and very conservative - estimate of "middling classes" puts them between 6 and 12 percent of the Roman Empire's overall population. While we cannot know with any certainty how accurate this might be, it is of little concern for the argument presented here. The main claim is that the Roman Empire did generate a sizeable middle class and a middle-class culture, and it is this middle class that generated the bulk of the archaeological evidence from Roman cities.[27]

Longenecker, although not using the term "class" because of its association with Marxist analysis, defends the existence of an economic middle group

---

25. "The transformation from agrotowns into economically and socially diverse cities created economic opportunities outside agriculture. As many items of daily use could no longer be procured through household production, artisans, peddlers, and shopkeepers made it their business to produce and sell them. This also applied to services. A series of recently discovered graffiti from a medium-sized house in Ephesus list a number of items and services that had to be accounted for. These are foodstuffs like bread, olive oil, and sausages but also items of daily use like laundry detergent and soap. Services are listed, too. They include entry fees to the bath, tips for the bath attendant, a haircut, and a laundry bill. The biggest item on the list is four *denarii* in legal fees. Obviously, Echion was correct: there was bread in practicing law. But interestingly, all other items are only valued with a few *assaria*, local small change in bronze." Mayer, 61.

26. Scheidel and Friesen, "The Size of the Economy and the Distribution of Income in the Roman Empire," 63.

27. Mayer, *The Ancient Middle Classes*, 21.

and proposes a table with percentages for all economic groups one would find in the empire. Below, I present Longenecker's table with a few necessary adaptations.[28]

Table 1. Adapted Friesen-Longenecker Economy Scale

Scale	Description	Includes	%
ES1	Imperial elites	imperial dynasty, Roman senatorial families, a few retainers, local royalty, a few freedpersons	0.04
ES2	Regional or provincial elites	equestrian families, provincial officials, some retainers, some decurial families, some freedpersons, some retired military officers	1
ES3	Municipal elites	most decurial families, wealthy men and women who do not hold office, some freedpersons, some retainers, some veterans, some merchants	1.96
ES4	Moderate surplus	augustales, apparitores, some merchants, some traders, some freedpersons, some artisans (especially those who employ others), military veterans	17
ES5	Stable near subsistence level (with reasonable hope of remaining above the minimum level to sustain life)	many merchants and traders, regular wage earners, artisans, large shop owners, freedpersons, some farm families	25
ES6	At subsistence level (and often below minimum level to sustain life)	small farm families, laborers (skilled and unskilled), artisans (esp. those employed by others), wage earners, most merchants and traders, small shop/tavern owners	30
ES7	Below subsistence level	some farm families, unattached widows, orphans, beggars, disabled, unskilled day laborers, prisoners	25

---

28. Longenecker, "Exposing the Economic Middle: A Revised Economy Scale for the Study of Early Urban Christianity." I retained the scales, descriptions, and components of the table presented in Longenecker (Steven Friesen's 'poverty scale'), but adjusted some figures according to the present research.

This table represents the best tentative schematics of the orders of the Roman Empire with the information currently available. Although deviating from a binary model of the Roman economy and being sensitive to the existence of a middle class (ES4), still around 80% of the whole Roman population (ES5–7) lived near the subsistence level. Therefore, the evaluation of Saller and Garnsey remains valid: "The Roman economy was underdeveloped. This means essentially that the mass of the population lived at or near the subsistence level."[29]

Since the wealth of the middle class (ES4) was not mainly connected to land, but to business, it is important to conclude that the empire itself and only 3% of the population (ES1–3) owned a huge proportion of land throughout the empire and as this chapter will show, they were buying more and more.

While the *honestiores* owned the land, the *humiliores* who lived in the country, composed of citizens, freedmen, peasants, tenants, and slaves (ES 5–6), were the ones who worked the lands. They did not have (enough) land themselves and consequently had no opportunity or perspective to improve their economic situation. They formed a large mass of people who could be exploited by the *honestiores*, and there was indeed much exploitation. Before looking into the exploitation, however, it is opportune to present briefly the history of land struggles and land bills from the inception of the Republic up to the Empire in order to show the importance this subject had at that time and the frustrated attempts made to abate the land injustice present in the empire.

2.2 Land Conflicts from the Republic to the Rise of the Empire

Historically, the injustice and exploitation related to land was not peacefully accepted by all inhabitants of Rome. Quite the contrary. This section shows the struggles of those who had no access to land in order to approve laws that could benefit them. These laws never worked as expected and the results of this failure was the maintenance of land injustices and the birth of the empire. The problems related to land injustice that characterized Israel during the New Testament times were not new nor localized.

---

29. Garnsey and Saller, *The Roman Empire*, 71.

The Roman conquests brought with it a rich history of land (*ager*) conflicts and laws. It is not possible to know exactly how the land of Rome was divided at first, but since the beginning of Rome the Patricians had a clear advantage against those who never had or who had lost the title of Roman citizens.[30] All land Rome conquered used to be at first denominated *ager publicus*, i.e. land pertaining to the people (citizens) of Rome. Then, depending on the terms of conquest or surrender, decisions would be made on how to use that land and charge taxes on it.

Cicero presents examples of agreements that Rome used with different people. He says that the Sicilian city-states had been "granted conditions of trust and friendship", paid a tithe to Rome, and had the right to "manage their own affairs themselves". For other people, however, Cicero says that "either a fixed tax has been imposed, which is called a 'tribute,' as for example that imposed on the Spaniards and most of the Carthaginians, which may be considered as the reward of victory and penalty of defeat; or else the taxation system is regulated by censors' contracts, as in Asia under the Sempronian Law."[31]

To be more specific, after the conquest and the declaration of all land as *ager publicus*, Rome would apportion this land unequally in four diverse ways.[32] First, part of this conquered land would be offered for public sale through auctions and, at first, only Roman citizens would be able to participate in those auctions. Second, small tracts of land would sometimes be assigned to the conquered people, depending on the terms of conquest, or to the establishment of Roman colonies of retired, decorated soldiers, or in later times, to impoverished plebeians. These people would transform these lands into family-farms, which had the subsistence as their main goal and, if possible, the production of a small surplus. Third, another part of the *ager publicus* would be retained as such and leased in periods of five years or perpetually with taxes of 10 to 20% being levied on the crops. Finally, large portions of the land which officially was *ager publicus*, would be "occupied" by wealthy citizens using slaves and cattle. This was an indefinite form of

---

30. Andrew Stephenson, *Public Lands and Agrarian Laws of the Roman Republic*, 11 et seq.

31. Cf. *In Verr.* 3.6.12–14. Livy narrates, for example, the conquest of the Ligurians, who have surrendered and were moved and placed in other conquered territory "at public expense". (*Liv.* 40.38)

32. Stephenson, *Public Lands and Agrarian Laws of the Roman Republic*, 17.

ownership the Romans used to call *possessio* or *occupatio*. These huge tracts of land formed large estates called *latifundia*.³³ Stephenson affirms that a great part of the wealth of the Romans consisted in domains of this kind.³⁴

Weber highlights the way in which this last kind of occupation contributed to the increase of social inequality:

> Essentially, *occupatio* grew out of an ancient institution used to put waste lands under cultivation. This was applied to the state in the course of its great expansion. Hence the significance of *occupatio* was entirely altered. Since cattle and slave owners could 'occupy' land with much greater success than free peasants, the result was that once commercial slavery penetrated Roman society there developed an agrarian capitalism of unequalled dimensions. The peasantry reacted to this with demands that conquered lands be divided equally among all citizens and assigned as private property (*ager privatus*).³⁵

As the monetary differences between citizens of high rank, citizens of low rank and plebeians grew stronger and stronger, Roman legislators started to try to use the force of the law to make things less unjust.³⁶ Thus, in 486 BC, the third-time consul Spurius Cassius proposed the first agrarian law. His proposal was to divide among Latins and plebeians some of the public land currently owned by the wealthy in form of *possessio*.³⁷ After the approval of

---

33. For more information on the types of landownership in the Roman Empire, see McGeough, *The Romans: New Perspectives*, 98–99.

34. Stephenson, *Public Lands and Agrarian Laws of the Roman Republic*, 18.

35. Weber, *The Agrarian Sociology of Ancient Civilizations*, 312.

36. Stephenson introduces the section on the Lex Cassia with the following remarks: "Every year added to the difference between the patrician and plebeian, the rich and the poor; a difference which had now grow so great as to threaten seriously the very existence of the state." Stephenson, *Public Lands and Agrarian Laws of the Roman Republic*, 24. Ahead, on page 26 he concludes: "The poor plebeian still continued to shed his blood on the battle field to add to Roman territory, but no foot of it did he obtain. Wealth centralized. Pauperism increased."

37. Livy describes the situation this way: "Of this the consul Cassius proposed to divide one half amongst the Latins and the other half amongst the plebeians. To this gift he wished to add some part of that land which, he charged, was held by individuals, although it belonged to the state. Whereupon many of the Fathers, being themselves in possession of the land, took fright at the danger which threatened their interests." (Livy 2.41) Appian describes the same situation as follows: "But the very opposite thing happened; for the rich, getting possession of the greater part of the undistributed lands, and being emboldened by the lapse of time to believe that they would never be dispossessed, absorbing any adjacent strips and their poor neighbors'

Cassius' law, much violence followed against those responsible for executing it.[38] Shortly thereafter, accused of aspiring against the royal power, Cassius was sentenced to immediate execution and stabbed in the middle of the forum.[39] This story would set a standard that endured many years in the Republic.

There were many attempts over the years to approve and establish an agrarian law that would give lands to the plebs. Some of the proponents of laws during these years were Spurius Licinius, Tiberius Pontificius, Quintus Considius together with Titus Genucius, and Lucius Icilius.[40] These laws, however, faced resistance of the patricians who would use the force of the Senate against these laws. It is worth noting that the historian Livy pairs himself with the patricians and scourges the proponents of the agrarian laws, naming these laws even as the "usual poison" of the Tribunes against the "Fathers".[41] During many decades, the land laws were the main cause of *turbulentia* among the orders.[42]

The next great event of the history of the agrarian laws in Rome happened in the career of Licinius Stolo. A plebeian married to a wise Patrician wife, Stolo was elected Tribune in 378 BC.[43] He proposed many laws favoring the plebs, including one limiting the size of *ager publicus* owned by *possessio* to 500 iugera, another changing the rules on money lending, another obligating the hiring of free men in large estates, and still another affirming that one of the consuls was to be elected from the plebs. Livy's reading of the situation after these proposals is very opportune: "Now when all the things that men immoderately covet, lands, money, and promotion, were jeopardized at once, the patricians became thoroughly alarmed . . .".[44] Stolo's career was rocketing

---

allotments, partly by purchase under persuasion and partly by force, came to cultivate vast tracts instead of single estates, using slaves as labourers and herdsmen, lest free labourers should be drawn from agriculture into the army." (Appian, *Civil Wars* 1.7)

38. Niebuhr, *The Roman History*, 24.
39. *Flor* 1.17.7
40. *Liv.* 2.43; 2.44; 2.52; 2.61.
41. *Liv.* 2.52
42. Livy uses similar terms in 2.61. In 2.63, Levy says: "It was clear that the plebs would endure no further postponement of the land-law, and were preparing to use violent measures . . .".
43. *Dio Cass.* 7.29
44. *Liv.* 6.35

to the point of being elected *dictator*.⁴⁵ One of the most important of Stolo's accomplishments, however, was also the reason for his decline. He was convicted of owning by *possessio* more than 500 iugera (300 acres) of land and sentenced to pay the fines that he himself had determined.⁴⁶ Even after all these endeavors, as the *lex licinia* lacked better systems of reinforcement, it did not change the real situation. So Stephenson:

> But in the main the rich still grew richer and the poor and mean, poorer and more contemptible. Such was ever the liberty of the Roman. For the mean and the poor there was no means of retrieving their poverty and degradation. These laws, then, had little or no effect upon the domain question or the re-distribution of land.⁴⁷

From the *lex licinia* (367 BC) to the Gracchan movement (133 BC), Patricians and plebeians enjoyed a time of relative peace. Many colonies were founded both to accommodate the Roman plebs and retired soldiers. These colonies had the important function of securing the new borders and Romanizing the new conquered people. Thus, the Senate itself started to distribute 5, 7 up to 10 iugera of land to people who were ignored before. These distributions of land also had the effect of augmenting the military force, since only those who owned land were apt to enlist.

At the same time, though, Roman military campaigns were going farther and farther, making it hard for the poorer colonists to maintain and keep their properties. Also, the Second Punic War, Hannibal's military campaign against Rome (218 to 201 BC), caused the destruction of many estates, cities and the loss of many lives. These facts, added to the influx of grains from abroad, made the life of poor colonists harder and the situation of the aristocracy easier, since the influx of money from the conquests made them even

---

45. "The Roman dictatorship was a constitutional office that only existed in times of emergency, when the normal constitution structures were considered unable to deal with a crisis in a satisfactory manner," Greene, *Permanent States of Emergency and the Rule of Law*, 6. "In the early history of Rome, it was regular for a dictator to be appointed in response to a severe threat from the outside." Golden, *Crisis Management during the Roman Republic*.

46. Plutarch, *Vit. Cat. Mai., Min.* 39.150; *Liv.* 7.16

47. Stephenson, *Public Lands and Agrarian Laws of the Roman Republic*, 45; Philip Kay, *Rome's Economic Revolution*, 102 et seq. Weber's conclusion on the agrarian reforms is that "after the full ownership of occupied land was confirmed, the whole of Italy was to a very large extent in the hands of estate owners." Weber, *The Agrarian Sociology of Ancient Civilizations*, 322.

more affluent and the poor more indebted.⁴⁸ Rome was facing inflation and the wealthy were adding more and more land and slaves.⁴⁹

What happened before in Italy, now was happening in the whole world. As Rome was conquering land almost uninterruptedly, *latifundia* were owned by the *honestiores* and run and operated by armies of slaves. It is in this context that Tiberius Sempronius Gracchus appears. Gracchus was the grandson of the great Scipio Africanus, the Roman general who defeated Hannibal in the Second Punic War. When elected consul, Tiberius Gracchus tried to approve another agrarian law. He vindicated the redistribution of public land occupied by wealthy aristocrats, only what exceeded 500 iugera plus 250 iugera per son, to poor plebeians.⁵⁰ The proposal faced strong opposition.

Stephenson explains this opposition to the law to the fact that, although the aristocracy of birth had ended, and the plebeians had conquered many rights and positions in the Republic, a new aristocracy based on wealth had developed and this *nouveau riche* alongside the old patricians were denying to others the access to wealth they enjoyed.⁵¹ Although the proposals of Tiberius Gracchus were approved and he was increasing in popularity by the minute, the Senate managed to stir up a riot and kill the reformer, who entered for the pages of history as both the destroyer and the reformer

---

48. "Debt we a direct consequence of poverty and land hunger, and itself gave rise to the condition of servitude to which many of the plebeians were reduced. The institution of debt-bondage us well attested in early Rome and has parallels in many other archaic societies." Joshel, "Slavery and Roman Literary Culture," 329.

49. Scullard, *From the Gracchi to Nero*, 18–21. How and Leigh present the moment as such: "But as the days of struggle ended and the external restraint of foreign rivals ceased to act, as the antique virtues which had justified command were corrupted by the influence of wealth and power, with despotism rampant abroad and capitalism at home, it was time for a new and internal check to be created sufficient to arrest decay." How and Leigh, *A History of Rome*, 331.

50. Plutarch on this: "And it is thought that a law dealing with injustice and rapacity so great was never drawn up in milder and gentler terms. For men who ought to have been punished for their disobedience and to have surrendered with payment of a fine the land which they were illegally enjoying, these men it merely ordered to abandon their unjust acquisitions upon being paid their value, and to admit into ownership of them such citizens as needed assistance. But although the rectification of the wrong was so considerate, the people were satisfied to let bygones be bygones if they could be secure from such wrong in the future; the men of wealth and substance, however, were led by their greed to hate the law, and by their wrath and contentiousness to hate the lawgiver, and tried to dissuade the people by alleging that Tiberius was introducing a re-distribution of land for the confusion of the body politic, and was stirring up a general revolution." (Plutarch, *Ti. Gracch.* 9)

51. Stephenson, *Public Lands and Agrarian Laws of the Roman Republic*, 56–57.

of the Roman Republic.⁵² To Weber, the main motivation for the Gracchan movement was a political reform in order to restore the ancient foundations of Rome's military systems.⁵³

Following Tiberius Gracchus' death, a revolution begun. His brother Gaius Gracchus became the main leader and continuator of Tiberius' ideas and faced the same fate as his. The subsequent years saw many proposals of agrarian laws always in practice resisted by the Senate, even when officially approved.

And why is all that important? This section shows how the subjects related to land were at the center of the political and social scene in Rome and the great relevance Luke adds to his work by dealing with this subject.

As we saw, many proposals of land reformation were being made. One of these proposals had in Cicero a fierce opponent. In *De Agraria Lege*, Cicero vociferates against a new agrarian law proposed to the Senate by the tribune Rullus. The first discourse addresses the Senate and the second and third speeches the Assembly of the people. Cicero's main accusation is that the new law would take the lands from the people of Rome and place it in the power of Rullus and other nine men, hence *decemvirs*. These *decemvirs* would be able to nominate public lands, set the taxes and sell *ager publica* as it suited them. Cicero says: "For it orders the same *decemvirs* to impose a very high tax on all public lands, so that they may be able to free any lands from it that they choose, and to declare any that they please to be public property."⁵⁴ A few pages ahead, he affirms that the *decemvirs* are the ones buying the land from the State after having expropriated them.⁵⁵ In his second discourse, Cicero vociferates against the new agrarian law as one that would not at all benefit the plebeians, but only a few who had written it.⁵⁶ One of Cicero's arguments in the third discourse is that his father in law would profit with this new law and, therefore, he was not against the law for personal reasons. He affirms:

---

52. Riddle, *Tiberius Gracchus*.
53. Weber, *The Agrarian Sociology of Ancient Civilizations*, 319.
54. Cicero, *Leg. agr.* 1.4.10
55. Cicero, *Leg. agr.* 1.5.14–15
56. In *Leg agr.* 2.6 he writes: "Thus I maintain, O Romans, that this admirable and popular agrarian law gives you nothing, but makes a present of everything to certain individuals; it holds lands before the eyes of the Roman people and robs them even of liberty; it increases the wealth of private persons and exhausts the fortunes of the State; lastly, the most disgraceful thing of all, a tribune of the people, a magistrate whom our ancestors intended to be the protector and guardian of liberty, is to set up kings in the republic."

> My father-in-law has some out-of-the-way waste lands; he will be able to sell them at whatever price he likes by virtue of my law. He has others of uncertain title, to the possession of which he has no right at all; they will be assured to him by the best possible title. He holds them as public property; I will make them private property. Lastly, as to those rich and productive estates, which he has bought one after the other in the district of Casinum, by the proscription of his neighbours as far as the eye could reach, until all these farms completed the appearance of a single large district and estate—these lands, which he now holds with a certain amount of apprehension, he will be able to possess without any anxiety.[57]

Note that under the current law, Cicero's father in law was able to use and add many lands to the point of becoming the *de facto* owner of lands and latifundia, but without guaranties. Under the new law, according to Cicero, he would be able to become the rightful proprietor of those lands acquired in questionable ways.

After a sequence of failed agrarian laws, Julius Caesar, in 59 BC managed to propose an agrarian law and put it into action. Julius Caesar proposed to buy land of those willing to sell it and use vacant land instead of those with owners. He also persecuted those who were against the bill as, for example, Cato, who was sent to prison.[58] Julius Caesar also alleviated the debt proposing a plan in which the properties' values would be reassessed, interests would be cut, part of the interests already paid would abate the debt, debtors would be able to keep part of their estates and creditors would receive the other part of it.[59] The plan was complex, but it had the positive side of not leaving any group completely disappointed. Julius Caesar's solutions to the land and the debt problems can be counted among the main reasons for his popularity among the masses but also for his assassination in 44 BC. The *pax* came only with the beginning of the empire under Caesar Augustus in 27 BC.

In conclusion, it is possible to say that almost since its birth, Rome divided its population between the honored citizens, whose main asset was land, and

---

57. Leg. agr. 3.4.14
58. Southern, *Augustus*, 17; Lintott, *The Romans in the Age of Augustus*, 64.
59. Lovano, *All Things Julius Caesar*, 280.

consequently, wealth and honor, and the poor plebs. For centuries the plebs claimed the right of having land, being constantly resisted by the Senate. The *ager publicus* was possessed and used by the aristocracy and from time to time small portions of land were given to settlers in order to forward the domination of distant provinces. The empire brought peace, but certainly failed to bring justice for all. The next section will present the ways in which the empire itself and the *honestiores* exploited most of the people.

2.3 The Agrarian Economy and Economic Exploitation in the Roman Empire

The first section of this chapter dealt with the social stratification of the Roman Empire and argued that more than 80% of its population lived close to the subsistence line. In the previous section, I presented the history of the class struggles with concern for land, from the old Republic until the rise of the empire. Both sections, therefore, made clear that there was an enormous gap between those who possessed land and those who did not have this privilege and also, that the first group would do everything possible to keep their positions at the expense of the plebs. This section will make it yet clearer how both the empire and its ruling class exploited those under them in the social pyramid.

2.3.1 Exploitation by the Empire

Greg Wolf defines empires in the following terms: "Empires are political systems based on the actual or threatened use of force to extract surpluses from their subjects. Imperial elites spend these revenues on the infrastructure necessary to maintain power, and retain a profit that is distributed to groups that are privileged by virtue of their place within the imperial hierarchy."[60] This definition fits perfectly the reality of the Empire of Rome.

---

60. Woolf, "Imperialism, Empire and the Integration of the Roman Economy," 283. After remembering that the story in the Bible happens in the context of different empires, Brueggemann lists three characteristic marks of all empires: "First, empires existed to extract wealth in order to transfer wealth from the vulnerable to the powerful. . . . Second, empires pursued a policy of commoditization in which everything and everyone was reduced to a dispensable commodity that could be bought and sold and traded and possessed and consumed. . . . Third, empires that practiced extraction and commoditization were fully prepared to undertake violence on whatever scale was required for the success of extraction and commoditization." Brueggemann,

Rome was fond of predatory practices since its foundation. Bang shows that through the episode of the abduction of the Sabine women.[61] This "predatory imperialism" continued in the conquests, by which the best of the possessions and land of the colonized people were confiscated and subjected to large taxes. Bang concludes his analysis affirming that "[t]he formation of the empire radically changed the capacity of hierarchical organizations, aristocratic households and government in particular. They were able to impose greater demands on wider populations. Land and mineral fields were confiscated, people enslaved or faced with higher demands for rents and taxes."[62]

Writing from a post-colonialist point of view, Mattingly states that "[e]mpires exploit territory and people, and there tend to be common patterns in the sequence of events that follow armed conquest of a region . . . The Roman sources, and the (rare) testimony of subject peoples such as the Jews, certainly suggest that the Roman state had an extraordinary capacity for swallowing up the wealth of the world."[63]

This opinion of Rome as the swallower of the wealth of the world is not a phenomenon of our time only, but witnesses from the first century

---

God, Neighbor, Empire, 2. He continues this insightful note by saying: "These policies and practices, moreover, were regularly legitimated by liturgical enactment of myths that allied the power of God to the power of the state. Such an understanding of god (gods) was perforce top-down, so that the claims of empire were theologically imposed by the empire of force." Other writers who deserve mention here are Ekholm and Freedman, who defend that ancient empires have the same capitalist core as new capitalist societies. They comment: "Our argument is that the general properties of imperialist-mercantilist expansion are common to ancient and modern worlds irrespective of specific local forms of accumulation. . . . Center/periphery systems are, by definition, imperialistic insofar as the center of a system accumulates wealth based on the production of a wider area. While the existence of larger exchange systems is linked to and reinforced by the emergence of local hierarchy and class domination, the c/p relation further integrates such local class structures into a differentiated pattern where the central class becomes increasingly elaborated into factions – landed aristocrats, bureaucrats, merchants, etc. – exploiting by direct taxation, slavery and even contract and wage labor, while the peripheral class structure is more or less restricted to a chiefly or feudal elite (that may become more elaborate in the developmental process) that mediates the export of raw materials and control all imports." Ekholm and Friedman, "'Capital' Imperialism and Exploitation in Ancient World Systems," 44–45.

61. Bang, "Predation." The abduction of the Sabine women is part of the Roman foundation myths. Not long after Romulus founded Rome with his mostly male followers, the Romans asked their Sabine neighbors to give their daughters to them in marriage, which they denied. The Romans then invited their Sabine and other neighbors to a great festival. In this festival, they abducted many Sabine women, who eventually became their wives.

62. Bang, "Predation," 213.

63. Mattingly, *Imperialism, Power, and Identity*, 146.

also framed Rome as such. Cornelius Tacitus presents the discourse of the Caledonian Calgacus, right before battling against the army of the Roman general Julius Agricola confirming this:

> Robbers of the world, now that earth fails their all-devastating hands, they probe even the sea: if their enemy have wealth, they have greed; if he be poor, they are ambitious; East nor West has glutted them; alone of mankind they covet with the same passion want as much as wealth. To plunder, butcher, steal, these things they misname empire: they make a desolation and they call it peace.[64]

One cannot lose sight, therefore, of the fact that the Roman empire was a huge structure built for the betterment of just one city, and by city we mean only the elites of that city, and especially the emperor's house.[65] The empire engaged in exploitation by subjecting conquered people to slavery, confiscating land, charging taxes, obligating specific cultures, obligating military service, imposing its culture of bread and circus, and the cult to the emperor.[66] By far, the most profitable of these exploitations, however, were those related to land. So, Finley:

---

64. Cornelius Tacitus, *Agr.* 30

65. "As great as the fortunes of wealthy private individuals were, the state was by far the largest landowner in the Roman Empire. The imperial government derived substantial revenues from state owned land, or imperial states, which were to be found in Italy and in all the provinces. These states came into imperial ownership from a variety of sources, including bequest to the emperor by grateful senators, the defaulting of property to the state when people died without heirs, and the confiscation of property of those unfortunate enough to be condemned for capital crimes or for tax arrears." Kehoe, "Landlords and Tenants," 298–99.

66. This remarkable passage of Tacitus speaking on the conquering of Britain illustrates well this point: "Children and kin are by the law of nature each man's dearest possessions; they are swept away from us by conscription to be slaves in other lands: our wives and sisters, even when they escape a soldier's lust, are debauched by self-styled friends and guests: our goods and chattels go for tribute; our lands and harvests in requisitions of grain; life and limb themselves are worn out in making roads through marsh and forest to the accompaniment of gibes and blows. Slaves born to slavery are sold once for all and are fed by their masters free of cost; but Britain pays a daily price for her own enslavement, and feeds the slavers; and as in the slave-gang the new-comer is a mockery even to his fellow-slaves, so in this world-wide, age-old slave-gang, we, the new hands, worth least, are marked out to be made away with: we have no lands or mines or harbours for the working of which we might be set aside." Tacitus, *Agricola* 31 in Tacitus. *Agricola. Germania. Dialogue on Oratory.* Translated by M. Hutton, W. Peterson. Revised by R. M. Ogilvie, E. H. Warmington, Michael Winterbottom. LCL 35. Cambridge: Harvard University Press, 1914.

> The commonplace that the land was the chief source of wealth in antiquity must be understood in the Roman Empire, from its beginning, to include the wealth of the state. That is to say, not only was the emperor himself by far the largest landowner but the bulk of the taxes fell on land. Although it is meaningless to assert, as do many historians, that in the early Empire taxation 'was not very oppressive', it is correct that the burden was bearable in the sense that grumbling led to appeals for a tax reduction, not to mass desertion from the land not to revolt.[67]

Finley highlights two areas in which the Roman state profited from its subjects related to land: land appropriation and taxes. Let us examine both beginning with Roman politics of land appropriation. Rome had different politics concerning land ownership rights to Rome and Italy on one hand and to the provinces, on the other.[68] In Italy, besides some *ager publicus*, there was full ownership of land available for Roman citizens, who would not have the burden of paying taxes.[69] The provinces did not have the same fortune. The conquered lands were confiscated and became public land. If the nation would submit peacefully and behave properly, some landowners would have the opportunity to keep their lands by paying taxes to Rome. Those nations and people who would not surrender were deported, enslaved and had their lands confiscated. The usufruct of this land would then be donated to retired military personnel, people who supported the conquest, and other influential people with access to the emperor.[70] As the last section has demonstrated, most of this land was historically kept by the *élites*.

Besides the territorial expansion by conquest the emperor had other ways through which he would acquire land. As Kehoe says, "These states came

---

67. Finley, *The Ancient Economy*, 89–90.

68. "In the last century of the Republic (we cannot tell the exact date or circumstances), the whole of the soil of Italy was assimilated to the original *ager Romanus*, the notion of *ager Italicus* took the place of that of *ager Romanus*, and the term *jus Italicum* designated the legal condition of land in the provinces which was given the privilege of full ownership, the occupiers of which had *dominium ex jure Quiritium*. Outside Italy, the ground was, on principle and save for exceptions, of provincial status, that is, it was subject to a tax and did not carry full ownership with it." Toutain, *The Economic Life of the Ancient World*, 272–73.

69. Thus, Cicero's accusation against Servilius Rulus, tribune of the people roughly a hundred years before the writing of Luke-Acts: "He is selling all the public property in Italy item by item." Cicero, *De Lege Agraria* 1.2 (LCL 240, p. 343).

70. Cf. Mattingly, *Imperialism, Power, and Identity: Experiencing the Roman Empire*, 157.

into imperial ownership from a variety of sources, including bequest to the emperor by grateful senators, the defaulting of property to the state when people died without heirs, and the confiscation of property of those unfortunate enough to be condemned for capital crimes or for tax arrears."[71] The consequence is that the State itself was the main landowner in the empire. This land could be ceded to tenants or administrated directly by the emperor's administration. Again, Kehoe: "The state maintained direct control throughout the empire of a substantial network of land and estates as well as other properties, including mines and quarries. These properties provided an important source of revenue, supplementing those achieved from direct taxes."[72]

These direct taxes were the second way through which the emperor would profit from land and maintain the power.[73] The Roman Empire had enormous expenditures. They had to sustain the military and its bureaucracy, feed and entertain the plebs of Rome and keep a continuous program of edification in Rome in order to produce jobs.[74] Sometimes the emperors would even distribute money to maintain their popularity (*congiarium*, *liberalitas*). Garnsey and Saller correctly comment that "It was the tax on agricultural land in all the provinces (but not Italy) which paid for the bulk of this expenditure."[75]

As affirmed above, although that was not so in Italy, the land in the provinces were subject to land taxes. It is hard to know exactly the total value of taxes someone living in a Roman province would need to pay, because each province had its own terms with the empire. Mattingly affirms that the taxes were a heavy burden and calculates that in Egypt one might have had to pay

---

71. Kehoe, "Landlords and Tenants," 298–99. See also Kehoe, *Law and Rural Economy in the Roman Empire*, 48–49.

72. Dennis P. Kehoe, "The State and Production in the Roman Agrarian Economy," 34.

73. "The system of land tenure that the Roman government maintained on imperial estates was a product of its efforts to achieve specific long-term economic goals. It is a likely hypothesis that the government maintained direct control over imperial estates, especially in important food-producing provinces, to ensure its access to crucial agricultural products, particularly grain and olive oil. Imperial estates in the provinces supplied revenues in kind that helped to provide food for the politically sensitive distribution programs in Rome, and the revenues from imperial estates, both in food-stuffs and in cash, also supplemented the revenues achieved by the taxation of private land to support the infrastructure of the government." Kehoe, *Law and Rural Economy in the Roman Empire*, 54.

74. Cf. Garnsey and Saller, *The Roman Empire*, 35.

75. Garnsey and Saller, *The Roman Empire*, 82.

up to 25% of grain production in addition to many other additional taxes.⁷⁶ Kehoe has another figure:

> Although it is difficult to be certain on this point, tax rates on private agricultural land were modest in the early Roman Empire, at least in comparison with other pre-industrial economies, generally in the range of about 10 per cent; at least they do not seem to have increased over time. Lands devoted to viticulture or olive culture, which were more productive in terms of revenue for each unit of land, were taxed at a higher rate.⁷⁷

Even this last figure, however, did not mean that the taxation system was just. The difficulty to access this number is that they depended on the specific province. Another possible variation is that while some provinces paid their taxes in crops and according to the size of the estates, others paid in money.⁷⁸ The censuses that became common in the empire had the objective of quantifying the properties of people in order to establish a more proportional taxation. Luke himself makes a clear reference to one of these censuses in Luke 2:1, specifying that Caesar Augustus expedited a decree requiring that all the world should be registered.

As the main landowners or renters of public land would sublease to people of more modest means, the tax burden would be heavy on these. As Finley affirms, "The social distribution of the burden was far more uneven. Land taxation lay most heavily, directly or indirectly, on those who actually worked the land, peasants and tenants."⁷⁹

This reality of taxes is present in the Gospel of Luke through it many references to publicans (3:12; 5:27–32; 7:29, 34; 15:1; 18:9–14; 19:1–10) and two important references to taxes. In Luke 20:25 Jesus utters the famous saying, "Then render to Caesar the things that are Caesar's, and to God the things that are God's." Through this answer, Jesus evaded the question about the justice of the taxes and at the same time made clear that there were more important things one should occupy the self with, i.e. the things related to God. The second reference to taxes that appear in the Gospel of Luke is one

---

76. Mattingly, *Imperialism, Power, and Identity: Experiencing the Roman Empire*, 152.
77. Kehoe, "The State and Production in the Roman Agrarian Economy," 37–38.
78. Richard Duncan-Jones, *Structure and Scale in the Roman Economy*, 187 et seq.
79. Finley, *The Ancient Economy*, 91.

of the false accusations against Jesus during his judgement before Pilate that he was "forbidding us to give tribute to Caesar" (Luke 23:2).

Besides land appropriation and taxes, the Roman Empire also would feel free to determine specific cultures and finalities for the farmers in the provinces. Garnsey and Saller comment, "In addition, some change of land use was forced on farmers, insofar as they had to provide the army with supplies, or alternatively, in areas lacking a substantial military garrison, produce goods that they could sell to raise money-taxes. This was exploitation, and in aggregate exceeded anything witnessed previously in the Mediterranean world."[80]

The result of this is that the state was the major exploiter of land and people in the first century AD. Conquering and subjecting peoples and their land at its own will, imposing taxes that would impact mainly the poor, and exerting freedom to decide cultures and finalities for crops. The emperor was the one who profited most from the large system of exploitation that was the Roman Empire.[81] But the *princeps* should not receive alone all the blame of this oppression. The ruling classes of Rome would also profit from abusing the *humiliores*, as will be demonstrated next.

2.3.2 Exploitation by the Ruling Classes

As I previously noted, the *honestiores* were the ones who, along with the emperor, owned most of the land throughout the empire. It was common for them to live in Rome or other cities where they held public offices. It was also common for the wealthy to own many lands in the city, near the city and in distant provinces and use workers to develop it. Garnsey and Saller affirm that "[t]he direct exploitation of labour by rich proprietors was a central feature of Roman imperial society."[82] It was through exploitation that the aristocracy

---

80. Garnsey and Saller, *The Roman Empire*, 82–83.

81. Kehoe contends that the fact the emperor was the main owner of land had a positive economic and social impact: "However, the growth and influence of private estates were to some extent mitigated by the considerable role that the state played as landowner. Since the state was by far the largest landowner in the Roman Empire, the administrative policies that it followed affected the terms of land tenure on a significant portion of the empire's most productive farmland. As I argue, the Roman state's policies in administering its estates were likely to have had enormous consequences for the Roman agrarian economy as a whole. To some extent, the state's fiscal interests may have worked to impede the growth of the large estates of the empire's elite." Kehoe, *Law and Rural Economy in the Roman Empire*, 48.

82. Garnsey and Saller, *The Roman Empire*, 134.

of Rome could reproduce a kind of omnipresence that generated wealth to them in many places throughout the empire at the same time.

Lucius Columella (AD 4–70) is the most important Roman writer on agriculture, having written 12 volumes of his *De Res Rustica*, translated as On the Agriculture. He deplores the way land was being used in his days, the fact that there were no specialists on agriculture and the common opinion that now, after many years of producing, the land was barren. Columella saw that as a completely wrong opinion. The problem, he explains, was that the land was being mistreated and "delivered over to all the worst of our slaves."[83] Columella affirms that one should buy land to live on it. However, as the political aspirations of his days were attracting people to the cities, he says, one should at least buy land in such a distance that he could visit it every day.[84] The reality of his time however was very different from this ideal, at least for the richest part of the population. He vividly describes what was happening:

> Therefore, as in all matters, so too in the acquiring of land, moderation shall be exercised. For only so much is to be occupied as is needed, that we may appear to have purchased what we may keep under control, not to saddle ourselves with a burden and to deprive others of its use and enjoyment after the manner of men of enormous wealth who, possessing entire countries of which they cannot even make the rounds, either leave them to be trampled by cattle and wasted and ravaged by wild beasts, or keep them occupied by citizens enslaved for debt and by chain-gangs.[85]

Thus, Columella refers to many forms of exploitation committed by those he calls "men of enormous wealth." First, they were depriving others of having land by becoming owners of entire countries. Second, they exploited the land itself using them for cattle or leaving them to wild beasts. Third, they were using "citizens enslaved for debt" as workers. Fourth, they were using slaves as manpower, both unfettered and "chain-gangs." Let us focus

---

83. Columella, *Rust* 1.0.3.
84. Columella, *Rest* 1.1.18–19.
85. Columella, *Rust* 1.3.11–12, emphasis mine.

on three of these forms of exploitation detected by Columella that relate to the exploitation of people.

2.3.2.1 The Problem of Latifundia

Latifundium is the Latin name for the large estates owned by the wealthiest families of the empire, mainly those with a historical high standing in society but also those who enjoyed special favors from the leaders of Rome.[86] These *latifundia* were created by *possessio* or at the expense of family farms, and would use mainly slaves and daily workers.[87] Sometimes these large estates were used for stock-rearing.[88] From time to time, even when Rome gave away 5 to 7 *iugera* to small colonists, the final destiny of these lands were the rich owners who would regain control of lands buy buying them, or entrapping the humble proprietors in debts and gaining practical control over their lands.[89]

---

86. "For this reason those seven iugera of Licinius, which the tribune of the plebs distributed to each man after the expulsion of the kings, rewarded the ancients with greater returns than our very extensive fallow-lands bestow upon us nowadays (*quam nunc nobis praebent amplissima veterata*). Columella, *Agr* 1.3.9–10.

87. David Mattingly, "The Imperial Economy," 289. Also Bowman and Wilson, "We have moved away from some traditional notions of a general linear progression towards 'latifundists' absorbing the independent peasantry, and an increase over time in the phenomenon of *agri deserti*. Although an appreciable amount of land changes hand, traditional patterns stubbornly persist in most rural areas. But, where there is quantifiable evidence, it suggests an increase (or at least no decrease) in the inequality of distribution of privately owned land and a clear trend away from state ownership and direct exploitation to private control, though caution is required in linking this to the supposed spread of 'feudalism' and the 'colonate', whatever we think these might be." Alan Bowman and Andrew Wilson, *The Roman Agricultural Economy*, 20–21. Garnsey and Saller, on another hand criticize the reconstruction in which ownership of small estates was diminishing drastically because of grand proprietors and affirms that "[o]wners-occupiers, tenant-farmers and farm labourers working for a wage were three overlapping categories thus owners-occupiers were a major recruiting ground for tenants." Garnsey and Saller, *The Roman Empire*, 102. See also Bunson, *Encyclopedia of the Roman Empire*, 301

88. Scullard, *From the Gracchi to Nero*, 19.

89. "Let me merely emphasize the fact that in the last period of the Republic most of the population settled on the lands in Rome's vast possessions were not protected by any treaty. Whatever rights to the land he had were revocable, their holdings were *precaria*. This applied especially to the peasants who actually worked the soil. . . . In other words, the peasants were subject to the arbitrary power of the provincial governors and, in so far as he did not intervene, to the power of tax farmers." Weber, *The Agrarian Sociology of Ancient Civilizations*, 333. See also, "We should also recognize that peasant farming was a dynamic and unstable system. Within a few years if the initial allocation of allotments, a kaleidoscopic process of division and amalgamation of the privately owned plots will have begun as the result of partible inheritance and sales, of some families prospering and other failing, some expanding and others dying out. Some will have increased their holdings and become employers of slaves and tenants, some will have had to resort to renting and laboring, others will have preferred to move off and take their

Sometimes, instead of having the sole responsibility of making the land produce, wealthy landholders would use the system of tenancy. They would buy a large estate and place many families to take care of it and make it produce profit. As I will show in chapter seven, Luke deals with the reality and some of the evils of tenancy in his gospel (Luke 20:9–18). The *latifundia* were a common phenomenon during the Republic, but they increased even more during the empire.[90]

In the center of these large estates was the *villa*.[91] This property and system of agriculture was characterized by the production of culture of subsistence for the villa itself and cash crops like wine and olive oil. A common villa would have several hundred hectares. There was a rotation in the cultures to maximize the use of land and slave labor. These slaves, living in a subhuman condition, were supervised by a bailiff, or *vilicus*, who commonly would be himself a slave of higher rank. Rich landowners would possess many *villae* in distinct parts of Italy and throughout the empire to minimize risk due to weather conditions. Archeology has helped scholars of this field by finding and reconstructing many of these *villae*.[92]

As we saw in Columella, not everyone in Rome was pleased with the phenomenon of *latifundia*. Pliny the Elder, for example, writing in the first century AD, deplores the current tendency of owning latifundia:

> In old times it was thought that to observe moderation in the size of farm was of primary importance, inasmuch as the view was held that it was more satisfactory to sow less land and plough it better; and I observe that Virgil was of this opinion. And if the

---

chances as urban poor. There are echoes of this in the literary sources." Dominic Rathbone, "Poor Peasants and Silent Sherds," 309–10.

90. Scullard, *From the Gracchi to Nero*, 327. "In the sphere of private landownership, Roman rule fostered the creation of large estates in the provinces, as the elite of the Roman Empire, including the senatorial and equestrian orders as well as the members of town councils, came to be made up of wealthy landowners throughout the more urbanized provinces. Over the course of the early empire, landownership became increasingly stratified, and it seems clear a greater portion of wealth was concentrated in fewer hands. Elite landowners took advantage of the commercial opportunities offered by the Roman Empire by producing cash crops, including wine and olive oil, for urban markets, and they used the wealth that they derived from agriculture to increase the extent of the land that they controlled." Kehoe, *Law and Rural Economy in the Roman Empire*, 45–46.

91. Kehoe, "Landlords and Tenants," 300.

92. See, for example: Annalisa Marzano, *Roman Villas in Central Italy*.

truth be confessed, large estates have been the ruin of Italy, and are now proving the ruin of the provinces too—half of Africa was owned by six landlords, when the Emperor Nero put them to death; though Gnaeus Pompeius must not be cheated out of this mark of his greatness also: he never bought land belonging to a neighbouring estate.[93]

It is evident that the existence of latifundia was a fact and, in Pliny's opinion, a deplorable one, since it was not in his view an honorable thing to possess too much land, especially if buying it from your own neighbors. Pliny's contemporary, Seneca the Younger shows a similar attitude towards latifundia in his epistle 88, in which he questions the right of an owner of latifundia (by *possessio*) in comparison to the right of the previous native owners of it.

There were many different farm sizes throughout the empire. Cato affirms in the second century BC that the best kind of farm was one of a hundred *iugera* (25 hectares) comprising all sorts of soil.[94] He also speaks about the necessary equipment for an olive yard of 240 *iugera* (60 hectares) and a vineyard of 100 *iugera*.[95] It is worth noting, however, that in the Gracchan movement, the proposal was to reduce the estates owned by *possessio* to 500 hundred *iugera* (125 hectares) plus 250 extra *iugera* for each son. Thus, there was a large variation in the sizes of estates in the Roman Empire and it is not possible to know precisely how many *iugera* were needed to consider a large estate a *latifundium*. The variation in size of estates one finds in the extant sources is from less than one *iugerum* to 3000 *iugera*.[96]

Cicero, for example, writes the *Philippic* to criticize Mark Antony in 43–44 BC and among the criticisms, he affirms that Antony gave three thousand *iugera* in the Plain of Leontini to his doctor (probably Antonius Musa) and two thousand to his professor (Sex. Clodius). He also describes the excesses the latter would practice in his own villa.[97]

---

93. Pliny, *Natural History*, 18.1.35, emphasis mine.
94. Cato, *Agr.* 1.2.
95. Cato, *Agr.* 1.10–11.
96. Duncan-Jones, *Structure and Scale in the Roman Economy*, 130. See also Kehoe, *Law and Rural Economy in the Roman Empire*, 46.
97. Cicero, *Philip.* 2.41.105–107; 3.9.22.

The consequence of the existence and propagation of latifundia was that there was not much land available for independent farmers and those who persisted in keeping their farms would have difficulties maintaining them and competing in the market to sell their surplus. Due to this situation, then, the wealthy *honestiores* were becoming richer and richer and other people would have had their possibilities of improving their economic situation through land curtailed. As this dissertation will show, Jesus used to live as someone destitute of land (Luke 9:58). At the same time he illustrated many of his teachings presenting himself and God as the main landowners. I will present the meaning of this apparent contradiction opportunely.

We conclude with Appian's remarks on this situation, which provide a good summary for all we are dealing with in this chapter:

> What happened was that the rich got hold of most of that land which was not distributed as allotments, and as time passed they assumed that no one would take it away from them; and they persuaded the poor owners of small farms bordering on their own to sell them, or even seized some farms by violence, so that they came to cultivate huge estates instead of individual farms; and they used bought slaves as cultivators and herdsmen, so that they wouldn't have to depend upon free man who could be called away from their work to serve in the army. And owning slaves was very profitable because they produced lots of children so that the number of slaves relentlessly increased because they weren't liable to military service. Those property owners who were powerful became extremely wealthy, and the number of slaves increased throughout the country, while the Italians became fewer and poorer, oppressed by poverty, by taxes, and by military service. And even if there was a period when they weren't away on campaign, they sat around without employment, because the land was owned by the rich and they used slaves to work instead of the free workers.[98]

A little ahead, Appian speaks about the results of the laws trying to make the situation more equal, as for example the law limiting the land of the

---

98. Appian, *B Civ.* 1.1.7.

Patricians to 500 iugera and obligating them to hire freemen: "They included all these things in a law and reinforced it with an oath and decreed a penalty, and they thought that the land that was left would soon be distributed to the poor in small allotments. But no one took any notice either of the law or of the oath".[99]

Kloppenborg helps us to better understand the effects of the creation of large estates:

> The creation of large estates, then, had profound effects on the structure of the economy: by reorientating production from local consumption to an export economy; by creating and exploiting a class of underemployed non-slave labourers; by forcing smallholders to marginal land; and by drawing on the labour inputs from underemployment non-slave labour and smallholders at certain key periods of the cycle of agricultural production.[100]

Thus, the creation of latifundia had many important consequences for Roman economy, most of them detrimental to those who were poor.

2.3.2.2 Free, But Enslaved by Debt

Another problem detected by Columella was the use of workers full of debt.[101] Debt was a historically considerable problem for many people in the Roman Empire. Luke also acknowledges the reality of debt in his gospel, as for example in Luke 7:41–42; 11:4; 16:5–7. Together with the attempts to change the laws on land possession, there were many legal projects trying to regulate debts and, from time to time, even discussions about widespread pardoning of debts.[102] Most times these laws were fiercely resisted and even when ap-

---

99. Appian, *B Civ.* 1.1.8.

100. Kloppenborg, *The Tenants in the Vineyard*, 289.

101. Varro, lists the possible workers of a farm in the following terms: "All agriculture is carried on by men—slaves, or freemen, or both; by freemen, when they till the ground themselves, as many poor people do with the help of their families; or hired hands, when the heavier farm operations, such as the vintage and the haying, are carried on by the hiring of freemen; and those whom our people called *obaerarii* [Those who work off a debt by labour.], and of whom there are still many in Asia, in Egypt, and in Illyricum." Varro, *Agr* 1.17

102. "Furthermore, the following two practices have alike been considered worthy of being most carefully guarded against in our laws and as deserving of execration and the most extreme penalties, namely, a proposal that debts be cancelled, or that the land ought to be redistributed." Dio Chrysostom, *Or.* 31.

proved the wealthy would find a way to find a loophole in them.[103] Culturally, debts were viewed as something one should flee from, but in practice, the norm was taking money from money lenders. Plutarch (c. AD 46 – 120), for example, writes a book specifically to advise people not to borrow money, in which he says:

> For debtors are slaves to all the men who ruin them, or rather not to them either (for what would be so terrible in that?), but to outrageous, barbarous, and savage slaves, like those who Plato says stand in Hades as fiery avengers and executioners over those who have been impious in life. For these money-lenders make the market-place a place of the damned for the wretched debtors; like vultures they devour and flay them, "entering into their entrails," or in other instances they stand over them and inflict on them the tortures of Tantalus by preventing them from tasting their own produce which they reap and harvest.[104]

In Roman law, creditors had the right of appending a stone on the neck of the debtors and taking them as slaves until they paid what they owed. Although not every free worker was a slave of debt, this situation was very common.[105] The interest in the epoch of the empire had an official ceiling of 12% per year.[106] Despite this being the law, many processes of the epoch reveal that the rates could reach even 48% per year.[107] This was the reality for

---

103. For there was now another pressing concern: the citizen body was overwhelmed by interest payments and, although profiteering had been checked by numerous laws relating to interest on loans, a loophole had been used to circumvent them by transferring debts to allies not covered by the statutes, so that debtors were being crushed by unrestricted interest charges. (Liv. 35.7)

104. Plutarch, *De Virt. Mor.* 4 Later, Plutarch adds: "So any man in debt sells, not his own plot of land, nor his own house, but those of his creditor whom by law he has made their owner." Plutarch, *De Virt. Mor.* 8

105. The situation of non-salve labor ranged very widely, from debt-bondage on the one hand, to relative independence on the other. Garnsey and Saller, *The Roman Empire: Economy, Society and Culture*, 111.

106. Zimmermann, *The Law of Obligations Roman Foundations of the Civilian Tradition*, 16; Homer and Sylla, *A History of Interest Rates*, 56.

107. In the Rome of the Civil Wars no shame was felt in lending money at exorbitant and fantastic rates of interest. 24% and even 48% did not seem excessive to the contemporaries of Cicero. The latter rate was that claimed by the publicans who in the course of fourteen years multiplied sixfold the total of their demand upon the cities of Asia Minor upon which Sulla had imposed war contributions. Louis, *Ancient Rome at Work*, 210.

both hired hands and tenants. Similar to slaves, free tenants "were unable to escape intense exploitation on account of their economic circumstances or lack of power."[108] The contracts of the tenants also made them susceptible to incur in debt.

> Renting to tenants had the advantage of reducing an owner's investment, since he did not have to put out the formidable sum it took to buy a staff of slaves. On the other hand, he rarely could count on getting the maximum a property could yield. The terms were usually a five-year lease at a fixed cash rental. Under such an inflexible arrangement, one year of bad crops inevitably put the tenants into arrears, once behind they rarely caught up, and the landlord found himself constantly lowering the rent.[109]

A good example of this is provided by Pliny the Younger, in a letter he writes to Paulinus. Pliny asks Paulinus to pardon his absence in his insulation as consul and explains the reason. Although long, the quotation is worth reading:

> It is not your nature to demand the conventional formalities from your personal friends when they are likely to be inconvenienced, and I love you too surely to fear you will misinterpret my intentions if I am not present when you take up your consulship on the first of the month; especially when I must stay here to arrange for letting my farms on *long leases* and I shall have to adopt a *new system* for this. During the *past five years*, despite the large *reductions I made in the rents*, the arrears have increased and as a result most of my tenants have lost interest in reducing their debt because *they have no hope of being able to pay* on the whole; they even seize and consume the produce of the land in the belief that they will gain nothing themselves by conserving it. I must therefore face this growing evil and find a remedy. One way would be to let the farms not *for a money rent but for a fixed share of the produce*, and then make some of my servants

---

108. Garnsey and Saller, *The Roman Empire*, 98; 112; Temin, *The Roman Market Economy*, 148; Bunson, *Encyclopedia of the Roman Empire*, 301.

109. Casson, *Everyday Life in Ancient Rome*, 26.

> *overseers* to keep a watch on the harvest. There is certainly no more just return than what is won from the soil, climate and seasons, but this method requires strict honesty, keen eyes, and many pairs of hands. However, I must make the experiment and try all possible changes of remedy for an obstinate complaint.[110]

We learn from Pliny that the payment from his renters was once in money, but his tenants had fallen into huge debt and because of that they even had despaired of paying the debts. Pliny decided then to try sharecropping as a form of payment supervised by overseers. Columella also recommends a disposition of the landowner to be flexible with his tenants, since this attitude will earn him more profit and, by demanding the law strictly, he says, the tenants would be in a situation of oppression.[111]

Cato exemplifies the portions of crop that a tenant could receive in a lease contract:

> Terms for letting the tending of the land to a share tenant: In the district of Casinum and Venafrum, on good land he should receive one-eighth of the unthreshed grain, on fairly good land one-seventh, on land of third quality one-sixth; if the threshed grain is shared, one-fifth. In the district of Venafrum the division is one-ninth of the unthreshed grain on the best land. If they mill in common, the caretaker shall pay for the milling in proportion to the share he receives. He should receive one-fifth of threshed barley and one-fifth of shelled beans.[112]

The share a tenant would receive by these figures presented by Cato would range from 11% to 20%. There are no other details of the contract here to be

---

110. Pliny, *Ep.* 9.37. (Emphasis added.)

111. "He should be civil in dealing with his tenants, should show himself affable, and should be more exacting in the matter of work than of payments, as this gives less offence yet is, generally speaking, more profitable. For when land is carefully tilled it usually brings a profit, and never a loss, except when it is assailed by unusually severe weather or by robbers; and for that reason, the tenant does not venture to ask for reduction of his rent. But the master should not be insistent on his rights in every particular to which he has bound his tenant, such as the exact day for payment, or the matter of demanding firewood and other trifling services in addition, attention to which causes country-folk more trouble than expense; in fact, we should not lay claim to all that the law allows, for the ancients regarded the extreme of the law as the extreme of oppression. Columella, *Rust* 1.7.2–3

112. Cato, *Agr* 1.136

able to make a better judgement, but it is clear why the tenants could have difficulties to subsist and would incur in debt in years of bad crop.

If the situation in the camp was so strenuous, why would people choose to remain in this position? Not everyone did. Many agrarian workers moved to the urban cities of the empire to have better opportunities. Some of them would manage to find an occupation, others however would become the abject poor, the beggars of the large cities of the empire. The ones who would not venture in the cities, would subject themselves to such exploitation, in part because of the system of patronage. They were not only hired by the estate owner, they were also their clients. From time to time, the patron would give them money, food, opportunities and means through which they could attain limited honor.[113] Because of this, almost everyone behaved according to convention.

However, most of the latifundia workers were not "free" workers, nor "free" tenants, most of them were slaves. In what relates both to hired workers and to tenants, what made *latifundia* worthwhile was the exploitation of the land.[114] The exploitation of slaves, however, was even bigger.

2.3.2.3 *Slavery in the Roman Empire*

In this chapter, we are diving into the unjust practices related to land that characterized the Roman Empire in the time Luke wrote his gospel and the book of Acts. The reason for that is providing a context for the ethics of jubilee Luke proposes in his gospel. The last two sections presented the problem of *latifundia* and debt. This section presents the problem of slavery related to land. Columella deemed slavery as another less than appropriate way to take

---

113. Cynthia Damon, in the introduction of Caesar's Civil Wars, expresses this reality: "The political, social, and economic divisions between social groups—senators, equites, propertied, landless—were to some extent blurred by patronage, or *clientela*, which facilitated the creation of mutually beneficial vertical links between individuals at different levels and (not coincidentally) discouraged the formation of broad interest groups within any given level." Caesar. *Civil War*. Edited and translated by Cynthia Damon. LCL 39. Cambridge: Harvard University Press, 2016.

114. "It is through exploitation that surplus value is extracted, and property becomes productive." Garnsey and Saller, *The Roman Empire: Economy, Society and Culture*, 133. "Roman landowners depended for their wealth on their ability to capture a portion of the surplus produced by the peasants in the countryside, whether they were working in their land as hired laborers or as tenants. So the development of the urban economy in the Roman Empire was a function, to a large extent, of the degree to which the urban elite controlled the surplus produced in the countryside." Kehoe, *Law and Rural Economy in the Roman Empire*, 5–6.

care of an estate. Slaves were the most common work force on large estates. Their presence was so pervasive that when employment became very difficult for a freeman to find, Caesar needed to approve a law limiting the number of slaves in a farm to two thirds and obligating the hiring of at least one third of free peasants.[115]

Slaves were considered property that could be bought, sold and inherited, including the future children of a female slave.[116] They were also considered part of the estate one could buy.[117] Dio defines a slave as a human being who is possessed in the strict meaning of that term just as any goods or cattle, and it is used by his owner as he or she pleases.[118] It is common to find references to slaves in the Roman sources as possession, chattel, equipment, and speaking tools.[119] They were also seen as animals.[120]

The owner had full power over his or her slaves, even for life or death.[121] Although lawfully this situation changed in AD 4 with a new law promulgated by Caesar Augustus, the praxis remained unchanged especially in the country. The mark of one's opulence was determined by the number and countenance

---

115. Scullard, *From the Gracchi to Nero*, 173.

116. P.S.I. 903. (AD 47)

117. "That these slaves are the property of Arethusius, and that I listed them in the inventory because they formed a part of his estate, I shall proceed to show you." Demosthenes, *Or.* 53.19.

118. Dio Chrysostom, *Or.* 15. A more contemporary definition says: "The slave was someone who had lost, or never had, any rights to share in society, and therefore to have access to food, clothing and the other necessities of physical survival. Typically this was because the slave had been on the defeated side in a war." Wiedemann, *Slavery*, 22.

119. Bradley and Cartledge, *The Cambridge World History of Slavery*, 1:215.

120. "Slaves were seen as similar to animals in three regards: First, they had to work like animals for their owners and were not paid for it. Like animals, sick and old slaves were considered a burden to be discarded rather than supported and maintained. Secondly, slaves' bodies could not be protected against physical abuse and sexual exploitation. Slaves had no control over their bodies, which were their owner's property. Thirdly, slaves were sold like animals and subjected to humiliating examinations of physical defects." Hezser, *Jewish Slavery in Antiquity*, 57.

121. Epictetus, a former slave, illustrates this in a dialog between a slave and his owner: "You are my slave; for it is in my power to prevent you from living as you will, it is in my power to lighten your servitude, or to humble you; whenever I wish, you can be happy again, and go off to Athens in high spirits." Arrian, *Epic Diss.* 24.75–76

of the slaves one had.[122] Athenaeus speaks that many people owned from ten to twenty thousand slaves or even more.[123]

It is difficult to determine the medium price of a slave, both because of the exiguity of sources dealing with the topic and because the price would vary much depending on sex, age, offer, location, and especially the level of specialization of the slave. The table below shows a few prices possible to find in the extant sources. In general terms, it seems possible to affirm that the prices had a deflation in the first and second centuries AD and a heavy inflation in the third and fourth century, when the emperor Diocletian had to set a limit for the prices of slaves.

---

122. Plutarch, *De Virt. Mor.* 5. Also Dio: "And similarly also within the city, each one has his own individual ambition—one to obtain as much land as possible, another silver, another slaves, another all these things together . . ." Dio Chrysostom, *Or.* 4. See also Seneca the Younger, *Brev. Vit.* 12.5.

123. Athen. 272. Pliny the Elder in *HN* 33.47 reports about a freedman in 8 B.C. who had lost much property and was still leaving in his will 4116 slaves, 3600 pair of oxen, 257000 other animals and a sum of 60 million sesterces in coins! Although very hard to access, the overall number of slaves was so large that inhibited the Senate to pass a law determining distinguish clothes for slaves, different from those of freeman in order that it was better that the first group was not aware of its numbers. Seneca the Younger, *Clem.* 24.1. There are also many instances of will, for example, in which someone leaves less than ten slaves. Cf. Wiedemann, *Greek and Roman Slavery*, 101.

Table 2.1: Price of Slaves in the Ancient Roman World

Source	Year	Slave's Description	Price (in the source)	Price in Denarius	Equivalent in US Dollars[124]
Pliny the Elder, HN 7.39	115 BC	A grammarian bought by Marcus Scaurus	700,000 sesterces	175,000	8,750,000
Plutarch, Liv. Luc.	73 BC	man-slave in war camp	4 drachma	4	200
Pliny the Elder, HN 7.12	40 BC	two very similar slaves (each)	200,000 sesterces	5,000	250,000
Martial, Epig. 10.31	AD 70	no description	1,200 sesterces	300	15,000
P.Oxy. 75.5051	AD 90	the slave Plousia alias Kalē Phasis, about 23 years of age	10 talents 5,000 drachmas in bronze	833	41,666
P. Oxy. 95.	AD 129	female called Dioscorous, aged about 25 years	1,200 drachmae of silver	1,200	60,000
P.Col.8.219	AD 140	slave girl born in Alexandria	1,000 silver drachmas	1,000	50,000
Plutarch, Liv., Mar. Cat. 4	170 BC	no description	1,500 drachmas	1,500	75,000
Plutarch, Mor.7	170 BC	no description	1,000 drachmas	1,000	50,000

---

124. All equivalence in dollars consider one day of work (denarius, drachma) as equivalent to $50.00.

Source	Year	Slave's Description	Price (in the source)	Price in Denarius	Equivalent in Dollars
Diocletian's Edict of Maximum Prices, *ZPE* 34	AD 300	male slaves between 16 and 40	30,000 denarii	30,000	1,500,000
		female slaves between 16 and 40	25,000 denarii	25,000	1,250,000
		male slaves between 40 and 60	25,000 denarii	25,000	1,250,000
		female slaves between 40 and 60	20,000 denarii	20,000	1,000,000
		boy and girl between 8 and 16	20,000 denarii	20,000	1,000,000
		male slave above 60 or under 8	15,000 denarii	15,000	750,000
		female slave above 60 or under 8	10,000 denarii	10,000	500,000

Although buying a slave was expensive, the overall treatment given to them could be very harsh. They could be struck and flogged at a whim, imposed fetters and chains, be burned with a burning iron even in the face; castrated; hanged up by the hands with weights attached to their feet; and be crucified, or burned by the will of their master.[125] Slaves would also be obligated to wear an iron collar with the name of his or her owner and instructions in case he and she escaped.[126] Also, it was assumed that slaves would tell the truth in trials only under torture.[127]

---

125. Prop. 4.7; Seneca the Younger, *Apocol.* 12.15; Petronius, *Sat.* 53. See also Seneca the Elder, *Controv.* 3.9 Juvenal, *Sat.* 6.215–216: "Crucify that slave." "What crime has he committed to deserve punishment? Who says they witnessed it? Who accused him? Give him a hearing! No hesitation is ever long enough when a person's life is at stake." "You idiot! Is a slave a person?" Cf. also Blake, *The History of Slavery and The Slave Trade, Ancient and Modern*, 52; Bradley, *Slaves and Masters in the Roman Empire*, 113–37.

126. ILS 8726–8733.

127. Wiedemann, *Slavery*, 23. See also Pliny the Younger, *Ep.* 96.

Plutarch illustrates in a very vivid way the promptness to impinge attacks on a slave based on minimal issues: "For which of us is so harsh that he scourges and chastises a slave because five or ten days ago he overroasted the meat or upset the table or came too slowly at our bidding? And yet these are the very things which cause us to be excited and in a cruel and implacable mood at the moment they happen and are still fresh in our memory."[128]

A slave was expected to treat his or her owner with *fides* (loyalty) and *obsequium* (obedience) since it was supposed that the slave owed his and her life to the owner. Therefore, they were to respond with a loyal and obedient gratitude.[129] For this reason, runaway slaves were a much-disdained class and were persecuted by specialized people (the *fugitiuarii*) who turned this into a business.[130]

Many thousands of slaves could be acquired in each battle, since while the combatants were killed, the non-combatants were taken as slaves.[131] From the fields of war, the slaves were bought by a slave-dealer and transported as cargo in ships to cities, where they were exposed naked on a platform to be inspected and sold in auction.[132] Slaves could also be home-bred or taken from the garbage-dump, where unwanted children were abandoned.[133]

Thus, the wars in which Rome was victorious resulted both in large tracts of land and an abundance of slaves. These two things were put together by those with access to influence and money.[134] The Elder Seneca, for example, reports a certain Vibius Gallus disdainfully defining wealth saying: "I do not

---

128. Plutarch, *Mor.* 11.460.

129. Bradley, *Slaves and Masters in the Roman Empire*, 33–39.

130. P. Par. 10.234.

131. Livy gives us an idea of their numbers: 2500, 5632, 8000 and 30000. See Liv. 29.29, 27.16, 41.12; 42.43; and 13.39.

132. Cf. Suetonius, *Gramm.* 1

133. P.Mich. inv. 133; P.Sel.Warga 8.

134. "But as the territories of the Roman estate were extended, the patricians obtained possession of large estates out of the public domain; since it was a practice of the Romans to deprive a conquered people of a part of their lands. These estates required a larger number of hands for their cultivation than could readily be obtained among the free population, and since the freedman were constantly liable to be called away from their work to serve in the armies, the lands began to be cultivated almost entirely by slave labor. Through war and commerce, slaves could be obtained easily, and at a cheap rate, and their numbers soon became so great, that the poorer class of freeman was thrown almost entirely out of employment." Blake, *The History of Slavery and The Slave Trade, Ancient and Modern*, 46.

like gangs of slaves whom their master does not know, slave-camps filling the countryside with their din for miles around."[135]

In large estates, slaves were divided among those who worked without fetters and the chain-gangs.[136] These latter were those with criminal records or those being punished by their master. They would work in chains. Also, while the first group slept in a *cubicle* (room), the last slept in a place called *ergastulum*, a sickening underground prison where they were kept in chains also during the night.[137]

Cato, Varro and Columella recommend that the slaves be treated with respect, consideration, and fairness and even that they should be recompensed for good production.[138] The motivation behind these instructions, however, is not the slaves' well-being, but an increase in their productivity.[139] Other characteristics of the treatment of slaves in large estates were the use of strong clothes that could endure all kinds of weather during two years;[140] that the bailiff should give the slaves a load of work to occupy them for the whole day, in order for them not to have time to turn their attention to anything other than food and rest;[141] and that the slave's food should be rationed and different portions were to be given to the free hands and the chain-gangs.[142]

It is clear, therefore, that among the slaves who worked on land throughout the Empire, there was much exploitation and abuse, even if sometimes these were disguised in forms of respect and apparent care.

---

135. Seneca (the Elder), *Controv.* 2.25
136. Columella, *Rust.* 1.7.1
137. Seneca (The Younger), *Ira* 15.3; Columella, *Rust.* 1.6
138. Columella, *Rust* 1.8.16. This recompense could include a dinner invitation from the bailiff or even freedom for woman who reared many children. Columella, *Rust.* 11.1.19; 1.8.19; Cato, *Agr.* 1.5; Varro, *Rust.* 1.17.
139. The following quotation illustrates well this attitude: "Nowadays I make it a practice to call them into consultation on any new work, as if they were more experienced, and to discover by this means what sort of ability is possessed by each of them and how intelligent he is. Furthermore, I observe that they are more willing to set about a piece of work on which they think that their opinions have been asked and their advice followed." Columella, *Rust.* 1.8.15
140. Columella, *Rust.* 1.8.9; 11.1.21; Cato, *Agr* 1.59
141. Columella, *Rust.* 11.1.26–27
142. Columella, *Rust.* 1.8.16; 1.8.19; Cato, *Agr* 1.56

2.4 Final Remarks

The Roman Empire was a huge machine of exploitation that operated primarily by means of controlling the land. The empire grew by conquering other lands and declaring these lands as belonging to Rome. Both the emperor and the opulent would make their fields productive by way of slaves, tenants and hired peasant workers, almost always in a system that extracted surplus by way of abuse. The *latifundia* would make land a hard asset to acquire and the concurrence unjust. The politicians were also the owners of *latifundia* and their laws were made in a way that insured their own continuous prosperity and acquisition of more land which led to wealth. The apparent benevolence shown in the system of patronage and rare approvals of laws benefiting the people were more to keep the order than to give real opportunity to the eighty percent of population that lived around the level of subsistence.

Thus, in order to be someone of significance in the Roman Empire, one needed to be rich and this was synonymous with having substantial portions of land producing surplus.[143] The rich had honor, access, admiration, power, and increasing chances of becoming wealthier. On the other hand, most people throughout the empire were slaves, hired peasants, and tenants who lived at the subsistence line, were explored by wealthy landowners, had massive debts and virtually no chance of improving their situation.

The gospel of Luke has another view about who has the right to own the land and how it should be used. Before entering this discussion, however, it is necessary to analyze how land was dealt with in Israel a few decades prior, and at the time when Jesus developed his ministry, up to about when Luke wrote his gospel. That is the focus of the next chapter.

---

143. "Wealth in Rome was not simply a focus of moral scrutiny (as it was in many ancient city states), nor was it important primarily because it was convertible to social or political capital. The institution of the census made wealth one of the most explicit and formal measures of an individual's social standing and a key component of his public identity." Greg Woolf, "Writing Poverty in Rome," 92. Also: "Vulnerability, exclusion and shame. Not everyone [in Rome] was poor by every one of these criteria; the excluded and the shamed overlapped, but were not co-extensive with the vulnerable. However, poverty in one respect might well lead to another, as shames contributed to social exclusion and social exclusion reinforced vulnerability, since the outcast could not rely on networks of reciprocity or patronage in times of crisis." Morley, "The Poor in the City of Rome," 35–36.

CHAPTER 3

Land Injustice in Israel

In the previous chapter, I presented the Roman Empire as a developed system of exploitation concerning land and demonstrated how both the emperor and the Roman aristocracy owned and abused land and people to augment their power and wealth. Jesus, Luke and their audiences lived under Roman dominion. At that time, Israel was but a small state-nation subject to the will of this enormous machine of exploitation that was the Roman Empire. In chapters ahead, we will see how Luke presents an antidote against this culture of exploitation characteristic of the Roman Empire. He does that by presenting land ethics built upon concepts of the jubilee law. Before seeing that, however, we need to focus on demonstrating how the general realities described in Chapter 2 apply specifically to the situation of first century Israel.

In this chapter I will argue that even before Roman domination, a local aristocracy developed in Israel which, together with and as an aid to the foreign powers, oppressed the people in matters pertaining to land with abusive taxes, indebtedness, misappropriation of land, and development of large estates with the manpower of dispossessed tenants, hired workers and slaves.

To reach our goal, this chapter will deal with Israelite land-related exploitation in two phases. The first phase covers the return from Babylon up to the Hasmonean rule, the intertestamental or Second Temple period. The second phase this chapter will cover is the period in which Israel was under Roman dominion. It looks at the situation during the kingship of Herod the Great and after.

3.1 Land Exploitation from the Return from Exile to Hasmoneans Rule

Although the period covered in this section does not relate directly to the epoch in which Jesus advanced his ministry, it is fundamental to see how the socio-economic dynamics related to land developed from the period in which the Old Testament finishes to the time covered by the New Testament. A few important questions this section aims to answer are: Who were the owners of land in Israel in Jesus's times and how did they reach their position? How did the land injustice found in Israel in the time of Jesus begin? To answer these questions, I present the history below.

When Judah was taken into the Babylonian exile, poorer Jews were left behind in the land and became, together with some gentiles brought by the emperor, the land holders of Canaan (2 Kings 25:12; Jer 39:10; 52:16). However, when the new Persian emperor Cyrus sent the Jews back home with gifts and support, these returnees became the new aristocracy, reclaiming their properties and subordinating those who were previously in the land to tenancy or small land holdings afar. "The return to Zion engendered conflict over landownership. The returnees became the large landholders at the expense of those who were already in the country."[1] Pastor believes that this is the background behind Nehemiah 5:1–5. What happened in Jewish history with respect to control of the land from the time of Ezra-Nehemiah to the conquest of Alexander the Great is uncertain[2] Thus, the focus here will be on the Macedonian conquering of Judah onward to the Maccabean period.

Understanding the concept of a client state is fundamental to grasping Israel's situation from the Persian Empire up to the Roman domination. A client or vassal state is a subaltern nation in a hierarchical relationship with a patron or sovereign state.[3] A nation becomes a vassal state mainly by losing

---

1. Pastor, *Land and Economy*, 14.
2. Miller and Hayes, *A History of Ancient Israel and Judah*, 474.
3. "A client state is a government that is dominated by another (imperialist) government; it is controlled by a foreign state. It is dependent on the economic or military support of a more powerful country. Other names for client states include satellite states, puppet government and vassal state." Mentan, *The State in Africa*, 217. "A *vassal state* subject to the suzerainty of another state does have some international personality, but it is subject to greater control by the suzerain state than is the case for protected states. The status of vassals may be defined both by treaty and by rather vague customary and personal relations which originated within feudal law." Hannum, *Autonomy, Sovereignty, and Self-Determination The Accommodation of Conflicting Rights*, 17.

a war, surrender, or treaty and there are different levels of submission in this kind of relationship. Commonly, the client state had some liberty to decide internal affairs while at the same time, paid tribute to the imperial state and received protection from other foreign powers. After the Babylonian exile, a weakened Israel became a puppet state in the hands of different foreign powers. Not taking into consideration the struggles and interruptions in these administrations, Israel's political situation from the end of the Old Testament period until the epoch New Testament can be represented as follows:

> 539 BC Under Persian domination (Cyrus)
> 332 BC Under Macedonian domination (Alexander, the Great)
> 320 BC Under Ptolemaic domination (Ptolemy I)
> 200 BC Under Seleucid domination (Antiochus III the Great)
> 167 BC Period of semi-freedom under the Maccabean Family
> 63 BC Under Roman domination (Pompey and Herod the Great)

Alexander the Great conquered Palestine in about 332 BC.[4] After Alexander's premature death in 323 BC, Judah was subject to the diadochi Ptolemy I Soter. Formerly, a successful and trusted general of Alexander, Ptolemy seized the opportunity of becoming the new Pharaoh in Egypt after Alexander's death.[5] Josephus affirms that he conquered Jerusalem peacefully on a Saturday and took many Jews captives to Egypt.[6] His son Ptolemy II Philadelphus, however, had a more sympathetic attitude toward the Jews. He promoted the translation of the Torah to Greek (the LXX) in partnership with the high priest who sent wise men to do the job. Philadelphus also sent one hundred twenty thousand Jewish slaves back to Jerusalem and invested large sums of money (one hundred and fifty talents) in Yahweh's temple.[7]

---

4. Josephus, *Ant.* 11.7.1. Schäfer, speaking about the government situation in Judea under Alexander, says: "For the formerly autonomous Persian province of Yehud this meant that the changeover of political power was unlikely to have resulted in any sudden radical changes and that Alexander was not going to intervene directly in Jerusalem affairs. He was probably satisfied with the recognition of Greek sovereignty by the High Priest acting as the representative of the people, and otherwise left the organizational structure of Judaea untouched, allowing the High Priest and the Council of Elders to remain the heads of state." Schäfer, *The History of the Jews in the Greco-Roman World*.

5. Bevan, *A History of Egypt Under the Ptolemaic Dynasty*, 28, 32.

6. Josephus, *Ant.* 12.1.1

7. Josephus, *Ant.* 12.1.2–5, 15. It is interesting to note that Cicero considered the Jews as "born to be slaves" (*De Prov. Cons.* 5.10). See also Josephus *Ant.* 11.210–211; Judith 14.13, 18 and Hezser, *Jewish Slavery in Antiquity*, 61–63.

However, if, on one hand, the Jews were experiencing freedom on internal laws and administration, on the other hand, the Ptolemies charged heavy taxes on the province of Yehud, the name of Judah at that time.

These taxes were especially high on land. "As the representative of the gods on earth, the Ptolemaic ruler had ultimate claim to the land under his control."[8] Thus, the Zenon Archive presents the example of Apollonius, the *dioiketes* (finance minister) of Egypt, who owned large tracts of land in Galilee, probably from a grant from the king of his own lands.[9] Although all land under the Ptolemies were ultimately their possession, Freyne convincingly defends that besides many state lands in Galilee, the Ptolemaic administration in general incorporated large Jewish owners of land into its own administration and left the small holders of land untouched.[10]

The burden of organizing the Greek administration of Egypt fell upon Ptolemy II Philadelphus. A document called *Papyrus Revenue Laws* shows in detail how he did that: Philadelphus developed an advanced system of revenue.[11] The land belonging to him as Pharaoh was auctioned for limited periods. The buyers could develop the land themselves or rent to tenants. After that, the owners imposed produce taxes, which were collected in kind or money by different companies of tax collectors. These companies reported to two officials whose offices were called *oeconomus* and *antigrapheus*. These

---

8. Adams, *Social and Economic Life in Second Temple Judea*, 146. Schäfer comments this situation as follows: "Not only the king's land in the narrow sense (*ge basilike*), which was leased to the king's farmers, but also the land allocated to the Egyptian Greek cities Alexandria, Ptolemais and Naucratis, was only held on trust (*en aphesei*) by the cities and belonged legally to the king. . . . Cultivation of the land could not in most cases be carried out independently, but the tenants had to act in accordance with the centralized planned economy of the state. The state had also claimed a monopoly on the most important economic goods, such as vegetable oils, salt, linen, and beer. Foreign trade was strictly controlled and high duties were imposed." Schäfer, *The History of the Jews in the Greco-Roman World*.

9. P.lond.7.1948 speaks about a estate with 80,000 vines, a well, a satisfactory building and producing good wine.

10. Freyne, *Galilee From Alexander the Great to Hadrian*, 156–60.

11. Grenfell and Mahaffy, eds., *Revenue Laws of Ptolemy Philadelphus*. Commenting on that, Manning says: "The Ptolemaic taxation system was extraordinarily complex, and it is still not well understood in some of its details. The regime received revenue in two basic forms, fixed rent from certain classes of land, mainly from royal land, and taxes, either in kind or money from other classes of land, or in money from the production in vineyards and orchards (the *apomoira*), and from production of certain industries, the oil crop being the most important, and from a poll tax. Taxes in money were generally guaranteed to the state by a system of tax farmers who bid auction each year for the right to collect a particular tax in an area." Manning, *Land and Power in Ptolemaic Egypt: The Structure of Land Tenure*, 53.

collectors were individuals who bought from the king the right to collect taxes.[12] Anyone could denounce a land owner who was late with his duties and keep a percentage of the amount payed with fines. There was a specific "tax guard" to guarantee the security of those who worked with revenue.

The tax on vineyards was of one-sixth (16.6%) of the wine. The tax for soldiers and less productive regions was one-tenth (10%). The tax on orchards was the equivalent to one-sixth in silver. If the producer failed to inform the tax collectors that he was producing wine and missed the due inspection, he was charged double that amount. There was in the law a limited liberty guaranteed for the tax collectors in the way they could impose fines over landholders as well as for the *oeconomus* and how he could charge the tax collectors. The tax collectors would keep the surpluses of what they collected in relation to what was agreed or pay the debts with their own money if the collection was shorter of the expected. Such is the tax system described in the *Papyrus Revenue Laws*. Although these laws were mainly applied in Egypt and represent an incomplete set of laws and there were idiosyncrasies in tax collection, there are no good reasons not to apply the same overall structure to the Palestine under the Ptolemies.[13]

The burden of all these taxes together was so great that Manning concludes, "The total tax burden on royal land, including various small charges for transportation, repayment of seed loans etc., approached half of the production each year."[14] This projection is confirmed by P. Cair. Zen 1 59016, which shows that the tax for transportation could reach up to 50% of the

---

12. Manning, *The Last Pharaohs: Egypt Under the Ptolemies, 305–30 BC*, 156–57.

13. After speaking of the Ptolemaic taxation as ranging from 14 to 21% of the GDP, Manning concludes: "If these estimates are anywhere near the truth, the Ptolemies must count as among the most impressive taxing powers and mobilizers of resources in antiquity." Manning, *The Last Pharaohs: Egypt Under the Ptolemies, 305–30 BC*, 127.

14. Manning, *Land and Power in Ptolemaic Egypt: The Structure of Land Tenure*, 59–60. On another place, Manning clarifies the tax policy under the Ptolemies: "The internal economic policy of the Ptolemies was designed for the maximization of revenue and may be summarized as follows: (1) extend and maximize cultivation where possible, (2) maintain old land tenure patterns while collecting the harvest tax, (3) tax production in the main industries, (4) tax transactions (sales, mortgages), (5) extend royal sale licenses in key industries (the so-called royal monopolies)." Manning, *Land and Power in Ptolemaic Egypt: The Structure of Land Tenure*, 141. With all these taxes, "The traditional figure for the annual internal revenue of Ptolemy II is 14,800 talents of silver and 1.5 million *artabs* of wheat [totalizing 4,000 to 5,000 thousand more talents]." Reden, *Money in Ptolemaic Egypt: From the Macedonian Conquest to the End of the Third Century BC*, 79.

goods.[15] Thus, as Grabbe says, "To the Ptolemies the region was just another milk cow, providing goods and revenues".[16]

The Zenon Papyri also has examples of loan contracts from the Ptolemaic Egypt. Based in this kind of documents, Von Reden affirms that there were five categories of interest arrangement in that time, the most common being the interest of 2 percent per month. There are also contracts with no interest from owners to tenants, interest added to the total sum of the loan, interests of more than 2 percent and interests of 50% of the loan with no due date.[17] There were also loans based on pledge and loans as part of other transactions.[18] Thus, besides the heavy burden of taxes, those who needed a loan would also need to work to pay for these.

With the constant struggle between the Ptolemies and the Seleucids, the tax burden was augmented, consequently increasing the oppression on the people. The author of 1 Maccabees narrates a decision by the Seleucid king Antiochus III, in which he indicates the taxes that were levied under the Ptolemies:

> I now free you and exempt all the Jews from payment of tribute and salt tax and crown levies, and instead of collecting the third of the grain and the half of the fruit of the trees that I should receive, I release them from this day and henceforth. I will not collect them from the land of Judah or from the three districts added to it from Samaria and Galilee, from this day and for all time. Jerusalem and its environs, its tithes and its revenues, shall be holy and free from tax (1 Maccabees 10:29–31, NRSV).[19]

The elevated level of taxes registered in 1 Maccabees indicates the possibility that all land in Judea was considered at that point government estate.[20] Besides the exorbitant taxes on produce, it is also evident in this quotation that

---

15. See P.Cair. Zen. 1 59016

16. Lester L. Grabbe, *Judaism From Cyrus to Hadrian. Volume One*, 215.

17. Reden, *Money in Ptolemaic Egypt: From the Macedonian Conquest to the End of the Third Century BC*, 160.

18. Reden, *Money in Ptolemaic Egypt: From the Macedonian Conquest to the End of the Third Century BC*, 162–204.

19. For a historic commentary explaining this text and taxes, see Bickermann and Tropper, *Studies in Jewish and Christian History*, 328 et seq.

20. Safrai, *Economy of Roman Palestine*, 323.

the Jews paid to the Ptolemies a multiplicity of taxes: (1) tribute, (2) salt tax, (3) crown levies, which at first were voluntary and later became compulsory, (4) a third of the grain; (5) half of the fruits and (6) taxes over the tithes, and (7) revenues. Besides those, there was also a transit tax applied even when transporting products between cities as we have seen already.[21]

Another characteristic of the Ptolemaic rule was the concession of large tracts of land to the priestly order (temple land) and charging them with heavier taxes. Much land was also given to active and retired military. Adams presents one of the results: "Such a hierarchical framework in the governing structure reduced the land available for private ownership, leaving many farmers with small plots (often called 'grant land' in Egyptian texts) or working in royal fields to which they had no claim."[22]

Thus, due to high taxes, unjust concurrence in disputing auctioned land leasing with the wealthy, the work of tax collectors, wars against the Seleucids,[23] local disputes,[24] and the favor of the rulers toward the rich local religious and political Judean leaders – the situation of the poor in Palestine at that time was not good. "Whereas the upper classes in particular were active participants in and beneficiaries of the new economic order, the simple rural population (*laoi*) were exploited even more intensively than before."[25] Freyne,

---

21. Neusner comments on the intentions of the Ptolemaic rulers: "The correspondence from that time and later shows a Palestine administered like one of the nomes of Egypt, apparently without a governor of its own (though this is disputed). The main concern of the Ptolemaic government was to see that the revenues from the region were extracted at their maximum practical level. To ensure this, they had administrative and revenue agents at every level down to the individual local village. Some of these agents were natives used by the Ptolemies, but descendants of the Greek conquerors also functioned in the tax-collecting service, often at the higher levels." Jacob Neusner, *Judaism in Late Antiquity*, 65.

22. Adams, *Social and Economic Life in Second Temple Judea*, 147.

23. During the Ptolemaic rule of Judea, there were five Syrian wars between Ptolemaic and Seleucid armies.

24. Josephus, *Ant.* 12.4.1

25. Schäfer, *The History of the Jews in the Greco-Roman World*. "The most easily influenced people came from the rising class of wealthy bourgeoisie; government officials, agents, tax-collectors, and merchants. For the first time their power could be felt, used and at times, manipulated. The bureaucratic class that became successful in Jerusalem, epitomized by the Tobiads, obtained their riches via tax collecting and tax farming, not trade." Derfler, *The Hasmonean Revolt*, 33. Horsley presents two examples of the inadequacy od being a poor Jew in its own nation at this time: "For example, Alexander and his successors founded numerous Hellenistic cities in Palestine, with their Greek-speaking citizens and their local gentry in control of the indigenous populations, who had no citizenship rights in the cities proper. . . . The high priest, for example, was responsible for the collection of taxes. Thus the Judean people saw its

considering the proliferation of large estates and the fact they were owned by outsiders says: "What is really taking place is the transformation of Palestinian agriculture in agribusiness, controlled and monopolized by outside agencies, to whom there was no recourse, unlike the days of social injustice under Nehemiah and the Persians (Neh 5:1–13)."[26]

The First Book of Enoch, which dates probably from the earlier Greek domination, in which Judah was under Alexander the Great and under the Ptolemies, corroborates this depiction of the economic situation of that time.[27] For example, one finds the aspirations of the Judeans in that time and they included cleansing of social oppression and abundance of produce.

> And then shall the whole earth be tilled in righteousness, and shall all be planted with trees and be full of blessing. And all desirable trees shall be planted on it, and they shall plant vines on it: and the vine which they plant thereon shall yield wine in abundance, and as for all the seed which is sown thereon each measure (of it) shall bear a thousand, and each measure of olives shall yield ten presses of oil. And cleanse thou the earth from all oppression, and from all unrighteousness, and from all sin, and from all godliness: and all the uncleanness that is wrought upon the earth destroy from off the earth (1 Enoch 10:18–20).[28]

Near the end of Ptolemaic rule over Palestine, the Tobiad family (the same of the book of Nehemiah) became politically strong and developed an opposition with the blood related high-priestly family. The High Priest Onias II was probably foreseeing a Seleucid domination of Palestine and denied sending the due tributes to the Ptolemean king (ca. 240 BC).[29] Joseph, son of Tobiah, gained popular support and strongly defended the Ptolemaic interests against

---

own representative, its mediator with its true divine King (God), collaborating closely with a foreign, pagan empire." Horsley and Hanson, *Bandits, Prophets and Messiahs*, 11.

26. Freyne, *Galilee From Alexander the Great to Hadrian. 323 B.C.E. 135 C.E.: A Study of Second Temple Judaism*, 171.

27. Grabbe, "The Seleucid and Hasmonean Periods and the Apocalyptic Worldview - An Introduction," 20–21.

28. Charles, ed., *Pseudepigrapha of the Old Testament*, 135. In 1 Enoch (Book of the Watchers), this chapter presents the eschatological solution for the corruption that happened because of the fallen angels. Virtually, the whole chapter speaks about the future social justice and plenty of produce.

29. Josephus, *Ant.* 12.4.2; Schäfer, *The History of the Jews in the Greco-Roman World*.

the high priest, who was obligated to send the tributes. After that, Joseph traveled to Alexandria, where, promising to double the earnings of the king in the regions of Coele-Syria, Phoenicia, Judaea, and Samaria, he won the bid to become the tax collector in this region.[30] Joseph fulfilled his promise to the king and through violence and oppression became yet more rich and powerful.[31] Collins comments regarding this epoch: "The splendid opportunities enjoyed by some, however, were bought at the expense of others. They were enjoyed primarily by the wealthy families of the Jewish aristocracy."[32]

After five wars, in 198 BC, the Seleucid king Antiochus III took complete control over Syria and Phoenicia, and this situation endured until the Roman domination (63 BC). Since in the end of the Ptolemaic rule the people were struggling under heavy oppression, the Jews welcomed the Seleucids with hope that life would become easier and indeed, Antiochus III did promise to restore Jerusalem in the beginning, which had been destroyed by war. In order to do that, he brought scattered Jewish people back to Jerusalem, gave the necessary material for the restoration of the sacrifices, restored the temple, allowed "a form of government in accordance with the laws of their country,"[33] instituted tax exemption to the religious and political leaders of the nation and tax exemption to everybody for three years, allowed freedom of those made slaves and their children and redeemed land to its original proprietors.[34] This was practically the enactment of a jubilee. With such a political platform, Antiochus III rapidly conquered popular support.

After that, however, Antiochus III made a treaty with Ptolemy V Epiphanes and decided to extend his empire even more into Asia Minor and Greece. The Romans, who were already powerful at this time, defeated the Seleucids in

---

30. Josephus relates this event in the following way: "Now when the day came around on which the rights to farm taxes in the cities were to be sold, bids were made by those eminent in rank in the various provinces. When the sum of taxes from Coele-Syria and from Phoenicia and Judaea with Samaria added up to eight thousand talents, Joseph came forward and accused the bidders of having made an agreement to offer the king a low price for the taxes, whereas he for his part promised to give double that amount and send over to the king the property of those who had been remiss toward his house; for this right was sold along with that of farming the taxes." Josephus, *Ant.* 12.4.4

31. Josephus, *Ant.* 12.4.5

32. Collins, *Jewish Wisdom in the Hellenistic Age*, 27.

33. Josephus, *Ant.* 12.3.3.

34. Although with a confused chronology, Josephus registers a letter sent from Antiochus III to the governor of Judea whose name was Ptolemy. See Josephus, *Ant.* 12.3.3.

the Battle of Magnesia (190 BC) and imposed a very heavy war compensation of twelve thousand talents over them. This crippled the Seleucid empire and changed their internal politics toward their client states. "The extent of the reparations plunged the empire into a desperate state, necessitating new and even more unscrupulous methods of acquiring the money."[35] The result was a tax burden similar to that under the Ptolemies.[36] Baesens calculates the oppressive situation of the peasants: "Finally, the peasant would therefore most probably be left with less than 25% of his earnings in the best case, with the two taxation systems [royal and religious] combined in the late Seleucid period."[37] Once again, the Jewish people were under great land related oppression.

At that period, land and land related taxes are at the center of all political changes the country is facing. Israel passes through times of more and less external oppression, but the oppression was always present, promoted by the foreign powers and by those of the country who are in alliance with the foreign powers. Those who belong to the low strata of society feel the oppression faster and harder. All of that is important in building the scenario in which Jesus develops his ministry.

Meanwhile, the tug of war between the high priest family (hierocracy) and the Tobiad family (aristocracy) for power in Jerusalem continued. Now, however, the Tobiad family was paired with the Seleucids and the high priest with the Ptolemies. In 175 BC, Antiochus IV Epiphanes rose to the throne of the Seleucid Empire. He decided to turn Judah into a Greek polis with the help of the Tobiad family. Receiving from them promises of augmenting the revenues, and consequently, the already heavy burden upon the people, Antiochus IV nominated Jason (2 Macc. 4:7–9) and Menelaus to the post of High Priest. This process of Hellenization of Jerusalem and the whole nation reached its peak with the prohibition of circumcision, the guard of the Sabbath and the desecration of the temple (1 Macc. 1; 2 Macc. 5–6; Dan 9:27; 11:31; 12:11).[38] The plan included distributing the properties of Jews to foreigners (1 Macc. 3:35–36). This attack against the Jewish institutions and people gave rise to

---

35. Schäfer, *The History of the Jews in the Greco-Roman World*, 33.

36. "On the whole, the Seleucids left the tax system in Judea as it had been under the Ptolemies." Malamat et al., *A History of the Jewish People*, 193.

37. Baesens, "Royal Taxation and Religious Tribute in Hellenistic Palestine," 196.

38. Josephus, *JW*, 1.1.2

the Maccabean revolt. Thus, Horsley affirms that "The Maccabean revolt was a struggle by the Judean peasantry for their own social-economic survival."[39]

Before speaking about the land situation during the epoch of the Maccabean, however, it is proper to summarize our findings up to here. The standard situation during the Ptolemaic and Seleucid periods was that most of the land in Israel was owned by the king (Ptolemaic or Seleucid); some large estates pertained to the aristocratic families, people with royal proximity, and the High Priest and priestly families; and many people who owned small tracts of land had serious problems keeping their lands due to taxes, wars, inclement weather, food crisis and political maneuvers.[40] "On surveying these various economic developments in Galilee in Hellenistic times one important fact emerges – the increased possibilities were clearly to the advantage of the few rather than the many."[41]

Such an oppressive situation whose major effects were on the small holders of land was alleviated in the time of the Hasmoneans, at least for those who were Jews.[42] Through revolts and social movements the Jews conquered tax exemption (1 Macc 10:30–31; 11:28, 34–35; 13:37–39), territorial expansion, and the subjection of other peoples to taxation and service, as well as social justice (1 Macc 11:34–35; 14:4–14; 15:33; 2 Macc 2:28–30).[43] The Hasmonean family acquired large amounts of land and the burden of sustaining the state

---

39. Horsley and Hanson, *Bandits, Prophets and Messiahs: Popular Movements in the Time of Jesus*, 21.

40. Pastor, *Land and Economy*, 22–52. To illustrate this a few quotations are in order: "Therefore, land is the property that is being taken from those who cannot withstand the economic pressures created by the demands pf the Ptolemaic period. The wealthy aristocrats who cooperated with the Ptolemaic rulers, and were in part, like Tobias and his son Hyrkanos, agents of the government, profited by the system, and probably enlarged their holdings. The majority suffered impoverishment and expropriation." Pastor, *Land and Economy*, 40. Adams also comments this situation: "When examining the available sources, it becomes apparent that authorities at all levels relied on taxes to generate revenue and maintain order. Stratification persisted during this period, and taxation contributed to income inequality and in certain cases to social unrest. Various obstacles made it challenging for households to retain their land and freedom." Adams, *Social and Economic Life in Second Temple Judea*, 128.

41. Freyne, *Galilee From Alexander the Great to Hadrian*, 176.

42. There is a discussion if the Hasmonean movement was mainly a religious movement or a socio-economic revolution. I tend to agree with Grabbe that is was complex movement with social, political, economic and religious aspects, but not mainly motivated by the economic aspect. See Grabbe, *Judaism From Cyrus to Hadrian. Volume One*, 247 et seq. See also Derfler, *The Hasmonean Revolt: Rebellion or Revolution*.

43. Grabbe, *Judaism From Cyrus to Hadrian. Volume One: The Persian and Greek Periods*, 268–69. See also Josephus, *JW*. 1.2.2.

fell on the foreign conquered people, who probably paid as much taxes as under Seleucid domination.[44] The book of Judith confirms the state of wealth the Jews were enjoying at that time, with money, estates, and slaves (Jdt 8.7, 27; 16.24).

This golden time did not endure, however. In 152 BCE, Jonathan Maccabeus was nominated high priest by the Seleucid usurper Alexander Balas. The fiscal situation of Judaea at that time was as such; besides all the taxes previously mentioned [the collective *phoros*, poll-tax, crown-tax, salt-tax, transit duties, slave trade, all sales and water rights] (plus a tax on livestock it seems), the Jews also paid a huge land tax: one third of the grain and half of the fruit harvest.[45] Thus, the family feud of the Hasmoneans in its power struggle, made the tax burden heavier and lastly supplanted the nation's freedom.

The Psalms of Solomon (PssSol) reveal some of the struggles and aspirations of those living by the end of the Hasmonean period.[46] In PssSol 4, for example, the author complains that "their eyes are upon the house of the man [who is] in security" (PssSol 4.9) and that "He laid waste a house on account of his lawless desire" (PssSol 4.11). The complaining is that some Jewish leaders are despising the Law and oppressing orphans and others. Atkinson comments on these texts, "The psalmist continued with a description of the sins that were committed by the Sanhedrin's leader and his supporters. The crimes now become even more appalling, for these individuals stole property (PssSol 4.9) and destroyed families (PssSol 4.10)."[47] This frustration with the Hasmonean rule, which had become corrupt, was probably the cause of the origin of the Essenes and the Pharisees, and also of the Sadducees as a supporter group of the priests.[48]

Therefore, the nation of Israel was oppressed both by Ptolemaic and by Seleucid rulers. The land was considered as a possession of the king and heavy

---

44. Schäfer, *The History of the Jews in the Greco-Roman World*, 66.

45. Baesens, "Royal Taxation and Religious Tribute in Hellenistic Palestine," 182.

46. The Psalms of Solomon is a collection of 18 psalms, or songs of praise and prayer, written in Hebrew between the first century BC and the first century AD. Despite their name, the psalms were not written by King Solomon, but rather by unknown authors who sought to express their faith and hopes for the future of the Jewish people.

47. Atkinson, *An Intertextual Study of the Psalms of Solomon*, 81.

48. Horsley and Hanson, *Bandits, Prophets and Messiahs*, 23–29.

taxes were demanded. Both regimens used Jewish aristocrats to take care of its interests in Israel and these families, together with some foreign officials, became more and more wealthy and influential. Large estates given by the king to loyal officials were developed by Jewish tenants and hired workers. The small free holder hardly managed to keep their possession and, as is common throughout this period, sometimes lost their possessions to his creditors.

Although this whole situation ameliorated during the first years of Hasmonean domination, in which Israel was practically sovereign, internal disputes, corruption and external pressures eventually made the Hasmoneans place a heavy yoke over their subjects. Israel also saw the rise of a new aristocracy composed by priestly families and those whom they favoured, military officers and traditional wealthy families.[49] This situation of political unrest opened the way to the Roman domination to which we will focus our attention in the next section. Before doing that, however, we need to present one more piece of evidence of the tyranny of the wealthy against the poor.

One of the institutions that confirm the favoured situation of the wealthy in Israel is called prozbul. The prozbul was created by Hillel the Elder (110 BC – AD 10). The text in the Mishnah[50] referring to Deuteronomy 15:9–10 reads:

> [A loan secured by] a prozbul is not cancelled. This was one of the things enacted by Hillel the elder; for when he observed people refraining from lending to one another, and thus transgressing what is written in the Torah, "Beware, lest you harbor the base thought, ['The seventh year, the year of remission, is approaching,' so that you are mean to your needy kinsman and give him nothing." Hillel enacted the prozbul. This is the formula of the prozbul: "I turn over to you, so-and-so, judges of such

---

49. Horsley and Hanson, *Bandits, Prophets and Messiahs: Popular Movements in the Time of Jesus*, 27–28.

50. While it is true that the Mishnah was not written until around AD 200, it is also important to note that the Mishnah was compiled from earlier oral traditions that had been passed down through generations of Jewish scholars. These oral traditions were likely in circulation long before they were finally recorded in writing. The Mishnah was compiled by a group of Jewish scholars known as the Tannaim, who lived and studied in the years immediately following the time of the Second Temple in Jerusalem. These scholars would have had access to earlier texts and teachings, as well as firsthand knowledge of the customs and practices of the Jewish people during the time of Hillel.

and such a place, that any debt that I may have outstanding, I shall collect it whenever I desire." And the judges sign below, or the witnesses.[51]

The prozbul is further explained in the Mishnah: "A prozbul is written only for [a debt secured by] land. But if [the debtor] has none, then [the creditor] can give him title to a share, however small, of his own field. If he had land in pledge in a city, a prozbul can be written on it. Rabbi Hutzpit says: a prozbul may be written for a man on the security of his wife's property, or for an orphan on the security of property belonging to his guardian."[52]

According to the Mishnah, the prozbul was created because wealthy people were not willing to lend money to those in need, because in the seventh year the land needed to be returned with or without the payment of the debt, since the debt itself was pardoned. Thus, Hillel created the prozbul in order to legally keep someone in debt even during and after the seventh year of remission. The Mishnah presents helping the poor as Hillel's motivation.[53] Some scholars however, affirm that the motivation of the prozbul was favoring the rich.[54] Although it is not safe to judge motivations, the fact is that the lenders were being helped with the maintenance of the debt, which according to Moses's Law should be forgiven.[55]

Thus, from the Babylonian domination until the time of the Maccabees, Judah was characterized not by living under the ethics of the jubilee, but by the same ethics found in other places and times. This ethics was one of oppression in which those with power and money used them to augment yet more their power and money at the expense and taking advantage of the poorer strata of society. When Rome dominates over Israel, the foreign power

---

51. Mishnah Sheviit 10.3–4. There are interesting discussions on the different Mishnaic exegetical traditions in play in the law, but they extrapolate our focus. The reader interested in those will benefit from Neusner, *From Politics to Piety the Emergence of Pharisaic Judaism*, 14 et seq.; Neusner, *Rabbinic Literature & the New Testament: What We Cannot Show, We Do Not Know*, 74 et seq.

52. Mishnah Sheviit 10.6

53. Marchant, Orlowek, and Fox-Ashrei, *Understanding Shmittoh: Its Sources and Background & Halochos of Shmittoh*, 86 et seq.

54. Herzog II, *Prophet and Teacher*, 65.

55. Collins calls attention to the fact that those using the legal fiction of the prozbul were not able to pray the Lord's prayer in sound conscience, since saying "And forgive us our debt, as we also have forgiven our debtors" would put them in a bad situation before God. Collins, *Wealth, Wages, and the Wealthy*, 104–5.

changes, but the situation of lacking conditions to keep the family land and land related oppression continues. This is the focus of next section.

3.2 Land Exploitation in Palestine during Roman Empire

Having presented the historical antecedents related to land and oppression, the focus of this dissertation now places itself in the time covered by the New Testament. The focus will be on the agrarian situation under Herod the Great and after him.

3.2.1 Land and Tax Under Herod the Great

King Herod the Great was the main owner of estates throughout Israel. These estates came to him from variegated sources. Some came as inheritance from his father (Antipater the Idumaean) and from his father-in-law (Alexander Maccabeus). Other estates he owned because they were state lands from the periods of the Ptolemies, Seleucids and Hasmoneans. He also amassed land by means of domination of other people. Finally, other sources were land whose owners were unable to support the heavy burden of taxes and grants given by Augustus.[56]

The rents Herod charged on his states were high and in times of peace, he would use soldiers to develop his estates.[57] One author affirms: "It may well be the case that half or even two-thirds of the entire Judaean state was his private domain."[58] Commonly these royal lands would be rented through tenancy and sometimes it would be developed by slaves and hired workers.

Besides lands belonging to the king, the rich in Israel also possessed land. While there were many plots in Palestine ranging from 1 to 15 acres (family estates, estates in regimen of tenancy), there were also large estates belonging to the elite.[59] Some of these estates were gifts distributed by Herod to those he favored.[60] Thus, the same phenomenon of *villas* found in other parts of

---

56. Rocca, *Herod's Judaea*, 213–15. See also Josephus, *BJ*. 1.20.4.
57. Stern, "The Reign of Herod," 97.
58. Grant, *Herod the Great*, 173.
59. Fiensy, *Christian Origins and the Ancient Economy*, 15.
60. "These scattered indications suggest that Galilee did not escape the advancing aggrandizement of the Herodian dynasty as more and more of the best lands of Palestine fell

the empire is present in the land of Israel, as witnessed by the archaeology and referred or inferred by literature. Safrai presents a list of Jewish *villas* and large estates, mainly found in the Talmud.[61] By analyzing this list, one concludes that the estates belonging to Jews were mainly owned by priestly families, rabbis, and sages.[62]

Although referring to the end of first century or beginning of the second, Yoma 35b speaks about the faithfulness of Rabbi Elazar ben Ḥarsum, who, despite inheriting a thousand villages on land and a thousand ships at sea, dedicated more time to study the Torah than to take care of his possessions. This number reflects someone extravagantly wealthy even to Roman standards. Certainly, the circle around high priests and Herod benefitted also from owning large estates. Safrai reminds us that the system of government of land itself was unjust, since their surplus and profit was necessarily transferred to those in the city at the expense of those who worked the land.[63]

One would also find successful merchants among the owners of large estates.[64] The proprietors of large estates commonly lived in large cities, mainly in Jerusalem, and hired people to administrate their properties and send them the profits. This aristocracy of Judea was deeply influenced by Greco-Roman life style and had money to spend in high priced and imported decoration

---

into their hands and were subsequently donated by them to suitable beneficiaries." Freyne, *Galilee From Alexander the Great to Hadrian*, 165. "As we just stated, there was a general trend from the small independent farm to large estates, whether private or imperial. The trend, however, was not in one direction. Imperial lands were occasionally given to the rich or to other supporters of the government." Safrai, *Economy of Roman Palestine*, 329.

61. Safrai, *Economy of Roman Palestine*, 85–99. "The estate in the Roman world usually belonged to the rich. In Judea, or Palestine, the owner of such an estate was usually a rich non-Jew, associated or identified with the Hellenistic culture and naturally identified with the interests of the government. . . . There were, however, Jewish estate owners such as Rabbi Judah the Prince who received estates from the emperor. (p. 85).

62. Although this applies more to the first part of the period than to the last, Mantel comment still reveals the power and wealth of the office of High Priest: "Throughout the period of the Second Temple the High Priests constituted the highest aristocracy of the land, both politically and socially." Mantel, "The High Priesthood and the Sanhedrim in the Time of the Second Temple," 267. Also Fiensy: "Thus, the literary evidence indicates that a wealthy, aristocratic class lived in Jerusalem in the Herodian period, many of whom, but not all, were from one of the influential priestly families." Fiensy, *The Social History of Palestine in the Herodian Period*, 52.

63. Safrai, *Economy of Roman Palestine*, 330.

64. Klausner, "The Economy of Judea In the Period of the Second Temple," 190.

items to their mansions.⁶⁵ As everywhere else in the empire, it was a common phenomenon to use tenants to make their land productive.

In Israel, like in Rome, there was an aristocracy that owned large estates and employed hired workers and tenants to develop their estates. Slavery, although present, was not as common a phenomenon in Israelite agriculture during the Roman period as in Rome.⁶⁶ The reader should remember the information of this and last chapters is the context of Jesus and his audience, as well as Luke and his original readers. Those hearing Jesus were well acquainted with terms like tenants, hired workers, day laborers, villas and all intricacies relating to the agrarian economy of Rome and Israel. I am proposing in this dissertation that Luke writes also in order to address the unjust system I am presenting here.

Between the large owners and the family farmer, there was a class of medium-sized land owners. They were the ones who loaned money to the peasants and not infrequently became proprietors of their land due to their debt.⁶⁷ This class was the main motor of economy since they produced food and other goods for internal consumption and exportation and paid in money for goods and services.

In the lower end of the landed classes, peasants who owned small portions of land had a hard life.⁶⁸ Taxes, wars, military service, corvée, and adverse

---

65. "Not only were Herod and his court attracted to the social ambience and material culture offered by Roman society; so, too, were the wealthy priestly and nonpriestly classes of Herod's Jerusalem. Excavations in the city's Jewish quarter after 1967 offer remarkable evidence of the extent to which this stratum of Jerusalem society imported and adopted the regnant artistic styles and material goods from the surrounding world. Among the most relevant finds in this regard are mosaic floors featuring geometric and floral designs, frescoes similar to those found at Pompeii featuring architectural designs, colored panels, imitation marble, stucco used in imitation of ashlar blocks or architectural and floral motifs, a glass decanter from Sidom, imported western and eastern terra sigillata, fine or thin walled ware, Pompeian red ware, Italian amphorae, and perfume bottles." Levine, *Judaism and Hellenism in Antiquity*, 48–49.

66. Rocca, *Herod's Judaea*, 224–25. "The peasant family supplied the backbone of the labor force for the ancient agrarian economy. This workforce was supplemented by animals and slaves. Slavery did not, however, play a great role in the agricultural production of Palestine." Oakman, *Jesus and the Economic Questions of His Day*, 22.

67. Klausner, "The Economy of Judea In the Period of the Second Temple," 189–90.

68. "The peasant was free only in relative terms, of course, since he was bound to the soil by tradition and by requirements of taxation and corvée labour, but he was not a slave to be sold or disposed of according to the whim of a master." Lester L. Grabbe, "Yehud: A History of the Persian Province of Judah," 191.

climate had the power to destabilize them in a very definitive way. Klausner clearly presents the situation of the common peasant living in Herod's time:

> In spite of his industry, however, the smallholder never became rich. Most of his produce went to feed himself and his family, and only a little remained for bartering or selling in the nearest market town, in exchange for the necessities of his household. He had no savings, so that after one or two years of drought, or a prolonged war, he often lost his land and became a hired laborer or journeyman. To avoid this the smallholder would sometimes borrow from a rich landowner, but if he failed to repay his debt, he finally forfeited his land. If even this was not sufficient to cover his debt, he could be taken in service as a "Hebrew slave"; sometimes, too, his wife and children went into bondage with him.[69]

The consequence of the situation described above was the augmentation of the social class who comes under the landed people, i.e., tenants and hired workers. Freyne comments on the situation of the tenants: "Indeed many tenants may have originally been owners of their own plots, but in a bad year had had to barter their land in order to pay tribute or buy grain for the following season and even feed their families. Once that had happened there was never any possibility of their retrieving the situation, and they were fortunate indeed if they could survive as tenants on what was formerly their own land."[70]

Tenants tended to suffer abuse from everywhere. They were oppressed by the Roman power with its taxes, by the Jewish aristocratic and hierocratic rulers with taxes and corruption, by the wealthy who owned their lands, and by unfavorable contracts on the rent of the land and money lending. Such a treatment makes it easier to understand a situation one reads both in the gospels

---

69. Klausner, "The Economy of Judea In the Period of the Second Temple," 189. He thus concludes the description: "Even if the farmer succeeded in holding on to his small plot of land until he died, only his eldest son, who according to the Torah prescription inherited double his brother's share – could hope to support himself and his family from the land. His brothers would often sell him their portion and join the ranks of the laborers. If they could not find regular work they had to make do with casual employment. Sometimes they became unemployable and ended up either as beggars or brigands." (189).

70. Freyne, *Galilee From Alexander the Great to Hadrian*, 195.

and in a Papyrus about tenants beating and killing the emissaries of the landowner (Matt 21:33–46; Mark 12:1–12; Luke 20:9–19, and P.Lond.7.1948).

In this class of land destitute people one finds also the hired workers. Their written or verbal contracts were per hours, days, or weeks up to the maximum of six years. The average wage was a drachma or a denarius per day. They worked in the royal estates, the large estates of the very wealthy, and the medium estates. Formerly small holders, some of them had completely lost their properties and were in a continuous situation of dependence and insecurity. They depended on the situation of the general economy. At the same time, it is this class of people, together with the tenants who commonly become conscious of the social injustice in which they lived and organized movements envisaging change.[71]

Although some scholars affirm the exiguity of slavery in Israel, it seems that the sources indicate that the practice was more familiar than commonly admitted.[72] P.Cair.Zen. 159076, for example, one of the many documents in the Zenon Archive is a letter from Tobias to Apollonius, referring to a gift of one eunuch and four slave boys, two of whom were circumcised.[73] Since circumcision was practiced in other cultures besides the Jewish it is not possible to guarantee the Jewish origin of the boys. However, considering that the one sending the presents was also a Jew, and an important one, it would not be a stretch to infer that the two circumcised boys were Jews or at least former slaves of a Jew. Other documents of the same archive also refer to slavery.[74]

In the Second Temple literature, one also finds references to slavery. Ben Sirach (ca. 180–175 BC) gives the following advice to his readers: "Do not abuse slaves who work faithfully, or hired laborers who devote themselves to their task. Let your soul love intelligent slaves; do not withhold from them their freedom" (Sir 7.20–21; cf. also 33.25–33; 41.24; 42.5). The Book of Judith (ca. 100 BC ?) affirms that her husband left her "men and women slaves" (Jdt 8.7). It is also common to find the triad 'women, slaves and minors' in Jewish

---

71. Freyne, *Galilee From Alexander the Great to Hadrian*, 197.

72. Rocca, *Herod's Judaea*, 224–25.

73. *P.Cair.Zen.* 159076; Anna Krautbauer, Stephen Llewelyn, and Blake Wassell, "A Gift of One Eunuch and Four Slave Boys: P.Cair.Zen I 59076 and Historical Construction," 305–25.

74. *P.cair.zen*.1.59077 makes reference to a slave-girl offered in Palestine as security in a transaction related to transport of oil. *P.cair.zen*.1.59093 speaks about slaves being transported from Gaza to Philadephia, Egypt. *P.cair.zen*.5.59804 mentions slaves that had run away probably from Gaza.

literature of the Second Temple period up to the second century AD.[75] And Josephus presents evidence of slavery in Israel, especially among the royalty.[76]

Thus, the lower strata of Jewish society also were the slaves. There were two types of slaves in Israel, the Hebrew and the Canaanite. Hebrew slaves received better treatment as fellow Jews. They attained freedom after six years of work and it was common to consider that their work and not their bodies were property of their owners.[77] The Canaanite slave, on another hand, was fully property of his or her owner. Some of the same abuses found in Rome would be found among Jewish owners, although not as frequent and widespread. The main owners of slaves in Israel were the aristocracy, the very rich Jews and foreigner owners of *latifundia*.

Fiensy confirms this picture with estimates. He calculates that the elite groups in Palestine, as in Rome itself, should not be very different than one percent, followed by about five percent of those called the retainers: minor religious leaders, state administrators, tax collectors, bailiffs, and magistrates.[78] These people were owners of medium and large estates, which ranged from two to three thousand acres.[79] Around the level of subsistence in ancient Galilee one would find small freeholders, which owned plots varying from 1 to 15 acres and tenant farmers, day laborers and slaves working mainly in the large estates of the wealthy.[80]

In the last pages, we are examining the agrarian economy of Israel in the times of Jesus. I have shown that the main owners of land in Israel were the king, the priests and their associates. After them, there was an elite class of proprietors that owned land and hired tenants, workers and had slaves. Among these three kinds of work force, there were people who had been owners of small tracts of land for the subsistence of their families but had

---

75. Hezser, *Jewish Slavery in Antiquity*, 69 et seq.; Flesher, *Oxen, Women, or Citizens?*

76. Eunuch slaves of Herod: Josephus *JW* 1.24.7; 1.22.7. Herod's slave girls: Josephus, *JW*. 1.30.3. Pheroras enamorated of a slave-girl: Josephus, *JW*. 1.24.5. Herod give eunuchs as gift to Archelaus: Josephus, *JW*. 1.26.6

77. Klausner, "The Economy of Judea In the Period of the Second Temple," 193.

78. Fiensy, *Christian Origins and the Ancient Economy*, 12–14. "The governing class and their retainers stood over the lower classes both in the urban centers and in the country. They extracted rents and taxes, the surplus, from the peasantry and others, and they lived mostly in the cities, usually in wealth and luxury." (p. 14)

79. Fiensy, *Christian Origins and the Ancient Economy*, 98–117.

80. Fiensy, *Christian Origins and the Ancient Economy*, 14–16.

lost everything because of the unfavorable conditions they faced. As in the Roman Empire in general, the situation of the agrarian economy of Israel was also one of oppression upon the weaker members of society. The messages of Jesus and Luke as I will show propose a critique and a solution against this *status quo*.

Going back to Herod, an important characteristic of his kingship was his building program throughout Israel and abroad. This program comprised the constructions of the temple of Israel, fortresses, palaces, mausoleums, temples in honor to Rome and Augustus, theaters, hippodromes, stadia, baths, gymnasia and cities such as Caesarea Maritima and Sebbaste (ancient Samaria).[81] If his projects abroad had the goal of presenting him as a good patron and grateful client, his projects throughout his kingdom had, among other reasons, possibly an economic one. Once a large construction was in execution, jobs and development would come to that respective region.[82] Galilee, however, was left outside of this development program undertaken by Herod, because of their former resistance against him when he was their governor.[83] Galilee, therefore, was not enjoying the same economic development as the other locations of the Herodian kingdom. As Oakman says:

> The early Roman economy in Galilee is a political-economy, and in many senses, only a semi-economy. Economic development functions for the sake of the urban and imperial elites, but only in basic and limited senses at the village level or on the lake. Distributed money does not circulate so much as affect the political will of the elites in keeping the masses in debt and the goods flowing toward the cities and the sea coast.[84]

All these construction projects were financed by a very developed system of taxation. There were many taxes one needed to pay during Herod's rulership, although it is not possible to know exactly their percentages. This uncertainty generates differing views on Herod's taxation. He demanded poll-tax, land tax, customs duties, tax on house property, tax on purchases

---

81. See a list of these projects in Josephus 1.21.1–10.
82. Richardson, *Herod: King of the Jews and Friend of the Romans*, 174–202.
83. Aviam, "People, Land, Economy, and Belief in First-Century Galilee and Its Origins," 16.
84. Oakman, "Execrating? Or Execrable Peasants!," 159.

and sales and voluntary. From the rich strata sometimes Herod demanded gifts for the king.[85] He also had monopoly over salt.

The effects of Herod's excesses are well illustrated by the fact that when he died, an entourage of Jewish leaders went to Rome to ask for the end of the Herodian dynasty. They accused Herod of looting the country through abusive taxes, obligatory gifts to himself and his friends, and expropriation of land in order to invest abroad.[86] Some scholars agree in general with this evaluation registered by Josephus. Klausner, for example, says that "During Herod's reign the level of taxes in Judea was particularly high."[87] Stern comments: "It appears that these complaints were largely due to the unequal distribution of taxes, the main burden of which rested on the shoulders of the Jewish farmers and tenants of the king."[88]

This heavy burden of taxes was assuaged by Herod's munificence in times of hardship. More than once, he reduced the taxes over the people. In 25 BC for example he practically sustained the nation during a drought that endured two years.[89]

From the end of the Hasmoneans' rule until the end of Herod's kingdom, Israel faced many changes. Different rulers, sizes of territory, taxation politics, and changes in the international and local politics all had impact on the whole nation, but especially upon those who worked the land, small holders, tenants, hired workers and slaves. Living on the subsistence level, they were an easy target for predators and unscrupulous governors, aristocrats and powerful landowners. This does not mean that all landowners were oppressors and all tenants oppressed, but the way society was built made this kind of situation easier and did not provide many ways for the lower strata to defend themselves.

3.2.2 Land and Tax After Herod the Great

The point of this chapter is showing that there was a culture of oppression in Israel in the times around the ministry of Jesus and the writing of the gospel

---

85. Grant, *Herod the Great*, 171–72.
86. Josephus, *Ant.* 17.11.2.
87. Klausner, "The Economy of Judea In the Period of the Second Temple," 204.
88. Stern, "The Reign of Herod," 97.
89. Grant, *Herod the Great*, 122.

of Luke. The last section has shown how this culture was lived during the times of Herod the Great and this section show the continuity of this culture after him. Below I present three evidences of the oppressive situation in which many peasants were living in Israel: high unemployment rate, the continuation of high taxation, and the movements of peasant's revolt. To those we turn.

With the death of Herod (4 BC), his kingdom was divided among his sons: Archelaus was made ethnarch of Judea, Idumea and Samaria; Herod Antipas, tetrarch of Galilee and Perea, and Philip was made tetrarch of Trachonitis, Batanea, and Gaulanitis. While the contenders for the throne were engaged in political strife in Rome, a massive rebellion erupted across Israel, engulfing the entire region. This riot was muffled with the mighty power of Rome through the general Varus and more than two thousand Jews were crucified in this process.[90] Thus, the era of Caesar's favor towards the Jews came to an end. Due to the fact that the political-economic situation in Judea and Galilee was very different at this time, I will present separately, starting with Judea.

In Judea after Herod the Great, unemployment and oppression became yet more common. Commenting on this, Klausner states, "The repeated mention in the Talmud of the פועל בטל ("idle worker") is evidence of a significant amount of unemployment in Judea during that period. This situation is corroborated by the parable of the workers in the vineyard (Matt 20:1–13). In this parable, the owner found idle workers at 9 a.m., 12 p.m., 3 p.m. and 5 p.m. These last workers tell him they were idle the whole day because no one had hired them. Also, according to Josephus, over 18,000 men were left without work when the rebuilding of the Second Temple was finally completed in 64 A.D."[91] This situation of unemployment was true in Judea and worse in Galilee.

After the kingship of Archelaus (4 BC to AD 6), Judaea was reduced to a province governed by a procurator of equestrian order. Klausner sheds light on the taxes on this period: "Taxes were also severe during the time of the procurators, and included a city tax, a water tax, a food tax (on meat, salt etc.)

---

90. Read about these events in Stern, "The Reign of Herod," 117–23.
91. Klausner, "The Economy of Judea In the Period of the Second Temple," 191. For what is possible to know, it seems that taxes in Israel were more or less steady from Herod to the time of the procurators up to the time of Nero, when the duties exigencies were augmented. Stern, "The Herodian Dinasty and the Province of Judea at the End of the Period of the Second Temple," 168.

and road tolls. Border tolls were particularly burdensome. [. . .] Though the official levy on goods was only 2.5% of their value, the operations of the tax farmers and publicans multiplied that figure many times over. The publicans and their assistants checked the goods as they passed through the customs house."[92] Besides the taxes, people would also be obligated to work without payment when requested by Roman authorities in a system of corvée.[93]

And how was the economic situation in Galilee after Herod's death? There is a great deal of debate concerning the economic situation of Galilee in the time of Jesus.[94] Although some scholars disagree, it is possible to affirm that Galilee in the first century AD was predominantly Jewish.[95] Some scholars propose that Galilee was a very poor part of the country and others, that the gap between Galilee and Judea was not so pronounced. Herod Antipas had a long and peaceful tetrarchy in Galilee from 4 BC to AD 39. While his father depleted Galilee of money and rebels, Antipas managed to rule Galilee without major incidents and created a new kind of man, "a man of the Hellenistic world *and* a Jew."[96] The lack of social unrest, however, should not be completely attributed to an enhancement of the quality of life of the small

---

92. Klausner, "The Economy of Judea In the Period of the Second Temple," 204.

93. Stern, "The Herodian Dinasty and the Province of Judea at the End of the Period of the Second Temple," 169.

94. Fiensy explicates these differences: "(1) Some look at Galilee through the lenses of cultural anthropology and macro-sociology, others look at Galilee through the lenses of archaeology and reject the use of social theories. (2) Some maintain that the relations between rural villages and the cities were hostile; others propose that the relationship was one of economic reciprocity and goodwill. (3) Some suggest that Galilee was typical of other agrarian societies – with poor peasants who lived in the rural areas and exploitative wealthy people who lived mostly in the cities; others respond that life was pretty good for everyone in Galilee and that is was an egalitarian society. Fiensy, *Christian Origins and the Ancient Economy*, 1–2. For a graphic representation of Lower Galilee economy, see Fiensy, *Christian Origins and the Ancient Economy*, 73.

95. Mark. A. Chancey, "Archaeology, ,Ethnicity and First Centuriy C.E. Galilee: The Limits of Evidence," 205–18. Freyne is still regarded as one of the best works to demonstrate the mainly Jewish character of Galilee throughout the political changes from Alexander to the time of the New Testament. Freyne, *Galilee From Alexander the Great to Hadrian*, 27–50.

96. Freyne, *Galilee From Alexander the Great to Hadrian*, 70. Speaking about the peace enjoyed in Galilee under Antipas, Freyne says: "One highly significant aspect of Antipas' reign is the fact that its stability meant that there was no need for direct Roman intervention in the internal life of the province. In view of the military, financial and social upheavals of the previous period this was indeed a great blessing for the ordinary people, and stands in sharp contrast to the situation in Judaea, where the insensitivity and brutality of the Roman procurators make a sorry story of mismanagement, and is generally accepted as one of the major causes for the revolt in 66 C.E." Freyne, *Galilee From Alexander the Great to Hadrian*, 69.

landowner and poor in general. "It must be presumed that for the ordinary people the advantages of a peaceful reign outweighed the disadvantages of having to support a Hellenistic-style monarch, since the heavy taxes on the produce of the land had been a fact of life for a very long time."[97] This peace did not last forever though, since the low classes started joining bandit groups to fight against Roman oppression.

The third evidence of the elevated level of oppression of the simple people who worked the land is the phenomenon of the proliferation of brigand groups supported by the peasant class. Richard Horsley writes a book defending this thesis. Following Eric Hobsbawm, he affirms that social banditry in peasant societies is a form of pre-political rebellion.[98] He says: "Social bandits emerge from incidents and circumstances in which what is dictated by the state or local rulers is felt to be unjust or intolerable. Underlying such incidents, however, are general social economic conditions in which many peasants are marginal and vulnerable."[99]

According to Josephus, there was indeed a proliferation of bands of brigands during the years that both preceded and succeeded the ministry of Jesus. One of these bands was ravaging the Syrian frontier led by a Jew called Ezekias. Herod the Great, just made governor of Galilee, caught Ezekias and killed him and some of his brigands.[100] This happened in 47 BC and gave rise to a protest and judgement against Herod because he killed Jews without the knowledge and judgement by the Sanhedrin. Josephus refers to cave brigands also active in 38 BC.[101] When Herod finally managed to conquer the whole territory of Israel, the brigands seemed to be inactive during his kingship. But, if there were no more brigands during Herod's kingship, it was not due to an

---

97. Freyne, *Galilee From Alexander the Great to Hadrian*, 192. Sharon affirms that instead of social banditry, those "bandits" were political rebels fighting against Roman domination. Nadav Sharon, "Judea under Roman Domination," 361–77.

98. Horsley and Hanson, *Bandits, Prophets and Messiahs*, 48.

99. Horsley and Hanson, *Bandits, Prophets and Messiahs*, 49. On another place he says: "A peasant society, however, is not simply a matter of two static classes, wealthy and poor. For the poor produce 'surpluses' which are controlled by the wealthy, with the result that conflicts between the two groups are almost unavoidable. The wealthy and powerful tend to use and abuse their power in ways that are detrimental and unfair to the peasants, and the peasants-producers build up hostilities and resentments which make the powerful anxious lest the poor strike back at them." Horsley and Hanson, *Bandits, Prophets and Messiahs*, 2.

100. Josephus, *JW.* 1.10.5

101. Josephus, *JW.* 1.11.2–4

amelioration of the socio-economic situation of the people, but to Herod's strong repressive attitude toward these movements.[102] The phenomenon again became quite common after the death of Herod the Great. There were many brigands under the leadership of Judas: the son of Ezekias, a royal slave called Simon, and a shepherd called Athrongaeus.[103]

After Herod Archelaus was deposed as governor of Judea and the equestrian Coponius became procurator, a different kind of group surged under the leadership of a Galilean called Judas. They were against paying tributes to the Romans. Josephus identifies these groups with the Essenes.[104] More violent groups, however, continued to exist. Josephus narrates about such a group of 'brigands and rioters who, under the leadership of Eleazar and Alexander, revenged the assassination of a Galilean in a Samaritan village.[105] He also speaks about the sicarii, 'a new species of banditti'.[106] Even leaving aside the companies of 'bandits' and 'brigands' active during the Great Revolt, it is clear that there was a deep unrest among the people.

In his description of the insurgence during the Great Revolt in AD 66, Josephus makes clear the connection between these movements and the indebtedness of the people: "The victors burst in and set fire to the house of Ananias the high-priest and to the palaces of Agrippa and Bernice; they next carried their combustibles to the public archives, eager to destroy the money-lenders' bonds and to prevent the recovery of debts, in order to win over a host of grateful debtors and to cause a rising of the poor against the rich, sure of impunity. The keepers of the Record Office having fled, they set light to the building."[107] Since the majority of the population was composed of peasants, it is impossible not to conclude that they were also the majority of people in these movements, who had as one of their main objectives the freedom of indebtedness, as this event well illustrates.

---

102. Horsley and Hanson, *Bandits, Prophets and Messiahs*, 64.

103. Josephus, *JW*. 2.4.1–3

104. Josephus, *JW*. 2.8.1

105. Josephus, *JW*. 2.12.1. Ahead, Josephus affirms that the brigand band headed by Eleazar ravaged the country for twenty years. Josephus, *JW*. 2.13.2

106. Josephus, *JW*. 2.13.3. In 2.14.1, Josephus call the brigands 'the principal plague of the country'.

107. Josephus, *JW*. 2.17.6

This thesis is not proposing that the sole reason for these unrests was oppression linked to land and tax, but that this was a very important factor.[108] These movements of revolt became strong. So Josephus: "Multitudes of Jews now joined him daily from Jericho and elsewhere, some drawn by hatred of Antigonus, others by his own [Herod's] successes, the majority by a blind love of change."[109] Why would the people have this "blind love of change" if not out of oppression? The demands made by the people in the death of Herod the Great are even clearer. As we have seen, they demanded the reduction of taxes and abolition of duties on sales to Herod Archelaus, Herod's son, and sent an embassy to claim for the autonomy of the nation before Augustus. One of the accusations of the group is that Herod "had sunk the nation in poverty."[110]

It is possible to find the economic element again in the brigands that ravaged the country in the decade that anteceded the Great Revolt: "The impostors and brigands, banding together, incited numbers to revolt, exhorting them to assert their independence, and threatening to kill any who submitted to Roman domination and forcibly to suppress those who voluntarily accepted servitude. Distributing themselves in companies throughout the country, they looted the houses of the wealthy, murdered their owners, and set the villages on fire."[111] Thus, even if one needs to be careful not to attribute the whole unrest caused by the brigands to economic oppression, it would be naïve to fail to acknowledge this as an important factor.

Hanson and Oakman shed light on this economic situation and define political presence in Palestine resulting from the relationship between the Herodian family and the Roman emperors as an "aristocratic empire", in which a very small elite of aristocratic families (around 2 percent) control

---

108. Writing after the fall of Jerusalem, Appian says "The Jewish nation still resisted, and Pompey conquered them, sent their king, Aristobulus, to Rome, and destroyed their greatest, and to them holiest, city, Jerusalem, as Ptolemy, the first king of Egypt, had formerly done. It was afterward rebuilt and Vespasian destroyed it again, and Hadrian did the same in our time. On account of these rebellions the tribute imposed upon all Jews is heavier per capita than upon the generality of taxpayers. The annual tax on the Syrians and Cilicians is one per cent of the valuation of the property of each." Appian, *Syr.* 8.50. Suetonius, speaking about the emperor Domitian, speaks about the rough treatment received by the Jews concerning taxes. Suetonius, *Dom* 12

109. Josephus, *JW.* 1.17.6

110. Josephus *JW.* 2.1.2; *JW.* 2.6.2. Not promptly attended, Jerusalem felt in constant ebullition after Herod's death and while they waited for a decision on who would be their leader. Josephus *JW* 2.13.6

111. Josephus *JW* 2.13.6

the land and the agrarian peasant families in order to maintain themselves in power.[112] Thus, taxes, tools, and tributes were not open to referendum, but imposed from above; and they were not collected to benefit the populace, but only for the elites.[113] Taxation in Roman Palestine, therefore, was extractive, that is, designed to assert elite control over agrarian production.[114] Grabbe presents an opportune illustration of the people treated as milk cows:

> The ancient imperial power seems to have had two main interests: taxes and military service. Its 'economic policy' was simply one of maximizing revenue from a short-term point of view, not in making what today we would consider longer-term investments. While it would be probably wrong to claim that the dominant power had no concern for the welfare of those ruled, this was not high on the list of priorities. Thus, there was not a great impetus to invest in the subordinate peoples and nations of the empire. These were treated simply as milk cows, as producers of wealth for the ruling power. Reasonable relations had to be maintained with the local administration which was often made up of the native elite.[115]

Thus, after Herod the Great, the situation both in Judea under the procurators and in Galilee under Antipas was one of land abuse through high taxes, lack of land to work, joblessness, obligatory work, and proliferation of popular movements repressed with strong violence. This is the context in Israel during Jesus ministry and in which Luke writes his gospel.

3.3 Final Remarks

While Chapter Two has demonstrated that the Roman Empire was characterized by an economical system that impaired the low strata of society in terms of land ownership and made them prey of many types of oppression,

---

112. Hanson and Oakman, *Palestine in the Time of Jesus*, 67–69. "Ancient commerce and economic development served the interests of elites and their storehouses. Participation at the village level was more in terms of labor exploitation, mortgages on subsistence, and distortion of traditional/local/peasant values". Oakman, "Execrating? Or Execrable Peasants!," 151.
113. Hanson and Oakman, *Palestine in the Time of Jesus*, 66.
114. Hanson and Oakman, *Palestine in the Time of Jesus*, 116.
115. Grabbe, "Yehud: A History of the Persian Province of Judah," 191.

this chapter has demonstrated how this situation was experienced in Israel in particular. Since the end of Babylonian captivity, those pertaining to Jewish aristocracy seized opportunities to expand their power and patrimony with the changes in international politics. Priestly and traditional families, while fighting against each other for power, tried to keep their position by accepting the foreign powers and became tools in their hands to deplete the people from land, money and freedom. Thus, since the Persian domination, Israel saw the appearance and establishment of a Jewish landed aristocracy, together with the emergence of rich foreign officials who owned land throughout Israel. This phenomenon continued through the Ptolemaic and Seleucid empires up to Roman times.

Not to ignore the differences of these epochs and their different regimens, but as a reminder and summary, it is good to call to memory a few important numbers:

> It seems that taxes of 33% of the grain and 50% of the fruits were steady in Palestine since the time of the Syrians (1 Macc 10:30) up to the time of Roman domination. Other taxes as the head tax (1 denarius/year), market taxes, transit tolls, port taxes, access to city-controlled resources and the need to labor for state projects, besides the head tax for the temple (1/2 shekel/year) resulting in a heavy burden on those working the land.[116]

During the epoch covered in this chapter, a few elements were more of a constant: (1) the kings or governors are the most successful proprietors of land and develop their lands through tenancy and rents with high taxation or cheap workforce in the face of joblessness. (2) The wealthy owners of large estates and villas live in cities and have people working for them. (3) These proprietors together with medium sized landowners are the minority of the population, but answer for the most part of the land, causing exiguity of land for the others. (4) The high unemployment rate, continued abusive taxation, wars, and compulsory military service make the life of tenants and hired workers miserable and make them a target to oppression, indebtedness, and slavery.

While many peasants just coped with this situation, it is possible to find expressions of unconformity and annoyance in the literature of the time and

---

116. Hanson and Oakman, *Palestine in the Time of Jesus*, 113–15.

in the companies of bandits ravaging the country in the first centuries BC and AD. I propose that both the coping and the grievance were connected to the 'small traditions', the teachings the peasants considered dear to them, expressed in the story of the Old Testament and in the affirmation that the land belongs to Yahweh. Thus, the teaching of the Old Testament on land is the focus of the next chapter, since it is this teaching that forms the basis of Luke's proposal of a jubilee land ethics.

CHAPTER 4

Land Justice and Injustice in the Hebrew Bible: Principles of a Jubilee Informed Ethics

In this dissertation, I am proposing that facing a situation of land related oppression in the Roman Empire in general and particularly in Israel, Luke, based in the Old Testament, proposes a jubilee related land ethic that affirms that since God is the main owner of land, all landowners have to use land according to the rules of God. These rules comprise using the land for the benefit of other people and not just for oneself, sharing land, and avoiding oppression. The last two chapters have demonstrated respectively that both the Roman Empire and Israel inside it had developed a societal system that favored those with large estates at the expense of those with small tracts of land or completely destitute of it. This chapter focuses on the Old Testament as the source from which Luke draws the principles of his jubilee land ethic.

While there was a "great tradition" believed and lived by those who used all opportunities to enrich, rule and dominate people and land, there was also a "little tradition" believed by the people who were at the margins of the society.[1] "The Little Tradition must have been a tradition that still clung to the old idea that the land belonged ultimately to Yahweh and was given

---

1. The term "Little Tradition" was created by R. Redfield to denote the tradition of the majority of peasants living in the country in contrast to the "Great Tradition" of the aristocracy living in the cities and forcing itself upon the peasants. See Redfield, *The Little Community and Peasant Society and Culture*, 41–42.

in trust to Israel as inalienable family farm plots. Land is not capital to be exploited but God-given means to subsist."[2]

I think it is possible to affirm that what Fiensy calls "little tradition" is the teaching of the Old Testament. Thus, presenting introductorily the teaching of the Old Testament on land and the ways Israelites used to alienate this teaching, this chapter prepares us for dealing with Luke's proposal, furnishing the theological and ethical background that bases Luke's teachings.

4.1 From Creation to the Promised Land: The Centrality of Land

As we have seen in the first chapter, land is a central theme in the Hebrew Bible.[3] The first two chapters of the Hebrew Bible present a very intimate relation between God, human beings and land. First, God creates the earth (Gen 1:1). He creates and organizes everything with light, time, waters above and below, and dry land, which receives the name of אֶרֶץ (earth, land) (Gen 1:1–10). By God's command, the אֶרֶץ sprouts (דָּשָׁא) all kinds of vegetation (Gen 1:11–12) and brings forth (יָצָא) living creatures (Gen 1:24–25). Finally, the man created in God's image and likeness receives dominion over all land and living beings on land, heavens and sea. God blesses the man with dominion over the land, the order to subdue it and the right to eat from its fruits (Gen 1:26–30).

The second chapter of Genesis presents the generations (תּוֹלֵדוֹת) of the heavens and the earth. In this chapter, we read that there was no vegetation yet in the earth (אֶרֶץ), because there was no man (אָדָם) to work the ground (אֲדָמָה) (Gen 2:5). Thus, God forms the man (הָאָדָם) from the dust (עָפָר) of the earth (אֲדָמָה) (Gen 2:7). God plants a garden to be the dwelling of the man, so he can work it and keep it (Gen 2:15). He also forms a female helper that can aid the man in his functions related to the land. The way the story is narrated, the linguistic relation between man (אָדָם) and land (אֲדָמָה), and the fact that the woman is created to help the man to fulfill his responsibilities

---

2. Fiensy, *The Social History of Palestine in the Herodian Period*, 3.

3. Von Rad, starts his study on Land in the Hexateuch with the remark: "In the whole of the Hexateuch, there is probably no more important idea than that expressed in terms of the land promised and later granted by Yahweh, an idea found in all the sources, and indeed in every part of each of them." von Rad, "The Promised Land and Yahweh's Land in the Hexateuch," 79.

toward the land stress the fundamentality of the relationship between man and land under God.[4]

The intimate relationship between God, humans and land is again presented in the account of the fall of Adam and Eve into sin. Once man and woman did what God had forbidden, he cursed them along with the serpent. However, one of the curses God imposes upon Adam is actually upon the land: "cursed is the ground (אֲדָמָה) because of you" (Gen 3:17). The other referred the man going back to his earthly origin: "till you return to the ground (אֲדָמָה), for out of it you were taken; for you are dust (עָפָר), and to dust you shall return" (Gen 3:19). Land is fundamental both in creation and in fall and continues to be so in the story of the sons of Adam and Eve.

Adam and Eve's first children were farmers. Abel is presented as a shepherd of sheep and Cain as a servant of the land (עֹבֵד אֲדָמָה) (Gen 4:2). When this one presents his offering of fruits of the land (אֲדָמָה) and God does not accept him nor his offering, he becomes angry and kills his brother in the field (שָׂדֶה) (Gen 4:8). From the earth (אֲדָמָה) the blood of Abel cries to God and God curses him: the already cursed ground (אֲדָמָה) will not give its strength to Cain and he will be a wanderer in the earth (אֶרֶץ) (Gen 4:9–12). From Genesis 5 to 11, the narrator progressively demonstrates that the land was full of violence and corrupt. Then the earth was emptied through the Flood and filled again by procreation. Different occupations, languages and peoples appear in various places along the earth.

---

4. "This means that in Genesis land is not merely a passive onlooker in the created order, nor is simply the material that God uses; it is actively involved in the process of creation, while other components of the universe, such as air and sea, remain passive. Furthermore, land as a unique relationship with the human beings and even provides the raw material from which the first man is made. The possession of land with clearly defined boundaries is the symbol of security and blessing, while the lack of a fertile piece of land is equated with insecurity and danger. The human beings are dependent on land for their continued existence, since it is their source for food. However, the dependence of humankind on land is just one side of the picture; the land is not self-sufficient and, without human beings to till and maintain it, cannot reach its full potential of fruitfulness. Thus, humans and land were partners, and the welfare of each depended on the other. A close relationship with God was necessary for this relationship to work properly, and any alienation between the humans and God affected their relationship with the land." McKeown, *Genesis*. "In comparison with Genesis 1, the picture in Genesis 2 has its own distinct drama. It tells of someone who is brought into union with the most human related elements of God's creation – soil and spouse. Genesis does not take an either/or approach to the soil and spouse. Though the Garden, it first secures the relationship to the soil/earth, and then goes on to establish the relationship to a spouse." Brodie, *Genesis as Dialogue*.

The related concepts of earth and land continue being central in the Abrahamic account. One of the main aspects of the Abrahamic covenant was the grant of the land of Canaan to Abraham's heirs (Gen 12:1, 7, 14–15; 13:17; 15:7–21; 17:8; 24:7).[5] Another fundamental aspect of Abraham's blessing is that all families *of the earth* would be blessed in him and in his offspring (Gen 12:3; 18:18; 22:18).[6] Yet another, third aspect of land in this covenant is that Abraham's descendants would be as the dust of earth (Gen 13:16). Also, in the context of Abraham's story in Genesis, God is as "possessor of heaven and earth" (Gen 14:19–20), "the judge of all the earth" (Gen 18:25), and "the God of heaven and God of the earth" (Gen 24:3).[7] The identity of God as "possessor of heaven and earth" (Gen 14:19–20) is fundamental for the whole Bible narrative and central for our purposes. It is a theological declaration that makes human beings dependent on God for their use of the soil, for it belongs to the Lord. This is the heart of a jubilee related land ethic. The promises God made Abraham are confirmed to Isaac and Jacob throughout Genesis.

In the final chapters of Genesis, one reads about reality outside the realms of the covenant. Joseph was made vice-king in Egypt and established a tax of 20% of all grains (Gen 41:34). That which was stored during the years of plenty was sold back to the Egyptians and to other people, since famine was over all lands (Gen 41:56–57). As a result of this severe famine, Pharaoh, with Joseph's help, stripped the people of money (Gen 47:14), animals (Gen 47:16–17), land (Gen 47:18–20), and freedom (Gen 47:21). Joseph, after buying everything for Pharaoh, kept the taxes of 20% on the people (Gen 47:23–26). In practice, in Egypt at that time, the supreme owner of the land was Pharaoh instead of God.

It is possible to say that this Egyptian culture of oppression was further developed in the following years and struck the Israelites hard. They were afflicted with heavy burdens and reduced to slavery: "So they ruthlessly made

---

5. "A conspectus of all the references shows that the promise of the land is of even greater moment than the promise of becoming a nation." von Rad, *Old Testament Theology*, 168.

6. "Land and progeny constitute the two primary elements of the promise." Birch et al., *A Theological Introduction to the Old Testament*, 78. See also Rad, *Old Testament Theology*, 168.

7. Bruce Waltke lists seven promises from God to Abraham: (1) make him into a great nation, (2) bless him, (3) make his name great, (4) make him a blessing, (5) bless those who bless him, (6) curse those who curse him, and (7) bless all the families of the earth through him." Waltke, *An Old Testament Theology*, 149.

the people of Israel work as slaves and made their lives bitter with hard service, in mortar and brick, and in all kinds of work in the field. In all their work they ruthlessly made them work as slaves" (Exod 1:13–14). The Egyptian oppression was getting worse and worse. So God decided "to bring them up out of that land to a good and broad land, a land flowing with milk and honey" (Exod 3:8). The rest of the Torah presents God fulfilling his word and teaching through Moses what the people needed to know to live in the land promised to Abraham while the people kept disobeying his statutes and suffering the consequences.

The promise of a specific land to a specific people which will bless the whole earth is central in the entire Torah (Gen 48:21; Exod 3:8; 6:4, 13:5; Num 14:8; 27:12; Deut 4:1; 6:18). The patriarchs come and go from Canaan until the children of Israel are enslaved in Egypt and God uses Moses to take them again to the land he promised to give them (Num 32;11). The land in Canaan is the inheritance (נַחֲלָה) God gives to Israel (Exod 15:17), and this inheritance from God to his people is to be divided according to the size of each tribe (Num 26:53–54; 33:54).

God is the one who gives land as inheritance to his people, and he did as he promised (Josh 21:43). As this inheritance is divided by the casting of lots (Num 26:55), it is clear it is Yahweh himself as the owner of the land who determined where each tribe would live.[8] God is also the one who unearthed the people from Canaan because they were not behaving properly towards him. Among all instructions on the new life in Canaan the one on land in Leviticus 25 deserves special attention. That is the subject of our next section. The focus here, in the next section and in Luke is that since the Creation, the flood, the promises to Abraham and the giving of the promised land to Israel as inheritance, God is recurrently presented as the one who has rights of ownership over the whole land.

4.2 The Jubilee Laws

This fourth chapter is presenting the theological reasoning over which Luke builds his land ethics. I am defending that the most important institution and

---

8. Davies, *The Gospel and the Land*, 28. As Davies points, in Ezekiel the division of land is directly defined by Yahweh without casting of lots (cf. Ez 47:13).

theological concept for Luke is the Old Testament jubilee. Thus, this section presenting the jubilee and the way it was appropriated in the Old Testament and Second Temple literature is central as theological and cultural context for Luke.

What I am calling loosely "jubilee laws" is the amalgamation of different Pentateuchal laws dealing with the sabbatical year, laws related to land, debt release, redemption, and freedom from slavery. These laws are found in Exodus 21:2–11; 23:10–11; Leviticus 25; Deuteronomy 15:1–18; and Deuteronomy 31:10–13. The comparison of these laws presents a few divergences that have generated different solutions among scholars. For example, both Exodus 21:2–11 and Deuteronomy 15:12–18 prescribe that a Hebrew slave is supposed to be freed in the seventh year, while Leviticus 25 prescribes that this release is to happen in the fifth year. Also, while Leviticus 25 does not refer to debt release in the Sabbatical year nor in the jubilee year (although it is implied), Deuteronomy 15:1–11 affirms that the seventh year is a שְׁמִטָּה year, i.e., a year of release of debt, which is confirmed in Deuteronomy 31:10–11.

The solution presented by Gerstenberger is that one can detect different strata of the development of the law in these texts and so, the laws of Leviticus 25 reflect an older and worse development when compared to the laws of Exodus 21:1–6 and Deuteronomy 15:12–18.[9] Daisy Tsai lists eight different solutions scholars have presented. She concludes that the laws of Exodus 21, Deuteronomy 15 and Leviticus 25 all refer to the undifferentiated Israelites and that the one in view on Lev 25 is the permanent slave referred to in the other texts.[10] I agree with Tsai's solution. As it would be beyond the limits of this dissertation to discuss this subject further, I proceed to the interpretation of the texts.

4.2.1 The Jubilee Laws in the Pentateuch

At this point, it is important to take time for a brief analysis of Leviticus 25, since this text is the only legislation on land ownership found in the Pentateuch.[11] This text is also important for the present argument, because,

---

9. Gerstenberger, *Leviticus*, 388, 395–98.
10. Tsai, *Human Rights in Deuteronomy*, 187–206.
11. Rooker, *Leviticus*, 300; Kaiser, "Leviticus," 1170.

as we will see in the next chapter, Jesus frames his ministry in terms of jubilee in the gospel of Luke (Luke 4:16–30).

Leviticus 25 is part of the Holiness Code (Lev 17–26), which together with the Covenant Code (Exodus 20:19–23:33) and the Deuteronomic Code (Deut 12–26) form the bulk of the legislative part of the Torah. This chapter begins (Lev 25:1, cf. also 26:46) with a reference to Sinai, adding authority and weight to the contents of chapters 25 and 26. Leviticus 25 can be divided into four sections:[12]

> 25:1–7: Instructions on the Sabbath Year
> 25:8–22: Instructions on the Jubilee Year
> 25:23–34: Instructions on the redemption of properties
> 25:35–55: Instructions on the redemption of people

The first of these sections, the instructions on the Sabbath Year (Lev 27:1–7), connects these instructions with the Creation account (Gen 2:2–3) and the fourth commandment (Exod 20:8–11), and is an expansion of the same law given in Exodus 23:10–11.[13] In the same way the Israelites are supposed to mimic God's rest in the seventh day of the week, they are also supposed to reproduce this pattern in relation to years.

Here, the main reason for the Sabbath Year is not sociological as in Exodus 23:10–11 (cf. also Exod 21:2–11 and Deut 15:1–8), but theological.[14] The land will keep a Sabbath "to the Lord" (Lev 25:2, 4). In light of the creation account and the Ten Commandments, this is a way to make the land holy as God's special possession.[15]

---

12. Gorman, *Divine Presence and Community*, 136–37. For a slightly different structure, see Wenham, *The Book of Leviticus*, 316.. For a very elaborated one, see: Kleinig, *Leviticus*, 545–46.

13. Jacob Milgrom presents a fine table showing that Leviticus 25:1–7 was written as an expansion of Exodus 23:10–11. He also affirms that Leviticus corrects some utopic views of the first text. See Milgrom, *Leviticus 23–27*, 2154–61. "This leads us to an important implication: *the law of the jubilee was an extension of the sabbatical principle of rest*. The sabbatical year law was primary; the jubilee laws were secondary. *The sabbatical year law was more fundamental than the jubilee land laws.*" North, *Leviticus*, 393. (Emphasis original)

14. "The law of God is theocentric. Whatever secondary applications it may have, a law's primary application always relates to God." North, *Leviticus*, 394.

15. Boyce, *Leviticus and Numbers*, 99–100; Kiuchi, *Leviticus*, 455. "Its concern is that, in a regular cycle, the land of each Israelite must lie fallow in acknowledgment that the Deity is its true owner. Human tenancy is thus to be relinquished temporarily so that the property may revert to its ultimate owner." Bailey, *Leviticus-Numbers*, 299.

Moreover, God is presented as the one who has the right to determine how the land is supposed to be used or not used. He is also the one who gives food for his whole creation without needing people's help to make the land produce. This is clearly expressed in Lev 25:20–22, where he promises that in the sixth year the land will produce the equivalent of three years in order for his people not to suffer need.

The Sabbath is also for the land itself (25:2, 4–5).[16] It is possible to name this the ecological aspect of this law.[17] This great Sabbath of one year is called by the superlative שַׁבַּת שַׁבָּתוֹן.[18] The land will have a great rest. This is yet clearer in the next chapter, when God presents the curses in case of disobedience by the people. One of the consequences of a possible exile is that the people would be sent far from their land and the land would rest its Sabbaths. Thus, since before entering the land God was giving, the Israelites knew that if they forbid the land from having its due rest (Lev 26:35), God would expel them. That was exactly what happened in Israel's history and the Bible makes it clear in 2 Chr 36:21.

The Sabbath Year also had an educational and a humanitarian reason. It was also for the people learning to trust God for their provision.[19] It required faith in order to put down their work tools for one entire year. The Sabbath

---

16. "The term Sabbath itself aggregates three meanings, seventh, rest and Saturday. As seen, it has many motivations, among them, rest for people and animals, solidarity for the poor, reminiscence of the liberation from slavery in Egypt, worship to God, rest for the Creator himself and pardoning of debts. The law of sabbatical rest originates in the conception that the land has its own rights, as do animals and human beings. This same concept needs to be recovered in the postmodern society, in which the land became an object of exploration. The Biblical Law fraternizes land, animals and people as creatures of God, with full rights. As God hears the cry of the oppressed people (Exod 3:7), he also hears the cry for help of the explored land". Silva, "Direito à Terra, Direito à Vida: Perspectivas Ecológicas a Partir de Levítico 25," 599.

17. "Since the land belonged to God, the Israelites were to return it to him every seven years. Thus, just as God had rested on the seventh day after creation (Gen 2:2–3) and had provided a regular day of rest for Israel on each Sabbath, so the land too was to observe a Sabbath to the Lord once every seven years (25:2, 4, 5). Like the Israelites on the Sabbath, the land was to acknowledge its God by resting from its work of agricultural production." Kleinig, *Leviticus*, 552.

18. ESV: Sabbath of solemn rest; NIV: Sabbath rest; NET: Sabbath of complete rest; LXX: σάββατα ἀνάπαυσις. Kaiser Jr. keeps the redundancy of the original expression translating it as a "Sabbath of sabbatism". Kaiser, "Leviticus," 1171.

19. "The sabbatical year was a system for forcing men to become self-consciously dependent on God's grace." North, *Leviticus: An Economic Commentary*, 401. This instruction included the reading of the whole Torah to the people in the Feast of Booths (cf. Deut 31:10–13). Harris, "Leviticus," 633.

Year envisioned also that the people could enjoy a physical and spiritual rest during one year in which they would have the opportunity to eat without working (Lev 25:6).[20] The humanitarian aspect is that during that year, everyone could have access to what naturally sprouted in anyone's fields and vineyards. The poor of the land would have abundance of free food and the rural workers during the Sabbatical year would be able to search for another occupation that could generate them some additional income.

The Sabbath Year was a very important opportunity to rest on God in faith and to rebalance some social disparities that the other six years had created.[21] Besides the sabbatical year, however, Israel had also another important institution called the jubilee year, which is presented in the remaining verses of Leviticus 25. As we shall see, these two are more or less conflated in the Lukan view of the jubilee.

The second section of Leviticus 25 presents the instructions on the Jubilee Year (Lev 25:8–22).[22] This was an exacerbation of the seventh seventh-year (the forty-ninth year) to a fiftieth year of redemption and rest.[23] The Hebrew

---

20. Boyce presents the Sabbath year as a demonstration of trust; an act of compassion, since the slaves and workers would rest together with the landowners; and a witness for others. Boyce, *Leviticus and Numbers*, 100. Hartley also emphasizes this humanitarian aspect of the law: "God wants his people to be free from continuous labor in order that they might enjoy the gift of the promised land and the grace of his blessings." Hartley, *Leviticus*, 433. North affirm that the landowners were completely forbidden of harvesting while other people would be able to do so. I understand that nobody could harvest in a commercial way, but anyone, including the owner could pick what was necessary for him and his family to eat. See North, *Leviticus: An Economic Commentary*, 399–400. Also: Kaiser, "Leviticus," 1171. Contra North and Kaiser, see Harris, "Leviticus," 633.

21. "Every seventh year the debts of all Israelites were to be canceled (Deut 15:1–2). Clearly, God was showing his people the greatness of his forgiveness and the implications of that forgiveness for their own behavior." Silva, "Freedom," 271. "The sabbatical year reinforced the fact that Israel had been set apart by God for rest (Lev 25:12), and that this goal involved the way they lived as well as the place where they lived. Moreover, even the land itself was only a foretaste of what God had promised." Shead, "Sabbath," 747.

22. It is probable that the Jubilee law is developed from the ANE practices and law of land tenure. For example, it was common that from time to time kings proclaimed a release of slaves, debts and return of lost land. There is no evidence, however, of a society doing that periodically by force of the law. It depended on the will of the king. For more information on that, see, for example Goddeeris, *Economy and Society in Northern Babylonia in the Early Old Babylonian Period (ca. 2000–1800 BC)*, 327.

23. Going against the clear evidence of the text (Lev 25:11–12; 20–22). North affirms the practical impossibility and having two unproductive years in a row and suggests that the jubilee was the seventh sabbatical year instead of the fiftieth. North, *Sociology of the Biblical Jubilee*, 72 et seq. Wenham on another hand, follows Hoenig in suggesting that the "year of jubilee" was a short year of forty-nine days long. It is possible that this is the meaning intended by Lev

word translated as jubilee is יוֹבֵל and possibly means "ram".[24] The reason is that the jubilee was inaugurated in the Day of Atonement with the blow of a ram's horn (trumpet, cf. Lev 25:9). There are two main aspects in the Jubilee Year – a theological and a socio-economical – and it also carries with it the aspects of the Sabbatical Year.

The theological aspect of the jubilee legislation has many facets.[25] The first facet is that the יוֹבֵל was proclaimed on the Day of Atonement (Yom Kippur). The Day of Atonement was the most important and solemn day of the Hebrew calendar. The high-priest would enter the Holy of Holies and God would appear above the mercy seat (Cf. Lev 16). Sacrifices were offered for the atonement of the sins of the people and the impurity of the sanctuary; and the emissary scapegoat would be released into the desert. This relation with the Yom Kippur presents the Jubilee Year with its regulations as a response to the fact that God pardoned the sins of his people.[26] As the people are clean from their inner defilement, they are able to act properly toward each other.[27] Thus, all socio-economical acts of liberation the people were obligated to obey were a response to the great spiritual liberation act that God had bestowed upon them. This is very important, for Luke also centralizes the expiatory work of Christ as fundamental to his ethical program.

A second theological facet of the Jubilee Year is that, as the Sabbatical Year, the Jubilee was to be a holy year (Lev 25:12). Throughout the year the

---

25:8. Wenham, *The Book of Leviticus*, 319. In this dissertation, I am interpreting the Year of Jubilee as a full year, following the seventh sabbatical year. This is one of the reasons the two are amalgamated in the tradition that followed.

24. Babcock, "Year of Jubilee." The LXX uses multiple words to express what is in this text: "ἐνιαυτὸς ἀφέσεως σημασία αὕτη ἔσται ὑμῖν" (a time of release, this will be a sign for you).

25. On this theological aspect, North affirms: "The theocentric meaning of the jubilee law was God's ownership of both the land and the people." North, *Leviticus: An Economic Commentary*, 408.

26. "The day of national liberation and family inheritance took place on the day of formal subordination to God. The imagery is obvious. *Only through submission to God can mane experience liberation.* Autonomy is not liberation. It is the antithesis of liberation. This is why modern humanism's free market economic theory, which is both agnostic and individualistic, is not the source of the free society that its defenders proclaim. If we begin our analysis with the presupposition of the autonomous individual in an autonomous cosmos, we begin with a hypothesis that cannot lead to liberty and maintain it." North, *Leviticus: An Economic Commentary*, 411.

27. Kiuchi, *Leviticus*, 456. In the same page, Kiuchi makes the apt comment: "it is stated in the commentary that holiness is a matter of the human heart, which is primarily characterized by an absence of the egocentric nature."

Israelites were forbidden from doing common agricultural activities. Both the Sabbath Year and the Jubilee Year, as well as the laws relating to land ownership and redemption, debt, loans and slavery are properly viewed as part of the Sabbatical laws, and consequently as an unfolding of the fourth commandment. It is also worth noticing that discussions on the right way of keeping the Sabbath are more important in Luke than anywhere else in the New Testament.

A third theological facet is the fear of the Lord, "You shall not wrong one another, but you shall fear your God, for I am the LORD your God" (Lev 25:17). Fear is an important concept in this chapter, repeating itself in verses 36 and 43. As the ultimate owner of the land (Lev 25:23), and of his people (Lev 25:17, 38, 42, 55), Yahweh has the right to dispose of both land and people at his will. He has power to bless the people (Lev 25:18-19; 26:3-13) and to curse them (26:14-39). The jubilee laws should lead the people to fear the Lord which should lead to their keeping of these laws. Fear is another central theme in Luke-Acts. The humanitarian aspect of the jubilee laws derives from this theological facet.

The fourth and most important theological facet is found in Leviticus 25:23 and deserves special attention.[28] The central statement of this whole chapter, and one of the most important in OT theology, and for the present study, is God's affirmation that "the land is mine". God, as the creator of the world has an inalienable right of ownership over the earth and all there is on it (Psalm 24:1; 50:10).[29] He is the king (Psalm 47:2, 7; Zech 14:9) and the Most High over the earth (Psalm 83:18; 97:9). He makes the land produce, brings rain and gives food to animals (Job 38:41; Psalm 67; 68; 104; 135:7). Consequently, Yahweh is the one who decides who will inherit what part of the land (Psalm 37:9, 11, 22, 29, 34; Prov 2:21) and who will not inherit

---

28. See a detailed study of this verse in Wright, *God's People in God's Land: Family, Land, and Property in the Old Testament*, 58–64.

29. By insisting that the land could not be alienated from the family who whom God has assigned it (cf. 1 Kgs 21:3), this law aims to preserver the idea that the land ultimately belongs to God. His people are but *resident aliens and settlers* in the land. In other words it does not really belong to them; they inhabit it thanks solely to the mercy and favor of their God, the great landowner (cf. 1 Chr 29:15; Ps 39:13 [Eng. 12]; Heb 11:13; 1 Pet 2:11). Wenham, *The Book of Leviticus*, 320. "The legislation for sabbatical and Jubilee years is an outgrowth of ideas associated with creation, exodus, and Sabbath. The Lord lays claim to the land of Israel on the basis of God's authority as creator." Willis, *Leviticus*, 216.

anything (Prov 2:22; 10:30; Isa 65:9; Ezek 39:28). He made a special covenant with Israel and promised to give them a specific land and relate with them and their land in a distinct way (Exod 19:5–6; Josh 22:19; Hos 9:3).

Thus, because God is the supreme landlord, he dispossessed the Canaanites (Gen 15:12–16; Exod 13:4, 23:28–30) and gave Canaan to Abraham's descendants according to his promise. He also demands from the Israelites the firstfruits (Lev 18:24; Deut 14:22; 26:9–15); the Sabbath (Exod 20:8–11; Deut 5:12–15); the sabbatical and jubilee years (Lev 25) and establishes laws that should be kept in order to maintain the land holy (Jer 16:18).[30]

Going back to Lev 25:23, the last clause is "For you are strangers and sojourners with me". This stresses the ownership of Yahweh, the provisional character of Israel's ownership, and the fact that God will take care of his people: "Just as an alien who is the guest of an Israelite comes under the protection of the head of the house, so too the families in Israel as resident aliens on the land owned by Yahweh come under his protection."[31] Summarizing: Yahweh is the definitive landlord. Accordingly, Israel is called to own land under him as his tenants. This point will be made clear ahead.[32]

The last facet of the theological aspect of the Jubilee Year is an eschatological one.[33] God promises future blessings for the Israelites if they keep, do, and perform these rules (Lev 25:18–19). In form of a chiasm, God promises them security and sustenance for the years ahead. This sustenance would be proven each sixth year, when God promises to multiply their crops threefold. This eschatological facet is further developed by the prophets, as I will show.

Up to here, we dealt with the theological aspect of the Jubilee Year. I have demonstrated five different facets of this theological aspect of the Jubilee Year. (1) It was a consequence of Yom Kippur. (2) It was a sabbatical year of

---

30. In the Torah four sins are presented are defiling the land: harlotry (Lev 19:29); shedding blood (Num 35:29–34; Deut 21:6–9; Psalms 106:38); leaving a corpse hanging on a three (Deut 21:22–23); and remarrying the same wife after she had married another person (Deut 24:1–4; Jer 3:1). Davies, *The Territorial Dimension of Judaism*, 19.

31. Hartley, *Leviticus*, 437.

32. See the development of some of these points in Davies, *The Gospel and the Land*, 24 et seq.

33. "The Sabbatical and Jubilee Year rulings are theologically important. They juxtapose images of Yahweh the creator and Yahweh the redeemer. They merge creation theology and a concern for social justice. In addition, they suggest an eschatological perspective that looks to a future day of redemption, rest, and release for persons and land alike." Gorman, *Divine Presence and Community*, 137–38.

rest in the Lord. (3) The laws of the jubilee should be kept out of a fear of Yahweh, the acknowledgement of his power and freedom. (4) It existed to demonstrate in a very practical way that all land belongs to Yahweh and the Israelites should use it according to God's will. (5) Finally, the Jubilee Year has an eschatological flavor into it. All these points and the next are important in the application Luke does of the jubilee laws. Now we turn to another aspect of the Jubilee Year, the socio-economical.

The second aspect of the יוֹבֵל is socio-economical and it also has multiple facets to it. These facets are developed in detail in the third (25:23–34: Instructions on the redemption of properties) and fourth (25:35–55: Instructions on redemption of people) sections of Leviticus 25.

The first facet of the socio-economical aspect of the jubilee is demonstrated in how the Jubilee Year begins with a proclamation of "liberty (וּקְרָאתֶם דְּרוֹר) throughout the land to all its inhabitants" (Lev 25:10). As the sequence of the chapter demonstrates, this proclamation of liberty to all inhabitants is better understood as a communicative act which not only announces freedom, but enacts it.[34] Indeed, the first of these proclamations is non-verbal. It is just the resonating of a trumpet. This sound however would mean and effect liberation to those who were oppressed by lack of property, debt, and slavery.

It is important to note that in the Septuagint, יוֹבֵל is translated in Lev 25:10 as the year of Pentecost: "And ye shall sanctify the year, the fiftieth year (πεντηκοστὸν ἐνιαυτὸν), and ye shall proclaim a release (ἄφεσιν) upon the land to all that inhabit it; it shall be given a year of release (ἐνιαυτὸς ἀφέσεως), a jubilee for you; and each one shall depart to his possession, and ye shall go each to his family. This is a jubilee of release (ἀφέσεως σημασία), the year shall be to you the fiftieth year (τὸ ἔτος τὸ πεντηκοστὸν ἐνιαυτὸς): ye shall not sow, nor reap the produce that comes of itself from the land, neither shall ye gather its dedicated fruits. For it is a jubilee of release (ἀφέσεως σημασία); it shall

---

34. This concept derives from Kevin Vanhoozer's speech act theory. Every speech act evolves many acts at the same time and produces different things: The locutionary aspect is the speech itself. The illocutionary aspect points to what the speech performs and the perlocutionary aspect points to the effects of the speech. Vanhoozer also stresses the importance of the covenantal context so that this communication and acts can occur. On this theory see: Vanhoozer, *Is There a Meaning in This Text?*; Vanhoozer, *First Theology: God, Scripture & Hermeneutics*; Vanhoozer, *The Drama of Doctrine*; Briggs, *Words in Action*.

be holy to you, ye shall eat its fruits off the fields." (Lev 25:10–12).³⁵ Lange makes clear the relation between the *Yobel* and the Pentecost: "The text is perfectly plain, using the same forms of language as in regard to the feast of Pentecost after the completion of the seven weeks, between which and this Pentecostal year there is a clear analogy."³⁶ Also, Milgrom affirms that the linguistic resemblance among Lev 25:8 and 23:15 is one of the indications that the jubilee cycle is based on the Pentecostal calendar.³⁷

Among the most important Greek words in the LXX of Lev 25:8–55, one finds the following: τὸ ἔτος τὸ πεντηκοστὸν, ἄφεσις, σημασία, ἐξέρχομαι and λύτρωσις. From these, ἄφεσις is the most emphasized. Some of these words will be very important in our study of the jubilee in Luke-Acts. Another Hebrew word that is very important is the word דְּרוֹר. It comes from דרר, which means to "stream," "be abundant," "run vehemently" and so on.³⁸ The form דְּרוֹר is a substantive that came to mean: "free run, liberty, freedom, emancipation, release, letting go, dismissal, personal freedom from servitude, confinement or oppression, liberation."³⁹ As we will see, the word is also used in Isaiah 61:1; Jeremiah 34:8, 15, 17, and Ezekiel 46:17.

A second facet of the socio-economical aspect of the jubilee laws is the tenancy pattern.⁴⁰ God declares in Leviticus 25:23: "The land shall not be sold in perpetuity, for the land is mine. For you are strangers and sojourners with me." It should be clear for the Israelites, consequently, that they were not

---

35. This English translation is from Brenton, *The Septuagint Version of the Old Testament: English Translation*.

36. Lange, *A Commentary on the Holy Scriptures: Exodus, Leviticus: Critical, Doctrinal and Himiletical, with Special Reference to Ministers and Students*, 189.

37. Milgrom, *Leviticus 23–27*, 2163. Ahead, he says: "There can be little doubt that the choice of the number fifty is based on the pentecostal structure of the calendar in chap. 23. That is, just as the seven weeks terminate in a fiftieth day, so the seven septennates terminate in a fiftieth year". (p. 2166)

38. Brown, Driver and Briggs, Hebrew and English Lexicon, "דרר."

39. See *The Lexham Analytical Lexicon of the Hebrew Bible*; Gesenius and Tregelles, *Gesenius' Hebrew and Chaldee lexicon to the Old Testament Scriptures*, 207; Brown, Driver, and Briggs, *Enhanced Brown-Driver-Briggs Hebrew and English Lexicon*, 204; and *The Lexham Analytical Lexicon of the Septuagint*.

40. "God deals with men as an absentee landlord deals with leaseholders who use his property. He gave Adam an assignment; then He left the garden. This is a continuing theme in the Bible. The Book of Job pictures God as normally distant from man. Jesus used the theme of the absentee landlord in several of His parables." North, *Leviticus*, 394. "The land belongs not to buyers and sellers. In truth, both are but 'aliens' and 'tenants' on the land; they are custodians of a title that only God can give." Balentine, *Leviticus*, 195.

receiving ultimate ownership of the land, but God was keeping the ownership to himself and giving them the usufruct of land.[41] As the ultimate owner, God reserved the right to determine that the land should lie fallow one year in seven, and eight years in fifty. He also decided that the usufruct contracts of the land would be renewed with the original tenant families each fifty years, and these original tenants would have constant right of redeeming the land if they had conditions.[42] The Israelites could negotiate the use of the land, but not the land itself, for it was not theirs, but the Lord's.

A third facet of the socio-economical aspect of the jubilee laws is a sympathetic ethic.[43] By this expression, we indicate an ethic based on Leviticus 19:18, "you shall love your neighbor (רֵעַ) as yourself: I am the Lord." Although the Hebrew word for neighbor is different, the concept of neighbor (עָמִית) appears four times in Leviticus 25 (v. 14 [twice], 15, and 17). The word עָמִית carries the ideas of associate, fellow, comrade; it levels two different people in the same plateau. Together with these words, God gives the instruction: "you shall not wrong one another" (Lev 25:14, 17), but, instead, they are to "fear the Lord" (Lev 25:17).

Another fundamental concept of this sympathetic ethics is that of brotherhood. Lev 25.14 uses the words neighbor (עָמִית) and brother (אָח) interchangeably. The concept of brother occurs even more frequently in this chapter (Lev 25.14, 25 [twice], 35, 36, 39, 46 [twice], 47, 48). God intended Israel not to lose sight of the fact they were a family, a brotherhood. Since this was the norm, they were supposed to act accordingly and promote fair trade with no exploitation. This meant promoting one another's liberty from debt and

---

41. An apt observation of Rosenberg and Weiss that strengthen this argument is related to the reason only the properties on the country were covered by these laws and not the urban properties. They say: "The key to this approach lies in the fact that the laws are concentrated around productive resources only – agricultural land (and the houses that service them) and workers (slaves). The purpose of these laws, according to this view, is to keep the resources spread out and to limit the ability of an individual to acquire too much economic power." Rosenberg and Weiss, "Land Concentration, Efficiency, Slavery and the Jubilee," 78.

42. "The right of redemption was based on God's ownership of the land. It was his royal estate. This meant that the Israelites too belonged to God as his royal servants. They, then, were not landowners. Rather, they resided on the land at his discretion, as if they were resident aliens. So, since both the land and the people belonged to God, he decreed that the people should provide for the redemption of the land." Kleinig, *Leviticus*, 549.

43. "All in all, the Jubilee years, while they are theoretically a time of liberation, challenge the condition of human hearts corrupted by an egocentric nature." Kiuchi, *Leviticus*, 467.

enslavement. Each one of them should also be ready to act as a redeemer (גָּאַל) for needy close members of the family..[44]

A last concept linked to the sympathetic ethic appears more clearly in the instructions on debt and slavery. For three times, God reminds his people that he is the one who brought them out of the land of Egypt (Lev 25:38, 42, 55). Since they were all slaves in Egypt, no one should feel having more rights to be rich and have well-being than the others. They were all equal in this sense. Thus, they are not supposed to take interest or profit from their brothers (another proof of the empathetic ethic, Lev 25:36), they are not to treat their fellow Israelites as common slaves, and they are to redeem their brothers from serving foreigners as slaves. All people of Israel are now God's slaves (Lev 25:42, 55) and this is one of the reasons they are to support the freedom of those who are in socio-economic hardship. Again, Luke uses repeatedly the concept of slaves to refer to Christians.

Thus, this sympathetic ethic would make them trade fairly both when selling and when buying. God specified the values as being the crop values until the next jubilee, which was a warning against oppression.[45] The sabbatical and jubilee laws, together with the laws of first fruits and tenths were a reminder and acknowledgement of Yahweh's ownership of the land.[46]

The laws of Leviticus 25 are impressively practical and sensible to the human nature. As seen in chapter 2, humans have the sinful tendency to subjugate and oppress each other. These laws worked as regulatory marks against the creation of latifundia, exaggerated accumulation of wealth and power, land speculation, indefinite and abusive slavery, debt bondage, and famine. Rosenberg and Weiss summarize the socio-economic goals of the jubilee laws in two points:

---

44. Words of this same root abound in this chapter (Lev 25:25 [twice], 26, 30, 33, 48, 49 [three times], 54), denoting the centrality of the concept of redemption.

45. "The text warns against becoming an economic oppressor. What must be recognized from the beginning is that in the case of buying and selling rural land in Israel, *economic oppression was a two-way street.*" North, *Leviticus: An Economic Commentary*, 441.

46. "Returning to the statement that the land is Yahweh's possession, it should now be added that of course all the cultic statements about the harvest which are codified up and down the Hexateuch also belong to the same complex as this conception; for the laws concerning firstlings, tenths, the leaving of gleanings, and so one, in so far as they fall within the context of Yahwistic religion, are certainly to be interpreted in the light of the belief that Yahweh is the real owner of the land and therefore claims 'a recognition of his right of ownership' from human beings." Von Rad, "The Promised Land and Yahweh's Land in the Hexateuch," 87.

The first is that discussed above – a desire to attain economic efficiency by 'spreading the wealth,' thereby limiting the ability of an individual to control resources, and thus monopolize markets. The second goal is to try to avoid the development of slavery within the Jewish nation. This goal also relies on limiting land concentration because too much concentration can lead to a situation in which poor farmers become dependent on loans from rich landowners, which, in the ancient world, often led to widespread slavery.[47]

I have presented two aspects of the jubilee law, a theological and socio-economic. From this last aspect, I presented three facets. The jubilee started with a proclamation of liberty; it had a tenancy pattern, and it was based on a sympathetic ethic which is related to the golden rule.

Against the background of chapters two and three, the jubilee laws seem to contain everything needed so that a society did not reach those levels of oppression and social injustice. Sadly, Israel did not follow these laws and the result was that many forms of oppression were the norm among God's people, as we have seen in the last chapter.

The other two texts (Lev 27:16–27 and Num 36:4) that refer to the jubilee in the Pentateuch deal more with situational laws. Leviticus 27:16–27 deals with norms for dedication to the Lord and remission of a field. By these norms, the price of the dedicated field should be calculated by the years until the Year of Jubilee. Also, if someone consecrated one's land to Yahweh, it would be necessary to add 20% of the value in case of redemption. Finally, if the field was not redeemed or if it was sold to someone else, then, after the next Jubilee it would be impossible to redeem the field in the future.[48]

The reference to the jubilee year in Numbers 36:4 is even more situational. In Numbers 27:1–11, the daughters of an Israelite killed in the desert called

---

47. Rosenberg and Weiss, "Land Concentration, Efficiency, Slavery and the Jubilee," 85.

48. "The case in vv. 20f is difficult to understand; here someone neither assigns to the temple a field consecrated to Yahweh, not purchases it back from the temple, but rather sells it elsewhere. In the first place, the free sale of land (inheritable land, no less!) is extremely restricted according to 25:23f. In the second place, this particular use of the field, which does, after all, violate the vow, would have to represent a serious insult to Yahweh. Comparably speaking, however, the legal consequences are extremely mild. The possibility for redemption is extinguished and the land comes into the possession of the priests (Yahweh) in the next Year of Jubilee." Gerstenberger, *Leviticus*, 444.

Zelophehad asked Moses for permission to inherit land and keep the name of their father alive, since their father had left only daughters. Moses accepted what they said, and promised they would inherit land like the other families. When the actual possession of the land was approaching, the men of clan of Gilead said to Moses:

> The LORD commanded my lord to give the land for inheritance by lot to the people of Israel, and my lord was commanded by the LORD to give the inheritance of Zelophehad our brother to his daughters. ³ But if they are married to any of the sons of the other tribes of the people of Israel, then their inheritance will be taken from the inheritance of our fathers and added to the inheritance of the tribe into which they marry. So it will be taken away from the lot of our inheritance. ⁴ And when the jubilee of the people of Israel comes, then their inheritance will be added to the inheritance of the tribe into which they marry, and their inheritance will be taken from the inheritance of the tribe of our fathers." (Num 36:2–4).[49]

The solution presented by Moses was that the daughters of Zelophehad should marry only with men from the tribe of Manasseh, so the ownership of land did not pass to another tribe in the jubilee year.

Thus, the law on the jubilee is given only once and it is not repeated in Deuteronomy. The law of the sabbatical year, on the other hand, appears again in Deuteronomy 15:1–6. These verses explain further the rules about the seventh year. The central concept in this text is the release (שְׁמִטָּה, LXX: ἄφεσιν) of debts and slaves. Moses instructs they should grant release of debts to fellow Jews. There would be a blessing for those who obey: "But there will be no poor among you; for the LORD will bless you in the land that the LORD your God is giving you for an inheritance to possess—if only you will strictly obey the voice of the LORD your God, being careful to do all this commandment that I command you today." (Deut 15:4–5). Although this commandment has broad impact in the social and communal life of the

---

[49]. On the daughters of Zelophehad, see also Josh 17:3–6; 1Chr 7:15–17

nation, its main thrust relates to God and his worship, that is why the event is called "the Lord's release" (שְׁמִטָּה לַיהוָה).⁵⁰

In v. 7, there is a hidden possibility that the law would not be completely obeyed, so the text opens the possibility of one brother becoming poor and instructs what should be done in this case (Deut 15:7–11). As in the case of Leviticus 25, throughout this whole chapter, there is an emphasis in kinship with a repeated use of the word brother (אָח).⁵¹ Besides the releasing of debts and the care for the poor, Moses also reminds the people that they had in the seventh year the obligation of releasing the slaves (Deut 15:12–18). This release, however, should be accompanied of liberality toward the former slave in order that he or she is able to restart his or her life with chance of establishing himself or herself.⁵²

The last text which refers to the sabbatical year is Deut 31:10–13. This chapter starts the last section of the book.⁵³ In these final instructions, Moses says: "At the end of every seven years, at the set time in the year of release, at the Feast of Booths, when all Israel comes to appear before the Lord your God at the place that he will choose, you shall read this law before all Israel in their hearing." (Deut 31:10–11). This intermingling between the year of release, worshipping the Lord, and being instructed in the Law is similar to the patterns found in Lev 25 that blend together the release with the Day of

---

50. Von Rad, for example, stresses this point commenting: "This custom was determined not primarily by social, still less by economic considerations, but was a definitely sacral arrangement. Even in the comparatively late regulations of Deuteronomy this ancient conception has not changed at all; it is a 'Yahweh's release' (v. 2b). . . . Here we clearly have to do with the manifestation of a primitive state of affairs, and more particularly of the original claim of God to the cultivated land (Lev 25:23). This sacral arrangement corresponded to a patriarchal peasant economy." Von Rad, *Deuteronomy*, 105. Patrick Miller also notes the primacy of the relationship with God in these laws: "Like the Sabbath, the laws of release in the seventh year have remembrance of God's redemptive activity as an aim (15:15) but are fundamentally set to provide rest and release from large burdens and obligations that otherwise would indefinitely oppress and enslave those so encumbered." Miller, *Deuteronomy*, 134. For the supposed difference between the laws of remission, see Lundbom, *Deuteronomy: Law and Covenant*, 488 et seq.

51. Miller, *Deuteronomy*, 136.

52. "The released bond slave is to be given the means of establishing a place in society again. A generous spirit and generous deeds, therefore, are what is required in the face of poverty and hardship, not a grudging, reluctant, half-hearted response." Miller, *Deuteronomy*, 137.

53. "Chapter 31 begins a second and final supplement to an expanded Deuteronomy, concluding with Moses' death and burial in ch. 34". Lundbom, *Deuteronomy: Law and Covenant*, 827.

Atonement.⁵⁴ It is clear that it is not possible in Israel to keep spiritual life and socio-economic matters apart. As Thomas Mann says, "Nonetheless, we should not ignore the theological implications of these traditions, above all, the recognition that economic systems – how property and work and money are distributed within a society – are matters of deep theological concern."⁵⁵ This is a lesson the jubilee and sabbatical laws in the Torah clearly teach.

4.2.2 Jubilee-Like Laws in the ANE

Although the laws of jubilee as they appear in Leviticus are unique in the ancient world, there is evidence of laws that hold some similarity with them in the ANE. These laws receive the name of *andarāru* or *mīšarum* laws, since the first is the Sumerian word for liberation and the second is the Akkadian word for justice and these words are used in the respective documents.

One of the first edicts of this kind that we have knowledge of comes from Entemena, king of Lagash around 2400 BCE. In his edict, he proclaims liberation of taxes and slavery.⁵⁶ Another Sumerian edict of this kind, comes from Uru-inimgina (reign: ca. 2351–2342 BCE), the last Sumerian king of the first dynasty of Lagash.⁵⁷ These edicts, that come from different times and documents include laws reorganizing the system of taxation for many areas of production, which were considered unjust, and promoting the freedom of prisoners.⁵⁸ McIntosh comments about the reforms of this king: "Around 2350 B.C.E. Uru-inim-gina became king of Lagash and brought in a series of domestic reforms aimed at improving the lot of the ordinary citizen, eliminating abuses practiced by officials, and restoring the eroded power of the temple."⁵⁹

---

54. "Every seventh year meant that the law was to be read in the Sabbatical year, when all Israelite debt slaves were released (Deut 15). The associations with harvest and debt release would have made the Feast of Tabernacle a fitting occasion to reflect on the law of Deuteronomy. It's concern for the poor and oppressed, and constant call to trust in God and obey him would have been especially powerful at that time." Hall, *Deuteronomy*, 458.

55. Mann, *Deuteronomy*, 288.

56. Bergsma, *The Jubilee from Leviticus to Qumran*, 22–23.

57. Hallo and Younger, *The Context of Scripture*, 407–8.

58. "A citizen of Lagash living in debt, (or) who had been condemned to its prison for impost, hunger, robbery, (or) murder — their freedom he established. Uru-inimgina made a compact with the divine Nin-Girsu that the powerful man would not oppress the orphan (or) widow." Hallo and Younger, *The Context of Scripture*, 408.

59. McIntosh, *Ancient Mesopotamia: New Perspectives*, 76.

Besides the above Sumerian law, the Babylonian laws, are important also as context of the jubilee laws in the OT. Some of these Babylonian edicts come from Samsu-iluna, who was the successor of Hammurabi as king of Babylonia. His reign was from ca. 1749 to 1712 BCE. In the eighth year of his kingdom, Samsu-iluna proclaimed a decree to reestablish equity for the land. In this edict, the king pardons the arrears related to the crown of many workers as farmers, shepherds and tenants. Also, those with specific forms of debts had their debts voided. Another aspect of the law, is that some kind of slaves would have their release granted.[60] In the twenty-fourth year of his kingdom, Samsu-iluna proclaimed another edict in which he proclaimed freedom to the people of Idamaraz whom he had conquered and made prisoners, giving them opportunity to go back to their land and helping them to rebuild it.[61] There is also another tablet which mentions that in the year 28 of Samsu-iluna, "The king cancelled the tablets of exchange of real property".[62]

Another very important *misharum* for the land, which comes from ancient Babylon is the edict of Ammisaduqa.[63] He was king from 1646 to 1626 and his edict is very similar to the one by Samsu-iluna. Again, in this edict, one finds the remittance of arrears and personal debts and the proclamation of freedom for debt slaves.

These edicts have in common that they are proclaimed by the monarch in times of need and they acknowledge that tax collectors and other agents may have perpetrated injustices. Those are the reasons for a "justice" decree for the land. The decrees which promote freedom for slaves include only debt slaves and not those born in the house of the owner or bought by money. Also, not every kind of debt is included in the remittance.

Thus, while the jubilee was to be applied to Jews of all social strata and regions in Israel, the *andarāru / mīšarum* were localized and limited to specific subjects.[64] Milgrom points another difference: "In sharp contrast with all

---

60. Hallo and Younger, *The Context of Scripture, Volume Two: Monumental Inscriptions from the Biblical World*, 362–64.

61. Hallo and Younger, *The Context of Scripture, Volume Two: Monumental Inscriptions from the Biblical World*, 258.

62. Charpin, *Writing, Law, and Kingship in Old Babylonian Mesopotamia*, 165.

63. Pritchard, *The Ancient Near Eastern Texts Relating to the Old Testament*, 526–28.

64. Milgrom, *Leviticus 23–27*, 2169. "The biblical decrees also seem aimed to effect a wider segment of the populace than the Mesopotamian decreed. Therefore, the biblical jubilee and sabbatical year are not simply Israelite *misharum* decrees. Nonetheless, the conceptual

ancient Near Eastern *andarāru* / *mīšarum* proclamations, the biblical jubilee was cyclical – ordained by God and not by an earthly ruler according to his whim or need – and could not be revoked or circumvented."⁶⁵ Finally, the last distinction between these edicts and the jubilee is that while the first promoted political capital for the king in times of evident injustice, the last one was a free gesture of God in order to keep justice in Israel.⁶⁶ Thus, it is possible to say that there is a relation between these laws, but there is not a dependence of the jubilee on the *andarāru* or *mīšarum* laws of the ANE.

4.2.3 The Jubilee Laws in the Prophets

The prophetic texts that clearly speak about the jubilee are Isaiah 61:1–11; 63:1–6; Jeremiah 34:8–22; and Ezekiel 46:16–18. I will present these texts albeit introductorily.

Isaiah 61 comes right after a text that pictures a cosmic restoration of Jerusalem (Isa 60).⁶⁷ The text reads: "The Spirit of the Lord God is upon me, because the LORD has anointed (מָשַׁח / ἔχρισέν) me; he has sent me (שְׁלָחַנִי / ἀπέσταλκέν με) to bring good news (לְבַשֵּׂר / εὐαγγελίσασθαι) to the oppressed, to bind up the brokenhearted, to proclaim (לִקְרֹא / κηρύξαι) liberty (דְּרוֹר / ἄφεσιν) to the captives, and release to the prisoners; to proclaim the year of the Lord's favor (לִקְרֹא שְׁנַת־רָצוֹן לַיהוָה / καλέσαι ἐνιαυτὸν κυρίου δεκτὸν), and the day of vengeance of our God; to comfort all who mourn; to provide for those who mourn in Zion— to give them a garland instead of ashes, the oil of gladness instead of mourning, the mantle of praise instead of a faint spirit. They will be called oaks of righteousness, the planting of the Lord, to display his glory." (NKJV with Greek from LXX).

---

parallels should be obvious." Bergsma, *The Jubilee from Leviticus to Qumran: A History of Interpretation*, 26.

65. Milgrom, *Leviticus 23–27*, 2169.

66. "At Sinai the Lord, the King of Israel, instituted something similar to that for his people. But he did not do it as a political gesture to gather support at the beginning of his reign; he instituted it as a liturgical benefaction that recurred periodically on each seventh year and fiftieth year. By means of it, the God who released Israel from slavery continued to release his people from slavery. It was part of his gracious provision for them in the land that he provided for them." Kleinig, *Leviticus*, 551.

67. See a table showing the connections between these two chapters in Paul, *Isaiah 40–66: A Commentary*, 536–37. Commenting on Isaiah 61:1–7, Witherington III says: "In some ways, this is the most important text in Isaiah for understanding Luke's portrayal of Jesus." Witherington III, *Isaiah Old and New: Exegesis, Intertextuality, and Hermeneutics*, 302.

There are a few evidences that this text in Isaiah deals with an eschatological image related to the Jubilee of Leviticus 25. The first one is the use of the Hebrew word דְּרוֹר, liberty. This word appears only seven times in the OT. The first one is Leviticus 25:10, referring to the proclamation of liberty in the jubilee year. Both the word for proclaim and the uncommon word for liberty are the same used in Isaiah 61. Thus, for the attentive reader that knows the Pentateuch, the line referring to "to proclaim liberty to the captives" has the first reference of the text to the jubilee.[68] The expression דְּרוֹר is also used in Jeremiah 34:8, 15 and 17, and in Ezekiel 46:17, all of them referring to similar jubilaic contexts.

The second evidence that Isaiah 61 is referring to the year of jubilee is the use of the theme jubilee throughout Isaiah. Motyer shows for example that Isaiah used the image of jubilee already in Isaiah 27:12–13 with references to harvest and trumpet as symbol for the restauration from the Babylon exile.[69] Note, however, that as happens in the jubilee year, also in the symbolic jubilee of Isaiah 27 an expiation moment will precede the liberation: "Therefore by this the guilt of Jacob will be atoned for, and this will be the full fruit of the removal of his sin".

Another text with an allusion to the jubilee is Isaiah 37:30: "And this shall be the sign for you: this year you shall eat what grows of itself, and in the second year what springs from that. Then in the third year sow and reap, and plant vineyards, and eat their fruit. And the surviving remnant of the house of Judah shall again take root downward and bear fruit upward." This generous production without the need of working the land is a specific provision God gave to his people in Leviticus 25:20–22.

John Oswalt also shows that the song of the servant of Yahweh found in Isaiah 49 also has themes linked to the jubilee: "As the embodiment of the covenant, the Servant will do several things: restore *the land*, apportion *desolate heritages*, and call forth the prisoners (v. 9). As mentioned above, this is the language of jubilee."[70] The name this epoch receives in Isaiah 49 is "time of favor" (בְּעֵת רָצוֹן), similar to the expression found in Isaiah 61:2.

---

68. Alexander, *The Later Prophecies of Isaiah*, 393. Motyer, *Isaiah*, 500; Gregory, "The Postexilic Exile in Third Isaiah: Isaiah 61:1–3 in Light of Second Temple Hermeneutics," 484.

69. Motyer, *Isaiah*, 225.

70. Oswalt, *The Book of Isaiah: Chapters 40–66*, 298.

Gregory adds another evidence that supports the overall importance of the jubilee in Isaiah:

> The allusion to Leviticus 25 is further strengthened when one considers the larger theological understanding of debt-slavery in Second Isaiah, where the exile is identified with debt-slavery into which Israel was placed because of her sins. "Proclaim to her that her service is completed, that her iniquity has been paid for, that she has received from the hand of YHWH double for all her sins" (Isa 40:2). According to Deutero-Isaiah, because of her sins, conceived as a debt, Israel was sold into debt-slavery (i.e., exile in Babylon). Once she had served her due, she would return to her land. [. . .] The fact that Second Isaiah understands the exile and the return in these terms must be accounted for in the development of the Trito-Isaianic material. It is clear that this concept of the exile as debt-slavery is in view in Isaiah 61, since later in the chapter there is an allusion back to Isa 40:2 (and Jer 16:18 as well).[71]

This long citation makes clear that the book of Isaiah develops the jubilee imagery as a symbol for the restoration from the Babylon exile. Due to the focus of this dissertation, I cannot develop this further, but in Isaiah, the Sabbath year and the jubilee year are conflated to build an eschatological image of restoration. This is the image evoked also in Isaiah 61:1–3.

The third evidence that Isaiah 61:1–3 makes a reference to the year of Jubilee is the expression the year of the Lord's favor (שְׁנַת־רָצוֹן לַיהוָה).[72] Although this phrase is not used in Lev 25, it expresses very well the idea of the jubilee in Leviticus and even better the use of the jubilee Isaiah is creating. Finally, Gosse affirms that another reason for Isaiah refer to the jubilee is the fact that the edict of Cyrus making the people free (538 BCE) came

---

71. Gregory, "The Postexilic Exile in Third Isaiah: Isaiah 61:1–3 in Light of Second Temple Hermeneutics," 484–85.

72. "In 49:8 the 'time of favour' was the preparation and coming of the Servant; in 60:7, 10 the Lord's favour was extended to the offering brought by Gentiles and expressed in the comparison which he showed to Israel and which magnetized the world to Zion". Motyer, *Isaiah*, 500.

49 years after the capture of Jerusalem in 587 BCE.[73] Isaiah 61, therefore, is using the Levitical jubilee as an image of restoration.

In Isaiah, there is no clear indication of who speaks the words Jesus quotes and scholars have different proposals, including Isaiah himself, another prophet, a communitarian person, Israel, the suffering servant, and the Messiah.[74] I think the last two options are correct.[75] In the context of Isaiah, therefore, the Messiah-Suffering Servant is the agent who will bring the reality described in Isaiah 60. The idea of a year of favor from Yahweh, and the whole concept of liberty and societal restoration is brought about through the proclamation of this agent of Yahweh.[76] The idea of each family returning to its inheritance includes the return from the exile; a double portion of land (Isa 61:7); and a situation in which the former foreign oppressors become servants of the Jews (Isa 61:4–7).[77] Those who were poor would be alleviated from their toils because of this one who has the Spirit. But who are these poor? They are those so broken their only hope is to claim to Yahweh.[78]

---

73. Gosse, "L' Année de Grâce Du Seigneur Selon Is 61,1–2a et Sa Citation En Lc 4,18–19," *Sci. Esprit* 69 (2017): 95.

74. See a brief history of this problem in Childs, *Isaiah*, 502.

75. The main reason for this identification is the literary links between Isa 61 and Isa 11; 42:1–9; 49:1–9; 50:4–9; 52:13—53:12; 59:21. On this, see Young, *The Book of Isaiah*, 458 et seq.; Motyer, *Isaiah*, 425–26; Oswalt, *The Book of Isaiah: Chapters 40–66*, 562–63; Blenkinsop, *Isaiah 56–66*, 220–23. "This is the prophet representing the Servant/Messiah in a climactic way." Oswalt, *The Book of Isaiah: Chapters 40–66*, 563.

76. "The series of infinitives which, down to the end of v. 3, set forth the purpose for which the messenger was sent are dependent on that verb (to send). Somewhat oddly, they combine the prophet's task with its purpose or results – 'to proclaim . . . to declare . . . to declare . . . to bind up . . . to comfort . . . to give'. All that he has to do is speak. Nevertheless, in and through this proclaiming he is to effect a change on those to whom he is sent. 'Thus, to proclaim salvation is almost as much as to summon it unto existence or bring it about.'" Westermann, *Isaiah 40–66*, 366. "Will the Servant/Messiah simply hurl words at the poor? No, for his words will accomplish what they speak of." Oswalt, *The Book of Isaiah: Chapters 40–66*, 565. "There is no evidence that the Year of Jubilee was ever actually put into effect. But it is a known and very effective metaphor for the freedom which God is providing for his people through his chosen instrument." Watts, *Isaiah 34–66*, 303.

77. Koole also acknowledges the land aspect of the jubilee in Isaiah: "In that case the word [דְּרוֹר] means not only a formal release but also a return to one's original property and so the opportunity for a new existence. This last aspect is mentioned again in vv. 4 and 7, though more than just economic prosperity is promised here. . . . The liberation is thanks to his rule and has its meaning in the recognition and acceptance of this rule." Koole, *Isaiah. Part III.*, 272.

78. "He declares the good news particularly to the *poor*. The connotation of this term is not restricted to financial or material conditions. Nor is there any justification in the context for limiting the reference to an oppressed minority of righteous persons. Rather, it speaks of all who are distressed and in trouble for any reason, including sin. Ps 25:16–21 explains this

This is not envisaged in the sense that the oppressors become oppressed, but the people of God will lead them in the service of Yahweh while they become their shepherds, plowmen and vinedressers (Isa 61:5).

Finally, in Isaiah 63:1–6, the jubilee is called "my year of redemption" (ESV) or "the year of My redeemed" (NKJV), in Hebrew, וּשְׁנַת גְּאוּלַי. There is an intimate relation between Isaiah 63:4 and 61:2. This is the reason why it is possible to be certain that the text is referring indeed to an eschatological jubilee.[79] While Isaiah 61 focuses on the aspect of liberation, Isaiah 63 focuses on the aspect of vengeance.[80] In Isaiah 61 and 63, therefore, the jubilee is an eschatological image of redemption; the coming year of liberation for the people of God will be at the same time the day of vengeance for the enemies of God.[81] He will deliver his people and punish their enemies.

---

larger sense of the word well.... Who are the poor? Those who are so broken by life that they have no more heart to try; those who are so bound up in their various addictions that liberty and release are a cruel mirage; those who think that they will never again experience the favor of the Lord, or see his just vengeance meted out against those who have misused them; those who think that their lives hold nothing more than ashes, sackcloth, and the fainting heaviness of despair. These are they to whom the Servant/Messiah shouts 'Good News'! Will the Servant/Messiah simply hurl words at the poor? No, for his words will accomplish what they speak of." Oswalt, *The Book of Isaiah: Chapters 40–66*, 565.

79. "God's interpretation of his action in vv. 4–6 is rendered initially by a repetition of the formula that occurs both in 34:8 and 61:2: 'the day of vengeance/the year of my redemption.' However, the liberating content of chapter 61 ultimately determines the formulation of 63:4." Childs, *Isaiah*, 517.

80. "The influx of the Gentiles into Zion having been described in the preceding verses, the destruction of her enemies is now sublimely represented as a sanguinary triumph of Jehovah or the Messiah". Alexander, *Commentary on the Prophecies of Isaiah: Vol II*, 413. "Aristotle's passionless Unmoved Mover is the farthest thing from the God of the Bible, whose love is more enduring than the mountains and whose fury is more white-hot than molten steel. Here, as the prophet has said again and again, God's rage is directed against those who would destroy and oppress his people. He is furious against all that would deprive them of the blessings he wishes to give them." Oswalt, *The Book of Isaiah: Chapters 40–66*, 597. "The marvelous poetry of chapters 60—62 anticipates the decisive intervention of Yahweh into the life of the world, whereby Jerusalem will be exalted and all its erstwhile enemies will become subservient, cast in menial roles". Brueggemann, *Isaiah: 40–66*, 225.

81. "The dramatic articulation is, in the end, a means whereby Israel's most elemental trust in Yahweh can be voiced. The substance of that faith is expressed as Yahweh's "day of vengeance" and "year for my redeeming work" (v. 4) that will bring victory (*ys'*; v. 5). At the heart of prophetic hope that here tilts toward apocalyptic expression is the deep conviction of Judaism that in due course – soon of late – there will be a time when Yahweh will act decisively to right the wrongs of the world and to establish a just, peaceable rule in the earth. The new rule, inevitably, will be a governance especially attentive to and protective of Jerusalem, and therefore aimed at elimination of the threat to Jerusalem embodied in other military powers." Brueggemann, *Isaiah: 40–66*, 227.

As the other uses of Jubilee in the prophets are not as important as the Isaianic use, their treatment will be briefer. In Jeremiah 31:8–22 one finds an important passage related to the Sabbatical year, the year of release. Judah was under the Babylonian siege (2 Kgs 24:10—25:7; 2 Chr 36:5–37:21). King Zedekiah cut a covenant with the people so he could proclaim liberty (לִקְרֹא דְרוֹר, vss. 8, 15, 17) to the slaves. So it happened, the whole people obeyed and freed their slaves (Jer 34:10).

In the next verse, however, we read: "But afterward they turned around and took back the male and female slaves they had set free, and brought them into subjection as slaves." The covenant and the consecration of the people did not last. It seems by the text that Zedekiah's motivations were noble, while the motivations of the slave owners could be egoistic from the beginning.[82] What one discovers only in the end of the text, is that in this gap, the Babylonian armies had temporarily withdrawn from the siege (Jer 34:21) and this motivated the slave owners to retreat from the word that they would free the slaves. God's interpretation of what had happened is in verses 15–16. "You recently repented and did what was right in my eyes proclaiming liberty, each to his neighbor, and made a covenant before me in the house that is called by my name, but then you turned around profaned my name when each of you took back his male and female slaves, you had set free according to their desire, and you brought them into subjection to be your slaves." For God, what the people did was a profanation of his name.[83] God does not separate

---

82. Reasons for their change of heart are not given, but several explanations have been proposed. The most likely reason for their decision to release the slaves is that while under siege it was not economically practical for the owners to feed and care for the slaves, so they released them to fend for themselves. Another possible rationale for freeing the slaves was the belief that they would be more likely to help defend the city if freed. Some owners may have believed that by obeying the law and freeing the slaves, they would gain favor with God and he would deliver them from the Babylonians. Huey, "Jeremiah, Lamentations," 308–9.

83. "The interface between theological intent and economic act is intense and remarkable. The two cannot be separated. Reenslaving debt slaves diminishes God's reputation; that is, it profanes God's name." Brueggemann, *A Commentary on Jeremiah: Exile and Homecoming*, 328. "Without doubt every ethical mandate is rooted in this story of weakness and helplessness. Here lies the crux of the people's wrongdoing. By reclaiming their freed slaves, both the king and the people exploit their place of privilege. By withholding mercy, the recipients of divine mercy become 'hard-hearted or tight-fisted' (Deut 15:7). By treating people as mere commodities, they do violence to their core identity as God's people: the once oppressed now become oppressors." Stulman, *Jeremiah*, 290.

social justice from relationship with him.⁸⁴ Because of that, God would call the curses of the covenant upon his people (Jer 34:17–22).⁸⁵

The last prophetic text with an evident reference to the jubilee is Ezekiel 46:16–18: "Thus says the Lord God: If the prince (הַנָּשִׂיא) makes a gift to any of his sons as his inheritance, it shall belong to his sons. It is their property by inheritance. But if he makes a gift out of his inheritance to one of his servants, it shall be his to the year of liberty (שְׁנַת הַדְּרוֹר). Then it shall revert to the prince; surely it is his inheritance—it shall belong to his sons. The prince shall not take any of the inheritance of the people, thrusting them out of their property. He shall give his sons their inheritance out of his own property, so that none of my people shall be scattered from his property." The commandment of returning the property to its original owners in the jubilee year is here confirmed and applied to the prince, who both should have his landed properties returned to his children and also were not supposed to abuse the power of his office by amassing property to himself.

4.2.4 The Jubilee Laws in Second Temple Judaism

Although the jubilee is not central in the Old Testament, it gained more and more importance in the second temple period. The importance of the jubilee is, first, a calendrical one, since it became a very important way of organizing the story of Israel.⁸⁶

---

84. "The economic leadership reneged and reinforced slavery, thus violating the Torah, nullifying the covenant, and reducing social relations between the haves and have-nots in the community to sheer economic power. Unbridled wealth and greed prevailed over neighbor solidarity. As the covenant is rejected, instead of covenant blessings, Judah receives one more unwelcome oracle from the prophet". Brueggemann, *A Commentary on Jeremiah: Exile and Homecoming*, 326. "A people who had experienced slavery in their past should have had a more compassionate attitude toward others who were enslaved." Huey, "Jeremiah, Lamentations," 309.

85. Nehemiah 10:31 also has a reference to a decision of keeping the Sabbatical year. It is possible also, that Daniel 9:24–27, with its references to the seventy sevens has also a reference to a Jubilee as a time of renovation. As the text is much encrypted, we did not include it in here. For more on that, see Ulrich, "The Need for More Attention to Jubilee in Daniel 9:24–27," 481–500.

86. With the focus on the Book of Jubilees, Segal affirms: "Other works from the Second temple period also describe periods of history using the terminology of 'jubilees' and 'weeks' (cf. Dan 9:24–27; the *Apocalypse of Weeks* [1 Enoch 93, 91]; *Testament of Levi 17*; *Assumption of Moses*; *Apocryphon of Joshua* [DJD 22]; *Apocryphon of Jeremiah* [DJD 30]; *11QMelchizedek* [DJD 23]), but *Jubilees* is the only one to apply this chronological system in a systematic, detailed fashion throughout the composition." Segal, *The Book of Jubilees: Rewritten Bible, Redaction, Ideology and Theology*, 7–8.

One sees this calendrical importance of the jubilee for example in the Book of Jubilees, also named The Little Genesis.[87] Jubilees belong to a genre called rewritten Bible.[88] Since the oldest manuscript of Jubilee dates from before 100 BC and considering some internal and external evidence, the date of the work is probably from around 155 BC.[89]

The book of Jubilees recounts the story found in Genesis and Exodus, reorganizing it in weeks of years and periods of forty-nine years that the author considers a jubilee. Thus, in this book, the Exodus happens in the fiftieth jubilee ("jubilee of jubilees") since the creation: "The entire chronological framework of *Jubilees* includes fifty jubilee periods of 49 years each; in the fiftieth jubilee the nation of Israel is freed from slavery in Egypt and returns, forty years later to its ancestral land of Canaan."[90]

It is clear, therefore, that the jubilaic chronology has an agenda. It aims to show that the Exodus is a time of release and return of Israel to its own former land, which is also clear in the Book of Jubilees.[91] Land ownership, therefore, is a very important concern and goal of the book.[92] Another lesson that the

---

87. "The book of Jubilees is arguably the most important and influential as all the books written by Jews in the Second Temple period." Kugel, "A Walk through Jubilees: Studies in the Book of Jubilees and the World of Its Creation," 1. "The Book of Jubilees is in certain limited aspects the most important book in this volume for the student of religion." Charles, *Pseudepigrapha of the Old Testament*, 1.

88. Segal, *The Book of Jubilees: Rewritten Bible, Redaction, Ideology and Theology*, 4–5; van Ruiten, "Abraham in the Book of Jubilees: The Rewriting of Genesis 11:26–25:10 in the Book of Jubilees 11:14–23:8," 3–7.

89. VanderKam, "The Origins and Purposes of the Book of Jubilees," 20; VanderKam, *Book of Jubilees*, 21. Todd Hanneken proposes a date in ca. 159 B.C. Hanneken, "The Subversion of the Apocalypses in the Book of Jubilees," 274. On the context of the book, he makes this comment: "The book of Jubilees was written at a crossroads in Jewish history. In the wake of the Maccabean revolt, the most fundamental issues of Jewish identity, practice, and authority were fiercely debated. Over time, multiple positions emerged, none of which matched the claims of Jubilees perfectly." Hanneken, "The Subversion of the Apocalypses in the Book of Jubilees," 1. For a different view on the date of Jubilee, see Segal, who contends that the book is contemporary with the sect of Qumran. Segal, *The Book of Jubilees: Rewritten Bible, Redaction, Ideology and Theology*.

90. VanderKam, "The Origins and Purposes of the Book of Jubilees," 17.

91. VanderKam, "The Origins and Purposes of the Book of Jubilees," 17.

92. "In a time when Judeans were subject to foreign powers who were at least interested in blending them into the surrounding culture, the writer of *Jubilees* articulated a powerful argument for freedom from foreign domination and Judean possession of their own land. The land was theirs by ancient right, the land of a people who would enjoy political blessings if they lived sincerely according to the covenant. God had accomplished their deliverance and liberty in the past and could do so again for a people true to the extraordinarily ancient covenant." VanderKam, "The Origins and Purposes of the Book of Jubilees," 22.

chronology of Jubilees teaches is that God sovereignly has appointed right times to act in history, so people can rest in God's way of moving it despite the current oppressive situation.[93]

In the book there is a reference to the law of jubilee, in 7:37, as if it had been given to Noah, which Charles translates as "And in the fifth year ... make ye the release so that ye release it in righteousness and uprightness, and ye shall be righteous, and all that you plant shall prosper."[94] Thus, as the author of Jubilees does with other laws, this one also he claims to be in existence before Moses.

Thus, besides being a marker of time, the jubilee in the Book of Jubilees is a symbol of the freedom God will proclaim and produce to his people, a symbol of Yahweh's sovereignty and an ancient law God's people should observe.

The Testament of Levi presents a somewhat similar view. The Testament of Levi is part of The Testaments of the Twelve Patriarchs, a Jewish collection of testaments interpolated by much Christian material.[95] In chapter 17 of T. Levi, history is narrated in terms of jubilees. The fifth jubilee is pointed as a time of release, return from exile and reconstruction of the temple, a reference to the return of Babylonian exile: "And in the fifth week they shall return to their desolate country, and shall renew the house of the Lord" (T.Levi 17:10).

A similar form of counting the time is found in Sanhedrin 97b. Although the personages of this tradition are from the third century CE, their tradition deserves mention in here: "Elijah the prophet said to Rav Yehuda, brother of Rav Sala Ḥasida: The world will exist no fewer than eighty-five Jubilee cycles,

---

93. "In his recounting of patriarchal history, the author of *Jubilees* was careful to divide his chronological history into jubilees as a way of invoking this idea. History, he seemed to be asserting with each new date, marches forward in multiples of these forty-nine year units. Indeed, he explicitly endorsed this notion at the end of the book, pointing out that precisely fifty jubilees (2,450 years) separate the 'time of Adam' (that is, the time od the creation of the world in six days from the time of Israel's crossing of the Jordan and entrance into the land of Canaan (*Jub*. 50.4–5). Surely that round number – fifty jubilees exactly! – could not be an accident, and it indicated that similarly large patterns were to be found in Israel's later history as well. So do not despair, the author was saying to his countrymen: the apparent disorder of a few hundred years disappears when you consider these larger patterns." Kugel, "A Walk through Jubilees: Studies in the Book of Jubilees and the World of Its Creation," 10.

94. Charles, *Pseudepigrapha of the Old Testament*, 25. Vanderkam translates the same text as: "During the fifth year arrange relief for it so that you may leave it in the right and proper way. Then you will be doing the right thing, and all your planting will be successful."

95. For a good introduction to the whole collection, see Kugler, *The Testaments of the Twelve Patriarchs*.

or 4,250 years. And during the final Jubilee, the son of David will come." Again, one finds the jubilees as a way of counting time and the final jubilee here is seen as the Messianic era.

A Jewish text fundamental to our dissertation as cultural and theological context is the Qumran manuscript 11Q13, also called 11QMelch or the Melchizedek document. The document is probably a *pesher* on Leviticus.[96] The part that it is possible to read, the second column focus on Leviticus 25:13 and the parallel Deuteronomy 15:2. The specific copy of this document found in cavern 11Q dates from ca. 75 BC.

11QMelch makes a connection between Leviticus 25:13; Deuteronomy 15:2 and Isaiah 61:1 with the expression "proclaim liberty to the captives" and "the Year of Melchizedek's favor". Besides, 11QMelch presents Melchizedek as a messianic figure, who is identified with the archangel Michael and is called Elohim, El and even Yahweh. He is presented as savior, judge, avenger against Belial and his evil spirits, anointed and is the one who brings the tenth jubilee about.

Xeravits says that in 11QMelch, Melchizedek is "an eschatological liberator, an agent of divide judgement", "a positive eschatological protagonist", "a leader of angelic hosts".[97] "Also attributed to Melchizedek is the atonement (*lcpr*, ii 8) of all belonging to him, on the eschatological Day of Atonement."[98]

Another characteristic of 11QMelch is that its jubilee has eschatological, social and redemptive tones: eschatological because it happens in the end of days, social because it is the release for the captives and redemptive because

---

96. Aschim, "The Genre of 11QMelchizedek," 17–31. There is discussion about the precise kind of pesher and the main text it envisage to interpret. Aschim states correctly that: "The most important structural feature in column 2 of 11QMlch is the alternation between explicit biblical quotations and interpretations. Both are introduced in a technical way, by the use of certain formulas. This is clearly an exegetical work. The structure of the text reminds one strongly of the so-called 'pesharim', like the famous Habakkuk commentary from Qumran cave 1 (1QpHab)." (p. 18–19). Xeravitis, on another hand, sees the work as a "thematic pesher on different parts of scriptural passages, of which Isa 61:1–3 seems to be the most important." Géza G. Xeravits, *King, Priest, Prophet: Positive eschatological protagonists of the Qumran library*, 195. James Vanderkam calls this document a thematic pesher on Melchizedek. VanderKam, *The Dead Sea Scrolls and the Bible*, 45.

97. Xeravits, *King, Priest, Prophet: Positive eschatological protagonists of the Qumran library*, 195–196.

98. Xeravits, *King, Priest, Prophet: Positive eschatological protagonists of the Qumran library*, 196.

it happens in the Day of Atonement and will produce forgiveness of the iniquities of the captives. Commenting on this, Bergsma says:

> The eschatological interpretation of these passages concerns 'captives' who are the 'inheritance of Melchizedek'. Melchizedek makes these captives return, proclaims liberty to them, and frees them from the debt of their iniquities (lines 4—6). Clearly, then, Melchizedek is seen as personally enacting a jubilee on behalf of the 'captives' who are somehow associated with him (his 'inheritance'), in much the same way that Isa 61:1–2 portrays a messianic figure personally enacting jubilee on behalf of the 'poor of Zion'.[99]

This Melchizedek therefore is at least one of the Messiahs expected in Qumran and his Messianic time is intimately related to a jubilaic proclamation with both spiritual and social overtones. He is savior against social oppressions and against the forces of Belial.[100]

It is clear by these and other texts, that in the intertestamental period, the jubilee was important mainly as a form of organizing history, it had

---

99. Bergsma, *The Jubilee from Leviticus to Qumran: A History of Interpretation*, 282. Robert Willoughby, after quoting a part of 11QMelch says: "Interestingly, forgiveness is now linked to liberation. The expected intervention has already become eschatological in character." Willoughby, "The Concept of Jubilee and Luke 4:18–30," 47.

100. "The remission of debts of the biblical text is interpreted as referring to the final liberation, which will occur during the Day of the Expiation. Melchizedek, the agent of this liberation, is presented as the eschatological judge mentioned in Ps 7:8–9 and Ps 82:1–2. He is also presented as the chief of the heavenly armies, the leader of the 'sons of God' who will destroy the armies of Belial, identifying his figure in terms of practical functions with the 'Prince of Light' (a figure we find in 1QS III 20, CD V 8, and 1QM XVIII 10) and with the angel Michael (a figure appearing in 1QM XVII 6–7). The victory of Melchizedek against Belial and the spirits of his lot will usher in an era of salvation, which is described in the words of Isa 9." Martínez and Tigchelaar, *Qumran Origins and Apocalypticism*, 209. "The author of the text expects a messiah-instructor, the anointed of the spirit (*mshya hrvh*), who stands on the mountains of the prophets and announces salvation; This salvation is comfort for the afflicted (*h'blym*) in the form of instruction about the periods of history and their ultimate end. This view of conceptual rather than or prior to material relief is similar to the eschatological vision of Instruction. It is Melchizedek who will free them from the hand of Belial. Since the hand of Belial is elsewhere associated with wealth (CD IV-VI), and since the term 'afflictions' can include financial hardship, it is legitimate to understand the messianic salvation as at least conceptual relief from the problems posed by the present affliction of the just, if not material relief from that affliction as well. This possibility is supported by the fact that eschatological redemption is envisaged as partially economic in several other Qumran texts, namely the constitutional literature, the Hodayot and Instruction." Murphy, "Wealth in the Dead Sea Scrolls and in the Qumran Community," 257–58.

a chronological importance.[101] However, commonly this way of marking the time would point to a point in history, a specific jubilee, in which the Messianic era would be inaugurated.[102] I also agree with Bergsma that the Jubilee and the Sabbatical year were fused in the Second Temple period and that is the context of these laws in the New Testament.[103]

Up to here in this chapter, we have seen the fundamental importance of land in the Pentateuch and the most important law God gave to Israel about land, the jubilee law. We have studied many aspects of the jubilee and how it became a symbol for a time in which God would liberate his people from their sins and oppression. Now we turn to the consequences of the fact Israel never practiced the ethics contained in the jubilee laws.

4.3 From the Promised Land to the Babylonian Exile: The Jubilee Ethics Despised and Its Consequences

More than fifty times throughout the Hebrew Bible one finds the affirmation that God gave the land to Israel. Together with the land, God gave instructions on how the land was supposed to be used and established a relation between keeping the law and keeping the land. This became a snare to disobedient Israel. As it happened in Eden, also in Israel's history, the curse of disobedience was intimately related to land. For example, the curses of the covenant included enemies eating their crops; lack of production; destruction of the livestock; and, finally, ejection from the land, i.e. exile (Lev 16:14–39; 20:22–26; Deut 28:15–68; Josh 23:15–16; Ps 106:24–27).

---

101. A few other texts that deserve future analysis because of their possible relation with the jubilee are: 4QApocryphon of Joshua (4Q378); 4QPsalms Pesher (4Q171 [4QpPsa]); 4QVisions of Amram" (4Q543); Wisdom Poems (4Q4i8 69–81); 4QMessianic Apocalypse (4Q521).

102. "The jubilee as a division of time is put to use in the Scrolls for roughly three purposes: historiographical, i.e. for charting the chronology of past events; cultic-calendrical, i.e., for calculating cultic activities such as the rotation of priestly service; and eschatological, i.e., for predicting the arrival of the final era of history." Bergsma, *The Jubilee from Leviticus to Qumran*, 251.

103. Bergsma affirms it seems that in Qumran the jubilee (Lev 25) was equated or conflated with the *shemittah* (Deut 15), and received an eschatological significance. He says that that is probably the reason why a literal jubilee was never referred to in qur'anic documents. "The jubilee continued to have a chronological and eschatological – but no longer legal – significance." Bergsma, *The Jubilee from Leviticus to Qumran*, 281–82.

Israel experienced some of these curses on the land already in the time of the judges. This is specifically referred to, for example, in Judg 6:3–6, where the author says that the Midianites were devouring the produce of the land and robbing the animals. Also, in Ruth 1:1 we are informed that the land was suffering famine. In this book one finds the jubilee redeemer in action (cf. Ruth 2:20; Lev 25:25). As Ruth and Naomi come back to Israel, Boaz, their redeemer, marries Ruth (Ruth 4). Although there is no evidence that the Sabbath and the Jubilee Years have ever being kept, there are a few indications of remission being exerted, as with the woman whose son Elijah restored to life. In this occasion, the king Jehoram ordained her land to be restituted to her (2 Kgs 8:1–6). Another instance of this role being fulfilled is when Jeremiah bought the field of his uncle even as they were going into exile (Jer 32:1–15). All of that relates to the aspect I called sympathetic ethics in the last section.

With the institution of the monarchy in Israel, Samuel made clear that the king would have the right to interfere with the way people used their land, imposing taxes and making slaves of the people (1 Sam 8:10–18). With this new regimen, the kings of Israel became very rich, owning many fields and vines.[104] This was the case of Saul (1 Sam 22:7–8); David (1 Chr 27:25–31), Solomon (Eccl 2:4; Song 8:11–12), and King Uzziah (2 Chr 26:10) just to name a few. The rights of the Israelite king were exacerbated by Ahab in the story of Naboth's Vineyard (1 Kgs 21).[105]

This account illustrates well the kind of oppression that was happening in Israel and Judah at that time. Naboth was faithful to God's instructions that the land should remain in the same family and thus refuses both to trade his land and vineyard with the king for a better one, and to sell it for money (1 Kgs 21:1–3). The vineyard was contiguous to the king's house. With Naboth's denial to sell his family's vineyard to the king, Jezebel, the king Ahab, and the elders and other leaders who lived in Naboth's city, with the aid of false witnesses, falsely accused Naboth of cursing God and the king, stoning him to death (1 Kgs 21:4–14). With Naboth dead, the king Ahab took

---

104. de Vaux, *Ancient Israel*, 124–25.

105. In the case of Saul, registered in 1 Sam 22:7–8; he affirms that David would not give, as he did, vineyards (and positions in the government) to the people of his tribe and birthland Gibeah. It is clear that since its beginning the kingship did not managed well its land rights.

possession of the vineyard (1 Kgs 21:15–16) and was sentenced by the Lord through Elijah (1 Kgs 21:17–24).

Sadly, this kind of oppression by the rulers became the norm also in Israel and Judah. Ezekiel, for example, received a prophecy from God regarding the future of the nation. In this prophecy he sees that the princes would have a portion of land of the same size of a tribe (Ezek 45:7–8) and God concludes: "And my princes shall no more oppress my people, but they shall let the house of Israel have the land according to their tribes." (Ezek 45:8).

From the monarchy on, there was an enormous change in the way Israel dealt with land.[106] Before the monarchy, there was more equality among the families. After the establishment of the monarchy and with the passing of years, it became more and more common to have very rich people, as Nabal (2 Sam 25). The archaeology seems to corroborate this when it shows that the similar sized houses of the tenth century gave space to richer and bigger houses in the eighth century which were built afar from poor and huddled houses.[107] De Vaux explains what happened:

> Between these two centuries, a social revolution had taken place. The monarchical institutions produced, as we saw, a class of officials who drew a profit from their posts and the favours granted them by the king. Others by hard work or good luck, made vast profits from their lands. Prosperity was the order of the day [Hos 8:14; 12:9; Amo 3:15, 5:11; 6:4; Isa 2:7; 3:16–24; 5:11–12] . . . On the other side we have the weak, the small men, the poor, who suffered from these burdens.[108]

---

106. "Israel's monarchy thus started to develop normally in the direction of a peaceful autocracy, with all the corresponding drawbacks particularly tax burdens and compulsory labor. Taken as a whole, it seemed as though Israel might fall in line with the general practices of the ancient Orient in becoming an imperialistic, ambitious, conquering, worldly nation, devoting all its forces to political and economic expansion." Baron, *A Social and Religious History of the Jews. Vol. 1*, 65.

107. De Vaux, *Ancient Israel: Its Life and Institutions*, 72–73.

108. De Vaux, *Ancient Israel*, 73. The biblical texts are quoted by De Vaux. Although long, this presentation of Elmslie of the same situation is worthy: "The institution of the monarchy was, of its very nature, a deeply disturbing influence, for it presented an alternative scheme of society – the nation and its boundaries, the king and his subjects. Nevertheless, the ancient sense of a covenantal brotherhood persisted. . . . In the period of the two centuries 800–6000 B.C., however, the political and economic conditions in Palestine changed disastrously, and the family ideal that had been the bond of society dissolved. Battles with the Syrian and Assyrian armies decimated the peasantry and reunited them economically. Authority and wealth rapidly

The injustices were not perpetrated only by the rulers of Israel and Judah, but also by the people. The prophets denounce the situation.[109] Matthews and Benjamin reconstruct this situation in the following terms:

> Rich households lent poor households money to pay their taxes, but secured these loans by taking their land and the labor which every member of the household was capable of doing as collateral. When households defaulted in repaying their loans, creditors foreclosed on their properties and sold the entire household – men, women, and children – as slaves. Legally, creditors were not buying the land or selling slaves, just holding the land as collateral and collecting the wages of its owners as interest until the debt was repaid (Lev 25:35–46; 2 Kings 4:1[–7]; Neh 5:1–5[; 2 Chr 28:8–15; Jer 34:14]).[110]

Thus, the prophet Hosea denounces the rich for using false balances; loving the oppression and enriching themselves (Hos 12:7–8). Isaiah pens a woe to those who buy properties along their fields, so they dwell alone in the midst of their fields, in other words, those who manage to have latifundia (Isa 5:8–10).[111] Isaiah also proclaims a woe of judgment upon those who make laws that facilitate the oppression and the destitution of widows and

---

concentrated in a few hands. New classes of men, lacking the old instinct of kinship-obligation, sprang up. The kings encouraged foreign trade; and now there were merchants pitilessly intent on gain (Amos viii.4–6. Large landowners needing slaves and hirelings to work the fields which the impoverished peasants sold or forfeited for debts (Isa. v.8); officials of the court ready to take bribes and deny justice to the landless, the widows, and the orphans now multiplied in both kingdoms. The two royal cities, Jerusalem and Samaria, became dominant, and were shockingly corrupt (Amos vi; Isa i.21–23). So complete was the moral degeneracy that the temporary prosperity from 780 to 740 B.C. served only to increase the debauchery of the powerful, and make more poignant the sufferings of the poor." Elmslie, "Ethics," 283–84. Quoted partially in Wright, *God's People in God's Land*, 107.

109. "When therefore economic changes and human greed later combined to attack and destroy large numbers os such small family landholdings, certain prophets were moved to denounce this, not merely on the grounds of social injustice but because it represented an attack upon one of the basic socio-economic pillars on which Israel's relationship with Yahweh rested – the family and its land." Wright, *God's People in God's Land*, 65.

110. Matthews and Benjamin, *Social World of Ancient Israel 1250–587 BCE*, 202.

111. Premnath defines "latifundization" as "the process of land accumulation (large estates, hence latifundia) in the hands of a few wealthy landowners to the deprivation of the peasantry." He defends that this problem reflected a substantial change in the economy of the country and was spread to the evil os peasants: "In this sense, 'growth' and 'development' contribute very little to the improvement of the condition of the common peasantry. The opulence of the rich is achieved at the expense of the poor. The consequence of all the aspects

orphans (Isa 10:1–2). Ezekiel denounces people for lending money with interests (Ezek 22:12; cf. Ezek 18:8–17; Prov 28:8; Ps15:5). Micah has a woe to those who plan evil. He exemplified the kind of evil they plan: "They covet fields and seize them, and houses, and take them away; they oppress a man and his house, a man and his inheritance" (Mic 2:1–2). Amos denounces the rich for speculating the price of the grains, using false balances, having no pity on the debtor, fomenting slavery and, in doing so, trampling the poor (Amos 2:6-8; 8:4-6). And while this happens, they keep their freedom by bribing the judges (Isa 1:23; Jer 5:28; Mic 3:11; 7:3).

Although many warnings against oppression related to land are found in the Law (Deut 24:14, 21; Lev 19:13), the Prophets (1 Kgs 8:37-48; Isa 1:7-8; Jer 7:5-7; 8:10; Joel 1; Hos 2:12-23, 9:3; Hag 1:10-11; Hab 3:17; Zeph 1:13; Mal 3:5), and the Writings (Prov 12:11; 13:23; 23:10; 24:27-34; 28:19; 31:16; Eccles 5:9; 2 Chr 6:28-38); the Israelites and Jews kept oppressing one another and suffering the covenant foresaid curses until the time of the Assyrian and Babylonian exiles. It is because of this situation of oppression and despise of the laws of the Lord, that "The jubilee became a distant vision, a hope carried by the prophets for a time when the messiah would come and bring in a kingdom of justice, righteousness, and social holiness, when all Israel would be able to enjoy shalom beneath their vines and fig trees (Mic 4:4; Zech 3:10)."[112]

After Israel and Judah passed through milder levels of covenant curses without repentance, God sent Israel to the Assyrian exile (2 Kgs 15:29; 17:3-6; 18:11-12; 1 Chr 5:25-26) and Judah to the Babylonian exile (2 Kgs 25:8-12; Jer 39:8-10; 52:12-16; Lam 5:1-18; 2 Chr 36:17-21). Although the main reason for the exiles were idolatry against Yahweh, the lack of sabbatical years is also remembered. That is the testimony of the Chronicler: "He took into exile in Babylon those who had escaped from the sword, and they became servants to him and to his sons until the establishment of the kingdom of Persia, to fulfill the word of the LORD by the mouth of Jeremiah, until the land had enjoyed its Sabbaths. All the days that it lay desolate it kept Sabbath, to fulfill seventy years" (2 Chr 36:20-21). The aristocracy of Judah, and among them those who oppressed the poorer people, was taken captive into Babylon

---

of latifundization is the steady deprivation and impoverishment of the peasantry." Premnath, "Latifundization and Isaiah 5:8–10," 301–12.

112. Tan, "Pentecost, Jubilee, and Nation Building," 76.

and part of the poorer population was kept in the land and took possession of it (2 Kgs 24:14; 25:12; Jer 39:10; Ezek 33:24).

The fact that God is the owner of all land is the basis for why he will give great part of it to Nebuchadnezzar. Jeremiah makes that clear when God sends him to deliver the following message to the kings of Judah, Edom, Moab, Ammon, Tyre, and Sidon: "'Thus says the Lord of hosts, the God of Israel: This is what you shall say to your masters: 'It is I who by my great power and my outstretched arm have made the earth, with the men and animals that are on the earth, and I give it to whomever it seems right to me.'" (Jer 27:4–5). Note that it is not just the land of Israel that belongs to Yahweh and is disposed at his will, but all lands.

Therefore, although God had given specific laws against exaggerated accumulation of wealth and land related oppression, he had advised his people that they would benefit from obedience and bring misfortune if they chose disobedience (cf. Deut 2–3 and 28–30), and had sent many prophets to admonish the people even with threats of exile, the rulers and people of Israel and Judah kept sinning against land, fellow Jews and God and for their sins they were sent into exile. The main reason was not oppression related to land, but this was one of the critical areas where they were adverted by the prophets and kept their wrongdoings. Thus, God kept his word and sent them to exile.

4.4 Prophecy and Reality: Life After the Return from Babylon

Von Rad makes the astute comment that one of the most interesting problems of the Old Testament theology is the fact that although fulfilled, the promise of land always remains as a promise:

> Here we come face to face with one of the most interesting problems of Old Testament theology: promises which have been fulfilled in history are not thereby exhausted of their content, but remain as promises on a different level, although they are to some extend metamorphosed in the process. The promise of the

land itself was proclaimed ever anew, even after its fulfilment,
as a future benefit of God's redemptive activity.[113]

One of the clues to solve this problem relies in the gap between what is foretold in predictive prophecy and what is accomplished in real history because of the sins of the people. This happened with the prophecies that foretold the return from the Babylonian captivity.[114] The same prophets who foresaw the exile also announced a redemption, a return from the exile to a renewed and improved land.

Isaiah, for example, prophesies rain, plenty of produce, fodder for animals (Isa 30:23–25), and even completely renewed heavens and earth (Isa 65:17–22; 66:22–23). Jeremiah speaks about the repossession of the land after the exile (Jer 30:3), plenty of vineyards on the mountains of Samaria (Jer 31:5), and deep gladness because of the abundant wealth of the fields (Jer 31:12). Ezekiel links the concession of a new heart and the outpouring of the Spirit (Ezek 36:26–27) with profuse crops (Ezek 36:30) and an Eden-like restoration (Ezek 36:35).

In Joel, the Lord promises to send his people sufficient grain, wine and oil to satisfy them (Joel 2:19), as well as fruits (Joel 2:22), rain in the right time (Joel 2:23), overflowing threshing floors and wine vats (Joel 2:24) and, finally, the Holy Spirit (Joel 2:28–29). Joel also foresees the day in which the mountains will drip sweet wine and milk and the land of Judah will be perfectly irrigated (Joel 3:18). Amos foresees extreme fertility in the land, mountains full of vineyards and orchards and an eternal inhabitation in the land (Amos 9:13–15). Do these prophecies find fulfillment in the return of the exile?

No. Cyrus made the decree in 538 BC allowing the Jews to go back to Canaan (2 Chr 36:22–23; Ezra 1, 6:3–5; cf. Isa 44:24–45:18; 48:14), but in the following years, the restoration was not as preannounced by the prophets. Indeed, the Jews were allowed to go back to their land, but there was not such an abundance. They were restored as a client state to Persia. Although there was some wealth amidst the people as one can see in Haggai 1:4 (ca. 520 BC), there was also infertility in the land (Hag 1:5). The reason, again, is that

---

113. Von Rad, "The Promised Land and Yahweh's Land in the Hexateuch," 92–93.

114. "With even minimally modest expectations unfulfilled, how far short the reality was of the glowing promises of Second Isaiah! As year followed disheartening year, the morale of the community sank dangerously." John. Bright, *A History of Israel*, 364.

Yahweh was not their priority and there was still injustice among them, as it is stated in Zechariah and Malachi, contemporaries of Haggai (Zech 7:1–14; Mal 3:5). Because of their infidelity to the covenant, God was already once again sending the milder versions of curse upon their land (Hag 1:10–11).

The Persian empire was organized in political regions called satrapies and these in smaller units embracing different states. These states were permitted to keep their religious and cultural idiosyncrasies.[115] It was around this time that a body of Jewish rulers was formed according to the example of Numbers 11:16–17. Josephus calls this body τῶν γερόντων ἄρχουσιν (the governing elders) and later this group of leaders develops into the Sanhedrin.[116] By the evidence of Ezra-Nehemiah, it seems that Judah was part of the satrapy called Beyond the River that had a governor (פֶּחָה).[117] Judah also had governors, but it seems that Judah was under the Beyond the River satrapy, especially considering that the money to rebuild the temple would come from their treasury (Ezr 6:6–13). Nehemiah was made governor (פֶּחָה / תִּרְשָׁתָא) of Judah (Neh 5:14; 7:65; 8:9; 10:1; 12:26). In Ezra 4, the governor of the Beyond the River satrapy complains to the emperor Artaxerxes that if he allows them to

---

115. "Royal officials wisely determined that culturally informed flexibility breeds loyalty. Consequently, those in charge of the bureaucratic system accepted differences across their diverse territories, and authorities used this tolerance to their advantage. Traditions involving a particular deity or other local practices might differ sharply from one region to another, but the Persians did not see this as an obstacle to stability. Rather, they allowed different customs to flourish, including cultic practices, and they encouraged local infrastructure projects and trading. In pursuing this course of strategic flexibility, the ruling authorities did not act out of compassion. While granting certain freedoms, these rulers also expected subject peoples to meet heavy taxation and tribute demands." Adams, *Social and Economic Life in Second Temple Judea*, 131–32.

116. Josephus, *Ant*. 11.4.7. In other places, Josephus call this ruling and religious body "ἡ γερουσία" (senate), *Ant*. 12.3.3; 13.5.8; "βουλῇ" (council), *Ant*. 20.1.2. Malamat comments about the gerousia in this way: "The High Priest was assisted by the Gerousia. Presumably, it ranked above him officially; such, at least was the case at the end of the third century. In addition to the leaders of the priesthood, the Gerousia also included heads of families who represented the interests of the provincial towns of Judea" Malamat et al., *A History of the Jewish People*, 192. The Gerousia develops into the Sanhedrin (συνέδριον) found in the New Testament and in Josephus. See, for example, *Ant*. 14.5.4; 15.6.2; 17.11.4; 18.4.5; 20.9.6. The first of these last references points to the event in which Alexander's mother asks him to form 5 sanhedrim in Palestine. For more on the Sanhedrin, see Mantel, "The High Priesthood and the Sanhedrim in the Time of the Second Temple," 274–81.

117. This is an Assyrian loan word appears only in the post-exilic books. Daniel 3:2 presents a list of the Babylonian officials probably in hierarchical order. פחה is third in the list. Miller, *Daniel*, 111. Both Shethar-bozenai and the governors in Judah as called by this word: Ezra 6:6.

build the walls of the city, they will stop sending tribute, custom, or toll (Ezr 4:13; cf. also v. 20; 7:24).[118]

With all these enemies and taxes, still in the time of Nehemiah (ca. 445 BC), Jerusalem's situation was precarious (Neh 1:3). Again, it is possible to find oppression, disloyalty and disobedience of the jubilee laws. Bright describes the situation in the following terms:

> The new community was, in fact, anything but the revived and purified Israel of the prophetic ideal. There were economic tensions, possibly attendant upon the scramble for land inevitable in any such mass repatriation, possibly aggravated as bad seasons drove the less fortunate into bankruptcy. Some knew how to turn the misfortune of others into their profit – while concealing their callousness behind a façade of piety (Isa 58:1–12; 59:1–8).[119]

The event narrated in Nehemiah 5 exemplifies this kind of situation. It narrates that the society at that point was divided between the people and the Jewish brothers (Neh 5:1), who are also called nobles and officials (Neh 5:7). The people were complaining because of lack of sufficient food (Neh 5:2), unbearable mortgages (Neh 5:3), debt bondage caused by abusive interest (Neh 5:4, 10), and slavery (Neh 5:5). After a hard rebuke from Nehemiah, the aristocracy of Jerusalem decided to apply the laws of Leviticus 25 (Neh 5:6–13).[120] Nehemiah himself, setting the example did not demand the bread of the governor, acting therefore in a different manner from his predecessors. He says:

---

118. The book *Oeconomica*, of anonymous authorship and wrongly attributed to Aristotle in the past, was possibly written during the times of Persian domination and it confirms the multiplicity of the taxes of the period: "The second kind of administration, that of the4 governor, is concerned with six different classes of revenue; those, namely, arising from agriculture, from the special products of the country, from markets, from taxes, from cattle, and from other sources. Taking these in turn, the first and most important of them is revenue from agriculture, which some call tithe and some produce-tax. The second is that from special products; in one place gold, in another silver, in another copper, and so on. Third in importance is revenue from markets, and fourth that which arises from taxes on land and on sales. In the fifth place we have revenue from cattle, called tithe or first-fruits; and in the sixth, revenue from other sources, which we term poll-tax, or tax on industry." (Aristotle, *Oec.* 2.1). There are authors who attribute this description to the Seleucid rule. Manning, *The Last Pharaohs: Egypt Under the Ptolemies, 305–30 BC*, 123.

119. Bright, *A History of Israel*, 367–68.

120. For an acid liberal economic critique of Nehemiah's actions, see Grabbe, "Yehud: A History of the Persian Province of Judah," 302–4.

> Moreover, from the time that I was appointed to be their governor in the land of Judah, from the twentieth year to the thirty-second year of Artaxerxes the king, twelve years, neither I nor my brothers ate the food allowance of the governor. The former governors who were before me laid heavy burdens on the people and took from them for their daily ration forty shekels of silver. Even their servants lorded it over the people. But I did not do so, because of the fear of God. (Neh 5:14–15).

Therefore, although promoting freedom for local cultures and religion, the Persian Empire had a heavy burden of taxes over its client states. Specifically, in Judah, this burden was made heavier still because of the taxes of the local governor, the tax for the temple (Neh 10:32) and the tithe of all produce (Neh 10:35–39). All these tributes and taxes, according to the prophets, would not be a problem if the people were faithful to their Lord. But that was not the case in the following years. Thus, instead of freedom and lavishness of the produce of the land, at the end of the Old Testament, although God's people are in their land, there is still oppression and they are slaves in their own land (Neh 9:36).

Another aspect into which Von Rad sheds some light is the tension between God as the one who gives land and as the one who is the ultimate owner of it.[121] How can these two apparently antagonist ideas coexist? Von Rad attributes this to the existence of two independent traditions in the Hexateuch. The older tradition, according to him, presents land as a promised gift and is related to the epoch of the patriarchs. The other tradition presents land as Yahweh's possession and brings with it many cultic laws to recognize that.[122]

---

121. Chris Wright defends that there are three main points in the Theology of Land of the Old Testament: "1. The land was given By Yahweh in fulfillment of the promise to the fathers – the historical tradition; 2. Nevertheless, Yahweh was still the ultimate owner of the land, a fact which was to be acknowledged in various legal and cultic ways; 3. Israel and its land were bound together in what Davies aptly describes as an 'umbilical' relationship, that is, a relationship determined by the nature of Israel's own relationship with God." Wright, *God's People in God's Land*, 9. Davies also acknowledge these two concepts as peculiar to Israel's view of land. Davies, *The Gospel and the Land*, 15, 24.

122. "It is now quite clear that this notion is of a totally different order from that of the promise of the land to the early patriarchs. It is a wholly cultic notion, as compared with the other which may be characterized as the historical conception." Von Rad, "The Promised Land and Yahweh's Land in the Hexateuch," 88.

Praising von Rad for his perspicacity in finding these two themes, Wright shows how the two themes presuppose each other and have the covenant as their common basis.[123] God cannot give a land that was not his in first place, and the cultic laws do not acknowledge only that God is the ultimate proprietor of the land, but are also a token of gratitude because he gave this land as inheritance to Israel.

Through what was demonstrated in the last portion of this chapter, it becomes clear therefore, that the 'little tradition', which helped the people to carry on amidst oppression and sometimes also rebellion, was based in the writings of the Old Testament. This tradition included the principle that God is the ultimate owner and giver of land. He is the one who defines the ethics that landowners are to pursue in their dealings with neighbors, brothers, workers and slaves.

4.5 Final Remarks

The main thrust of this chapter was demonstrating the theological basis over with Luke proposes an ethics related to land that is influenced by the jubilee and other theological tenets of the Old Testament, especially the theological point that God is the owner of all earth and everything on it. The jubilee instructions were the central law regulating on land use and avoiding land abuse and people abuse related to land.

Thus, the first section of this chapter presented the importance of land in the Pentateuch. The second section presented the law of the jubilee and its posterior interpretations and applications. The third part has shown that as the people of God despised the jubilee justice they suffered the covenant consequences of the disobedience and were ultimately expelled from their land. Finally, the last part of the chapter dealt with the prophecies announcing restoration and justice. This future time announced in the prophecies was not fulfilled in the return from the Babylonian exile. Quite the contrary, many of the same injustices were perpetrated among the people returning from Babylon.

At the end of the Old Testament, therefore, in what concerns land justice, one has a frustration and an expectation of a time in which God will

---

123. Wright, *God's People in God's Land*, 10–13.

accomplish the transformation he announced through his prophets, including an eschatological jubilee promulgated by the one who God promise to bring on the scene, the Messiah.

CHAPTER 5

Land Justice in Luke-Acts

The preoccupation of the third evangelist with economic justice is well known and well researched.[1] The unique aim of this present dissertation is analyzing this concern with relation to the specific subject of land ownership. I propose here that against a background of profound social inequality and injustice, Luke demonstrates that the faith in Jesus Christ implicates also in a way of dealing with land that acknowledges God as the principal land owner and treats land according to God's will. This I am calling a "jubilee land ethics" since, on one hand, that is an appropriate name for the Old Testament teachings on the use of land and, on another, Luke himself centralizes the jubilee in his gospel, as it will be shown.

The path this dissertation made up to here was as follows. Chapter Two demonstrated that there was much land-related oppression in the Roman Empire. Most land belonged to the emperor and the ruling classes and they exploited lower classes by means of high taxation, exiguity of land, indebtation and slavery. Although there were popular movements requiring justice, they were silenced by a politics of bread and circus, patronage and imperial worship.

Chapter Three has shown that since the return from Babylon, Israel witnessed the formation of two privileged classes, the aristocracy and the hierocracy. Although the nation had been under different patron-nations, the

---

1. Just to mention a few studies, see: Donahue, "Two Decades of Research on the Rich and the Poor in Luke-Acts," 129–44; Phillips, "Reading Issues of Wealth and Poverty in Luke-Acts"; Metzger, *Consumption and Wealth in Luke's Travel Narrative*; Hays, *Luke's Wealth Ethics: A Study in Their Coherence and Character*; Hays, *Renouncing Everything*; Rodriguez, *The Liberating Mission of Jesus*.

constant, with the exception of a small interim in the Maccabean state, was one in which these two classes were favored by amassing land and wealth while the people were burdened with high taxes, military service, joblessness, debt and unjust contracts of tenancy. Jesus developed his ministry and Luke wrote his gospel under this kind of circumstance. The contention of the present chapter is showing that Luke proposes in the jubilee land ethics a solution for this abuse, at least among the community of faith.

The previous chapter, the fourth, presented the teaching of the Old Testament on land as well as the detours Israel took from these teachings. The OT teaches that God is the ultimate proprietor of all land and even of the whole earth. Thus, he is the one who gives land to whom he pleases and establishes how this land is to be used. He wants his people to use land not in a selfish way, but with concern for their neighbors, brothers and even foreigners. Also, the people of God were not supposed to use slavery, debts and *latifundia* as a way to perpetuate their power over the land. Thus, the Sabbath year and the jubilee year were created to reset the land, debt and slavery situation on the nation, giving an opportunity of a fresh start for the next generation of a poor family. The fourth chapter demonstrated also how the literature of the second temple applied the jubilee legislation in an eschatological and Messianic way. The fourth chapter also demonstrated that since the beginning of the monarchy, this ethics was perverted and this process was almost continuous up to the Babylonian captivity.

Now, in this chapter, I begin to establish the primary claim of this dissertation, namely, that Luke writes his work, in part, to subvert the oppressive socio-economical structures of his time, at least among those who decide to follow Jesus's teachings. Luke's answer to this problem is the presentation of an ethics informed by OT and Jewish traditions of jubilee in which Yahweh is the supreme landowner, and thereby the one who has the right to bless those who use the land for justice and to curse those who keep and use land as if it were only their own.

With this objective, this chapter will first present a study of Luke 4:14–30, presenting the reasons it is considered a programmatic text. I will show also that one of the programmatic aspects of Luke 4:16–30 is the jubilee theme that appears in the text and is spread throughout Luke-Acts. Then, exploring different texts of the gospel of Luke, I will show that, following the teaching of the Old Testament, Luke presents God as the ultimate owner of land.

After that, this chapter will explore texts in which Luke proposes that those who share land are blessed and, alternatively, those who treat the land as if it belongs exclusively to themselves are cursed. This chapter also demonstrates that Luke presents Jesus as identifying himself with the landless. Finally, the last part of Chapter Five will show that the book of Acts advances the same land ethics found in the Gospel of Luke. By following the program stated above, the goal of this central chapter is to demonstrate the existence and importance of a jubilee informed land ethics in Luke-Acts.

5.1 The Centrality of the Jubilee in Luke

The present section bases itself on a syllogistic reasoning. The premises are, first, that the OT institution of the jubilee is fundamental to Luke. The second premise is that land was central to the OT jubilee, as I have demonstrated in the last chapter. Thus, if these two premises are right, one can expect that land is also an important subject in Luke-Acts. This section aims to demonstrate the importance of the concept of jubilee to the gospel of Luke, analyzing one of its most important, programmatic pericopes, Luke 4:14–30.

5.1.1 The Programmatic Character of Luke 4:16–30

That Luke 4:16–30 is a programmatic text is a consensus among Lukan scholars.[2] The text, also called a messianic manifesto, is programmatic in the sense that it works as the annunciation of the agenda or plan of Jesus's ministry.[3] The context, themes and consequences of this announcement work as a paradigm for the rest of the gospel.

The writer himself gives a special treatment to this passage, giving to this event much more importance than Mark and Matthew, and making it the first passage in Jesus's ministry that he writes with "scenic detail".[4] The pas-

---

2. "This scene is programmatic for Luke-Acts, as one grows almost tired of reading in the literature on the passage." Sanders, *The Jews in Luke-Acts*, 165. "It has become axiomatic in studies of Luke that Jesus' sermon at Nazareth (4:16–30) is programmatic for our understanding of the mission of Jesus in the Gospel." Green, *The Theology of the Gospel of Luke*, 76. "In fact, this account is one of Luke's most detailed events and contains many themes that he will continue to develop. Luke 4:16–30 is a representative sample of Jesus' ministry, a paradigm for his ministry." Bock, *Luke 1:1–9:50*, 406.

3. Hofheinz, "Good News to the Poor," 42.

4. Tannehill, *The Narrative Unity of Luke-Acts*, 61.

sage also reports Jesus's first spoken words in the gospel.[5] The themes this passage brings up are expanded throughout the gospel. These themes are: (1) the centrality of the Holy Spirit for ministry; (2) the ministry toward the poor; (3) the revelation of the identity of Jesus; (4) the importance of the Old Testament as Scripture; (5) the mission toward the gentiles; (6) the reversal of the kingdom; and (7) the acceptance of Jesus by some and the rejection of Jesus by others, especially the leaders of Israel.

To each of these we turn briefly in order to prove the programmatic character of Luke 4:16–30. First, the importance of the Holy Spirit to Luke-Acts can hardly be overstated.[6] One finds 20 references to the Holy Spirit in the gospel and 60 in Acts.[7] The Spirit is intimately connected to Jesus birth (Luke 1:35) and ministry (3:22, 4:1, 18; 10:21). He fills people already in the gospel (1:15, 17, 41, 67, 2:25–27). In the gospel, the Holy Spirit is also the one with whom Jesus will baptize people (3:16) and the gift and promise of the Father (11:13, 24:49). In the book of Acts, Luke presents the fulfillment of all these promises and the Holy Spirit is yet more in the spotlight.[8]

Luke 4:16–30 is also a programmatic text, second, because of the emphasis it places on the poor. The poor is not just the economically poor, but also a category that encompasses different kinds of marginalized people.[9] The breadth of the subject throughout the gospel makes it one of the most

---

5. Green, *The Theology of the Gospel of Luke*, 76.

6. "The Holy Spirit plays a major role in God's program and in Luke-Acts. . . . The Spirit is a driving force for Luke's portrait of salvation, energizing and guiding events both in Luke and especially in Acts." Bock, *A Theology of Luke and Acts*, 211–12. "The Spirit is a major uniting theme within his double-volumed work, indeed nothing less than the driving force of the "salvation history" and mission that Luke describes." Turner, "The Work of the Holy Spirit in Luke-Acts," 146–53.

7. These references can be found in Luke 1:15, 17, 35, 41, 67, 80; 2:25, 26, 27; 3:16, 22; 4:1 (2x), 14, 18; 10:21; 11:13; 12:10, 12; 24:49 and Acts 1:2, 4, 5, 8, 16; 2:4 (2x), 17, 18, 33, 38–39; 4:8, 25, 31; 5:3, 9, 32; 6:3, 5, 10; 7:51, 55; 8:15, 17, 18, 19, 20, 29, 39; 9:17, 31; 10:19, 38, 44, 45, 47; 11:12, 15, 16, 17, 24, 28; 13:2, 4, 9, 52; 15:8, 28; 16:6, 7; 19:2 (2x), 6, 21; 20:22, 23, 28; 21:4, 11; 28:25.

8. For one of the most important books on the role of the Holy Sprit in Luke-Acts, see Dunn, *Baptism in the Holy Spirit*.

9. The phrase in Luke 4 'to bring good news to the poor' refers to the new socio economic order, which includes transformation of the situation of all indebted, landless, enslaved, and unemployed. . . . The poor were all those who were at the bottom of the economic scale suffering for survival. They were the members of the society that suffered exploitation by the rich. The phrase 'to preach or to bring good news to the poor' refers actually to all those in desperate need'. All of them will act in response openly and honestly to Jesus". Gunjević, *Jubilee in the Bible*.

important for Luke.[10] Many studies have shown the fundamental importance of this subject in Luke-Acts and the present dissertation resides in this field.

Thirdly, another subject presented in Luke 4 and clearly developed in the whole gospel is the revelation of the identity of Jesus.[11] Jesus is evidently the center of the gospel of Luke and the center of Acts of the Apostles. "Luke's presentation of Jesus begins mostly in regal and prophetic terms and ends with an emphasis on his lordship and the authority of his name in Acts."[12] Gunjevic, speaks about this aspect in reference to the jubilee and says:

> The gift of the spirit of the Lord, the anointment of the Messiah and the year of the Lord's favour create the unity in Luke's quotation of Is 61. This unity clarifies that without the king there can be no kingdom. The Messiah, who is the Anointed One, brings that kingdom and salvation. The anointing in Is 61 and Luke 4 refer to the coming of the Lord's salvation. Jesus interconnects himself with the promise of the coming Messiah who will bring the good news, free the needy and heal the broken-hearted.[13]

The fourth element that characterizes Luke 4:16–30 as programmatic is the use of the Old Testament Scripture. In this text, Jesus quotes an edited version of Isaiah 61:1–2 and Isaiah 58:6. Isaiah, by its turn, refers to the OT jubilee of Leviticus 25. Jesus affirms that the Scriptures he just quoted were being fulfilled as they were hearing and some hearers start to question the origins of Jesus.[14] Thus, facing their doubts, Jesus refers to two stories of the Old

---

10. All these texts somehow deal with the subject of poverty and wealth in the gospel of Luke: 1:46–55; 3:1–14; 4:16–30; 5:1–11, 27–29; 6:20–26; 7:18–35, 36–50; 8:1–3; 9:1–6; 10:1–12, 25–37; 11:37–44; 12:13–21, 22–34, 35–48, 54–59; 14:7–14, 15–24; 15:8–10, 11–32; 16:1–13, 14–17, 19–31; 18:18–30; 19:1–10, 11–27; 20:9–18, 19–26; 21:1–4; 22:3–6.

11. O'Toole, *Luke's presentation of Jesus: A Christology*, 118–20. A classic study in this sense is, Malherbe, "Christology in Luke-Acts 2," 115–27.

12. Bock, *A Theology of Luke and Acts*, 177. Later, Bock affirms: "Jesus is bound inseparably to God's program as Messiah-Servant-Prophet-Son of Man-Savior, and above all as Lord. Luke presents Jesus as a divinely vindicated figure who now rules alongside God in a way that enables Jesus to mediate salvation." (209)

13. Gunjević, *Jubilee in the Bible*.

14. "When Christ said that *this day is this prophecy fulfilled in your ears*, He did not mean that the prophecy was exhausted on that particular day, but rather that the time had now come of which Isaiah spoke, and that the prophecy would be fulfilled throughout the course of the Church upon earth. The passage brings to the fore the great work of redemption that the Messiah accomplished, and the proclamation of the Gospel that He and the disciples under His authority carry out." Young, *The Book of Isaiah*, 460.

Testament: Elijah helping the gentile widow of Zarephtah (1 Kings 17) and Elisha healing the gentile Naaman (2 Kings 5). This heavy use of Scripture is an important characteristic of Luke-Acts. Müller speaks about this centrality of Scriptures in Luke-Acts: "To a much higher degree than in the other two synoptic gospels the Jewish Bible plays an important role for the theological argumentation in the Lukan writings. In Mark and Matthew, it was fundamentally the faith in Jesus that threw light over Scripture. But in the Lukan writings the Jewish Bible becomes more important in itself."[15]

Fifthly, Luke 4:16–30 makes clear that the gospel Jesus brings will encompass not only Jews, but also gentiles. This is not completely clear during Jesus's ministry, but becomes clearer as one reads the whole work, Luke-Acts. Luke 4 foreshadows this aspect by the reference to the ministries of Elisha and Elijah.[16] Other texts in the gospel that foreshadows the ministry toward the gentiles are Luke 2:32; 18:32.

The sixth programmatic aspect in Luke 4 is the reversal. Luke 4:16–30 presents a reversal that characterizes the kingdom Jesus came to establish.[17] The salvation he brings is to those who are poor, captives, blind, and oppressed (Luke 4:18–19). The kingdom of God is of a kind in which "some are last who will be first, and some are first who will be last." (Luke 13:30). That is why Mary sings in her song that God: "has brought down the mighty from their thrones and exalted those of humble estate; he has filled the hungry with

---

15. Müller, "The Reception of the Old Testament and in Matthew and Luke-Acts," 322. Speaking about the importance of the Jewish Scripture for Luke, Jervell also says: "Everything in the Old Testament is Scripture, everything is important, everything is binding. Luke is the fundamentalist within the New Testament. There is in Luke-Acts no criticism whatsoever of Scripture, such as we find in Matthew and Mark, not to mention Paul. Not even the idea that the Scriptures as a whole contain the promises whereas the gospel gives the fulfillment – which puts the Scriptures in a secondary position compared to the gospel – is present. Jervell, *The Theology of the Acts of the Apostles*, 61. On the use of the Old Testament in Luke, see also Litwak, *Echoes of Scripture in Luke-Acts*.

16. Siker, "'First to the Gentiles,'" 73–90.

17. "To affirm the world does not mean to approve all human conduct or structures. The prophetic imagery of Luke-Acts is joined to a prophetic critique of human religious expectations and social values. In the "visitation of the people" by the Prophet, a great reversal is proclaimed and enacted". Johnson, *The Gospel of Luke*, 22. "Within this account we find several important Lukan theological emphases. One that is dealt with at length is the theme of reversal. The humble are exalted, and the arrogant are brought low. . . . Clearly Luke saw in Jesus' coming a great reversal of the world's value system." Stein, *Luke*, 94. "One of the pervasive themes of Luke's Gospel is eschatological reversal, especially involving rich and poor." Goodacre, *Thomas and the Gospels*, 89. "More than either Mark or Matthew, Luke portrays the final judgment as a time of eschatological reversal." Olmstead, "Judgement," 461.

good things, and the rich he has sent away empty" (Luke 1:52–53). Also, in the kingdom of God, "everyone who exalts himself will be humbled, and he who humbles himself will be exalted" (Luke 14:11).[18]

Thus, despite the powers and powerful of this world (Luke 1:5; 2:1–3; 3:1–2, 14, 19–20; 4:5–6; 5:14; 9:7–9; 13:31; 20:21–26; 23:2, 7–12; Acts 4:25–28; 12:1–23; 17:6–7; 23–27:1), Luke shows that the focus of God's action and the people he uses are the barren (Luke 1:7, 25), women (1:24–25; 1:26–38; 7:11–17, 36–50; 8:1–3, 43; 10:38–42; 13:10–13; 24:10); shepherds (2:8), homeless (3:2; 9:58), poor (4:18–19; 6:20–24; 16:19–31; 18:24–25), demon possessed (4:31–37; 8:26–34), fishermen (5:8–11), physically ill (5:12–26; 14:1–6, 21), publicans (5:27–32; 18:9–14; 19:1–10), sinners (5:32; 15:1, 10); Samaritans (10:25–37; 17:15; Acts 8:25); small ones (10:21; 12:32), children (18:15–17), and gentiles (Acts). This is the great reversal of the kingdom, foreshadowed in Luke 4:16–30 and presented throughout the gospel and Acts.[19]

The last characteristic that makes Luke 4:16–30 a programmatic text relates to the theme of rejection. The rejection appears unexpectedly. Deeply impressed with Jesus's words, those men at the Synagogue argued: "Is not this Joseph's son?" Nolland comments that the force of this question is unclear. In the flow of the text and comparing it with Mark 6:3, it seems to imply criticism to Jesus. "A suggestion of illegitimacy (cf. John 8:41) or a contempt based on familiarity and/or humble origins is possible."[20] Bovon affirms that nothing points to rejection in the question of the men present at the Synagogue, to the contrary, "The audience has only gone halfway toward faith (v. 22), and has not completed the decisive second half. For this reason, Jesus puts them to test."[21] Hendriksen, on another hand, is of the opinion that the question needs to be read against the affirmation of Jesus that he was the fulfillment of the prophecy of Isaiah 61:1–2. He says that Jesus's hearers liked to hear that the prophecy was being fulfilled in their time, but their familiarity with Jesus caused them to doubt and despise him.[22] Garland has another proposal,

---

18. See more on this theme of reversal in Dennison, "The Eschatological Jubilee: Luke 4:16–30," 31–36.

19. For a more complete treatment of the theme reversal on Luke and Acts, see York, *The Last Shall Be First the Rhetoric of Reversal in Luke*.

20. Nolland, *Luke*, 199.

21. Bovon and Koester, *Luke 1*, 155.

22. Hendriksen, *Exposition of the Gospel According to Luke*, 256.

"Implicit with this recognition is the expectation that they will reap special favors from him".[23] Considering that θαυμάζω does not always convey an implicit approval, and the flow of the narrative, it seems to me that Nolland and Hendriksen are correct in affirming that this phrase implied some form of criticism against Jesus in the sense that they were doubting that he was the one he affirmed to be.[24]

Jesus's response to them could hardly be harsher.[25] He quotes two proverbs: 1) "Physician, heal yourself" and 2) "no prophet is acceptable in his hometown" and gives them the example of Elijah and Elisha as prophets who ministered to gentiles instead of Israelites. Using the concept of inter-narrativity, when an author alludes to a personage/episode/context alluded to in various texts, the whole story of Elijah-Elisha is used by Luke to form an image of Jesus in the reader, not in a precise way, rather in an elusive one.[26] The three images Huddleston chooses to present this connection between Jesus and Elijah-Elisha is the performing of miracles, the confrontation with rulers and the anointing of successors.[27] Our text has its own set of comparisons: Elijah-Elisha were prophets, both had a special measure of the Spirit of God, their message was rejected by Israel, they announced salvation and damnation, and they directed their ministry to outsiders (interestingly, economically rich people).

Prompted by Jesus's words, "all in the synagogue were filled with wrath" and they made an attempt against Jesus's life, taking the rejection to the ultimate level of assassinate. They expelled (ἐξέβαλον) Jesus from the city and led (ἤγαγον) him to the brow of the hill with the aim of throwing him

---

23. Garland, *Luke*, 202. "Jesus splashes cold water on their eager anticipation that his local family connections will mean special advantages for them. There will be no nepotism in the reign of God". (203)

24. "In summary, the congregation testified to the amazing wisdom of Jesus, but at the same time expressed astonishment and suspicion of his message as well as his messianic claim to be the eschatological fulfillment of Isaiah 61:1–2. He had proclaimed the year of the Lord's favor, but not the day of vengeance. Both Jesus and his message were rejected." Hertig, "The Jubilee Mission of Jesus in the Gospel of Luke," 170.

25. "Jesus himself, by virtue of this prophetic message, will provoke conflict." Carroll, *Luke*, 113.

26. "By comparing Jesus to Elijah and Elisha, perhaps Luke suggests to his audiences (even if unwittingly) that Jesus too is strange, surprising, and confounding." Huddleston, "What Would Elijah and Elisha Do?," 280.

27. Huddleston, "What Would Elijah and Elisha Do?"

down (κατακρημνίσαι) the cliff. Somehow, Jesus passed through (διελθὼν) the middle of them and went away (ἐπορεύετο).

Luke shows right in the first sermon Jesus preaches, that his preaching and person would face fierce rejection and indeed, that is what one finds throughout Luke and Acts. Both Jesus and his followers face persecution, abuse and sometimes death. As Simeon had adverted (Luke 2:34), Jesus was repeatedly a sign of refusal and opposition (σημεῖον ἀντιλεγόμενον), being persecuted, and betrayed to the death.[28]

Luke makes clear the theme of rejection with other personages also. John the Baptist faced persecution, imprisonment and martyrdom (3:18–20; 9:7–9). Jesus's disciples and apostles faces opposition and rejection during the ministry of Jesus and after his resurrection (Luke 5:30, 33; 6:2; 10:10–11; 21:15–17; Acts 2:13; 4:1–3, 29; 5:17–42; 8:1–3; 9:1–2; 12:1–6), especially Peter (Acts 4:7, 17–18; 11:2–3; 12:3). Other disciples who were persecuted and rejected were Stephen (Acts 6:8–60), James, the brother of John (Acts 12:2), Jasom (Acts 17:5–9), Sosthenes (18:17) and, especially Paul (Acts 9:23–25, 29–30; 13:45–46, 50; 14:2–6, 19; 16:19–24, 39; 17:5, 13, 32; 18:6, 12; 19:9, 23–31, 20:22–25; 21:11–13; 27–40; 22–28).

It is clear by these six features, therefore, that Luke 4:16–30 is indeed a programmatic text, setting the stage for many of the themes that Luke will develop in both volumes of his work. Thus, just by way of revision, the six characteristics that appear in Luke 4 which are developed throughout Luke-Acts are (1) the centrality of the Holy Spirit for ministry; (2) the ministry toward the poor; (3) the revelation of the identity of Jesus; (4) the use of the Old Testament as Scripture; (5) The mission toward the gentiles; (6) The reversal of the kingdom; and (7) The rejection of Jesus and his followers by many Jewish leaders. The jubilee is an eighth theme that is present in Luke 4:16–30, which is also programmatic, but due to its importance to the present dissertation, we will deal with it in a separate section.

---

28. The following list presents the texts in Luke-Acts in which one finds Jesus being rejected: Luke 5:21; 6:7, 11; 7:19–20, 23, 34, 39, 49; 8:37; 8:53; 9:22, 44, 53, 58; 10:13–16, 25, 40; 11:15–16, 38, 53–54; 12:9, 49–53; 13:14, 31–33; 14:1; 15:1–2; 16:14; 17:17–18; 25; 18:31–33; 19:7; 39, 44, 47; 20:1–2, 14–17; 19–26; 22:2–6, 22–23, 34, 47–71; 23:1–56; Acts 1:16–17; 4:25–28.

5.1.2 The Fundamental Importance of the Jubilee in Luke 4 and throughout Luke-Acts

In Chapter One of this dissertation (topic 1.2.1), I presented a review of literature dealing with application or appropriation of the jubilee theme in Luke-Acts. I presented there three ways in which scholars have dealt with the theme. Some scholars defend a historic reading as if Luke presents Jesus announcing the inauguration of a literal jubilee. Other academics affirm that Luke presents an eschatological view on the jubilee. A third group of researchers contends that Luke uses the jubilee just as an adequate symbol for representing Jesus's ministry. This dissertation finds itself in the second group of those who sees Luke developing the jubilee theme as a symbol of an eschatological reality inaugurated by Jesus ministry.

The last chapter has demonstrated that the jubilee in the Pentateuch had both theological and social reasons and consequences. The jubilee itself was a consequence of the Yom Kippur; it was a sabbatical year of rest in the Lord; and it existed to demonstrate in a very practical way that all land belongs to Yahweh and the Israelites should use it according to his will. In the prophets and in the Second Temple literature, the jubilee gained eschatological and Messianic overtones. In Isaiah and in 11QMelch, for example, the jubilee is presented as a future time of spiritual and economical deliverance.

I also demonstrated in chapter 4, that some of the most important words in the LXX for the jubilee are λύτρωσις, σημασία, πεντηκοστός, σάββατον, κτῆσις, and ἄφεσις. Of these, the most important concept is the last one, which appears in almost all texts of the LXX that refer to the Year of Jubilee (Leviticus 27:16–27; Numbers 36:4; Isaiah 61:1–11; Jeremiah 34:8–22; Ezekiel 46:16–17; exceptions: Isaiah 49:5–13; Isaiah 63:1–6). Another important concept for the jubilee theology in Luke is the Isaianic expression ἐνιαυτὸν κυρίου δεκτὸν (Isa 61:1–2).

In this section, I will demonstrate that many of these terms are very important in Luke-Acts. After analyzing the occurrence of jubilaic themes scattered in the OT passages in Luke 4:18–19, Smith correctly says that "Luke's intensification of a weak linguistic connection between these passages relationship suggests that, whatever the original intertextual relationship among them may have been, Luke likely understood them together as referring to a climactic eschatological release analogous to the Jubilee."[29]

The question that drives this section, therefore, is if it is possible to speak about a jubilee theology in Luke springing from Luke 4 throughout the Gospel and Acts? This section will contend that this is exactly the case. In Luke 4 Jesus quotes the important jubilaic text of Isaiah 61 and says that it was fulfilled in the ears of those present at Nazareth's synagogue. This is even more important, because Luke is the only synoptic writer to quote this passage in this event (cf. Mark 6:1–6 and Matthew 13:54–58). Commentators diverge about the jubilee background of this text. Bock, Marshall, and Green, for example, agree that the jubilee is the context behind Jesus's announcement.[30] Tannehill, Johnson and Stein on another hand are against such a reading.[31]

---

29. David Andrew Smith, "'No Poor Among Them,'" 148.

30. "The deliverance imagery parallels the description of the Jubilee year (Lev 25: 8–17), when debts were canceled and slaves were freed every fiftieth year. It is a picture of forgiveness and spiritual liberation, which is at the center of Jesus' message." Bock, *Luke 1:1–9:50*, 406. J. D. Yoder is responsible for popularizing the hypothesis that in Luke 4:16–30 Jesus was proclaiming a "year of jubilee" with social and economic as well as spiritual consequences.[32] An exegetical foundation for this hypothesis is offered by R. B. Sloan who stresses that the jubilee concept is *primarily* religious; but while the presence of the motif cannot be doubted, my feeling is that it is much less prominent and decisive in Luke. than Sloan suggests. Marshall, *Luke: Historian & Theologian*, 233–34. "The third major theological feature of Jesus' missionary program grows out of a further way of construing "release" in the Lukan narrative—namely, as "release from debts" (cf. 11:4). This draws our attention to Jubilee legislation (Leviticus 25) - the freeing of slaves, the cancellation of debts, the fallowing of the land, and the returning of all land to its original distribution under Moses. The jubilary theme is most evident in 4:18–19 by the repeated use of "release" (cf., e.g., "the year of release" – Lev 25:10) and the phrase, "the year of the Lord's favor," borrowed from Isa 61:2. It is now widely recognized that Isaiah 58 and 61 develop jubilary themes, describing the coming redemption from exile and captivity in the eschatological language of jubilary release. Other texts follow a similar interpretive maneuver, moving away from more literal applications of Jubilee legislation to the employment of jubilary themes to signify the eschatological deliverance of God (with its profound social implications). This interpretive tradition encourages a reading of Luke 4:18–19 as the announcement of the eschatological epoch of salvation, the time of God's gracious visitation, with Jesus himself presented as its anointed herald." Green, *The Gospel of Luke*, 212. At the same time, in the same page, in footnote, Green says: "It seems more prudent, then, to speak of 4:18–19 as encouraging our reading of Jesus' mission against the backdrop of the theme of the eschatological jubilee, but not our concluding that Luke thus develops or is controlled by a theology of Jubilee."

31. "While it seems clear that Isa 61:1–2 develops themes from the Jubilee year, it is not so clear that the author of Luke-Acts was aware of the connection between this passage and the law of Jubilee. This remains a possibility but has not yet been proved.[49] This is not to deny that the social concern expressed in the Jubilee law is also present in Luke, for the "good news to the poor" does reflect a concern for economic justice, as Jesus' later teaching will make clear." Tannehill, *The Narrative Unity of Luke-Acts*, 1:68. "The language of "release" and "year of the Lord" has suggested to some readers that Luke wishes to portray Jesus as announcing

However, we have already seen in the last chapter that Isaiah 61 refers to the jubilee. Thus, affirming that Jesus or Luke did not see this connection is attributing a short view to them in matters of Scripture, while they show otherwise throughout Luke-Acts. Also, the fact that the jubilee had a messianic tone since the biblical prophets and especially in the Second Temple literature, as last chapter demonstrated, would make such a reading adequate to the historical context of Luke.

Besides using Isaiah 61, a text with a clear reference to the jubilee, the Lucan Jesus edits the quotation of Isaiah 61 in order to include the LXX of Isaiah 58:6, ἀπόστελλε τεθραυσμένους ἐν ἀφέσει [Isa 58:6]. By doing that, the text of Isaiah 61, which includes only one reference to ἄφεσις, now has two references to this central concept of the jubilee and also presents an echo of Deut 15:12.[32] In sum, the edited version of Jesus is yet more "jubilaic" than the original version of Isa 61.[33]

What kind of ἄφεσις is Jesus announcing in Luke 4? In accordance with the prophetic vision of the jubilee and with the Second Temple Judaism's perspectives on the matter, Jesus announces a broader release than that of the Torah jubilee, including release (ἄφεσις) for the captives (αἰχμαλώτοις) and oppressed (τεθραυσμένους), good news to the poor (εὐαγγελίσασθαι πτωχοῖς),

---

the eschatological Jubilee year, when all debts would be remitted and all slaves manumitted (cf. Lev 25:10–18). This is possible, but the Gospel does not offer further support for this being Luke's point. Rather than picturing Jesus' work in terms of a political or economic reform, Luke portrays his liberating work in terms of personal exorcisms, healings, and the teaching of the people. The radical character of this mission is specified above all by its being offered to and accepted by those who were the outcasts of the people." Johnson, *The Gospel of Luke*, 81. "Although Isa 61:1–2 develops certain themes from the concept of the Jubilee Year (cf. Lev 25:8–55), Luke did not seem to have been thinking of this here." Stein, *Luke*, 157.

32. "The insertion by Luke of Isa 58:6 into Isa 61:1–2 introduces an additional echo from Deut 15:12, in which instructions are given for the Sabbath year release of those sold into debtor slavery." Smith, "'No Poor Among Them': Sabbath and Jubilee Years in Lukan Social Ethics," 147.

33. "The inclusion of the clause ἀπόστελλε τεθραυσμένους ἐν ἀφέσει from Isa 58:6, however, needs further examination. The connection with Isa 61:1–2 seems to be made with ἄφεσις, a word that appears in both Isa 58:6 and 61:1. The clause from Isa 58:6 is identical with the LXX reading except for the change from the imperative ἀπόστελλε to the aorist infinitive ἀποστεῖλαι to conform to the other subordinate infinitives. The connection of the two Isaianic passages through the word ἄφεσις should be understood as an example of "deliberate exegesis". The clause may have been inserted to emphasize the idea of release and therefore the connection with the Jubilee of Isa 61:1. more importantly, this insertion highlights Jesus not only as one who proclaims the arrival of the Jubilee, but also as the one who is appointed to accomplish the inbreaking of the new era through his power to bring about ἄφεσις. Pao, *Acts and the Isaianic New Exodus*, 73.

and recovery of sight to the blind (τυφλοῖς ἀνάβλεψιν). As I will show below, this ἄφεσις is not just socio-economic, but is mainly from sin.

Thus, "Jesus' claim to 'fulfill' Isaiah 61 must be seen as a claim to inaugurate the eschatological Jubilee of God's people, the time when their freedom from captivity and oppression would be permanent."[34] Sloan correctly sees in the expression κηρύξαι αἰχμαλώτοις ἄφεσιν (to proclaim liberty to the captives), a reference to the year of jubilee, with both spiritual and practical implications.[35] The outcast whom Jesus came to free are those oppressed in the Roman-Jewish society. Throughout Luke-Acts, the poor are the landless, indebted, slaves, oppressed tenants, mendicants, lepers, gentiles and demon-possessed. All of those people enslaved by life can expect deliverance through Jesus.

Now, if the jubilee is such a central concept in the programmatic text of Luke 4:16–30, then it is correct to expect the appearance of the jubilee concept throughout the whole work of Luke-Acts.[36] And that is indeed the case.[37] Throughout Luke and Acts, one finds Jesus and the apostles releasing many people from their oppressions and especially from their sin. Of the 44 occurrences of ἀφίημι and ἄφεσις in Luke-Acts, 23 are related with releasing from sin (Luke 1:77; 3:3; 5:20, 21, 23, 24; 7:47 [2x], 48, 49; 11:4 [2x]; 12:10 [2x]; 17:3, 4; 23:34; 27:47; Acts 2:38; 5:31; 8:22; 10:43; 13:38; 26:18) and 3 with release from suffering (4:18, 39).

This shows that Luke is in line with the literature of Second Temple Judaism, especially with 11QMelch, that shows the releasing of the jubilee as being mainly a release from sin.[38] This release from sin is followed, how-

---

34. Bruno, "'Jesus Is Our Jubilee'. . . But How? The OT Background and Lukan Fulfillment of the Ethics of Jubilee," 98.

35. Sloan, "Jubilee," 396–97.

36. "In the foundational episode at the Nazareth synagogue in Luke 4, Jesus casts his entire ministry in terms of the prophetic hopes surrounding the Jubilee year—hopes which, at least in some Second Temple writings, included release from moral-spiritual debt and hopes that are clearly developed in this direction throughout the rest of Luke-Acts." Edward Sri, "Release from the Debt of Sin: Jesus' Jubilee Mission in the Gospel of Luke," 194.

37. "It is obvious that Luke has used some of the Old Testament themes that are connected to the year of Jubilee. The themes such as God's kingdom, the poor, the good news, release to the captives, recovery of sight to the blind, freedom for the oppressed, need to be interpreted and understood in correlation with Luke 4:16–21 and its eschatological vision for Jubilee." Gunjević, *Jubilee in the Bible*, 182.

38. "Finally, and most significantly, 11QMelchizedek spiritualizes the significance of the Jubilee by envisioning a release from moral or spiritual debt. The priestly, kingly Melchizedek

ever, by the release of other kind of oppressions.³⁹ As Sloan says: "This word (ἄφεσις) represents doubtless the primary theological and verbal connection, and reference to, the levitical proclamation of Jubilee."⁴⁰

At the same time, without necessarily using the concept of releasing, Luke shows Jesus and his apostles freeing many people from demonic oppression (Luke 4:31–37; 4:41; 6:18; 7:21–22; 8:1–2; 8:26–34; 9:37–43; 10:17; 11:14–26; 13:10–17; Acts 5:12–16; 8:6–7; 16:16–18; 19:11–12), illnesses (Luke 4:38–39; 4:40; 5:12–16; 5:17–26; 6:6–11; 6:7–19; 7:1–10; 7:21–22; 8:1–2; 8:42–48; 9:6; 14:1–6; 17:11–19; Acts 3:1–9; 5:12–16; 8:6–7; 9:32–35; 14:8–18; 19:11–12; 28:7–10), blindness (Luke 7:21–22; 18:35–43) and even death (Luke 6:11–17; 8:40–56; Acts 9:36–43; 20:9–10). Thus, the jubilaic liberationist ministry announced by Jesus in Luke 4 is being described in the following pages of the double work of Luke.

It is also worth noting that throughout Jesus's ministry, these "releasings" are on one side comprised of his deeds and on the other side, his proclamation. The concepts of κηρύσσω and εὐαγγέλιον that are very important in the citation of Isaiah 61:1–2 are also important in Leviticus 25:10 and Deuteronomy 15:2, 12. Also, they appear scattered in Luke-Acts, many times in relation with Jesus's ministry of releasing people from their sins and oppressions.⁴¹

Another word family that is very important in the LXX of Leviticus 25 and is used in Luke-Acts is linked to the root λύτρον (λυτρόω and λύτρωσις), meaning "to redeem or to liberate". These words appear 13 times in Leviticus 25. The concept appears also in Isaiah 63:1–6, qualifying the jubilee as the ἐνιαυτὸς λυτρώσεως (the year of redemption). The gospel of Luke is the New

---

figure is expected to come 'to free them from [the debt of] all their iniquities [11QMelch, line 6].'" Sri, "Release from the Debt of Sin," 190.

39. Willoughby is wrong when affirms that the jubilee deliverance presented in Luke is more Isaianic then similar to that of 11QMelch. It is similar to both. See Willoughby, "The Concept of Jubilee and Luke 4:18–30," 53.

40. Sloan, *The Favorable Year of the Lord*, 36–37.

41. Occurrences of the root ευαγγελιον: Luke 1:19; 2:10; 3:18; 4:18, 43; 7:22; 8:1; 9:6; 16:16; 20:1; Acts 5:42; 8:4, 12, 25, 35, 40; 10:36; 11:20; 13:32; 14:7, 15, 21; 15:7, 35; 16:10; 17:18; 20:24; 21:8. Occurrences of the root κηρυσσω Luke 3:3; 4:18, 19, 44; 8:1, 39; 9:2; 11:32; 12:3; 24:47; Acts 8:5; 9:20; 10:37, 42; 13:24; 15:21; 19:13; 20:25; 28:31. See a nice table with the similarities between the OT texts on the Jubilee and Luke 4:18–19 in Smith, "'No Poor Among Them': Sabbath and Jubilee Years in Lukan Social Ethics," 146.

Testament book with more occurrences of the word (5 in Luke-Acts from 20 occurrences in the NT).⁴²

The meaning of λύτρωσις in Luke relates with the history of redemption. God is the one redeeming his people (Luke 1:68). Anna speaks about Jesus to those who were waiting the redemption of Israel (Luke 2:38). The coming of the Son of Man is the sign that the redemption is near (Luke 21:28). The disciples of Emmaus were frustrated because they thought Jesus was the one who would redeem Israel (Luke 24:21), and Moses is presented by Stephen as the redeemer of the people (Acts 7:35). Jubilee and history of salvation are interwoven in these references.

Besides the emphasis in the concept of ἄφεσις, the presentation of many different types of liberation and the use of the concepts εὐαγγέλιον, κηρύσσω, and λύτρωσις, the emphasis in the Sabbath found in Luke-Acts is also an evidence of the presence of this jubilee theology throughout the gospel and Acts. In Leviticus, the sabbatical year is a kind of maximized Sabbath and the Jubilee is a maximized sabbatical year.⁴³ In the books of the Second Temple period, the jubilee is the epitome of many weeks of years, again, a maximized Sabbath. Thus, a great way to argue for the inauguration of the Messianic jubilaic era is showing the work of liberation happening especially in the Sabbath.

Luke is the gospel with more occurrences of the word for Sabbath.⁴⁴ Jesus's announcement of the arrival of the jubilee happens in a Sabbath (Luke 4:16) and immediately, his ministry is shown as happening mainly on Saturdays.⁴⁵

---

42. Ocurrences of λυτρον in the LXX of Lev 25: 25:25, 29 [2x], 30, 31, 32, 33, 48 [2x], 49 [3x], 54. Ocurrences in Luke-Acts: Luke 1:68; 2:38; 21:28; 24:21; and Acts 7:35.

43. The relation between the Sabbath and the Jubilee is missed in M. Daniel Carroll R., "La Cita de Isaias 58:6 En Lucas 4:18: Una Nueva Propuesta," 61–78.

44. The gospel has 20 occurrences of the root σαββατον and Acts has 10. For comparison, Luke and John have 13 each, Matthew has 11, 1 Corinthians, Colossians, and Hebrews have 1 occurrence each. The other books of the New Testament do not use the word.

45. "The fiftieth year, which came after every seven Sabbath years, was regarded as an intensified Sabbath year when the release of all citizens and the restitution of their patrimony were required. The Servant's proclamation is compared with the crying of the herald announcing this release to those in slavery because of debt. Now in Luke the salvation of the end time depicted in terms of Sabbath year of jubilee us seen to be inaugurated in the coming of Jesus; "Today this Scripture has been fulfilled in your hearing" (Luke 4:21). Both κηρύσσειν ("to proclaim") and εὐαγγελίζεται ("to preach good news") are used of Jesus' mission here. His herald's cry, like the trumpet of the priest in the Old Testament, announces the good news of jubilee. This mission is an eschatological event through which all in principle is fulfilled and where it only remains for this to work itself out. The great year of jubilee, the intensified Sabbath year of restoration and liberation, an institution that had never really functioned as intended,

Jesus preaches, teaches, and heals on Saturdays and defend the Sabbath as a day of releasing people from their sufferings against the pharisaic interpretation of strictly guarding the Sabbath (Luke 4:31; 6:1–5, 6–11; 13:10–17; 14:1–6).[46]

Saturday is also important in the ministry of the apostles in Acts (Acts 13:14, 42, 44; 16:13, 17:2; 18:4). Two other references of the word are especially important. Twice Luke uses the expression μιᾷ τῶν σαββάτων (first [day] of the week). This is a reference to the Sunday, but making it intimately related to Saturday (Luke 24:1; Acts 20:7). All these evidences point to the fact that Luke wanted to stress the Sabbath as a special day in which Jesus fulfilled his ministry of releasing, his jubilee ministry.[47]

In this section I am presenting evidences that Luke has a jubilee informed theology in his gospel. Another evidence is that in the LXX of Leviticus 25 there are two references to the jubilee year as the πεντηκοστὸν ἐνιαυτὸς (the year of Pentecost, Lev 25:10–11). Considering this fact, it is possible to guess that the inauguration of the church as a catholic community in τὴν ἡμέραν τῆς πεντηκοστῆς is not just a coincidence also, but part of the construction of this jubilee theme that Luke is developing throughout his work.[48] It is important to remember that there is a deep link between the inauguration of Jesus's ministry in Luke 4 and the inauguration of the ministry of the church in Acts 2, both being dependent of the anointing of the Holy Spirit.[49]

Besides these concepts spread through Luke-Acts, there are specific texts in Luke-Acts in which it is possible to find the jubilee theme behind the scenes. Sun-Jong Kim following a suggestion made by Fitzmyer affirms that the parable of the prodigal son illustrates the proclamation of the "Lord's year

---

now becomes a reality for all those who find salvation (in the fullest sense of the word) in Jesus the Messiah." Lincoln, "Sabbath, Rest, and Eschatology in the New Testament," 201–2.

46. See more on the relationship between the healings and the Shabbath in Smith, "'No Poor Among Them,'" 152.

47. "That is, the person of Jesus is now the embodiment of Jubilee, of sabbath writ large. Jesus in Luke subverts the entire system of coercion upon which society operates." Brueggemann, *A Mandate to Be Different: An Invitation to the Contemporary Church*, 182.

48. See article by Tan in which he develops the similarity between the birth of Israel as nation and the birth of the church. He says that what Israel had in law to care for the poor, the church fulfilled by the power of the Holy Spirit: Tan, "Pentecost, Jubilee, and Nation Building."

49. Smith, "'No Poor Among Them': Sabbath and Jubilee Years in Lukan Social Ethics," 159.

of favor". He compares this parable with Leviticus 25 and sees four similarities between the parable and the law.⁵⁰

The first similarity is between the social status of the people who got out of Egyptian slavery and the status of the prodigal son, who was working for food. The second similarity is not complete. Kim compares the reasons for slavery in both cases. He says that while the prodigal son had become a slave because of his sin, the causes for the slavery referred in Lev 25 are not expressed. Despite the reason for the slavery, however, both find a possibility of return. The third similarity is that in both cases someone goes from servitude to freedom. The final similarity stressed by Kim is that is both cases one finds a land jubilee. The Israelites went back to the land of their fathers, which belongs primarily to Yahweh. The prodigal son received a welcome back to his father's land. Kim affirms that it is hard to affirm with certainty that the parable was written with Leviticus 25 in mind, but he also says that the programmatic text of Luke 4 is an argument in this direction.

James Sanders presents Luke 7:36–50 as another specific example of a Lukan text with a jubilaic background.⁵¹ Although Luke is the only evangelist who does not quote Deuteronomy 15:11 in this event (see Mark 143–9; Matt 26:6–13; John 12:1–8), he is the one who most preserves the jubilaic context of the referred text. The most evident connections with the jubilee legislation found by Sanders are the parable of the creditor (Luke 7:40–43), the use of the verb χαρίζομαι ("freely remit or graciously grant"), the four uses of ἀφίημι in three verses in Luke 7:47–49, and the emphasis on the forgiveness of her many sins (αἱ ἁμαρτίαι αὐτῆς αἱ πολλαί). Thus, for Sanders, Luke wrote this passage in such a way as to present Jesus as the one who brings about the jubilee of God.⁵²

---

50. Sun-Jong Kim, "Lecture de La Parabole Du Fils Retrouvé À La Lumière Du Jubilé.," 211–21. Fitzmyer suggestion is that "In the Lucan Gospel as a whole the story exemplifies the proclamation of the Lord's year of favor, which Jesus was sent to announce to the downtrodden (4:18–19). As the Son of Man who has come to seek out and to save what was lost (19:10), he will not be deterred from such a proclamation by the attitude of those who might prefer their own sense of uprightness to joining in joy and love for those who react with repentance to such a proclamation." Fitzmyer, *The Gospel According to Luke*, 1086.

51. Sanders, "Sins, Debts, and Jubilee Release," 84–92.

52. "What Luke wanted to establish for the reader and hearer is that Jesus was indeed the one who was to come (7:20), the herald of the arrival of God's jubilee. God's acceptable year (Isa 61:1–2a; Luke 4:19) of release of sins. This was not simply a Jubilee Year indicated by the calendar; this was the introduction of God's jubilee, indeed God's kingdom of love, faith,

After analyzing some of the evidences which are also presented in here, Smith presents the following conclusion, which is very adequate to present in here also:

> The foregoing survey is sufficient to demonstrate that Luke's portrayal of the economics of the kingdom of God, both in the ministry of Jesus and in the social practices of the early church, stands in the tradition of the generous, compassionate, self-consciously communal Israelite economy typified by the institutions of the Jubilee and Sabbath years and the prophetic poetry of Isaiah. Themes, images, and vocabulary from Leviticus 15 and Deuteronomy 15 echo throughout Luke-Acts, at some points louder than others, but with a noticeable consistency.[53]

What kind of jubilee, then, is Luke proposing to his reader?[54] Luke proposes that the ministry Jesus came to develop was mainly a ministry of ἄφεσις, the release from sin and all evil sin produces in the individual and in society. Jesus came to inaugurate the eschatological jubilee and to present himself as the Messiah who enacts the liberation entailed by it. Now, does this jubilee announced by Jesus have any implications for the distribution and use of land, as the original jubilee had? I believe so and this is what the remaining of this dissertation is about.

5.2 God as the Ultimate Landowner in Luke

As the last chapter made clear, one of the most important theological aspects of the jubilee legislation is that God is the ultimate owner of all land (cf. Lev

---

salvation, peace, and forgiveness (7:50). Sanders, "Sins, Debts, and Jubilee Release," 90. On another place, Sanders writes: "Luke's gospel may well be called 'the Jubilee Gospel' because throughout the gospel, and even in Acts, Jesus is understood to be the herald sent by God to proclaim God's jubilee for the whole world." Sanders, *The Monotheizing Process*, 48.

53. Smith, "'No Poor Among Them,'" 160–61.

54. "The question we are faced with is to what extent Luke's Jesus is recalling his hearers to a literal enactment of the Jubilee legislation of the Old Testament with its redistribution of wealth and its curtailment of the power of the rich and influential. Alternatively, has the hope of such socio-economic egalitarianism been simply shunted off into a spiritual future with no real expectation in concrete terms? Already we have observed considerable reinterpretation of the Jubilee motif. The concrete specifications of earlier legislation dissolve into metaphor and vision of future, indeed eschatological, hope." Willoughby, "The Concept of Jubilee and Luke 4:18–30," 48.

25:23). This teaching is also present in other OT texts, such as Exodus 19:5; Deuteronomy 32:8; Psalm 24:1; and Isaiah 54:5. Luke presents his own version of this theological point. He does that, for example, in the words of Jesus who calls God "Lord of heaven and earth" (Luke 10:21). The primary way Luke presents God and Jesus as the supreme owners of all land in the earth, however, is through parables, which repeatedly and symbolically present God or Jesus as the owners of a land property and who frequently leave the property for someone else to take care in their absence.

This argument, however, promptly raises a question of method. Is it justifiable to emphasize a point that is not the main one of the parable? Or, to put in another way, is there a hermeneutical warrant that allows readers to extract more than one point from each parable? Moreover, is it possible that by the repetition of a similar parabolic image Luke intents to convey an important theological point?

This dissertation approaches Jesus's parables as allegories, which commonly have more than just one point.[55] A parable can have ethical prescriptions and at the same time teach about the character of God. Blomberg proposes that the main points of a parable are intimately related to the number of its main characters.[56] When he explains how to interpret what he calls complex three-point parables, he affirms that the 'monarchic' or authoritative character of a parable points to God:

> One cluster concerns the nature of God. He preeminently exhibits grace to the undeserving, giving generously far beyond what one expects. He considers all people as equal and emphasizes that even human enemies should be considered neighbors. He waits patiently, repeatedly summoning people into his kingdom, even when they rebel against him. He entrusts all individuals

---

55. Agreeing with the most recent developments in Parabolic hermeneutics, as expressed for example by Snodgrass, *Stories with Intent: A Comprehensive Guide to the Parables of Jesus*, 16; Blomberg, *Interpreting the Parables*, 192–93; Longenecker, *The Challenge of Jesus' Parables*, 46. Another approach to parables that acknowledges the validity of multiple interpretations is found in Zimmermann, *Puzzling the Parables of Jesus: Methods and Interpretation*. The difference is that Zimmermann bases his hermeneutics in contemporary theories on memory and emphasizes the human process in reminding and writing the parables. Consequently, he valorizes the gospel versions of the parables but also believes is it possible to have even valid contradictory interpretations of the same parable.

56. Blomberg, *Interpreting the Parables*, 197 et seq.

with resources and abilities and expects them to be good stewards of what they have been given.[57]

According to Blomberg's proposal of parable interpretation, therefore, it is correct to identify the main character of a parable to God and extract from that character lessons about the nature of God and what God expects from his people (ethics). This is the approach to parables used in this dissertation. The interpreter needs to be careful, however, not to attribute to God moral flaws that belong to the character of the parable. One way of doing that is searching on Luke's work if that aspect is attributed to God somewhere else or if God is presented on another light. On another hand, God's image portrayed by Luke will sometimes be more disturbing for twenty first century ears, especially when confronting human dignity and God's freedom to use violence.

The fact therefore that Jesus repeatedly characterizes the main figure of a parable as a landowner, I claim, points clearly to God (and sometimes to Jesus himself) as the main landowner. This is the main form through which Luke confirms one of the most important tenets of the jubilee, namely, that God is the owner of all land. I will present the evidences for that.

The first time Jesus is metaphorically compared to a landowner is in Luke 3:16–17 (cf. Matt 3:11–12). John the Baptist compares Jesus to a small landowner who works his own farm and gathers wheat in his barn. The focus of this passage is Jesus as the one who divides humanity (cf. Lc 2:34–35) by means of salvation (baptism with the Holy Spirit) and damnation (baptism with fire). As John's illustration lacks a plot, it is possible to say that Luke just started to characterize Jesus as a landlord, without deeper developments.

In Luke 10:1–2 (cf. also Matt 9:37–38), God is presented as τοῦ κυρίου τοῦ θερισμοῦ, the owner-manager of a large property with a harvest so abundant that he needs to hire extra hands to take care of the work.[58] Most interpreters agree that the Lord of the harvest represents God the Father, instead of Jesus.[59] Again, the focus is not related to agriculture in first instance, but with discipleship. It is worth noting that one finds the same saying in the Gospel

---

57. Blomberg, *Interpreting the Parables*, 338.

58. Nolland, *Luke*, 551.

59. So: Carroll, *Luke*, 235; Bock, *Luke 9:51–24:53*, 995; Fitzmyer, *The Gospel According to Luke*, 846; Marshall, *The Gospel of Luke: A Commentary on the Greek Text*, 416. These interpreters say it is Jesus: Edwards, *The Gospel According to Luke*, 305; Gundry, *Commentary on Luke*.

of Thomas, but without the qualification "of the harvest", which is present in both Luke and Matthew. Oakman proposes that the text is about tax collectors (workers) and the Roman empire (lord of the harvest) and has an irony to it.[60] His interpretation, however, although socially engaging, completely ignores the point of the passage. Even so, it is wise to gather the impact that this characterization of God as the main landowner will have later in other parables.

In the parable of the faithful and wise servant (Luke 12:42–48; cf. also Matt 24:45–51), Jesus is represented for the first time as the owner of a large estate who traveled for a while and left the slaves under the care of a higher rank slave.[61] Chapters two and three presented important information about the character types shown in this parable: the οἰκονόμος (Latin: *vilicus*), a slave responsible for taking care of other slaves; the slaves (θεραπείας); and the landlord (κύριος).[62] The landlord was commonly a rich landowner with slaves working his lands and who commonly used all levels of violence to punish his servants. As we have seen, usually the lord lived in the city, coming from time to time to supervise his property and take possession of its profits. This person was not commonly cherished by the peasants who were the majority of Jesus's hearers. Still, Jesus portrayed himself as an absentee landowner who will come back and oversee the work of his administrators with possibility of recompensing them with the administration of his entire

---

60. "Irony continues in this statement. 'The laborers' and 'the lord' refer not to religious missionaries of God, but to customary tax collector and the Crown. Irony comes in because Jesus and his audience know that the laborers now operate under the eminent domain of God to make sure of the harvest remains in the village and the Crown is deprived of its due." Oakman, *Jesus, Debt, and the Lord's Prayer*, 106.

61. Although approaching the subject from completely another angle, Uytanlet reches the conclusion that Jesus is presented by Luke as the one with rights to inherit the land: "In summary, Jesus' genealogy cannot be understood apart from the accounts of Jesus' baptism and temptation. These three accounts, read together as a complete unit, portray Jesus as the Son of God and the legitimate heir of God's land. As demonstrated in chs. 8 and 9, genealogies in Greco-Roman and Jewish writings were used to legitimize the reign of the kings or one's ownership of lands. Both themes are also expressed in Luke's narrative: Jesus as God's appointed ruler and heir to God's land. The theme of land continues in Jesus' claim as herald of the jubilee, and in the same account, he was portrayed as the rejected one. Same themes are brought up in the parables of the tenants." Uytanlet, *Luke-Acts and Jewish Historiography*.

62. "The larger, more estimable the estate, the greater the degree of differentiation of responsibilities and specialization of roles within the slave staff. As one who manages the affairs of another, the steward was chosen for precisely the characteristics Jesus enumerates, faithfulness and prudence (v 42), as well as such other qualities as zeal, competence, and industriousness." Green, *The Gospel of Luke*, 504.

estate, or punishing them with an elevated level of violence, uncommon even for the standards of that time.[63]

Thus, this parable presents three foci: (1) Jesus Christ is like this Lord who is absent and will return to deal with his slaves according to the way they dealt with their colleagues; (2) those who are slaves of Christ are supposed to know and to perform the responsibilities he gave to them; and (3) the way the slaves act will determine what happens next, unpredicted blessings or grievous punishment. In so doing, the parable also builds up the characterization of Jesus as the landowner who has complete right to define the way his servants are supposed to behave, and the servants are like that οἰκονόμος, who has to decide in what way he will use his authority to treat the other servants of their common lord.

The Parable of the Barren Fig Tree (Luke 13:6–9) compares God, instead of Jesus, with the owner of a vineyard. The fact that this man has a vinedresser (ἀμπελουργός) who calls him "sir" (κύριε) points to someone of at least good economical means. This κύριος is sovereign over his vineyard (or orchard), over his vinedresser, over his fig tree and over his soil. He acknowledges the value of the soil, since he does not want the fig tree using it unprofitably.[64] The main focus of the passage is on the impending judgement of God the Father over impenitent Israel and it is possible to affirm that the vinedresser represents Jesus.[65] In what concerns the purpose of this dissertation, God is represented as the one who owns the estate in which the fig tree is planted and have complete sovereignty over it. God's people in this text are compared not to workers but to a fig tree.

The Parable of the Prodigal Son (Luke 15:11–32) also has an agricultural context. The main character of this parable is the father, who clearly represents

---

63. Suetonius exemplifies the cruelty of the emperor Caligula, narrating that once he punished a slave who had robbed a strip of silver of a coach ordaining that the slave's hand was cut off and hung around his neck upon his breast and that the slave was paraded in front of the guests. Suetonius, *Cal.* 32.2 Blomberg considers Jer 34:18–20 as a possible context for this punition, evoking the curses of the covenant. Blomberg, *Interpreting the Parables*, 234.

64. "Because it not only takes up room but also exhausts the soil in which it grows, the owner wants it to be cut down." Norval Geldenhuys, *Commentary on the Gospel of Luke*, 372. See also Bock, *Luke 9:51–24:53*, 1208.

65. Lenski, *The Interpretation of St. Luke's Gospel*, 730. Blomberg see this interpretation as an exaggeration of the allegory. Blomberg, *Interpreting the Parables*, 363. Calvin interprets the vinedresser as representing the ministers. Calvin, *Commentary on a Harmony of the Evangelists Matthew, Mark, and Luke*, 154.

God.⁶⁶ The family is definitely not poor, nor very rich either, since they live in the country instead of the city and the elder son works the land. They are well-to-do, considering the fattened calf the father orders to commemorate the return of his son, the ring he gives him, the hired workers (μίσθιος) working the land and faring well, and the fact they have slaves (παῖς) who work in the house. Instead of having an absentee owner, one finds in this parable the absence of the younger son preceded by his request of his share in the family possessions (τὸ ἐπιβάλλον μέρος τῆς οὐσίας) and the accord of the father, who divided to both sons their shares in the estate (διεῖλεν αὐτοῖς τὸν βίον).

As the earlier chapters of this dissertation demonstrated, wealth in that society was mainly land. When the text, therefore, refers to οὐσία (Luke 15:11, 13) and βίος (15:12, 30) it is pointing to all the father had amassed throughout his life, which was especially invested in his land(s). God, therefore, is portrayed as this family farmer who shares his possessions with two undeserving sons. Although Holgate exaggerates in excluding other interpretations, he is right in the following affirmation:

> The parable reveals Luke's support for the ideals of the common ownership and shared use of possessions. It also shows that he advocates the practical virtues of moderation and liberality in the use of possessions. Unlike many other Jewish and Christian texts on the topos, the parable does not constitute an attack upon the rich. Instead, Luke's message is that those who have wealth ought to share it. This accords with Luke's teaching elsewhere in Luke-Acts.⁶⁷

Thus, besides teaching that there is an opportunity for repentance and conversion; a welcoming love from God and an invitation of Jesus which extends even to the Pharisees, this parable also uses the example of God as a

---

66. "The most important character is the father. His central structural position and individualization concentrate attention upon him, and suggests that Luke intended his behavior to be a positive example for his readers. He forms the standard by which all other behavior is to be judged. His home is the central place. His workers and servants reveal his liberality, and his sons evoke his compassion. Holgate, *Prodigality, Liberality and Meanness in the Parable of the Prodigal Son*, 67. Holgate proposes a moral interpretation of this parable which does not emphasize the identification of the father as God.

67. Holgate, *Prodigality, Liberality and Meanness in the Parable of the Prodigal Son*, 248.

family farmer to teach the readers about their duty to share their land, which in ultimate instance belongs to God.[68]

In Luke 16:1–13, the Parable of the Dishonest Manager, God is equated with a rich man (ἄνθρωπός τις ἦν πλούσιος) who had an administrator (οἰκονόμος) over his business.[69] The οἰκονόμος calls him my lord (ὁ κύριός μου). The context is agricultural, since the options of jobs the administrator considers after being dismissed are digging (σκάπτω) the land or begging (ἐπαιτέω).[70] The setting seems to be a village that grew around the farm of that landowner, who probably did not use to live in the property.[71] Thus, the houses in which the οἰκονόμος hopes to be received are the houses of the tenants and small proprietors around the villa of his boss. Another common characteristic for that epoch is that the rich man is a creditor to many of those workers. The parable presents two examples of debt, one of 875 gallons of olive oil and the other being the equivalent of thirty-seven thousand liters of wheat.[72] Both figures are impressively high and reveal the enormous wealth of the rich man, but also the possibility that the debtors are merchants instead of tenants.

Herzog proposes that this parable presents the struggle between retainers (the manager), expendables (tenants) and the wealthy (the landlord). In his reconstruction, the expendables engaged in a successful campaign against the manager in order to alleviate their hard situation under oppression. They were using common survival strategies and something he calls weapons of the weak.[73] The manager was a representative of the master, who used the manager to impose abusive and unlawful interests on his debtors. At the end

---

68. For the referred three points, see Blomberg, *Interpreting the Parables*, 367.

69. For a summary of more than fifteen interpretations this parable has received both historically and recently, see Snodgrass, *Stories with Intent*, 406–9.

70. "Digging is the hardest kind of work." BDAG, 926.

71. "The master depicted in the parable is described as *plousios*, a clear indicator of wealth and prestige. Whether the master is an absentee landlord who visits his estates on occasion or a member of the local nobility who lives closer to his estates, perhaps in a nearby urban center, he belongs to the elite class. The figures on the contracts indicate large holdings of land, including orchards." Herzog, *Parables as Subversive Speech*, 240.

72. In Bock's calculation, the oil debt amounted to one thousand denarii and the wheat debt to two and a half and three thousand denarii. Bock, *Luke 9:51–24:53*, 1331.

73. "The hostile charges brought against the steward need to be seen in his context. They are not moral charges that cast a shadow over the character of the steward but tactics in the endless resistance that is part of everyday life in agrarian societies. The charges are brought to sabotage the steward, undermine his authority, and place the villagers or merchants in a stronger bargaining position." Herzog, *Parables as Subversive Speech*, 252.

of the parable, all people retained their previous position, but a more just system had been instituted (less interests on the oppressed) by means of their active use of the weapons of the weak.[74]

Herzog´s interpretation is socially sensitive and, in many ways, reconstructs well the ways of the Jewish Roman society in first century. It does not do justice, however, to the canonical form of the text with its commentaries and interpretations. It follows the same approach of Dodd, who finds three different interpretations in the text itself and famously comments that there are apparently three different sermon outlines appended to it.[75] Blomberg, on another hand, goes to the heart of the question, equalizing the three personages (or group thereof) to three referents and consequently to three different applications: "(1) All of God's people will be called to give a reckoning of the nature of their service to him; (2) Preparation for that reckoning should involve a prudent, shrewd use of all our resources, especially in the area of finances. (3) Such prudence and shrewdness, demonstrating a life of true discipleship, will be rewarded with eternal life and joy."[76]

Relating this text yet more to its agricultural context and to the focus of this dissertation, this parable reveals that all possessions, evidently including land, belong not to the managers (the readers), but to their master (God). Also, what the Lord wants from their stewards is that they use his property (all property and money they administrate) in a way that benefits others and is consequently profitable to their eternal future. The land belongs to the Lord and all his people are but stewards who are to benefit others using property shrewdly.

The last of these parables presenting Jesus as the landowner is the Parable of the Ten Minas (Luke 19:11–27). Van Eck shows how much this parable relates with its historical context:

> Luke's version of the parable fits well into what has previously been indicated as typical of Jesus the Galilean's message: the parable is evidence of the social stratification, patron–client relationships, the exploitative relationship between elite and nonelite and conflict and peasant resistance that formed part

---

74. Herzog, *Parables as Subversive Speech*, 233–58.
75. Dodd, *The Parables of the Kingdom*, 17.
76. Blomberg, *Interpreting the Parables*, 325.

and parcel of 1st century Palestine as an advanced agrarian society under the control of the Roman Empire, issues addressed in almost all of Jesus' parables.[77]

From this correct reconstruction of the context and also a reconstruction of the parable, Van Eck concludes that the villain of the parable is the nobleman and the third servant is the hero.[78] When one is conscious of the social role that most noblemen exercised in that time and society, it is almost impossible to affirm that the nobleman represents Jesus. But this is exactly one of the punchlines of this parable. It maximizes the idea of divine land-ownership, presenting Jesus metaphorically not just as a rich proprietor, but as a king. As the third chapter has shown, it was not unheard in Palestine to have a postulant to the throne traveling to the capital of the empire in order to confirm his rights. Herod the Great went to Rome and was confirmed king by Cesar Augustus. His sons Archelaus, Antipas and Philip, after the death of his father, tried the same before the same emperor. This kind of situation therefore was known especially in Palestine.

Thus, it is a common situation that one finds in this parable, a king asking his slaves to manage his money while he is absent. One mina is the equivalent to one hundred denarii, each denarius roughly corresponding to the wages earned in one day of work. Thus, in this last parable with the same theme, Jesus is not only the landowner, but he is represented as a well-born noble man (ἄνθρωπός τις εὐγενὴς) who will be confirmed as the king of his people. He is the one who has the right to define how his possessions are to be managed by his slaves. Therefore, Luke is showing that Jesus, not the emperor nor the Jewish leader or the elite, is the ultimate owner of land.[79]

As we reach the conclusion of this section, Uytanlet's remarks are very proper:

---

77. Van Eck, "Do Not Question My Honour," 3. Van Eck uses a form critical approach to defend that Luke 19:12b–24, 27 represents the most original version of this parable which was eschatologically reworked by Matthew. My conviction is that the parables and biblical books in general should be dealt with in their canonical final forms. Van Eck's social scientific approach, however, brings fruits to the reconstruction of Jesus' context.

78. Van Eck, "Do Not Question My Honour." One finds the same type of reading in Herzog, *Parables as Subversive Speech*, 150–70.

79. Luke 20:9–18 also presents God as the owner of a vineyard, but as we will work this parable in another chapter, we will not deal with it here.

In the Third Gospel, God's claim over all territories under the emperor's jurisdiction was made clear through the territories associated with earthly rulers (Luke 1:5; 2:1–2; 3:1–2). God's rule over these territories would be realized through his Son, whose legitimacy as heir was stressed in several accounts (baptism, genealogy, temptation, Jesus' claim as herald of 'the year of the Lord's favor,' and the parable of the wicked tenants). Luke's presentation of Jesus as the embodiment of the Law, a stark contrast with his presentation of the earthly rulers, makes it clear that Jesus is the only one who qualifies as God's co-regent in God's land.[80]

Up to here in this section, I presented seven discourses in Luke in which Jesus present God or himself as landowners. Commonly a lord representing God or Jesus becomes absent of his property. This was a very frequent characteristic of large estate owners in Roman times. They had slaves and servants administering and working for the production of surplus and profit in their absence. I contend that Luke does that intentionally and the reason is to forward the theological point that God is the proprietor of all land.

While accepting that the main focus of these parables is not related to agricultural questions per se, it is the contention of this thesis that the repetition of this image of God and Jesus as the main landowners is purposeful and furthers the jubilee idea that God, and now Jesus also, are the main landowners and those who decide how their tenants and slaves are supposed to use their estates.

According to Uytanlet, another way Luke claims the ownership of God for the land is through the geographical movements found in his gospel: "The geographical movement in Luke-Acts is evidence of Luke's interest in the theme of the land. His concern is not just to provide his readers with special information, but to claim these territories as belonging to God, over which the God of Israel is sovereign and within which the lordship of Christ must be proclaimed."[81]

---

80. Uytanlet, *Luke-Acts and Jewish Historiography*. Uytanlet reaches this conclusion based in the similarity of Luke's account with the ancient accounts of migration and conquests.

81. Uytanlet, *Luke-Acts and Jewish Historiography*, 198.

Thus, God is the proprietor of all land. As such, he is also the one who has the right to establish how the land is to be used. This ethical aspect related to land is dealt with by other discourses of Jesus proposing blessings for those who use the land according to a jubilee ethics and curses for those who do not use it that way. That is the focus of next section.

5.3 Blessings and Curses Related to Land Administration

In the previous section, I dealt with a few Lukan texts that present God or Jesus metaphorically as the main owners of land. The argument is that Luke repeats this image in order to make the point that the land belongs to God. It follows from this that those who have land are supposed to deal with their property in a way that pleases the owner – God. If they do so, the human owner will receive blessings and alternatively, if they do otherwise, they will need to face the anger of the one to whom the land ultimately belongs.

This theme of administrating the land as a representative of the rightful owner relates intimately with Lukan emphasis in stewardship (οἰκονομία, οἰκονόμος). Kim affirms that stewardship is "one of the major themes of Luke's Gospel". He defines the steward as "[. . .] a slave whom his master entrusts with, and leaves in charge of, his assets and material possessions (12:42; 16:1; 19:13). Thus it is discovered that he has nothing of his own and all he has belongs to his master."[82] This concept of stewardship or slavery toward God is at the heart of the jubilaic notion of use of land. While stewardship is a very important subject in Luke-Acts (Luke 12:13–21, 35–48; 16:1–13; 17:7–10; 19:11–27; 20:9–18; Acts 4:29; 13:2; 16:17; 20:19, 24), it will not be developed in here.

Although this point will be made in yet more detail in the next two chapters, I will present below the parable of the Rich Man and Lazarus (Luke 16:19–31) and the text of the conversion of Zacchaeus (Luke 19:1–10) as part of the argument that God blesses those who share land and curses those who deal with it in a self-centered way.

---

82. Kim, "Stewardship and Almsgiving in Luke's Theology," 166.

5.3.1 The Parable of the Rich Man and Lazarus (Luke 16:19–31)

The parable of the rich man and Lazarus is a very clear example of someone who did not use his house, possessions and wealth to the good of others and was punished by that. Although there is some divergence among scholars, it is clear that the main sin of the rich man was the selfish way he used his possessions despite the evident needs of Lazarus. Scholars agree that the rich man is presented as a bad example, but what is the sin that makes him suffer? Most interpreters argue that he was condemned because he was wicked or at least restrained himself from helping poor Lazarus. A few more recent scholars, however, seemingly in agreement with Abraham's words in Luke 16:25, affirm that the reason for the condemnation of the rich man was just his extravagant wealth. It is not without reason, therefore, that Darrell Bock affirms that "Luke 16:19–31 is one of the most complex of Jesus' stories."[83]

Luke Timothy Johnson says that the rich man was arrogant, hard of heart, and idolatrous because he did not help Lazarus. He says that "if he had fed the poor man who 'longed to be filled from what fell from the table' he could have avoided his present condition."[84] Joel Green agrees with this interpretation and calls the rich man presumptuous, audacious, and indifferent and charges him with neglecting the poor.[85] Bock affirms that the rich man was extravagant, self-indulgent and without compassion and that this was the reason of his fate.[86] Hock, based on the similar story of Lucian, Cataplus, charges the rich man of hedonism and affirms that probably, according to

---

83. Bock, *Luke 9:51–24:53*, 1377. Bovon lists the following problems of interpretation in this parable: "Is Abraham's severity compatible with Christian pity? Is the description of life beyond death true and normative? Is there an allusion to Jesus Christ's resurrection in v. 31? Was Lazarus consoled because of his poverty or because of his piety? Conversely, was the rich man punished for being rich or because of his lack or charity? Why did the poor man have a name, but not the rich man? Is this story truly a unit? Are we not dealing instead with an original story (vv. 19–26) to which a dialogue has been added (vv. 27–31)? Is not Jesus quoting a well-known Egyptian, Jewish, or Greek story that would be the basis of his own? Is it possible to attribute a story this unusual to the historical Jesus?" François Bovon, *Luke 2*, 473.

84. Johnson, *The Gospel of Luke*, 256.

85. Green, *The Gospel of Luke*, 608–10.

86. "The lesson is in the reply, for in effect Abraham says that the rich man's extravagant wealth and lack of compassion on earth has resulted in spiritual poverty and absence of mercy eternally. . . . The rich man is not condemned because he is rich, but because he slipped into the coma of callousness that wealth often produces." Bock, *Luke 9:51–24:53*, 1372.

the example of Megapenthes, he is also guilt of committing sexual offenses, wrongdoings and oppression.[87]

Along with these interpretations that attribute an active sin to the man, there is an interpretation that connects the rich man's suffering with his lack of compassion. I. Howard Marshall represents this position: "The main point is clear: the rich man and his associates did nothing to help the beggar, beyond possibly throwing him some scraps. It is quite false to infer that the rich man's lack of charity does not figure in the story."[88] Stein, Calvin, Lagrange, Tannehill, Nolland, Carroll, Garland and Bovon also blame the rich man's lack of generosity for his damnation.[89] Schweizer even affirms the innocence of the rich man, but even so still blames him at the same time: "Neither is the rich man a villain, but his innocence does not excuse him. It is a form of stupidity that ignores a fellow human being lying in plain sight at one's doorstep and thereby ignores God".[90] Ireland adds that the lack of compassion is worsened in face of the eschatological hope that should characterize people facing the arrival kingdom of God.[91]

Recently, at least two scholars affirmed that the only reason the rich man was condemned was not an active sin, nor his lack of compassion, but the mere fact of being excessively rich. Richard Bauckham writes: "What is wrong with the situation in this world, according to the parable, is the stark inequality in the living conditions of the two men, which is vividly and memorably conveyed simply by the juxtaposition of the rich man's expensive luxury and the poor man's painfully beggary. Therefore, there is no mention of the moral qualities of the two men".[92] Thus, for Bauckham, this parable makes the point

---

87. Ronald F. Hock, "Lazarus and Micyllus," 459–60.

88. Marshall, *The Gospel of Luke*, 636.

89. "The rich man suffered reversal in the afterlife not because he was rich but because he was rich and lacked compassion for the needy." Stein, *Luke*, 427. "But the chief accusation brought against this man is his cruelty in suffering Lazarus." Calvin, *Commentary on a Harmony of the Evangelists Matthew, Mark, and Luke*, 184. Lagrange, *Évangile selon saint Luc*, 442–43; Tannehill, *Luke*, 251; Nolland, *Luke*, 827; Carroll, *Luke*, 338–39; Garland, *Luke*, 675–76; Bovon, *Luke 2*, 479.

90. Schweizer, *The Good News According to Luke*, 262. In another page he says: "The rich man is not depicted as a profiteer. He lives according to contemporary standards, considers wealth and poverty the gift of God, who knows why. The terrible thing is the innocence with which he lives his life of ease, avoiding contact with what surrounds him." (260)

91. Ireland, *Stewardship and the Kingdom of God*, 217–18.

92. Bauckham, "The Rich Man and Lazarus: The Parable and the Parallels," 232.

that it is immoral to have luxury coexisting with starvation: "In effect, therefore, it is true that the rich man suffers in the next life just because he was rich in this life, while the poor man is blessed in the next life just because he was poor in this life."[93] Any other explanation for the fate of the rich man is, in Bauckham's view, the introduction of an alien explanation in the passage due to the difficulty of accepting Abraham's explanation as sufficient.

James Metzger agrees with Bauckham. However, he portrays the richness of the rich man as sin, by affirming, "Thus, had the rich man opened the gate and given alms to Lazarus *yet remaining wealthy*, he would not have improved his chances of joining Abraham and Lazarus on the other side of the chasm. Relinquishing his wealth (so that he could no longer be classified as 'rich' would have been the first and most important step in attaining a position of honor at the patriarch's side".[94] Metzger concludes: "Personal wealth is not permissible under any circumstances, even if accompanied by generous almsgiving. It is, quite simply, incompatible with service to God".[95]

Which of these interpretations is correct and how does this parable relate to my argument? As virtually all commentators of Luke 16:19–31 affirm, one idiosyncratic characteristic of this parable is that it is the only one of Jesus's parables in which a personage receives a name –the poor Lazarus. The rich man remains anonymous.[96] It is worth noting that Λάζαρος (לְעָזָר) is the rabbinic abbreviation of the Hebrew name אֶלְעָזָר which means God helps.[97]

According to the jubilee ethics Luke is constructing throughout his gospel, the rich man should have helped poor Lazarus with his property, food and money. Lazarus had no shelter, the rich had a very big estate in which he could have helped the homeless.[98] Lazarus had no food, the rich had plenty and did not share. Lazarus was sick and the rich had all the means to help his fellow human being. God could have helped Lazarus through the rich, but the rich man did not view his wealth as something pertaining to God and

---

93. Bauckham, "The Rich Man and Lazarus: The Parable and the Parallels," 232–33.
94. Metzger, *Consumption and Wealth in Luke's Travel Narrative*, 146.
95. Metzger, *Consumption and Wealth in Luke's Travel Narrative*, 147.
96. That is the reason why applying any name to him, as Dives, Nineveh or Phineas corrupts an important characteristic of the parable.
97. BDAG, 581.
98. The Greek word that appears in Luke 19:20 to refer to the rich man's door, πυλών, refers to large and portentous gates that were used to cities and temples.

a blessing given by God, but as his own. Herzog comments on the meaning of the parable:

> The parable is not a story about abstract social types but a story about representatives of two social classes, the urban elites and the desperate expendables, those who had nearly everything and those who had almost nothing. In this case, wealth may indeed lead to Hades, for such wealth could be obtained only by the systemic exploitation of the poor, and it could be maintained only by their continual oppression.[99]

Herzog is right in the sense that the economic element is central in this parable, but the parable itself does not speak about active oppression as he argues, but to the lack of using one's means to alleviate the suffering of others. In the parable, the rich man and Lazarus meet again in the afterworld. Although there is an abyss separating them (as the gate was separating before), it is still possible for the rich to contemplate Lazarus at Abraham's bosom. Also, the fact that the Lord made both is evident in the passage in the sense the he lords over both, defining their final destinies based on how they lived their lives.

The account does not make explicit what were the wrongdoings of the rich man simply because the problem was not one of committing something, but one of not doing what he was supposed to. The rich himself expresses that his brothers, who apparently had the same attitude as him, should repent (μετανοέω, Luke 16:30) so that they would not to have his same fate. Longman affirms that this retribution principle can only be considered an "ultimately true principle" in the light of New Testament texts that speak about the fate of the wicked in the afterlife.[100]

The rich man of the parable had a mansion with a portentous gate. Sheltered in his mansion he wears very expensive clothes and feasted in banquet every day. He used to live as if all the material blessings he had were only his, for his own pleasure. He forgot that his villa was God's property placed under his care in order to be used for the betterment of others. That was his sin and that was the reason of his fiery punishment. God punishes those who

---

99. Herzog, *Parables as Subversive Speech: Jesus as Pedagogue of the Oppressed*, 128.
100. Longman, *Proverbs*, 405.

use their property as if it were only their own. The text of Zacchaeus' conversion has the same teaching, but presented in a positive way.

5.3.2 The Conversion of Zacchaeus (Luke 19:1–10)

The account of the conversion of Zacchaeus (Luke 19:1–10) has a special importance in this gospel, since, together with the parable of the ten minas (Luke 19:11–27), it concludes the travel narrative (9:51–19:27) and recalls several important Lukan themes.[101] The first link between this text and the present study is the fact that Zacchaeus is presented as an ἀρχιτελώνης, a chief tax collector. Tax collectors were deeply despised in Jewish society of that time, being commonly compared to sinners (Matt 9:10–11; 11:19; Mark 2:15–16; Luke 5:30; 7:34; 15:1); gentiles (Matt 18:17) and harlots (Matt 21:31–32). This is well illustrated, for example, in the prayer of the Pharisee in Luke 18, "God, I thank you that I am not like other men, extortioners, unjust, adulterers, or even like this tax collector." (Luke 18:11).

This class of people was so despised that they were not considered full members of Jewish society, being prevented, for example, of witnessing in jury.[102] Donahue affirms that the τελώνης of the New Testament should be equated to toll collectors instead of land tax collectors.[103] His main argument is that the Talmudic Hebrew presents two different words, one for tax collector (גבאין) and other for toll farmer (מוכסין) and only the second figure is compatible with the publicans of the New Testament. B. Shabbat 78b:6, however, clearly refers to tax collectors (land and/or head) eight times using the word מוכסין and related. Therefore, the words were used interchangeably. The Greek word is not that specific and is applied to both tax and toll collectors. As this dissertation has demonstrated already, the tax over land was

---

101. "Its conclusion (19:10) functions as a summary of Jesus' ministry in the travel narrative." Stein, *Luke*, 466. "This episode thus brings to an end that part of the Lucan travel account which has been called the 'Gospel of the Outcast.'" Fitzmyer, *The Gospel According to Luke*, 1218. "The final story in the long account of Jesus on his journey to Jerusalem is meant to be a climax in the ministry of Jesus, and it brings out several notable features which Luke considered important." Marshall, *The Gospel of Luke*, 694. "It is a story in which multiple Lukan themes jostle and link together: walking, wealth, the desire to see, the reversal of values, encounters, salvation as a current event, and Jesus' identity and mission." Bovon, *Luke 2*, 592. On the links between this passage and the previous, see Bruehler, *A Public and Political Christ*, 202.

102. Jeremias, *Jerusalem in the Time of Jesus*, 311.

103. Donahue, "Tax Collectors and Sinners," 39–61.

the most important in the Roman Empire and it would be strange if the New Testament did not mention this kind of publican.

In the Talmudic literature one learns that tax collectors sometimes were self-nominated and that the Jews considered it allowed to lie to tax collectors, affirming that a specific amount of money was an offering to God (Mishnah Nedarim 3:4; B. Sanhedrin 25b). B. Shevuot 39a illustrates the social status of a tax collector, affirming that his whole family was considered as unworthy as the tax collector himself. This status is confirmed by the following facts: coins of tax collectors could not be used for charity, nor change, because it was assumed they were obtained illegally (B. Bava Kamma 113a:12); a house in which a tax collector entered should be considered impure (Mishnah Tahorot 7:6); and, as already referred, tax collectors testimonies were not accepted in court (B. Sanhedrin 25b). B. Bava Kamma 113a:12 affirms that it is very difficult for a tax collector, as well for a shepherd, to repent, since it would be hard to find all people from whom they would have stolen. Besides the fact that tax collectors worked directly or indirectly for the domineering foreign power and many of them were corrupt, tax collectors were despised also for representing an abusive system through which poor people could lose their property (B. Bava Batra 55a:5) and even their freedom (B. Yevamot 46a:12).[104]

This despising attitude toward tax farmers was not exclusive of the Jews. Suetonius affirms that the tax collector, because of his extortion is more odious than the tax itself.[105] Epictetus says that a man cannot be a philosopher and at the same time a tax collector because one cannot be good and bad at the same time, not a philosopher and a vulgar (ἰδιώτης).[106] Hence, it is not surprising that "they all grumbled" seeing Jesus being hosted by an ἀρχιτελώνης.[107]

Because of the exiguity of a middle class at that time, when Luke calls someone rich (πλούσιος), he is referring to someone that is extremely wealthy,

---

104. "In a corrupt system, the loftier one's position, the greater one's complicity in that system. While nothing of the private life of Zacchaeus is revealed in the story, this much we know on principle: no one can be privately righteous while participating in and profiting from a program that robs and crushes other persons." Craddock, *Luke*, 218.

105. Suetonius, *Agr*.19

106. Epictetus, *Disc*. 3.15

107. Although there is no evidence for this expression in Greek, in Shabbat 78b:6 one finds the expressions מוכס גדול ומוכס קטן ("a senior tax collector and a junior tax collector") to refer to different tax collectors who could want to see a receipt of paid taxes, pointing to a land and/or a head tax.

with multiple land properties; a large house in the city; slaves, hired workers and tenants; and a job connected to the imperial or local government – consequently, someone very well connected and powerful.[108] Zacchaeus was such a man. The main point of this *pericope* is Jesus's initiative to save the outcast.[109]

From an economic-ethic point of view, this text shows a tax collector, i.e., someone who participated in an oppressive system in which land was the main asset and means of oppression. He was also personally guilty of extortion, since the first-class condition εἴ τινός τι ἐσυκοφάντησα ἀποδίδωμι τετραπλοῦν (if, or, better, since I have defrauded anyone of anything, I restore it fourfold) assumes the veracity of the extortion.[110] Zacchaeus was hated and despised because he was an important symbol, part, and tool of what the Roman Empire used to do to perpetuate its own power and the power of the aristocracy in Israel.

After receiving Jesus, however, Zacchaeus becomes a symbol of the economic reverberations of an existential encounter with Jesus.[111] His oppression and extortion that was certainly linked to land were transformed into a fourfold restitution, going far beyond what was commanded in the Law (see Exod 22:1; 2 Sam 12:6; Lev 5:16; Num 5:7). His participation in an unjust system converted into donation of half of his wealth, which certainly comprised landed properties, to the poor. Consequently, he became a son of Abraham and an heir of promises which also encompass land, as seen in last chapter.[112]

Both the parable of the rich man and Lazarus and the narrative of the conversion of Zacchaeus, just analyzed, and the parables of the rich fool

---

108. See Chapter Two.

109. Bock presents the following structure for the text: "a. Jesus' association with Zacchaeus (19:1-6): i. Setting (19:1); ii. Zacchaeus's efforts to see Jesus (19:2-4); iii. Jesus' initiative to stay with Zacchaeus (19:5-6). b. The crowd's murmuring (19:7). c. Jesus' explanation (19:8-10): i. Zacchaeus's defense (19:8); ii. Jesus' vindication and the lesson: The Son of Man seeks the lost." Bock, *Luke 9:51–24:53*, 1515.

110. See an explanation of first class condition in Wallace, *Greek Grammar Beyond the Basics*, 690. The verb συκοφαντέω is strong and had the meaning: "(1) to put pressure on someone for personal gain, harass, squeeze, shake down, blackmail"; and "(2) to secure something through intimidation, extort" (BDAG, 995).

111. "Not only is his household involved but also the poor who will be beneficiaries of his conversion as well as all those people whom he may have defrauded. His salvation, therefore, has personal, domestic, social and economic dimensions." Craddock, *Luke*, 220.

112. I disagree with Bock, who sees here only a "purely racial designation", a reference to the fact that Zacchaeus is a Jew. Bock, *Luke 9:51–24:53*, 1522. This ignores the central theological importance that Abraham has in this gospel.

(Luke 12:13–21) and of the wicked tenants, which will be analyzed in the next chapter, demonstrate that Luke presents a version of the jubilee land ethics in which those who are willing to share their land receive blessings from God and those who are not willing to do so face his judgement and condemnation. This jubilee ethics has another aspect in Luke, which is the fact that although Jesus is presented as the main landowner, he also identifies with the landless, as the next section shows.

5.4 Jesus Identifies with the Landless

This thesis has demonstrated already that Luke presents God and Jesus as the supreme landowners, placing them many times in parabolic discourse in the function of a lord who owns land and give orders to his servants. It is quite interesting; therefore, that Luke also presents Jesus as the one who identifies with the landless.

This happens already in the Jesus's birth narrative (Luke 2:1–20). The context is "the first registration [census, ἀπογραφὴ] when Quirinius was governor of Syria" (Luke 2:2).[113] The reason for the Roman census was to register land properties and the number of people of each family of the empire had in order to determine their land tax, other taxes, and service in the army.[114] This last reason did not apply to Jews, who were exempt from serving in the Roman army. The census was one of the main marks of Roman domination and was commonly received with strong opposition by many nations.[115] Israel, in particular, was not fond of censuses. Not only did they probably remember the consequences of David's census (2 Sam 24; 1 Chr 21); but they were also unwilling to accept pacifically this token of Roman oppression. Josephus, for example, narrates the strong opposition that a certain Judas made against the

---

113. Scholars debate on this historicity of this chronology in Luke. Nolland, for example, a bit inconsistently, affirms that is Luke as wrong in his depiction of the census, but then adds many qualifiers to preserve Luke's overall correct perspective of this event. Nolland, *Luke*, 99–102.

114. Niebuhr, *Lectures on the History of Rome*, 112. "The census went much further than merely ascertaining a citizen's wealth and classifying him accordingly; it also determined his military and fiscal obligations an d political privileges, but it cannot be said that any of these decisions were historically prior to others. Nicolet, *The World of the Citizen in Republican Rome*, 52.

115. Ando, *Imperial Ideology and Provincial Loyalty in the Roman Empire*, 352 et seq.

census in AD 6.[116] Thus, it is possible to affirm that Luke places the birth of Jesus in a context of land oppression and right after that expresses that Jesus's parents did not have a place to stay in Bethlehem, resulting in Jesus being born and placed in a manger (Luke 2:7).[117] Joseph and Mary were submissive to the Roman Empire exigencies and were, at least temporarily, landless.[118]

Also, Jesus's first visitors were shepherds who were 'living out in the fields' (ἀγραυλοῦντες). These were nomadic shepherds, commonly very despised in society and who used to live in the fields, having no property of their own.[119] Already at the dawn of this gospel, therefore, Jesus identifies himself not only with the poor in general, but also specifically with the landless poor.

The accounts of Jesus's birth (Luke 2:1–40) and the travel to Jerusalem as a teenager (Luke 2:41–52) are concluded with similar remarks on the development of Jesus (Luke 2:40, 52). They are also the middle element in a chiastic structure:

    A: John the Baptist in the wilderness (Luke 1:80)
        B: Powerful people (Luke 2:1–2)
            C: Jesus birth (Luke 2:3–40)
            C¹: Teen Jesus in Jerusalem in Passover (Luke 2:41–52)
        B¹: Powerful people (Luke 3:1–2)
    A¹: John the Baptist in the wilderness (Luke 3:2)

---

116. Josephus, *Ant.* 18.1.1. Luke also alludes to this event in Acts 5:37. On the alleged chronological problems of Luke's account, see Coogan, *The Oxford History of the Biblical World*, 61 et seq.; Hoehner, *Chronological Aspects of the Life of Christ*, 13 et seq.; Puig i Tàrrech, *Jesus: An Uncommon Journey*, 70 et seq.

117. "If we are to understand that Mary and Joseph were excluded from the *kataluma*, then the definite article favors reference to the public inn at Bethlehem (cf. Jer 41:17), tough the guest-room of the family home remains possible." Nolland, *Luke*, 105.

118. "For Luke the census, historical or not, serves as a dramatic apologetic device. Joseph and Mary, and therefore Jesus, are seen as adhering to the demands of the Roman government: travel anywhere when one is about to give birth, let alone by donkey over the rough terrain between Galilee and Bethlehem, surely proves dedication to duty. This loyalty is contrasted with another event, and another Galilean, mentioned both by Luke [Acts 5:37] and Josephus in conjunction with the census, and this other reference illustrated the problems created by the Roman policy." Coogan, *The Oxford History of the Biblical World*, 61.

119. "Nomadic shepherds who were separated from human communities and culture for long periods of time were inevitably subjected to suspicion and scorn. Popular lore accused them of failing to observe the difference between "mine" and "thine." Because they could prey on lonely travelers, they were often suspected of practicing "the craft of robbers" (*m. Qidd.* 4:14)." Edwards, *The Gospel According to Luke*, 74.

This structure reveals the importance of the wilderness theme and how it is used to present a marked contrast between John the Baptist and those powerful politicians and religious authorities presented in B and B^I.[120] The contrast is not just between powerful people and John the Baptist, but also geographical. The desert is where the Jewish people spent forty years without land, walking to their promised land. It seems that John the Baptist is also being represented as someone who is not a landowner in contrast to those who own and rule the land.

The identification of Jesus with the landless is even clearer in Luke 9:58, "Foxes have holes, and birds of the air have nests, but the Son of Man has nowhere to lay his head." As an itinerant preacher and teacher, Jesus did not have a house of his own and depended on the not always certain hospitality of people (cf. Luke 7:44–46; 8:37; 9:51–56; 10:10–12; 11:38). Jipp, commenting on that says:

> While Luke is unconcerned with providing an exact itinerary for Jesus and the disciples, the section of Luke 9:51–19:44 is suffused with reminders that they are journeying to Jerusalem, and thus the programmatic remark: "he set his face to journey to Jerusalem" (αὐτὸς τὸ πρόσωπον ἐστήρισεν τοῦ πορεύεσθαι εἰς Ἰερουσαλήμ). This remark along with the repeated references to Jesus' journeying and being 'on the way' (e.g., 13:22, 31–33; 14:25; 17:11; 18:31, 35–36; 19:11, 28) characterize Jesus as a traveling itinerant prophet within Luke 9:51—19:44.[121]

---

120. "With acid irony, Luke reports that 'the word of God came to John son of Zechariah in the wilderness' (v. 2). The names before John are accompanied by titles and offices: emperor, prefect, tetrarch, high priest. John has no title or office. The names before John are associated with places of importance: Rome, Sepphoris, Jerusalem. John lives in a place with no name, 'in the wilderness.' People must leave their comforts and securities and *go out* to the wilderness. In Israel's history the wilderness represents a place of testing, repentance, and grace." Edwards, *The Gospel According to Luke*, 106.

121. Jipp, *Divine Visitations and Hospitality to Strangers in Luke-Acts*, 183–84. The paragraph continues: "Within Luke 9:51–62 alone there are five references to a form of πορεύομαι (vv. 51, 52, 53, 56, 57), three to Jesus setting his face for the journey to Jerusalem (vv. 51, 52a, 53), and one to Jesus and the disciples traveling 'on the way'. Thus, while the connections between individual sections of the travel narrative are loose, there can be no doubt about Luke's characterization of Jesus as a sojourner on his way to Jerusalem."

Thus, Jesus is pictured as homeless when he was born, and he is still a homeless now that he is starting his journey to die in Jerusalem.[122] As the context is one of discipleship, Jesus is making clear to those who want to follow him that, if necessary, they too need to be willing to be homeless. Evidently, in light of the other texts presented in his chapter, this landlessness is not a demand of the jubilee land ethics, but a disposition of making oneself homeless in order to bless others.

5.5 Land Giving in Acts of the Apostles

I am proposing in this chapter that Luke proposes a land ethics informed by the Old Testament institution of the jubilee. Luke does that first by making the jubilee a central theme of his gospel. Then, by the imagery constructed in some parables, Luke builds the concept that God is the rightful owner of all land. After that, I demonstrated that Luke gives examples of people being punished for not using their landed properties in a proper way, while others are praised for doing the opposite. Finally, the last section demonstrated how Luke characterized Jesus and the apostles as poor, homeless, and landless people. In his section, I will show that what Luke presents in principle and through the example of Jesus, He presents as reality in the daily life of the church on Acts of the Apostles.

5.5.1 The Community of Goods of Acts

It is not possible to speak about the role of land in Acts without speaking about the community of shared material goods and the common basket depicted especially in Acts 2:42–47 and 4:32–37.[123] Thus, in this section I will argue that the community of goods presented in Acts is a vivid communitarian performance of the jubilee ethics, which Luke presents as a possible model for the church.

---

122. "'Homelessness' has been Jesus' fate from his birth." Bock, *Luke 9:51–24:53*, 978.

123. For a useful reviews on the history of interpretation of the community of goods depicted in Acts and its application for the church, see Finger, "Cultural Attitudes in Western Christianity Toward the Community of Goods in Acts 2 and 4," 235–70; Capper, "The Judaean Cultural Context of Community of Goods in the Early Jesus Movement," 29–49.

In Acts 2:42–47 one finds the first of the summaries Luke presents on the state of the church.[124] In order to keep our focus, I will deal only with the points of the text that have a direct relation to the subject in hand. One of the characteristics of the church was the persevering (προσκαρτεροῦντες) in the κοινωνία (2:42).[125] This concept is clarified in vs. 44–45: "And all who believed were together and had all things in common [κοινὰ]. And they were selling their possessions and belongings and distributing the proceeds to all, as any had need". A superficial reading of these verses suggest that the believers used to live together (ἦσαν ἐπὶ τὸ αὐτὸ), that all of them were selling everything they had, and that they had in fact a common basket into which they placed the proceeds of everything they were selling and from which people could take money according to their needs. This common basket could be an emulation of the purse Jesus and the disciples seem to have shared (cf. John 12:6).[126]

This reconstruction of the community of goods, however, does not hold itself completely together in a close reading of the text. In the next verse, Acts 2:46, Luke explains that the believers were "breaking bread from house to house" (NKJV) (κλῶντές τε κατ' οἶκον ἄρτον). This multiplicity of houses in which they were eating can be understood in two ways. Either the community of goods of the believers in Jerusalem had more than one house in which a few families would live together, or, in another possible reading, each family was living in its own house and the communality was not as comprehensive as the verses 44–45 seem to imply.

It is important to remember that at least some of those three thousand new converts were not originally inhabitants of Jerusalem, but were Jews who had come from other countries (cf. Acts 2:5–11). The apostles and other disciples were from Galilee and not from Jerusalem either. Thus, it is possible, that at least in some measure, these communities of good were indeed of a more

---

124. "Evidently the church's unity and the community of goods that expressed that unity most tellingly were of special interest to the narrator, who emphasizes them in the first two summaries and introduces related scenes." Parsons, *Luke*, 48.

125. According to BDAG (p. 552), κοινωνία is a "close association involving mutual interests and sharing, association, communion, fellowship, close relationship". Although in our text the concept is explained in very practical terms, Peterson is right in remembering that "this sharing was clearly a practical expression of the new relationship experienced together through a common faith in Christ." Peterson, *The Acts of the Apostles*, 160.

126. See more details on this relation in Capper, "Holy Community of Life and Property amongst the Poor," 113–14.

comprehensive type, sharing house, food and life together. Also, among the number of converts, it is possible that at least some of them were already from Essene communities of goods, who only transferred their way of living to the community of Christians.[127] Thus, it seems mandatory to accept that at least a number of the first disciples were living in a community of goods, albeit not everyone.

In Acts 4:32-37 Luke presents another summary and, again, there is a heavy focus on the economic aspects of the unity of the church. Luke illustrates the affirmation that each one of the believers were "one heart and soul" with the information that "no one said that any of the things that belonged to him was his own, but they had everything in common [κοινά]" (v. 32). This verse is very important because it illustrates in very practical terms the meaning of the communality experienced by the church in Jerusalem. Since people had things that belonged to them (τι τῶν ὑπαρχόντων αὐτῷ), this communality did not preclude the right of having private property. At the same time, there was a disposition of letting other people use what rightfully belonged to one of them. In this sense, they had everything in common. The things each one of them owned continued being a property of the original owner, but this original owner had a heart and soul disposition of letting everyone else use what belonged to him.[128] Smith presents the result and link with Jubilee precisely: "The result of this practice is stated in Acts 4:34: "There was not a needy person among them (οὐδὲ γὰρ ἐνδεής τις ἦν ἐν αὐτοῖς)." This is the clearest reference to a socially rich Pentateuchal text in Luke-Acts, reproducing very nearly the result of the Sabbath year debt forgiveness outlined in Deut 15:4: "There will be no one in need among you (οὐκ ἔσται ἐν σοὶ ἐνδεής)."[129]

Both the vocabulary and the reality Luke describes in his summaries draw upon Greco-Roman ideals of friendship. The oneness of soul is spoken about by Aristotle, Cicero and Plutarch.[130] A partial kind of property communality is envisioned by Seneca and Plato, and enacted by Cynic and Pythagorean

---

127. Capper, "Holy Community of Life and Property amongst the Poor," 121.

128. This interpretation is defended by: Walton, "Primitive Communism in Acts?," 99–111; Tannehill, "Acts of the Apostles and Ethics," 281.

129. Smith, "'No Poor Among Them,'" 160.

130. See examples and references in Talbert, *Reading Acts*; Walton, "Primitive Communism in Acts?"; Van Der Horst, "Hellenistic Parallels to the Acts of the Apostles," 58–59.

communities.¹³¹ Alan Mitchell is correct when he affirms that the Greek traditions on friendship are not equal among themselves, that friendship would only occur among equals, and that instead of a mere descriptive and literary function, Luke uses this *topos* as ". . . a vehicle for encouraging the rich of his community to benefit the poor, by transferring to them some of the normal benefits well-off friends took for granted."¹³² Mitchell also shows that the picture presented by Luke is more similar to Aristotle's and Cicero's proposals of a society in which property is a mix of common and private ownership.¹³³ Luke´s goal, therefore, is reshaping the friendship tradition in order to motivate the believers in Jerusalem to emulate these ideals in a way that previous socio-economic divisions would not stand in the way of sharing property especially with those who needed more.¹³⁴

Another important background for the community of goods practiced in the church of Jerusalem were the communities of goods of the Essenes. The main current advocate of an identification between the *modus operandi* of these two is Brian Capper. He affirms that the Essenes were the "dominant social and religious force amongst the laborers, artisans and needy of the villages and towns of rural Judea", with around four thousand male celibate strict practitioners and "several tens of thousands" married Essenes of a second and less radical order.¹³⁵ The economy and social conditions of Judea facilitated the propagation of Essenism and possibly of other similar groups.¹³⁶

---

131. See examples and references in Talbert, *Reading Acts*, 48–49.

132. Mitchell, "The Social Function of Friendship in Acts 2:44–47 and 4:32–37," 258.

133. Mitchell, "The Social Function of Friendship in Acts 2:44–47 and 4:32–37," 262.

134. "Luke, however, uses friendship to equalize relationships in his own community. He portrays the early Jerusalem community in Acts as a community of friends to show how friendship can continue across status lines and the poor can be benefited by the rich. Redefining friendship this way helps Luke to achieve his social objective: encouraging the rich to provide relief for the poor of his own community." Mitchell, "The Social Function of Friendship in Acts 2:44–47 and 4:32–37," 272. A very similar interpretation is defended by Zimmerman, "Neither Social Revolution nor Utopian Ideal," 777–86.

135. Capper, "Holy Community of Life and Property amongst the Poor," 116.

136. "Overpopulation and scarcity of resources characterized [sic] the ancient agrarian economy. The needy were frequently compelled to migration, perhaps to seek work in the large coastal cities, to soldiering, or to work on large estates as servants or slaves. Women were frequently forced into prostitution. Essenism offered different options for the needy of Judaea. Children who could not be fed in poor local families could be adopted into Essene communities, where they received training in work, economic security, and education in holy tradition." Capper, "Holy Community of Life and Property amongst the Poor," 117.

John the Baptist's and Jesus's discipleship groups were such kind of groups.[137] To Capper, therefore, following the example of Jesus's disciples, the whole Christian community lived for one year or so in a regimen of complete communality of goods, emulating the inner group of the Essenes, situation that changed, he suspects, after the event of Ananias and Sapphira's death.[138] He says: "When we find, therefore, in the Acts of the Apostles, the early church of Jerusalem sharing their property and joining together in daily common meals, we are observing a well-established feature of Judaean cultural and economic life, practiced by the primary Essene order and perhaps other groups too. It was, of course, a 'virtuoso' way of life practiced by only a very small minority of Judaea's inhabitants."[139]

Capper's reconstruction of the early Jesus movement is very well researched and defended. He is right, I think, that there existed inside the church in Jerusalem more radical kinds of communities of goods. The weakness of his reconstruction, however, is the imposition of the rigid rules of the Essenes to the earliest Christian group as a whole. Without the rigid rules of Essenism, it is possible to reconstruct the Christian movement in a way that more radical versions of communal life coexisted with less radical forms. It seems that this view does more justice in light of the record of Luke in Acts.

Going back to Acts 4:34–35, one finds the other illustration of the Jerusalem church's communality. Now Luke gives an example of the χάρις μεγάλη that was present among all of them, i.e., there was no needy person (ἐνδεής) among them. The ἐνδεής in this context is important because although it is a *hapax legomena* in the New Testament, it appears in a very suggestive context in the Septuagint, i.e., Deut 15; the Deuteronomic repetition of the jubilee laws of Lev 25: ὅτι οὐκ ἔσται ἐν σοὶ ἐνδεής (for there will be no need one among you, Deut 15:4). It seems that through this vocabulary reference, Luke is presenting the community of goods of Jerusalem as a community in which the purpose of the jubilee ethics is being reached, i.e. the eradication

---

137. Capper, "The Judaean Cultural Context of Community of Goods in the Early Jesus Movement: Part II."

138. Capper, "Holy Community of Life and Property amongst the Poor," 121.

139. Capper, "The Judaean Cultural Context of Community of Goods in the Early Jesus Movement: Part II," 36.

of poverty inside the community.¹⁴⁰ The practical illustration is that "as many as were owners of lands or houses sold them and brought the proceeds of what was sold and laid it at the apostles' feet, and it was distributed to each as any had need." Literally, this text affirms that everyone among the believers who owned fields and houses sold and donated them to the apostle's fund. The text does not affirm that the proceeds were placed in a common purse to which everyone had access, but that there was a special fund administered by the apostles that existed to meet the needs of those who needed more.¹⁴¹

Luke wants to make very clear this characteristic of the church. Thus, in Acts 4:36–37 and in Acts 5:1–11 he presents examples of real people who did that; a good example and a bad one. The good example is the one of Joseph, best known as Barnabas. Luke uses these verses to present the personage Barnabas and his good example as one of the people who sold a field that belonged to him and laid it at the apostles' feet. Barnabas was living what the jubilee land ethics entails.

The bad example is the one of Ananias and Sapphira (5:1–11). In this pericopae, one learns some of the characteristics of the community of goods: The selling of fields and houses and other possessions was not compulsory. We know that from Peter's rhetorical questions in v. 4: "While it remained unsold, did it not remain your own? And after it was sold, was it not at your disposal?" Ananias and Sapphira could have continued being part of the church without selling their property or giving the money. Another characteristic one learns from this account is the gravity of the matter. Although many commentators try to detach the lie from the economic context, it is impossible to do so. From Acts 4:32 onward, Luke's focus is in the communality of goods as a mark of the unity of the church. Ananias and Sapphira were not just lying, but lying in a very important matter, something that had

---

140. "Thus Luke presents the messianic community in Jerusalem as fulfilling the hopes and ideals embodied in the Torah for a community life in which no one was poor or in need.... Accordingly, property and money are held in trust on behalf of their divine owner: the forgiving of debts every seven years, as well as the radical Jubilee legislation, were signals of limits on the 'rights' (if we may use such a term in relation to biblical thought) os private property under the sovereign rule of Yahweh." Walton, "Primitive Communism in Acts?," 105.

141. "This suggests a strong desire at work in the community that no one be in need, rather than that all members should have the same amount." Zimmerman, "Neither Social Revolution nor Utopian Ideal," 780.

to do with the essence of the church at that point. Both these examples will be more deeply treated further in this dissertation.

The last reference one reads in Acts about to the community of goods is found in Acts 6:1–7. Some scholars affirm that this narrative is the way Luke uses to show the problems and the end of the community of goods. Finger explains this text affirming that the widows were not the ones receiving the food, but the ones in charge of the preparation of food and the problem between Hebrew and Greek speaking widows was a relational one.[142] This reconstruction, although creative, does not make sense in light of the canon.

The administration of the διακονεῖν τραπέζαις was so important that it was part of the apostolic function and it needed to be assumed by spiritually qualified men who were in a sense ordained as church representatives to do this service.[143] As the focus of the book departs from the church in Jerusalem to Samaria, Antioch and Rome, Luke stops describing the community of goods that characterized the church in Jerusalem.[144] Yet, one finds evidence of sharing needs and providing hospitality throughout the rest of Acts (see esp. Acts 9:25–28; 11:27–30; 12:12; 16:40; 18:1–3, 7, 18; 20:33–35; 21:15–16; 27:3).

It is not correct to doubt Luke's integrity and affirm that he created this community of goods according to the same utopian descriptions of it in the Greek world. Neither it is correct to blame the economic crisis that hits the church in Jerusalem to the fact that they used to live such a practice, since the book itself nowhere represents this attitude as being wrong or misguided; quite the contrary, Luke presents this community of goods as a reality and an example of the practice of the church in its better moments and original form. Among those who affirm that the community of goods was a fact, one will find scholars who relativize the application of this reality to contemporary times attributing the existence of that community to a situational ethics. There are also scholars who defend that the community of goods should be the ethical norm for the church of all times.[145]

---

142. Finger, "A Theology of Welcome."

143. Thomaz de Aquino, "Atos 6:1–7: A Gênese Do Ofício Diaconal?," 9–20.

144. For more information on the way Luke portrays the church of Jerusalem, see Bruce, "The Church of Jerusalem in Acts of the Apostles," 641–61.

145. Acuña, "'No Había Entre Ellos Ningún Necesitado,'" 35–53.

Having secured the existence and property of the community of goods one finds in Acts of the Apostles, the next section presents the way in which this reality was lived in the regards to land properties and houses of the believers.

5.5.2 The Community of Goods in Acts of the Apostles and Land

In the previous section I defended that there was indeed a community of goods in the church of Jerusalem that lived in property communality, but with different levels of voluntary sharing. While some people sold everything, they had to live in complete material communality, others kept their properties and used them for the good of those in need. This section aims to present how this reality impacted the attitude of the early believers related to their landed properties.

The first aspect of the land jubilee ethics in Acts is the selling of land properties in order to contribute to the common good and to the poor. This is referred to in Acts 2:45; 4:34–35, 36–37; 5:1–11; texts that we will briefly analyze again, with a specific focus on land.

The first of these texts is Acts 2:45. We need to answer two questions in this verse: The first is, does this verse refer specifically to landed property? And the second, does the imperfect tense of πίπρασκον and διεμέριζον implies that these were recurrent practices done whenever need arose?[146] The two Greek words used by Luke to refer to property are κτῆμα and ὕπαρξις. This second word is defined in the sense of "that which one has, property, possession".[147] It is used with the meaning of clothes (Aristophanes, *Ecclesiazusae* 654), the attribute of a science (Aristotle, *Eth. Eud.* 1.1218b), armament (Demosthenes, *Exordia* 30.1), business affairs (Plato, *Epistles* 7.339c), livestock (LXX of 2 Chr 35:7), everything necessary to explore the ocean (Julian the Emperor, *Epistulae* 1) or general belongings (LXX of Ezra 10:8).[148] This word is a very generic one, pointing to belongings and properties in general. In Acts 2:45,

---

146. This position implied in the last question is taken by, among others, Witherington, *The Acts of the Apostles*, 162; Newman and Nida, *A Handbook on the Acts of the Apostles*, 65.

147. BDAG, 1029. Cf. also Louw-Nida 57.16; EDNT, 395

148. Check this and other references of this word in Greek works by visiting: http://www.perseus.tufts.edu/hopper/searchresults?target=greek&all_words=u%28%2Fparcis&all_words_expand=on&phrase=&any_words=&exclude_words=&documents=

therefore, this word should be taken as referring to anything that could be sold to make money, like clothing, furniture, tools, field production and so on.

The first word, κτῆμα, I contend, has a more restricted idea. BDAG presents two meanings for it: "(1) that which is acquired or possessed", in which they place the occurrence of Acts 2:45 and, "(2) landed property, field, piece of ground", about which they comment "in later usage, κτῆμα came to be restricted to this meaning". The scholars behind BDAG place the occurrence in Acts 5:1 among this second sense.[149]

I argue that BDAG is wrong in attributing the first meaning to Acts 2:45 and that the word should be read as landed property. First, in the LXX there are twelve occurrences of this word; seven of which have the narrower sense of field and five with the sense of general possessions.[150] Second, in the New Testament there are four occurrences of κτῆμα, all of them, I contend, better interpreted as field, landed property or estate.[151] Third, in the context of Acts 2:45, κτῆμα appears together with ὕπαρξις with has the meaning of general properties, making obsolete the use of κτῆμα with this same meaning. Fourth, in Acts 5:1, κτῆμα is used interchangeably with χωρίον (Acts 5:3, 8), which means "a piece of land, field" (BDAG, 1095). Finally, although κτῆμα is used in the same epoch of the New Testament mostly with the meaning of possessions in general, even when the word is used in this sense, it carries many times land as one of the possessions referred, even because the most important kind of possession one could have in the first century, as I demonstrated in chapters 2 and 3, was land.

The second aspect of this summary deserving comment is the use of the imperfect and the possible implication of frequent action. Recent studies on the imperfect question the idea of time on it. Campbell, for example, affirms that "the imperfect indicative grammaticalizes both imperfective aspect and spatial remoteness".[152] Decker agrees with Campbell.[153] Runge, on another

---

149. BDAG, 572.

150. Proverbs 12:27; 23:10; 29:34; Job 20:29; 27:13; Wisdom of Solomon 8:5; 13:17; Sirach 28:24; 36:30; 51:21; Hosea 2:15; Joel 1:11.

151. Matt 19:22; Mark 10:22; Acts 2:45, 5:1.

152. Campbell, *Verbal Aspect, the Indicative Mood, and Narrative*, 78.

153. "The substantive difference between the present and imperfect forms is *remoteness*. The imperfect is used in statements that are more remote than statements using the present. The imperfect may be logically, temporarily, physically, or focally remote compared to the present tense-form. The imperfect often has a *discourse function* in the narrative: it supplies

hand, still keeps the idea of time in the imperfect.¹⁵⁴ Whether or not the imperfect grammaticalizes time, the imperfects of Acts 2:42–47 are to be interpreted as iterative imperfects, indicating repeated or customary actions.¹⁵⁵ This use of the imperfect is evident in the passage by the deictic use of the verb προσκαρτερέω in v. 42, denoting to persist or persevere (BDAG, 881), and the double use of καθ' ἡμέραν in v. 46 and 47.

Thus, Luke's focus in this first summary in what concerns land is showing in a highly condensed way that the first group of Christians was applying in a very practical way the jubilee ethics presented in his gospel. He will make this even clearer and yet more central in the next summary.

In Acts 4:32–35, Luke presents more details on how the land jubilee ethics was being applied by the church: those who had χωρίων or οἰκιῶν (note the plural), were selling at least some of them and bringing the money to be administrated by the apostles.¹⁵⁶ These summaries emphasize subjects Luke wants the reader to pay special attention to as he narrates the history.¹⁵⁷ Thus, this land ethics is something the reader should pay special attention, especially considering that it becomes the center of the narrative from 4:32 to 5:11. The use of houses, about which we will see in the next section, the nature of the summaries' customary actions the narrator wants to stress instead of events and the examples Luke presents to the reader to point that

---

background information or sometimes introduces dialogue or summary statements". Decker, *Reading Koine Greek*.

154. "Since both present- and imperfect-tense forms grammaticalize imperfective aspect, theoretically either one could be used for offline information in narrative, but this is not the case. Since the imperfect-tense form is associated with the past time and the present with present time, there is a preference for using the form that best matches the temporal setting. The imperfect is the default means of signaling the offline information in a past-time setting, freeing the present-tense form for use as prominence marker." Runge, *Discourse Grammar of the Greek New Testament*, 130.

155. See Köstenberger, Merkle, and Plummer, *Going Deeper with New Testament Greek*.

156. "Thus it is entirely compatible for Luke to write of people selling their property and the proceeds being distributed to those in need (2:45; 4:34–35) alongside references to private homes where the believers met (e.g. 2:46, κατ' οἶκον; 12:12). Indeed, it seems likely that these references imply that believers did not sell their own houses, but other properties which belonged to them." Walton, "Primitive Communism in Acts?," 103–4.

157. "Evidently the church's unity and the community of goods that expressed that unity most tellingly were of special interest to the narrator, who emphasizes them in the first two summaries and introduces related scenes." Tannehill, *The Narrative Unity of Luke-Acts*, 44.

the selling and donation was voluntary and those who donated probably also kept other properties.[158]

In order to illustrate this important aspect of the life of the church, the communion of goods even at the expense of their own land, Luke presents two examples, the Levite Ἰωσὴφ Βαρναβᾶς and the couple Ἀνανίας and Σαπφίρη, which we will briefly analyze.

According to the Old Testament, although the Levite tribe did not receive a portion of land (Deut 10:9; Josh 10:14), the Levites could own houses inside cities and fields for pasture adjacent to the cities (Num 35:1–2; Deut 18:6–8; Neh 13:10). Besides that, in the first century, these laws had been relaxed and as it was demonstrated in previous chapters, the priests were part of the elite in Israel and had land, which was also true for Levites, as one can see with the family of Mark, who was Barnabas' cousin (Acts 12:12–13; Col 4:10). Thus, it is not possible to know if Barnabas' field was in Jerusalem or in Cyprus, nor the size of the field, neither if he had other properties, which he probably did have.[159] The fact is that he deposited the whole proceeds of the field at the apostles' feet.

The second example Luke presents of people living the land jubilee ethics is a negative one. The couple Ananias and Sapphira had a κτῆμα (5:1), a χωρίον (5:3, 8), a piece of land which, as Barnabas', was rented to one or more tenants, or was developed by themselves and their family, or by hired hands. The fact is that a piece of land in that time was always a producing field, rarely an idle one. It produced the subsistence for a family that managed to keep its field amidst the pressure of taxes or the surplus that enriched the wealthy. The text does not present the reader with all information one would like to read. What was the context of the giving, a worship service or something else? Did the laying of money at the apostles' feet imply giving everything or did Ananias tell Peter he was giving everything, and Luke does not tell us that?

---

158. "It is important to note that this sharing of possessions was voluntary and occasional. Their needs were related to the physical and social environment in which they found themselves. Their progressive isolation from unbelieving Israel must have made the economic situation of many quite precarious. Here was no primitive form of 'communism', but a generous response to particular problems in their midst (cf. 4:34–5)." Peterson, *The Acts of the Apostles*, 163.

159. Barnabas' selling of the field, as significant as it was, ought thus to be understood not as a complete surrender of property but rather as a partial disposal of that property for charitable reasons." Kollmann, *Joseph Barnabas: His Life and Legacy*, 12. For a provoking article on Barnabas, see Read-Heimerdinger, "Barnabas in Acts," 23–66.

Once Ananias and Sapphira were giving the money, would they be able to benefit from the common basket as if they were destitute? Did Ananias and Sapphira have other properties?

The function of the exegete is not creatively providing information the text does not have, but working with the text as Luke wrote it. The sin of Ananias and Sapphira is described in the text as keeping back or embezzling (νοσφίζω) part of the money (v. 2 and 3); allowing Satan to fill their heart (v. 3), and placing that deed in their hearts (v. 4); lying to the Holy Spirit (v. 3), and lying to God (v. 4); and, finally, agreeing in testing the Holy Spirit (v. 9). The first six accusations appear in the first part of the text which deals mostly with Ananias, and the last accusation is the one Peter makes to Sapphira. The first six are presented in the text in form of pairs and each part of the pair explain the other. It seems that Luke took care not to stress any of the main three accusations above any of the others. He starts with the concept of νοσφίζω and then makes it part of what Satan filled Ananias' heart with. He presents the lying as part of what Satan placed in the heart of Ananias and then concludes with this idea. Finally, he affirms that Ananias was responsible for having placed this deed (πρᾶγμα) in his heart. To Sapphira, Peter affirms that their sin was having agreed to put the Holy Spirit to test.

The concepts of lying and acceding to the satanic temptation are clear, but the νοσφίζω needs to be further clarified. Most versions agree to translate it as "keep back" (ESV, NIV, NKJV, RSV). BDAG presents the following definition: "to put aside for oneself, keep back, of engagement in a type of skimming operation".[160] Capper makes a strong case for embezzling.[161] Analyzing occurrences of this word in other places we find that it is used only one other time in the New Testament, in Titus 2:10, an instruction to slaves not to pilfer (ESV) or steal (NIV). In the LXX, one finds this word used in the event of Achan. The text is introduced affirming: "And the children of Israel committed a great sin and took for themselves (ἐνοσφίσαντο) from the cursed city." (Josh 7:1). The only other instance in the LXX is in 2 Maccabees 4:32.[162] Both texts carry the idea of something misappropriated. In Philo one finds thirteen occurrences

---

160. BDAG, 679.

161. Capper, "The Interpretation of Acts 5:4," 117–3.

162. But Menelaus, thinking he could seize a convenient opportunity, stole (νοσφισάμενος) some golden vessels from those of the temple.

of the word; all of them have this same idea of misappropriating.[163] One of them is very interesting because of the repetition of a few terms and ideas that occur in our text: "For all things (πάντα κτήματα) belong to God; so he who attributes anything to himself is taking away (νοσφίζεται καὶ) what belongs to another, and receives a very severe blow and one difficult to heal, namely, arrogance, a thing (πρᾶγμα) nearly akin to imprudence and ignorance."[164]

Based in the evidence above, the use in the text, and the semantic use of νοσφίζω in other works of the same epoch, we are compelled to conclude that Ananias and Sapphira's wrongdoing was not only the fact that they lied, succumbed to Satan's temptation in their heart, plotted together to tempt the Holy Spirit, but also that they robbed God, they schemed in order to keep a money that did not belong to them anymore. We are not able to know if this was clear by placing the money at the apostles' feet, if that was a rule of the Christian community in light of Qur'anic practices,[165] or if Ananias had declared to be giving everything, but the text makes clear that at that point he was robbing from God, although before and after selling the property, it was lawfully his (Acts 5:4).

Thus, through the good examples of the community of goods and Barnabas and through the bad example of Ananias and Sapphira, Luke presents a clear demonstration of people enacting the jubilee land ethics in the church, as well as of the consequences of ignoring or acting against this principle.

5.5.3 Land Jubilee Ethics and Christian Hospitality

The second aspect of the land jubilee ethics one finds in Acts is Christian hospitality.[166] In the first chapter of Acts we find the eleven apostles with

---

163. Concerning Noah's Work as a Planter 103; Who Is the Heir of Divine Things 106, 107; Who Is the Heir of Divine Things 107; On Mating with the Preliminary Studies 75; On Dreams 2.99; On Joseph 258, 260; On the Life of Moses 1.253; The Decalogue 171; The Special Laws 4.34; Flaccus 69; On the Embassy to Gaius: The First Part on the Treatise on Virtues 199.

164. "Allegorical Interpretation," 3.33 In Philo of Alexandria and Charles Duke Yonge, *The Works of Philo*, 53.

165. Capper, "The Interpretation of Acts 5:4."

166. See detailed study of this topic and Luke-Acts and in the whole Bible in Jipp, *Divine Visitations and Hospitality to Strangers in Luke-Acts*; Jipp, *Saved by Faith and Hospitality*. As an introduction to the theme see Jipp: "the God of the Christian Scripture is a God of hospitality, a God who extends hospitality to his people and who requires that his people embody hospitality to others. Stated simply, God's hospitality to us is the basis of our hospitality to one another. . . . Hospitality is the act or process whereby the identity of the stranger is transformed into that of a guest. While hospitality often uses the basic necessities of life such as the protection of one's

Mary and Jesus's brothers in a cenacle (ὑπερῷον).¹⁶⁷ The text informs they were living there, since the verb καταμένω has the connotation of dwelling, or inhabiting temporarily somewhere.¹⁶⁸ Although it is not possible to be certain of the location of this ὑπερῷον and if it was rented or borrowed, it is certain that the apostles and other associates were living together. There is a chance that this room is the same as for other meetings between Jesus and the disciples, but it is not possible to be sure.¹⁶⁹

In Acts 2, we find the group of around one hundred twenty people (the πάντες in 2:1 refers back to Acts 1:15) sat in a house (οἶκον, Acts 2:2). Again, there is no information about the owner of this house and if the apostles were renting, borrowing or had bought it. The fact is that the whole congregation is together in a very large house that allows for one hundred and twenty people to sit together.

As Luke's account of the church develops, it becomes very clear that hospitality towards the Christian movement is of central importance. The church meets from house to house, people host churches, itinerant gospel workers need to count on the hospitality of believers to spread the word around the world. The exiguity of space does not allow us to develop this aspect more deeply, but the citation of the occurrences of Christian hospitality in Acts suffice to our argument:

2:2 Disciples meeting in a house

2:46 Christians ate together from house to house

5:42 Christians preached from house to house

9:43; 10:17, 32 Peter in a house of Simon, a tanner

10 Cornelius receives Peter and a church in his house

---

home and the offer of food, drink, conversation, and clothing, the primary impulse of hospitality is to create relationships and friendships between those who were previously either alienated, at enmity, or simply unknown to one another. Thus, the language of 'friendship' or 'fictive' kinship is closely related to hospitality to strangers". Jipp, *Saved by Faith and Hospitality*, 2.

167. "*The room* is literally 'the room upstairs,' and this word is used elsewhere in the New Testament only in Acts 9:37, 39 and 20:8. The type of room referred to is a tower-like construction built on the flat roof of an oriental house and reached by a stairway from the outside. Nothing further is known regarding the identity of this particular room." Newman and Nida, *A Handbook on the Acts of the Apostles*, 22.

168. Cf. LXX Gen 6:3; Num 20:1; 22:8; Josh 2:22; 7:7; Judith 16:20; and also TestLevi 9:5; Josephus Ant. 6,249; 7,180.

169. The cenacle Jesus borrowed to eat the last supper with his disciples is called κατάλυμα in Luke 22:11 and ἀνάγαιον in Luke 22:12 and Mark 14:15.

10:23 Peter hosts the group from Cornelius

12:12 Mary, mother of John Mark welcomed a many people in her house

16:15, 40 Lydia welcomes Paul and Silas and the church

16:30–34 The jailer welcomed Paul and Silas in his house

17:5, 7 Paul and Silas are welcomed and protected in Jason's house

18:3 Paul dwells with Aquila and Priscila

18:7 Titius Justus hosts Paul, Silas and Timothy

20:20 Paul affirms that he taught the word from house to house

21:8 Paul, Luke and other are hosted by the evangelist Philip

21:16 Paul and a group of disciples from Caesarea are hosted at Mnason's house

28:6 Paul stays with Publius in his villa at Malta Island

28:11 The brothers in Puteoli ask Paul and his entourage to stay with them for seven days

28:16, 30 Paul welcomes everybody in his house prison

The number of instances related to hospitality in Acts makes clear the importance of the subject to the Christian church and the fact that this, besides the selling of fields and houses, was also a way to apply the jubilee land ethics.

5.6 The Expansion of the Holy Land

The focus of this dissertation is mainly ethical, about how Luke applies the jubilee laws to his Christian readers. I made clear in the beginning that the focus of the present work is not the rightful ownership of the territory God has promised to Abraham. My focus is instead on how those who accepted Jesus Christ as the Jewish Messiah and Savior of the world are supposed to deal with any land God has entrusted to them.

This does not mean that this author ignores the importance of the land of Israel, and especially of Jerusalem in the literary and theological scheme created by Luke in his double volume work. That Luke writes his two-volume work in such a way that Jerusalem is at the center is well known.[170]

---

170. "However, Luke is also interested in geography and space: at a basic level this is shown by the way he structures his gospel's main narrative in three main geographical sections

There is heavy discussion among scholars if the role Luke attributes to Jerusalem and the holy land is temporary with or with no restoration in the future. Peter Walker, for example, defends the position that Luke-Acts presents the temporary importance of Jerusalem, its role in accrediting the gospel message and the Christian church and its ultimate rejection from God, which eventually makes Jerusalem a common place as any other. He sees no future restoration for Jerusalem and consequently the holy land in Luke-Acts.[171] He argues that the centrality of Jerusalem gives way in the narrative to the importance of other places.[172] Levine concurs with Walker.[173] Tannehill affirms that Acts is a tragic story for the promises of the beginning are not fulfilled inside the book. He opens the possibility however of a restoration of

---

(Galilee, 4:14–9:50; Jordan, 9:51–19:27; and Jerusalem, 19:28–24:53) and then radiates out from Jerusalem to the ends of the earth in Acts (1:8)." Burridge, *Imitating Jesus: An Inclusive Approach to the New Testament Ethics*. The classical work on this subject is Conzelmann, *The Theology of St. Luke*, 70 et seq.

171. Walker, *Jesus and the Holy City: New Testament Perspectives on Jerusalem*, 59.

172. "There are frequent returns to Jerusalem, but these become fewer, and give way to Paul's extended journey away from Jerusalem towards Rome. There is a gradual severance from Jerusalem, with the city becoming increasingly 'dispensable'. . . . God is not tied to Jerusalem, and those holding such ideas may make Jerusalem and even God's temple into an idol." Walker, *Jesus and the Holy City*, 81–82. Ahead, he says: "This theme of *centrifugal* going-out of the gospel from Jerusalem needs to be contrasted with the more predominant *centripetal* notions that were current at the time, as expressed both in the phenomenon of pilgrimage, and also in the belief in the eschatological 'ingathering of the Gentiles' to Jerusalem. Such notions kept Jerusalem very much at the centre. Now there were inverted: the message of Christ turned to prophetic hopes into a new direction." (83)

173. "One can regard the various predictions of Jerusalem's destruction (13:33–35; 21:20–24; 23:27–31) as 'pathetic, not vindictive,' and Jesus does weep over Jerusalem (19:41–44), but the result is the same. The last lines of the Gospel state that Jesus' followers 'returned to Jerusalem with great joy; and they were continually in the temple blessing God' (24:52–53), but this setting is at best a stopgap measure. Their new location is not Jerusalem but the ends of the earth (Acts 1:8; cf. Luke 24:47). The Gospel hints at what Acts displays: the Jerusalem community eventually disappears, so that no one is left to support Paul; churches are formed outside the land of Israel and thus fully detached from the sacred space of the 'Jewish religion.' Further, it is only Jesus' followers who are found blessing God in the temple." Levine, "Luke and the Jewish Religion," 395.

Jerusalem and Israel for the future.[174] Fusco also speaks about this possibility.[175] Brawley on another hand contends that the fate of Jerusalem, the land, and the people of Israel is open-ended.[176]

Although these scholars do not agree about the theological and practical future of Jerusalem in the theology of Luke, they all agree that there is in Luke a transference in importance from Jerusalem to the rest of the world. Indeed, geographical references appear more than four hundred times in Luke-Acts.[177] From these, Jerusalem appears 90 times. The rest of the occur-

---

174. "After the mission's initial success in Jerusalem, the emphasis in Acts falls on Jewish resistance and rejection. Even this does not mean that the hope for Israel is dead. After all, the kingdom for Israel was promised by God through the prophets, and it is not likely that the author of Luke-Acts would admit that this important aspect of God's purpose has been finally frustrated. However, the story in Acts, so far as the author takes us, is not the story of the fulfillment of this hope but the story of a tragic turn away from fulfillment. The repeated references to Israel's messianic hope during the transition from Luke to Acts remind the reader that this hope is not yet fulfilled and prepare for this tragic turn." Tannehill, "Israel in Luke-Acts," 76–77.

175. "Walking towards Jerusalem, fully aware of the hostility awaiting him there (9:51), at a certain point Jesus breaks out in a lament over the city (13:31–35; par. Matt 23:37–39). First Jesus foretells his own death in Jerusalem and its consequences for the city— 'See, your house is left to you. And I tell you, you will not see me . . .' — but then adds: '. . . until the time comes when you say "Blessed is the one who comes in the name of the Lord!"'. This latter statement seems to offer a glimmer of hope. Within sight of the city, Jesus weeps on account of its fate which is already sealed, but attributes it to the blindness which at this moment (νυν) has enveloped Jerusalem (19:41–44). Later on, he concludes his public teaching at the temple (Luke 21:5 diff. Mark 13:3), foretelling the destruction of the city (Luke 21:20–24a), but even then he adds a mysterious allusion to its future: 'And Jerusalem will be trampled on by the Gentiles, until the times of the Gentiles are fulfilled' (Luke. 21:24b)." Fusco, "Luke-Acts and the Future of Israel," 10–11.

176. "With such a focus on Paul's mission in Asia Minor, Macedonia, and Greece, it is true that the growth of the Jerusalem congregation fades into the background. But not entirely. When Paul returns to Jerusalem in Acts 21:20, James informs him "how many myriads" among the Jews have believed (literally, 'how many tens of thousands')." Brawley, "Ethical Borderlines between Rejection and Hope: Interpreting the Jews in Luke-Acts," 420. In the next page, Brawley says: "But turning to Gentiles in the previous cases does not mean an end to Paul's mission among Jews. On the contrary, at the end of Acts Paul still has a measure of success among Jewish people. Thus, a number of pointers indicate that, as harsh as the quotation from Isaiah is, it does not mean that Luke writes off the Jews. . . . Just as at the end of the story of Simon the Pharisee the question of his response is left open, so also at the end of Acts the response of Jewish people to the proclamation about Jesus is left open. It is obviously possible for readers to fill in the ending with the conclusion that Luke-Acts rejects the Jews. But my reading above is evidence for the possibility (I would actually contend "probability") that Luke does not close the door on the Jews.

177. "With the help of semantic domain lexicons, a close examination of the New Testament writings shows that only the book of Revelation comes anywhere close to the consistent quantity and variety of geographical terms found in Luke and Acts. Thus, while Luke was not a geographer per se, he was interested in geography, and it will be instructive

rences are about half referring to other places in Israel and half dealing with other places in the world. The "international" references occur mainly in the last half of Acts of the Apostles.

In the gospel of Luke, one finds references to places like Syria (Luke 2:1; 4:27); Ituraea, Trachonitis, and Abilene (Luke 3:1); Zarephath in the land of Sidon (Luke 4:26); Tyre and Sidon (Luke 6:17; 10:14); country of the Gerasenes, which is opposite Galilee (Luke 8:26), Sodom (Luke 10:12); ends of the earth (Luke 11:31); east and west, and from north and south (Luke 13:29); far country (Luke 15:13; 19:12); the whole land (Luke 23:44); all nations (Luke 24:47).

In some of these instances, Luke is showing God or Jesus expanding their blessing outside of Israel (Luke 4:26–27; 8:26) and the centripetal force of God or Jesus of attracting people from outside Israel (Luke 6:17; 11:31; 13:29). The last international geographical reference of the gospel is very suggestive and central to the narrative Luke is writing: "Thus it is written, that the Christ should suffer and on the third day rise from the dead, and that repentance for the forgiveness of sins should be proclaimed in his name to all nations, beginning from Jerusalem" (Luke 24:47).

The book of Acts starts where the gospel stopped, making a reference that the gospel is to be preached to the end of the earth (Acts 1:8). The next reference points again to the centripetal force of the gospel, attracting people "from every nation under heaven" (Luke 2:5). The text presents the list: "Parthians and Medes and Elamites and residents of Mesopotamia, Judea and Cappadocia, Pontus and Asia, Phrygia and Pamphylia, Egypt and the parts of Libya belonging to Cyrene, and visitors from Rome, both Jews and proselytes, Cretans and Arabians—we hear them telling in our own tongues the mighty works of God." (Acts 2:9–11). In the discourse of Stephen, he makes clear that God appeared to Abraham in Mesopotamia (Acts 7:2), was present with Joseph in Egypt (Acts 7:9), appeared to Moses "in the wilderness of Mount Sinai" (Acts 7:30), and revealed himself in the tabernacle in the desert (7:44). The idea Luke is showing through these references if that God is still God outside of Israel and the whole world belongs to him.

---

to create a map of Luke's symbolic world based on his literary texts." Parsons, "The Place of Jerusalem on the Lukan Landscape," 158–59.

Continuing the book, Luke shows the resurrected Jesus Christ in action in Damascus in the conversion of Saul (9:1–25), Peter preaching to a gentile in Caesarea and "those who were scattered because of the persecution" preaching in "Phoenicia and Cyprus and Antioch" (Acts 11:19).[178] A major geographical change happens in Acts 11 since from now on Antioch instead of Jerusalem becomes central to the advance of the gospel throughout the world. The list of references to geographical markers one finds in the rest of Acts of the Apostles, almost always with Paul passing through them, is astonishing both because of the quantity and the coverage.[179]

Uytanlet is right when he interprets this fact in this way: "The geographical movement in Luke-Acts is evidence of Luke's interest in the theme of land.

---

178. "Peter's role as traveling missionary to the house of a Roman centurion at Caesarea occasions the first significant shift in the geography of Acts, away from the regions of Judea and Samaria, and to the households located at the 'ends of the earth' (Acts 1:8). The paradigmatic position of the Cornelius story is evident from the way that the narrator delays reporting a systematic mission to the Gentiles (11:19–21) until after the climatic events transpiring in Cornelius's house. Thereafter, Paul is free to begin his work among the Gentiles (13:1–28:31)". Matson, *Household Conversion Narratives in Acts: Pattern and Interpretation*, 128.

179. 13:1 Antioch, Cyrene; 13:4 Seleucia, Cyprus; 13:5 Salamis; 13:6 Paphos; 13:13 Paphos and came to Perga in Pamphylia; 13:14 from Perga and came to Antioch in Pisidia; 13:17 Egypt; 13:19 Canaan; 13:49 whole region [of Antioch]; 14:1 Iconium; 14:6 Lystra e Derbe, cities of Lycaonia; 14:8 Lystra; 14:19 Antioch and Iconium; 14:2 Derbe; 14:21 Lystra, Iconium and Antioch; 14:24–25 Pisidia, Pamphylia, Perga, Attalia; 14:26 Antioch; 15:3 Phoenicia; 15:22 Antioch; 15:23 Antioch, Syria and Cilicia; 15:3 Antioch; 15:35 Antioch; 15:38 Pamphylia; 15:39 Cyprus; 15:41 Syria and Cilicia; 16:1 Derbe and Lystra; 16:2 Lystra and Iconium; 16:6 the region of Phrygia and Galatia, Asia; 16:7 Mysia, Bithynia; 16:8 Mysia, Troas; 16:9 Macedonia; 16:11–12 Troas, Samothrace, Neapolis, Philippi, which is a leading city of the district of Macedonia and Roman colony; 16:14 Thyatira; 17:1 Amphipolis and Apollonia, Thessalonica; 17:10 Berea; 17:11 Berea, Thessalonica; 17:13 Thessalonica, Berea; 17:16 Athens; 17:19 Areopagus; 17:21 Athens; 17:22 Areopagus; 18:1 Athens, Corinth; 18:2 Pontus, Italy, Rome; 18:5 Macedonia; 18:12 Achaia; 18:18 Syria; 18:19 Ephesus; 18:21 Ephesus; 18:22 Caesarea; 18:22 Antioch; 18:23 Galatia and Phrygia; 18:24 Ephesus, Alexandria; 18:27 Achaia; 19:1 Corinth, the inland country, Ephesus; 19:9 hall of Tyrannus; 19:10 Asia; 19:17 Ephesus; 19:21 Macedonia e Achaia; 19:22 Macedonia, Asia; 19:26 Ephesus, Asia; 19:27 Asia; 19:35 Ephesus; 20:1 Macedonia; 21:2 Greece; 21:3 Syria and Macedonia; 21:4–6 Asia, Berea, Thessalonica, Derbe, Asia, Troas, Philippi; 20:13 Assos; 20:14 Assos, Mitylene; 20:15 Quios, Samos, Miletus; 20:16 Ephesus, Asia; 20:17 Miletus, Ephesus; 20:18 Asia; 21:1 Cos, Rhodes, Patara; 21:2 Phoenicia; 21:3 Cyprus, Syria, Tiro; 21:7 Tyre, Ptolemais; 21:8 Caesarea; 21:16 Caesarea, Cyprus; 21:27 Asia; 21:39 Tarsus in Cilicia; 22:3 Tarsus in Cilicia; 22:5 Damascus; 22:6 Damascus; 22:1 Damascus; 22:11 Damascus; 23:11 Rome; 23:23 Caesarea; 23:31 Antipatris; 23:33 Caesarea; 23:34 Cilicia; 25:1 Caesarea; 25:4 Caesarea; 25:6 Caesarea; 25:13 Caesarea; 26:12 Damascus; 26:20 Damascus; 27:1 Italy; 27:2 Asia, Thessalonica; 27:3 Sidon; 27:4 Cyprus; 27:5 Cilicia and Pamphylia, Myra in Lycia; 27:6 Alexandria, Italy; 27:7 Cnidus, under the lee of Crete off Salmone; 27:8 Fair Havens, the city of Lasea; 27:12 Phoenix, a harbor of Crete; 27:13 Crete; 27:16 small island called Cauda; 27:17 Syrtis; 27:21 Crete; 27:27 Adriatic Sea; 28:1 island was called Malta; 28:12 Syracuse; 28:13 Rhegium, Puteoli; 28:14 Rome; 28:15 Forum of Appius and Three Taverns; 28:16 Rome.

His concern is not just to provide his readers with special information, but to claim these territories as belonging to God, over which the God of Israel is sovereign and within which the lordship of Christ must be proclaimed."[180]

What one finds in Luke-Acts, therefore, is not the exclusion, but the expansion of the concept of "holy land". Munther Isaac is correct when he says that "The boundaries of the land of the kingdom have expanded to achieve the original vision of universal dominion. The book of Acts is a testimony to the beginning of the realization of this vision. In Acts, the gospel of the kingdom expands, and the reign of God is declared in new lands—not just the Promised Land."[181] In the next page he summarizes nicely: "In short, the newly inaugurated kingdom claims as its sacred turf, not a single piece of territory, but the entire globe."[182]

That is the reason one can apply the land ethics practiced by the church of Jerusalem to the universal church, because the land promises made to Abraham and throughout the Old Testament started being fulfilled in Acts and the plan of God includes Jerusalem but also the ends of the world.

5.7 Final Remarks

The argument of this chapter was that Luke-Acts presents a land ethics to his readers based in the jubilee injunction that all land belongs to God. Those who become followers of Jesus are to use their estate in a way that is compatible to their belief. They are not to adapt to the unjust and oppressive way of negotiating with land, which was common in the Roman Empire and in Israel.

With this goal in view, this chapter started by demonstrating that Jesus announced his ministry in terms of jubilee and that this has, as one should expect, implications related to land. Thus, in the gospel, Jesus is presented both as the ultimate landowner, but also as the one who identified with the landless. Jesus is also the one who teaches his followers to use their land as if

---

180. Uytanlet, *Luke-Acts and Jewish Historiography*, 198.

181. Isaac, *From Land to Lands, from Eden to the Renewed Earth*, 310.

182. Isaac, *From Land to Lands, from Eden to the Renewed Earth*, 311. "The territory associated with this kingdom thus necessarily will expand outwards—no longer confined to the Promised Land. It will become any land where the risen Jesus is declared and followed as *the Christ*: Israel's Messiah and king of the world. In this new era, inaugurated by Jesus, the original "land of promise" has been left behind, and a new, larger "land of promise," has been laid enticingly before the eyes of Jesus's disciples—the whole inhabited world." (311–312)

it was not their own, but God's. Also, those who use their fields and houses for the benefit of others, receive blessings, while those who do not are accursed by God.

Finally, I demonstrated the practical implications of these teachings in the second volume of Luke's work. The fact that the first believers lived at least a partial community of goods and many were willing to sell their fields and donate to the church is evidence of what this dissertation calls jubilee land ethics. The account of Ananias and Sapphira shows that the curses announced in the gospel for those who treat the land in an egoistic way are indeed enacted in the church. This land jubilee ethics is also clear in Acts by the willingness the believers had to use their houses to practice hospitality toward one another.

After this bird's-eye survey, the next chapters will deal with two parables in the gospel of Luke in a deeper way, showing the details of this land jubilee ethics and the payback one have for living or not conscious that God is the owner of all land.

CHAPTER 6

Luke 12:13–21: The Parable of the Rich Fool

In the previous chapter I presented an overall picture of land justice in Luke-Acts and the way this subject relates to the jubilee theme. The contention of that chapter was that Luke presents a land ethics that those who call themselves Jesus's disciples are supposed to enact. Also, the fifth chapter proposed that God gives blessings or curses as consequences of living out or despising this jubilee land ethics that Luke forwards.

Now, in this and the next chapter the reader will find the exegesis of two Lukan parables that will seek to establish how Luke deals with the quest of land rights and uses it in a more focused way. This chapter will analyze what one can learn of this land ethics in Luke 12:13–21, the parable of the rich fool, and the next chapter will do the same with the parable of the wicked tenants (Luke 20:9–18).

Luke 12:13–21 is part of the journey to Jerusalem (9:51—19:46), the central section of Luke's gospel.[1] The small section to which our text belongs goes from 12:1 to 13:9 and deals with subjects related to discipleship in light of the approaching eschatological times, and emphasizes the themes of persecution,

---

1. While the beginning of the journey to Jerusalem narrative is agreed upon in Luke 9:51, there is much disagreement on the verses that end it. I concur with Matera's literary reasons for ending it in 19:46: "I maintain that the journey ends at 19:46 for two reasons. First, Jesus does not enter the city of Jerusalem until 19:45. Secondly, 19:47–48 and 21:37–38 form a literary inclusion which marks the beginning and ending of Jesus' ministry in Jerusalem: καὶ ἦν διδάσκων τὸ καθ' ἡμέραν ἐν τῷ ἱερῷ (19:47); Ἦν δὲ τὰς ἡμέρας ἐν τῷ ἱερῷ διδάσκων (21:37)." Matera, "Jesus' Journey to Jerusalem (Luke 9:51–19:46)," 57–58.

possessions, and perseverance.² The question in Luke 12:13 prompts a change of subject from perseverance to possessions, which continues until Luke 12:34. Jesus's teachings on possessions in 12:13–34 adds to the many other teachings on the subject both in the travel narrative and in the gospel in general.³

The change of subjects from 12:12 to 12:13 is very abrupt.⁴ An unidentified man asks Jesus to arbitrate between him and his brother in a matter related to their inheritance. "He has already decided what he wants and he tries to *use* Jesus," says Bailey.⁵ It is possible that the man is a Pharisee or a Jewish leader, but there is no way to be certain of that.⁶ It is probably secure to affirm, however, by the use of διδάσκαλε instead of κύριε, that the man treats Jesus in a formal and distanced fashion, albeit not disrespectfully. This man was probably not a follower of Jesus. In addition, he is not worried about the subjects Jesus was dealing with, related to persecution and perseverance, but was instead, worried about his earthly supposed rights and belongings. Carroll calls the man presumptuous.⁷ It was common for a rabbi to deal with this kind of problem, but, since Jesus was able to detect the underlying motivations of the heart, Jesus was not a common rabbi.⁸

---

2. Green, *The Gospel of Luke*, 27; Carroll, *Luke: A Commentary*, x; Tannehill, *The Narrative Unity of Luke-Acts*, 1:240 et seq.

3. These is the list of texts dealing with possessions (wealth and poverty) in Luke: 1:46–55; 3:1–14; 4:16–30; 5:1–11, 27–29; 6:20–26; 7:18–50; 8:1–3; 9:1–6; 10:1–12; 10:25–37; 11:37–44; 12:35–48, 54–59; 14:7–24; 15:8–32; 16:1–31; 18:18–30; 19:1–27; 20:9–26; 21:1–4; 22:3–6.

4. The Savior had just been discussing the deepest and holiest matters and was perhaps still in the act of doing so (verses 1–12) when someone from among the multitude, without giving any sign that he had paid any attention to Jesus' words, asked Him to deal with a purely earthly affair. Geldenhuys thinks that the brother was also present. Geldenhuys, *Commentary on the Gospel of Luke*, 354.

5. Kenneth E. Bailey, *Poet & Peasant and Through Peasant Eyes*, 59. [emphasis original]. Bailey goes on the same page and says: "To say 'Rabbi, my brother and I are quarreling over our inheritance; will you mediate?' is one thing; To order Jesus to implement his plan is something else." Maybe it is not correct to stress this point since it is common that one who searches for judgment commonly is the one who thinks they are right.

6. The indefinite pronoun "someone" (Gk. *tis*) and especially the address to Jesus as "Teacher" may indicate the questioner is a Pharisee or Jewish leader, for ten of eleven addresses to Jesus as "Teacher" in Luke come from such, whereas disciples usually refer to Jesus as "Lord" or "Master." Edwards, *The Gospel According to Luke*, 369.

7. Carroll, *Luke: A Commentary*, 266.

8. "A rabbi would often settle such disputes about inheritance because the regulations on them appear in the Pentateuch and the rabbi interpreted Torah." Bock, *Luke 9:51–24:53*, 1149. Cf. also, Bailey, *Poet & Peasant and Through Peasant Eyes*, 58–59.

Because of the nature of the agrarian economy of that time and the kind of parable Jesus tells afterwards, it is almost certain that the inheritance about which the man is asking has its main part as land (fields and houses).[9] The inheritance could be comprised also of slaves, silver, gold and cattle, which only make sense if the person has fields.[10] It is not possible to know the details of the dispute; if the brother who approaches Jesus was right or wrong, or the quantity of wealth evolved in the quarrel.[11] Wright suggests that they are probably from a poor family, but that is uncertain.[12] The law established that the older brother had the right to a double portion of the family's estate (Deut 21:17).[13] When the field of the family was too small to be separated, it was common for the younger sibling to move out to find another way of

---

9. The dispute centers on the estate. A brother has refused to divide the inheritance, and this other brother hopes that Jesus will prevail upon him to be more generous. Possessions were often held jointly as undivided shares. But it is not clear whether the complainant was getting nothing or whether he wanted his own piece of the pie, independent of the family. No more details are given concerning the problem. Is the one making the request the younger brother? Is the fault simply that of the other brother (Psa 133:1 raises another perspective on the dispute)? Bock, *Luke 9:51–24:53*, 1149.

10. Hiers, "Transfer of Property by Inheritance and Bequest in Biblical Law and Tradition," 123.

11. Some of the possibilities for this quarrel among these brothers could be: (1) the younger brother wanted half a portion when he had right to less than that. Cf. Marshall, *The Gospel of Luke*, 522. (2) The younger brother wanted his rightful share, but the older brother was not giving it to him. (3) Being an unlawful son, the asking brother wanted a part in the inheritance, but he had no right to it. About the law underlying the third possibility, Hier says: "But who are to be counted as "sons" for purposes of inheritance? Biblical traditions refer to the situation of sons by their fathers' concubines, their wives' maids, by slaves, and by harlots. It seems that any such sons might inherit, absent steps being taken to prevent their doing so." Hiers presents Judges 11:1–2 as evidence of this possibility. Hiers, "Transfer of Property by Inheritance and Bequest in Biblical Law and Tradition," 127. (4) Another possibility is that the father, through a testament, had left all that he had to one of his sons (cf. Gen 24:36; 25:5–6; 48:21–22), and the other son was complaining to Jesus.

12. "The man was probably from a peasant family. Wealthy families would have had their own means to get what they wanted, and probably would not have resorted to seeking advice from a wandering teacher." Stephen I. Wright, "Parables on Poverty and Riches (Luke 12:13–21; 16:1–13; 16:19–31)," 221. Such a judgement is uncertain because it was not the family who was seeking advice, but one of the children. They could properly be a rich family whose father had decided to give the whole inheritance to only one of the sons, or maybe that man was unjustly not satisfied with his share.

13. Hier affirms that Deut 21:16–18 is the only texts that affirms the right to a double portion by the firstborn and that is it strange that the Bible does not refer to that in any other place. He elucidates that this could be an oral law. Hiers, "Transfer of Property by Inheritance and Bequest in Biblical Law and Tradition," 144–45. Traditional Jewish texts confirm the double portion of the firstborn: Mishnah Bechorot 8:9; Mishnah Bava Batra 8:3–4; 123a. just to cite a few.

subsistence, sometimes even being forced into begging.[14] Bailey affirms that the Jewish law guaranteed the division of the estate if one of the brothers demanded it and the Roman law would require an agreement between the siblings.[15]

The fact is that it is not possible to know the exact situation of the dispute, but it is clear that Jesus was harsh to the man who was asking and detected his motivations as being related to πλεονεξίας, i.e., greed (NRSV, NIV), covetousness (ESV, NKJV).[16] I concur with Butler when he says that "Not making a legal judgment, Jesus did make a moral one."[17] To whom did Jesus pronounce the content of verse 15? The text affirms that he said it to "them" (αὐτούς). This could refer to the brothers involved in the dispute (note the plural you [ὑμᾶς] in verse 14), to the crowd referred to in verse 13, to Jesus's disciples, or to all of them.

Jesus's answer to that man comprises a rhetorical question, a warning against covetousness and a parable. The question is "Man, who made me a judge (κριτὴν) or arbitrator (μεριστὴν) over you?" Through this question, Jesus was making clear to that man he was not there in the quality of a divider of inheritances, a role played by Joshua (cf. Josh 13–22).[18] Jesus's answer, properly speaking start with, "Watch out, and be on your guard against all covetousness, for one's life does not consist in the abundance of his possessions" (Luke 12:15). This verse together with verse 21 form the frame in which one should read the parable. The problem that Jesus detected in the man was greed. Stein defines greed as "an insatiable desire and lust for more and more. It is all-consuming, so that all of life becomes focused on the accumulation of wealth. There is no room for anything else, not even God. This is why it is so hard for a rich person to enter God's kingdom (18:25)."[19] This definition

---

14. Herzog, *Parables as Subversive Speech: Jesus as Pedagogue of the Oppressed*, 65.

15. Bailey, *Poet & Peasant and Through Peasant Eyes*, 59.

16. The use of the vocative ἄνθρωπε implies harshness. Cf. J. Reiling and J. L. Swellengrebel, *A Handbook on the Gospel of Luke*, 469; Bock, *Luke 9:51–24:53*, 1149. Edwards, however, thinks that it is just an Hebraism that conveys a direct and emphatic address. Edwards, *The Gospel According to Luke*. On the use of the term πλεονεξίας and its meaning, see above note on the Greek text.

17. Trent C. Butler, *Luke*, 204.

18. Wright, "Parables on Poverty and Riches (Luke 12:13–21; 16:1–13; 16:19–31)," 221.

19. Stein, *Luke: An Exegetical and Theological Exposition of Holy Scripture*, 344. "Greed receives mention because it can fuel disagreement and disharmony. The danger of the pursuit of possessions is that it can make one insensitive to people. Greed can create a distortion about

has support in the text, when Jesus affirms that the ζωὴ (life) of someone is not found in the abundance of his possessions.[20] Jesus was revealing what was happening in that man's heart.

That wealth has the power to dominate one's life is also a teaching spread throughout Luke. For example, in Luke 6:24, Jesus said: "But woe to you who are rich, for you have received your consolation". Note that the woe to the rich in this verse has as explanation the fact that consolation is not expected from God, but from money. Another text that makes this competition between God and money very plain is Luke 16:13, "No servant can serve two masters, for either he will hate the one and love the other, or he will be devoted to the one and despise the other. You cannot serve God and money." It is impossible to be a servant of God and a servant of possessions at the same time. Wealth has a way to possess its owner and drag him or her out of God and this is what Jesus will explain through his parable.[21] And it is good to remember that wealth in this text is inseparable from land.

The parable starts by affirming that the field (χώρα) of a certain rich man (ἀνθρώπου τινὸς πλουσίου) produced plentifully (εὐφόρησεν). This last Greek word means, "to produce unusually well, bear good crops, yield well, be

---

what life is, because the definition of life is not found in objects, but relationships, especially to God and his will. To define life in terms of things is the ultimate reversal of the creature serving the creation and ignoring the Creator." Reiling and Swellengrebel, *A Handbook on the Gospel of Luke*, 473.

20. "The Greek language had three words for 'life' that Luke could have chosen. One was *bios*, which referred to *quantitative* life, i.e., how long one lived, how many goods one acquired. Another was *psychē*, which referred to *qualitative* life, i.e., to the values and relationships that constitute personhood. The third was *zōē*, which referred to *quintessential* life, i.e., to the life offered to humanity in the call to follow Jesus, and through him to live in a personal relationship with the Father. The first form of 'life,' *bios*, could, in fact, be measured by one's possessions. Luke does not use *bios*, however, but rather *zōē*, the word that describes God's life and the abundant God-life offered to the world in the gospel (John 10:10). *Zōē* cannot be reduced to, measured by, or satisfied by stuff. We do not earn or merit *zōē* but receive it freely and undeservedly from God through the person of Jesus Christ. *Zōē* is relational rather than material, I-Thou rather than I-It, eternal rather than temporal and fading. *Bios* leaves us restless and insatiable, hungering for more; *zōē* produces contentment, peace, and joy. 'Be on your guard,' says Jesus, against trying to achieve and satisfy *zōē* with things!" Edwards, *The Gospel According to Luke*.

21. "According to the Bible, idolaters do three things with their idols. They love them, trust them, and obey them. 'Lovers of money' are those who find themselves daydreaming and fantasizing about new ways to make money, new possessions to buy, and looking with jealousy on those who have more than they do. 'Trusters of money' feel they have control of their lives and are safe and secure because of their wealth." Timothy Keller, *Counterfeit Gods*, 56–57. See also Brian S. Rosner, *Greed as Idolatry*, 159 et seq.

fruitful" (BDAG, 414). Because of such a harvest, this already rich man would become even richer. The attitudes of the man start to be depicted in verse 17.

Edwards correctly calls attention to the fact that, by starting to focus on the producing field, Jesus makes clear that the overproduction was not due to any effort of the rich man.[22] God and the land are the most important characters in this parable and the main entities responsible for the overproduction.[23]

Another feature of this parable noted by Edwards is the soliloquy of Luke 12:17. This scholar says that "Inner monologues such as this are a unique feature of the Third Gospel, occurring nearly a dozen times, and always in sections of Luke not paralleled by Mark or the double tradition. Not surprisingly, these soliloquies frequently reflect, as they do here, the human will in defiance of the divine will (also 7:39; 11:38; 12:45; 16:3; 18:4–5, 11–12)."[24] Besides this, these soliloquies also point to Jesus's ability of knowing and revealing the human heart, which sympathetically approximates the reader to the character who reveals his dilemmas.[25] The monologues in Luke point to crisis, reveal the foolishness of the one who speaks with the self and are also a way to invite the reader to be transformed by what happens with the

---

22. "The opening line of this parable is important, for the subject of the sentence is not the rich man but the 'ground.' The prosperity of the rich man is not his doing but a consequence of the productivity of land. His prosperity derives from a source other than himself. It is, in other words, an inheritance, even a *gift*. But the rich man cannot (or will not) acknowledge this." Edwards, *The Gospel According to Luke*.

23. "But it is not really the rich man's story. Along with God's stunning direct appearance in 12:20 (the only time Jesus introduces 'God' within a parable), God implicitly plays the lead role throughout as Creator of all (land, grain, humanity) and Lord of life and death. And the part of best supporting actor is played by the earth endowed with God's creative energy. Note well the subject of Jesus' opening statement: "The land (ἡ χώρα) of a certain rich man brought forth a bumper crop (εὐφόρησεν)" (12:16, my translation). This follows the primordial pattern, when the God-generated 'earth brought forth vegetation: plants yielding seed of every kind, and trees of every kind bearing fruit with the seed in it' (Gen 1:11–12) and 'the Lord God formed an earthling (אדם (from the dust of the earth (2:7)' (אדמה, my translation). Humans are naturally and integrally grounded in the God-made humus of the earth. F. Scott Spencer, "To Fear and Not to Fear the Creator God," 241. "In this lone instance, however, that authority appears as God himself rather than as a character who represents God". Blomberg, *Interpreting the Parables*, 266.

24. Edwards, *The Gospel According to Luke*. Luke's character soliloquies often include the troubled question 'What shall I do' (τί ποιήσω, Luke 12:17; 16:3; 20:13), as the characters look at their circumstances and debate the proper course of action." Mark Goodacre, "The Protoevangelium of James and the Creative Rewriting of Matthew and Luke," 72.

25. Philip Sellew, "Interior Monologue as a Narrative Device in the Parables of Luke," 239–53.

character who's thoughts are showed.[26] This specific soliloquy is a clear way of letting God outside of the rich man's plans for the future as the parable clearly demonstrates. In his own plans, the rich man did not allow space for receiving any input from God for knowing the better course of action.

The problem the man in the parable detects is that he does not have a place to store such an abundant harvest. His solution is tearing down his current storehouses (ἀποθήκας, note the plural) and building bigger ones (again, plural). The man thinks that by implementing his plan he would be solving the very practical problem of not having where to store his abundant harvest. The word for storehouse or barn appears again in this same chapter, when Jesus calls his hearers to imitate the ravens in their attitude of trusting God to receive what they need: "they neither sow nor reap, they have neither storehouse nor barn (ἀποθήκη), and yet God feeds them" (cf. Luke 12:24). By this semantic connection, it is possible to affirm that one of the sins of the man in the parable is lack of trust in God to provide – for him, not following the example of the birds. He was not resting in God, but was anxious (cf. Luke 12:22).

Bock demonstrates how Luke, by his narrative mastery, points to another aspect of the sin of this man:

> He quite naturally wants to preserve his crops, but there is a hint of a problem in his perspective, for throughout these verses the major stylistic feature is the presence of the pronoun μου (*mou*, my), not to mention the numerous first-person singular verbs. The fruit of the land and other elements of the parable are repeatedly described with μου: *my* fruit, *my* barn, *my* goods, *my* soul. Such language suggests exclusive self-interest, a focus that is often the natural product of "earned" wealth.[27]

After deciding what to do to solve his problem, the man in the parable plans what he will say to his soul. This is very interesting, because here the reader finds a soliloquy inside another. The man plans to say to himself: "Soul,

---

26. Michal Beth Dinkler, "'The Thoughts of Many Hearts Shall Be Revealed,'" 373–99. "For Luke, as well as for much of the ancient world, thinking to oneself is a negative indication: it suggests something one would be ashamed to speak openly, or a plot one connives." Levine and Witherington, *The Gospel of Luke*, 212.

27. Bock, *Luke 9:51–24:53*, 1151–52.

you have ample goods laid up for many years; relax, eat, drink, be merry." (Luke 12:19). The man seems to be ecstatic in his hedonistic dreams without God. He is absorbed in a way of thinking that was characteristic of that very materialistic society of his.[28]

In a similar fashion as Jesus was interrupted by the man's request (Luke 12:13), the monologue of the rich man is interrupted by God himself calling him a fool (ἄφρων). This word points to lack of prudence or good judgement, foolishness, and ignorance.[29] It appears in Luke 11:40, an indictment to the Pharisees, whose exterior was clean while the interior was full of greed and wickedness. In that text, the solution proposed by Jesus was giving alms (Luke 11:38–41). The reasons God calls this man a fool is that while all his providence completely ignores God, God is the one who can subvert his situation of wealth and even his soul overnight. "The rich fool did not realize that he 'owned' nothing. All he had – even his life – was on loan and could be called in at any time."[30] The concept of fool can also point to immorality, although this is not clear in this passage.[31] This aspect that the land and the harvest were a loan from God to the man is central to the teaching of Luke throughout the gospel, that God is the ultimate owner of all land and other possessions and all earthly owners are but stewards of God who are supposed to administer the land and goods for God.

Besides calling him a fool, God also poses a question: "This night your soul is required of you, and the things you have prepared, whose will they be?" God clearly tells the character of the parable that he would die that very

---

28. "Having made plans to resolve his problems, the man concludes that he can now live in total leisure and self-indulgence. . . . His future perspective is entirely self-centered and self-indulgent. As 12:21 will make clear, he has laid up treasure for himself alone. He has morally mismanaged his wealth, giving no thought to the needs of others or thanking God." Bock, *Luke 9:51–24:53*, 1152–53. Blomberg, *Interpreting the Parables*, 267.

29. cf. BDAG, 159. "This word points to the contrary of being φρόνιμος, i.e. "pertaining to understanding associated with insight and wisdom, sensible, thoughtful, prudent, wise". (BDAG, 1066).

30. Stein, *Luke*, 353. "He did not regard his possessions as things *lent* to him by God's grace and to be used by him in the service of the Lord (for instance, in helping the needy). On the contrary, he considered that everything belonged exclusively to *him*, and that he had the full monopoly of it to use it for his own pleasure and enjoyments." Geldenhuys, *Commentary on the Gospel of Luke*, 355.

31. "Foolishness often has overtones of immorality in the Old Testament and intertestamental literature and is not just an epithet for stupidity. Important background texts include Job 32:24–28; Psalm 14,1; Psalm 49; Ecclesiastes 2:1–11; and Sirach 11:19–20." Blomberg, *Interpreting the Parables*, 267.

night. It was not a possibility, but a certainty expressed by the one who has means to make it happen. The language shows that even his own soul was not the rich man's, since it would be demanded (ἀπαιτοῦσιν, cf. BDAG, 96) from him "by them".[32] His very soul did not fully belong to him.[33] There is a discussion about the identity of this "them" in the parable. This could refer to God, angels or demons.[34] By the impossibility of an objective answer, it is better to leave the identity of "them" undefined. God's question in the end of the parable exposes the inutility of reducing all value and meaning of life to material things. At the end, that rich man would die, and his bold plans, plentiful harvest, large barns, and large field or fields and other properties would be left to someone else. He would not have enough time to enjoy the things he owned.

---

32. "The verb for demand" (ἀπαιτέω) means "ask for something back, ask to be returned," as in transactions of lending and borrowing (cf. 6:30; Deut 15:2–3; Sir 20:15). A creditor has the right to call in or "demand" payment on a loan, with or without interest. The concept is most apt for the calculating rich man, whose fortune was likely built through shrewd credit arrangements, including land foreclosures. What he has not accounted for, however, is that he has received his entire life and possessions on theological and terrestrial credit: everything comes from God and God's land and will revert back to these life sources in Gods time. Like all creation, the rich man lives on borrowed time and resources. He just does not know it or, better put, he denies knowledge of his finitude and dependence. And that makes him a damn fool. His presumed arrogant control over his God-fashioned, earthbound the marks the same impudent attitude of the idolater exposed in the Wisdom of Solomon: "And, toiling perversely, he molds a futile god out of the same clay, he who a little before came into being out of the earth and after a while returns whence he was taken, when the soul (ψυχῆς), which was lent him is demanded back (ἀπαιτηθείς)" (Wis 15:8, nets). Spencer, "To Fear and Not to Fear the Creator God," 243. Henry Johannes Mugabe, "Parable of the Rich Fool," 70.

33. "By using the same term [ψυχή] thrice Luke effectively brings out the contrast between what the rich man thinks to be the case, viz. that he is master of his soul just as he seems to be of his goods, and what God knows it to be, viz. that he is to lose both." Reiling and Swellengrebel, *A Handbook on the Gospel of Luke*, 473. "God's direct speech is striking; God is given voice only here in a Lukan parable. The rhetorical question God poses begs the answer 'someone else.' It is not clear who demands the forfeiting of the rich man's life; 'they' resemble the unspecified 'those' in 12:4 who are capable of killing the body but can do no further damage. The basic point is clear: life centered in one's own prosperity and security is illusory." Carroll, *Luke: A Commentary*, 267.

34. "The oddity of the verse is the third-person plural: 'they demand your soul from you.' This has been understood in one of two ways: either as the angelic execution of the task (Grundmann 1963: 258 [the angel of death, Satan; Heb 2:14]; Marshall 1978: 524) or as a Semitic idiom for God (Job 4:19c; 6:2b; Prov. 9:11b; Creed 1930: 173; Fitzmyer 1985: 974). It is hard to be certain, since both possibilities make good sense. The point is that a heavenly call for death has been made and will be executed. It is perhaps more natural to see God referred to here, since the context discusses him and not angels. Either way, death is his sovereign call." Bock, *Luke 9:51–24:53*, 1153.

Now the parable has ended, Jesus finishes the frame he started in verse 15, and concludes: "So is the one who lays up treasure for himself and is not rich toward God" (Luke 12:21). It is possible to say that the pronoun οὕτως reveals the pointlessness of a life built over material things without acknowledgement of God.

Words of the root θησαυρ appear five times in Luke: 6:45; 12:21, 33, 34; and 18:22. In Luke 6:45 Jesus makes clear, that one can have either a good or an evil treasure in his or her heart. In the last occurrence, in Luke 18:22, Jesus calls people to sell everything they have and give to the poor so that they may have a treasure in heaven. Luke 12, however, is the chapter that most uses the concept of treasure. Besides our text, verses 33 and 34 also refer to treasure. Verse 33 precedes the instruction of 18:22. In it, Jesus affirms that when his followers sell their possessions and give to the poor, they will have a treasure in heaven. Then, Jesus makes clear in verse 34 that the heart of someone will follow their treasure. It is implicit that either one can have his treasure in heaven or on earth, as the rich man of Luke 12:13–21. The way in which one makes clear her treasure is in heaven is by being willing to dispossess from material earthly things in order to help those who are in need.

The problem of the rich man in the parable was that he held his treasure only for himself and on earth and that he was not rich (πλουτῶν) toward God. This is the only occurrence of this word in Luke referring to something good. Being rich in Luke is commonly something bad and deserving of curses, but now, Jesus affirms that his followers should be rich not in the sense their society used to define, but rich toward God. The text that follows teaches that being rich toward God can be interpreted as trusting God for subsistence, investing one's life in his kingdom and being willing to give up one's own possessions in order to support those in need.

Joshua Noble wrote a very illuminating article about this expression εἰς θεὸν πλουτῶν, (rich toward God).[35] He defends that it points to a benefactor-recipient relationship and conveys the idea that being rich toward God is giving someone's own wealth to God through almsgiving. His arguments to defend this interpretation are both syntactic and contextual.

---

35. Joshua A. Noble, "'Rich toward God': Making Sense of Luke 12:21,'" *Cathol. Biblic. Q.* 78 (2016): 302–20.

The syntactic arguments are that (1) the Greek construction εἰς + accusative is sometimes used in Greek to code relationship between beneficiary and recipient and that (2) in the other extant occurrences of πλουτέω + εἰς + accusative in Lucian (*Saturnalia* 24), Philostratus (*Vita Apollonius* 4.8), and Paul (Romans 10:12), the object of εἰς is the one receiving wealth as beneficiary. The contextual arguments are both textual and cultural. (3) In the flowing of the passage, to be rich toward God is the antithesis of treasuring for oneself. Besides, Luke 12:33 explains that the way to amount treasures in heaven is by doing almsgiving. The last argument Noble presents is (4) that one of the most important texts related to almsgiving both for Jewish and for Christians is Proverbs 19:17, against whose background, Luke 12:21 makes plain sense as referring to someone giving one's own wealth to God when assisting the needy.

I agree with Noble and accordingly think that the man is convicted of not being rich in helping other people and consequently not being rich toward God. He lacked a serving attitude by means of almsgiving. Other texts of the Old Testament that serve as canonical context for this parable are Psalm 49; Eccl 2:1–11; Job 31:24–28 and the extra canonical Sirach 11:18–20 and 1 Enoch 97:8–10. All of these texts stress the stupidity of trusting wealth instead of God and the drastic consequences of doing that.

Sin is not simple, but deep and multifaceted. The reason for that is because the human heart is complex, full of concomitant motivations and concurrent attitudes toward or against God. Thus, the sinful attitudes this text is combating, present in the brother who asked Jesus for help and especially in the rich man of the parable are multiple. The text clearly points to greed (love for money and abundance of possessions). The context of Luke points also to the sin of being dominated by money, i.e. having money as lord and ultimate consolation. Subjacent to these sinful attitudes, one can suppose the rich man was also guilty of selfishness,[36] lack of conscience of his own finitude,[37] lack of

---

36. "The parable of the rich fool is an attack on selfishness, individualism, and egocentrism." Mugabe, "Parable of the Rich Fool," 69.

37. "Such a way of life fails to reckon with the possibility of sudden and swift crisis." Marshall, *The Gospel of Luke*, 524.

gratitude[38] and pride.[39] Although there is no evidence in the text or context, it is possible also that there was a lack of sense of gratitude toward the land itself and despise for the workers who worked for him.[40] Finally, it is possible that the plan of the rich man was to take grain out of circulation in order to inflate the market and making more money at the expense of the poor, a sin referred to in Prov 11:26 and Amos 8:4–5.[41]

Although we cannot be sure this whole list was part of the sinful heart dynamic of the rich man's soul, some of them are evident in the text and context of Luke, and these are the reasons the man in the parable is called a fool and Jesus rebukes the asking brother. On the other hand, Wright correctly calls attention to the danger of attributing especially terrible sins to this and other parable characters in a sense that they stop representing human nature in general.[42] This man represents the fallen condition of the heart of all human beings.

---

38. "In this parable and these pronouncements the Saviour does not condemn the possession of worldly goods as such, but what He disapproves of is the covetous and carnal attitude with regard to earthly wealth, the trust in worldly things instead of in God, and the fault of not regarding one's possessions gratefully as God's gracious gifts and using them in His service and according to His will to the glory of His name." Geldenhuys, *Commentary on the Gospel of Luke*, 355–56.

39. "His folly is his oblivion to God. There are many forms of pride, but the worst of them is to think that one has no need of God. He does not acknowledge the source of his blessings. Rather, he gathers to himself and serves himself, and as such is a practical atheist." Edwards, *The Gospel According to Luke*, 371.

40. "Apart from neglecting to reciprocate God's and the earth's bountiful goodness, the rich man also discounts other people's contributions to his fortune, such as tenant farmers, harvesters, and storehouse builders." Spencer, "To Fear and Not to Fear the Creator God," 242.

41. "The plans of the rich man are not neutral; he is probably removing grain from circulation in order to maximize profits. Once grain was stockpiled, hunger and shortage followed, allowing the monopolist to earn excess profits." Mugabe, "Parable of the Rich Fool," 69. Bock thinks otherwise: "It is important to note that the parable is initially neutral concerning the man's attitude. There is no hint of avarice, cheating, or immorality, contra the claim of Schottroff and Stegemann (1986: 97) that this man was hoarding his crop to charge a higher price in case of famine. Bock, *Luke 9:51–24:53*, 1151.

42. "We miss the force of the story if we see the rich man as being especially wicked. Commentators sometimes describe the characters of the parables in very lurid colors, and so they become figures that the pious love to hate. But the point here, as in many another tale, is not that this man was a monster, but that he is typical – that is, typical of the class of people and typical of a whole social system. His thought-processes are normal. They encapsulate the whole basis of an exploitative, agrarian society that seeks control over land and wants to use surpluses to finance luxury. They are thought-processes that exclude God and other people – who both, alike, inevitably reassert themselves at the end." Wright, "Parables on Poverty and Riches (Luke 12:13–21; 16:1–13; 16:19–31)," 223.

Blomberg, classifying this parable as a "two-point parable" presents an application about not being ruled by money and includes another one about God's judgement: "The two main point deriving from the actions of the fool and of God follow naturally. (1) A purely selfish accumulation of possessions is incompatible with true discipleship. (2) This incompatibility stems from the transience of earthly riches and the coming reckoning which all will face before God."[43]

Therefore, this parable clearly teaches that not living out a land ethic that makes clear that God is the ultimate owner of land results in curse from God. The sin of the man in the parable related to land was the fact that he considered the land and its production as being only his and not God's. His plans were egotistic and hedonistic and he had no place for God and other people in them, not in the elaboration, nor in the results. The parable does not present the rich man actively oppressing people; he only did not think of anybody else besides himself. Both the asking brother and the man in the parable loved their possessions and had them in the center of their thinking and preoccupation.

Thus, because of his egocentric and idolater thinking and behavior related to his land and its production, the man in the parable faced death and, in the face of Luke 16:19–31, he would probably face hell afterwards. Thus, both the brother who asked Jesus to act as a divider of inheritance, the other brother (if he was present), Jesus's disciples, the multitude and the reader of Luke were and are called to evaluate their relationship with money in general and land in particular. God is the rightful owner of all land. He is the one who lends land in order that people make it productive in a way that honors him. He is the one who gives inheritance to his people. If men forgets that God is the real proprietor and lender in their plans and actions, they will face his wrath. The parable of the wicked tenants that we will analyze in the next chapter will make that even clearer. God is the owner of all land and consequently, humans are required to use it in a way that is pleasing to him.

---

43. Blomberg, *Interpreting the Parables*, 267.

CHAPTER 7

Luke 20:9–19:
The Parable of the Wicked Tenants

The previous chapter presented the contribution of Luke 12:13–21 (The Parable of the Rich Fool) to the subject of land justice in the Gospel of Luke. This chapter will do the same with the parable of the wicked tenants (Luke 20:9–19).[1] It is the contention of this chapter that although this parable does not have the main objective of teaching about land ethics, it explores the subject by using an unjust situation related to land in order to illustrate the fact and absurdity of the rejection of the Messiah by the Jewish leaders. The parable also teaches about God's lordship over the land. Before presenting an exegesis of the parable, it is useful to present a brief history of its interpretation.[2]

---

1. "The most difficult of the parables referring directly to the existing situation is that of the Wicked Husbandmen." Dodd, *The Parables of the Kingdom*, 96. "This is one of the most significant, most discussed, and most complicated of all parables, and not surprisingly, one about there is enormous debate." Snodgrass, *Stories with Intent*, loc. 6200. "The Parable of the Tenants (Mk 12:1–12; Mt 21:33–45; Luke 20:9–19; GThom 65–66) is one of the most debated of all the parables ascribed to Jesus. Situated at the intersection of a host of important issues in Gospels scholarship—ranging from the synoptic problem, to the use of the OT in the NT, to the historical Jesus—it has generated a seemingly overwhelming quantity of secondary research in recent decades." Lanier, "Mapping the Vineyard," 74. Kloppenborg identifies three sets of problems related to this parable: "The first concerns issues in the history of the interpretation and the profound effect of ideology on texts and interpreters. Second, there are source-critical problems having to do with reconstructing a tradition history of the parable that accounts for its four extant textual performances. And, finally, we have socio-cultural issues related to the mechanics of ancient viticulture, the typical social levels of landlords and tenants, and the combination of factors that made ancient viticulture a unique conflicted sector of the agrarian economy." Kloppenborg, *The Tenants in the Vineyard*, x.

2. For an article about recent interpretations of this parable, see Klyne Snodgrass, "Recent Research on the Parable of the Wicked Tenants," 187–216.

The interpretation will be followed by a discussion on the teachings of this parable for the quest for land in Luke.

7.1 History of the Interpretation: An Introduction

In the *Catena Aurea* of Thomas Aquinas, one finds good examples of the patristic and medieval interpretation of this parable.[3] Eusebius, for example, calls this parable a foretelling and identifies that while Isaiah's prophecy foreshadows punition for Israel as a whole, the parable of the wicked husbandmen chastises only the cultivator of the vineyard, i.e., the elders of the people. Eusebius also interprets the rock, saying that it represents Christ's earthly body. Theophilus affirms that the fruit of the vineyard is the knowledge of God, which he himself bestows and requires. The hesitation shown by the owner of the vineyard represents the preservation of men's free will. Finally, Bede identifies the three servants as Moses, through whom God sent the law; David, who tried to generate fruits in the people through music and psalms; and the company of the prophets. All of them were rejected by God's people in themselves or through their descendants. Bede also affirms that the fact that the son was thrown out of the vineyard represents he was first driven out of the heart of unbelievers before going to the cross. He also interprets the one who stumps on the rock as a Christian sinner shaken but preserved through penitence.

I stressed only the interpretations of some fathers who take the allegory too far. While not every detail of a parable needs to have a specific referent, the medieval interpretation tried to do exactly that by using the *regula fidei*. They interpreted the text in the light of doctrines and of other biblical texts that had similar images or vocabulary. The result is that some of the referents they find in the parables are indeed correct while others are anachronistic or do not make sense in light of the literary and historical context.

Dodd affirms that although altered by the early church, the general plot of this parable is originally from Jesus.[4] To Dodd the context of the parable fits perfectly in first century Galilee with its peasantry revolts. The reference to the killing of the beloved son and the destruction of the husbandmen

---

3. Aquinas, *Catena Aurea*, 653–60.
4. Dodd, *The Parables of the Kingdom*, 96 et seq.

makes sense in light of the end of the earthly ministry of Jesus, not as specific references, but as a reading of the times pointing to the future destruction of Jerusalem and its leadership. The explicit references to Jesus as the beloved son with the stone saying, and his death out of the vineyard are, for Dodd, the editing work of the church.[5]

Joachim Jeremias presents a similar interpretation. To him the least altered version of this parable is found in the Gospel of Thomas 65 and all the allegorical elements found in the synoptic gospels were posterior additions and consequently were not originally proffered by the historical Jesus.[6] After dismissing all allegorical features of the parable, Jeremias shows what he thinks to be the original meaning intended by Jesus:

> Like so many other parables of Jesus, it sets out to justify the offer of the gospel to the poor. You, it says, you tenants of the vineyard and leaders of the people, you would not listen, but have opposed to God again and again, and now you reject the last of his messengers. The cup is full. God's vineyard, therefore, will be given to 'others' (Mark 12:9). As neither Mark nor Luke indicate who the 'others' may be, we must follow the analogy of the related parables and think of them as the poor (cf. Matt 5:5).[7]

The main problem of interpreters like Dodd and Jeremias is that they despise the canonical version of the evangelists and try to perform the impossible work of restoring what Jesus really did and said. After this highly speculative work, they try to interpret the parable. Also, as they believe that parables are not allegories and have only one *tertium comparationis*, they extract pale general lessons from the parable. In the case of our parable, for example, they affirm Jesus was detecting what was happening politically and pointing to a revolt that probably would happen if things continue as they were.[8] Also,

---

5. "The parable therefore stands on its own feet as a dramatic story, inviting judgement from the hearers, and the application of the judgement is clear enough without any allegorizing of the details." Dodd, *The Parables of the Kingdom*, 101.

6. Joachim Jeremias, *Rediscovering the Parables*, 57 e seq.

7. Jeremias, *Rediscovering the Parables*, 63.

8. De Moor does a pertinent critic of this kind of reading when he says: "All consequent attempts to purge the parable from its allegorical elements result in a bloodless story which can only be given sense by attributing to it some undocumented meaning," De Moor, "The Targumic Background of Mark 12:1–12," 65.

they are not always consistent with the principles they themselves establish and, thus, Jeremias feels obligated to assume that the use of the vineyard is an allegorical aspect in the parable which is probably original from Jesus.

Dan Otto Via proposes that some allegorical elements of this parable are probably original (vine as Israel, beating as rejection of God's servants, son as Jesus, wicked tenants as Jewish leaders of Jesus days) and others (Christological reference of the stone, the adjective beloved applied to the son) are due to the editorial role of the gospel writers. His proposal of meaning and application, that he calls existential-theological interpretation is as follows:

> When The Wicked Tenants is seen as a parable of unfaith, then sin becomes man's self-centered effort to reject any and all limitations which the being and will of God impose upon him. Man's self-defensive drive for security, engendered by a lack of faith in the benevolence of the universe, may express itself in more than one way. If man cannot believe that there is a transcendent reality which undergirds him and fills his emptiness, he may act as little as possible or he may be driven to violent action. In both cases the power that would have sustained him had he been responsible causes his downfall when he is irresponsible.[9]

Via's interpretation uses similar tools as Dodd's and Jeremias' interpretations. He accepts however, that the parable was originally an allegory and, consequently, is willing to accept some allegorical references as original. His drive to extract existential lessons from the parable leads him to present a broad application that does not make justice to the specific features presented in the parable.

Herzog proposes a very different reading. First, he questions the identification of the owner of the vineyard with God, based in the fact that the owner is introduced as a man.[10] This man was simply a very rich Jew who probably lived in Jerusalem. His second action is to consider the construction of the vineyard as something bad:

> As already noted in chapter 5, the creation of a vineyard would, on economic grounds alone, have disturbed the hearers of the

---

9. Via, *The Parables*, 137.

10. Herzog, *Parables as Subversive Speech*: 102.

parable. Because land in Galilee was largely accounted for and intensely cultivated, 'a man' could acquire the land required to build a vineyard only by taking it from someone else. The most likely way he would have added the land to his holdings was through foreclosure on loans to free peasant farmers who were unable to pay off the loans because of poor harvests.[11]

As demonstrated in the quotation above, Herzog's third analysis in his interpretation includes the view of a class struggle between the very rich landowner who had money to speculate in the plantation of vines (which took four to five years to produce) and the oppressed tenants who lived in the subsistence line and who, he says, were probably the very ones who had lost the ownership of that large field.

A fourth aspect of Herzog's interpretation is very clever. He affirms that the allusion the evangelists make to Isaiah 5, instead of envisaging the identification of the owner of the vineyard with God, has the goal of remembering the readers of Isaiah 5:7–8, which reads: "For the vineyard of the Lord of hosts is the house of Israel, and the men of Judah are his pleasant planting; and he looked for justice, but behold, bloodshed; for righteousness, but behold, an outcry! Woe to those who join house to house, who add field to field, until there is no more room, and you are made to dwell alone in the midst of the land."

A fifth feature of this interpretation is that the blows to the first servant were probably due to the fact that the tenants were making the point that they had been spending their own money in this first year of the vineyard and the owner had no rights to demand anything from them.[12]

The sixth move is the equalization of the progressed violence described in the parable to phases of spiral of violence, i.e., the tenants could not endure their oppression anymore and started to act violently against their oppressors, who, in turn, paid back with even greater violence.[13] The violence of

---

11. Herzog, 102.
12. Herzog, 106.
13. "As the literature on social banditry and peasant revolts makes clear, peasants resorted to violence not to usher in an ideal order of justice but to restore what they had recently lost. In this parable, the tenants have rebelled for the purpose of restoring the patrimonial holdings, a situation that renders their actions and motive (v. 7) perfectly clear. Herzog, *Parables as Subversive Speech*, 110.

the oppressed class is, in Herzog's words, like a "holy war" similar to those of Joshua. On another hand, the fact that their rebellion is suppressed "codifies the futility of violence under these circumstances".[14] But this anticlimactic note is not the fulcrum of the passage. The author concludes his explanation by saying that; "The parable may codify the futility or armed rebellion, but it does more. By exploring the themes of ownership, inheritance, and heir, it calls into question the accepted version of those generative themes and undermines their credibility."[15] Schottroff presents a very similar interpretation but relates the parable to the situation of the revolts that lead to the fall of Jerusalem. She concludes that "The parable narrates in a condensed form experiences of violence in many levels."[16]

Herzog's interpretation is very creative and provocative. To his credit, he takes into serious consideration the canonical form of the parable searches for connections with the Old Testament and dives into the sociocultural context of first century Palestine. He reads parables more as pointing questions than answers, as codifications and "out of a liberationist framework".[17] With a historical-critical approach, he does not take into account the narrative context in which the parables appear, which is antagonistic to the fact that he uses redaction criticism and gives importance to the canonical version. Throughout the explanation of this specific parable, he stressed the fact that he did not want to take theology out of the parable of the wicked tenants. The result of this set of presuppositions is an explanation that shuns some obvious references, as the equalization of God as the owner of the vineyard and Jesus as the beloved son, but at the same time, brings to light important references to social justice that other interpreters do not see.

Hultgren's interpretation belongs to the newer approach to parables that rescued allegory. He says, "In all three Synoptic versions the parable is rich in allegorical detail. Their various items and their referents are easily identifiable."[18] The most unexpected referent he proposes to the parable is seeing the disciples of Jesus as the "others" to whom the vineyard is given,

---

14. Herzog, 113.
15. Herzog, 113.
16. Schottroff, *As Parábolas de Jesus: Uma Nova Hermenêutica*, 31.
17. Herzog, *Parables as Subversive Speech*, 1–4.
18. Hultgren, *The Parables of Jesus*, 357.

i.e., the disciples substitute the corrupt leaders of Jesus times: "For Luke, the people of God consist of the repentant of Israel and repentant Gentiles added to them. The leaders of renewed Israel are the apostles and those who come after them."[19]

Blomberg, also of this renewed allegorical approach to the parables, classifies this parable as a "complex three-point parable".[20] He then presents an interpretation that identifies the vineyard owner with God, the first tenants with Israel's leaders and the second group with religious leaders that replace the first set. He raises the possibility of this one being a four-point parable, with the identification of the vineyard's son with Christ, but leaves this interpretation open and subsumes it to the other three points.[21]

As Snodgrass points out, the history of interpretation of parables made a full circle from allegorizing to allegorizing.[22] This is clear in the history of interpretation of this specific passage. First, we see the patristic and medieval interpreters trying to find a theological referent for each detail of the parable. Then, critical schools and scholars struggling to undress the parable of any allegorical meaning clearly present in the canonical gospels and rebuild a "historical" version of the parable. The existentialist scholars brought allegory to bear in the interpretation in a good way, but apply the passage too broadly. The liberationist school interpreting the parable based in Marxist presuppositions finds a historical struggle in the passage and divests it completely from any theological significance.

Finally, the renewed allegorical school try to interpret the parable in its canonical form, finding referents that make sense to the time of Jesus and the theology that emanates from the text itself. Some scholars of this school, trying to avoid the excesses of the medieval interpretation show themselves overly careful in their restrictions of possible referents to the personages and details of the parable, as the last case well illustrates. The interpretation I present below finds itself in this last school of interpretation of parables,

---

19. Hultgren, *The Parables of Jesus*, 377.
20. Blomberg, *Interpreting the Parables*, 247.
21. Blomberg, *Interpreting the Parables*, 248–49.
22. "We have come to a full circle. For if patristic and medieval interpreters allegorized the parables by reading into them their own theologies, modern scholarship is no less guilty in reading into them its own agenda. We have gone from allegorizing to allegorizing – in some cases straying even further from hearing the voice of Jesus." Snodgrass, "From Allegorizing to Allegorizing," 26.

but also draws on the warranted insights of other schools. I completely agree with de Moor when he says, "In its present form the Parable of the Wicked Tenants does not make sense unless it is read as an allegory."[23]

7.2 Interpretation of the Parable

Before dealing with the parable *per se*, it is worthwhile to look at its literary context. The section of the journey to Jerusalem (9:51–19:46) ends and gives space to the concluding section of the gospel (19:47—24:53). This section presents events that happened in Jerusalem, including augmented and more aggressive opposition, Jesus's last teachings, the passion and the resurrection. The Lukan version of the parable of the wicked tenants appears in the first subsection of this last part of the gospel, a part we can call augmented controversy (Luke 19:47–21:4).

In this subsection, the emphasis is in the fact that "The chief priests and the scribes and the principal men of the people were seeking to destroy him" (Luke 19:47) and they try to do that by means of snaring Jesus with captious questions whose answer could somehow make Jesus guilty of heresy or treason (Luke 20:1–21:4). Jesus answered their questions with teachings to the disciples and the people, and accusations against the Jewish leaders.

The question that prompts the parable, asked by the chief priests, the scribes and the elders of the people, appears in Luke 20:2, "Tell us by what authority you do these things, or who it is that gave you this authority." Considering that Luke made clear that the leaders of the Sanhedrin were searching for an opportunity to destroy Jesus (19:47), it is evident that their question is not sincere. These men were criticizing and questioning Jesus's authority.[24] Thus, after making them speechless with a question about John the Baptist's ministry, Jesus tells the parable of the wicked tenants.

This parable is not that hard to interpret if one is willing to let the canonical text speak with liberty to be an allegory. Even Joachim Jeremias is clear in

---

23. De Moor, "The Targumic Background of Mark 12:1–12," 63.

24. "The leadership does not believe that Jesus has the right to do what he is doing, despite the evidence. Their reaction stands in stark contrast to the popular reaction of 19:48." Bock, *Luke 9:51–24:53*, 1585.

affirming the allegorical nature of the parable in its canonical versions and presents a clear summary:

> The vineyard is clearly Israel, the tenants are Israel's rulers and leaders, the owner of the vineyard is God, the messengers are the prophets, the son is Christ, the punishment of the husbandmen symbolizes the ruin of Israel, the 'nation' (Matt 21:43) is the Gentile Church. The whole parable is apparently pure allegory.[25]

After this summary, Jeremias goes on despising the canonical versions and trying the rebuild the 'original' non-allegorical parable. It is comical that he summarizes the correct interpretation of the parable with precision before dismissing it. Let us examine the parable.

Luke (together with Thomas) presents the vineyard (ἀμπελῶνα) without making specific references to Isaiah 5 (as do Matthew and Mark). When reading Luke, therefore, Isaiah 5 cannot be taken as a special background text, but figures together with other Old Testament texts exploring vineyards as symbols for Israel.[26] From these texts, Isaiah 3:14 has a more striking relation with our text, since in it God charges the elders and rulers of the people for mistreating his vineyard. Isaiah 3:14, includes an economic explanation for the accusation: "The Lord will enter into judgment with the elders of His people, and with their oppressors; because ye have robbed my people, the spoil of the poor is in your houses." Jeremiah 12:10 has a similar use for the metaphor of the vineyard. The difference with the parable, however, is that in these two texts, the rulers are destroying the vineyard instead of taking possession of it as in the parable.

A few scholars try to make a more precise indication for the vineyard than Israel, as for example, indicating it as the promise of God or the privileged

---

25. Jeremias, *Rediscovering the Parables*, 57. Geldenhuys has a similar summary: "To a greater degree than most of the other parables, this one should in many respects (though not in all respects) be interpreted allegorically. The vineyard thus symbolizes, as it often does in the Old Testament (cf. Isa 5:1–7; Jer 2:21, etc.), the chosen people, and the husbandmen the Jewish leaders to whom the care of the people has been entrusted." Geldenhuys, *Commentary on the Gospel of Luke*, 497–98.

26. These texts include, for example, Exodus 15:17; Numbers 13:22–24; Psalm 80:8–19; Isaiah 3:14; 5:1–7; 27:2–6; Jeremiah 2:21; 5:10; 6:9; 12:7–13; Ezekiel 15:1–8; 17:1–21; 19:10–14; Hosea 10:1–2.

position of Israel.²⁷ The most common and evident allegorical identification for the vineyard, however, based in the Old Testament is really the nation of Israel as the chosen people of God.

The identification of the vineyard as Israel and the fact that he has a son who is murdered identifies the ἄνθρωπος who is the owner of the vineyard with God and the γεωργοῖς with the leaders of Israel. There are evidences in the literary context as a base for such an interpretation. As I said before, this text appears in a highly polemical context. When one reads it closely, one sees that the polemic is not about the person of Jesus Christ, but about the different conceptions that Jesus and the Jewish leaders had about God.

The pericope preceding our text deals with the origin of Jesus's authority. The reader of the gospel knows that the authority of Jesus comes from God since he is the son of God (Luke 1:35; 4:41), the holy one of God (Luke 4:34), the Christ of God (Luke 9:20), and the announcer and definer of the good news of the kingdom of God (Luke 4:43; 8:1; 9:11; 13:18, 20; 17:20–21; 18:16–17). Jesus has authority that comes from God even to pardon sins and manifest God's power and majesty (Luke 5:21–24; 9:43; 11:20). Jesus has clear authority originated in God, but the leaders of the people are questioning it. This difference in the conception about God continue after the parable.

After this parable, when he was answering a trick question that intended to make Jesus commit treason, Jesus proffered "Then render to Caesar the things that are Caesar's, and to God the things that are God's" (Luke 20:25). The implication is that Jesus's interlocutors were not giving what was rightfully due to God. When it was Jesus's turn to make them a question, he asked about the correct interpretation of Psalm 110, which deals with God's given authority to a figure that David calls Lord, but who is at the same time David's son (Luke 20:41–44).

These texts found in the context of our parable reveal that the confrontation between Jesus and "[t]he chief priests and the scribes and the principal men of the people" (Luke 19:47) were about God and to whom he gave authority: to Jesus or to the leaders of the people. These references make the identification of God as the owner of the vineyard and the vinedressers as the leaders of Israel very compelling. There is also an interesting relation

---

27. Respectively, see Bock, *Luke 9:51–24:53*, 1591; 1597; Stein, *Luke: An Exegetical and Theological Exposition of Holy Scripture*, 491.

between 20:5 and 20:14 showing that both the leaders of the people and the vinedressers were plotting against their enemy.

The fact that the man in the parable "went into another country for a long while" (Luke 20:9) does not point to the delay in the parousia, since it represents God instead of Jesus and points to another time in the history of salvation, covered by the Old Testament, culminating in the coming of the Son.[28] The most probable reason for referring to the delay is related to the time of four to five years a vineyard takes to come to full production.[29]

The parable goes on to say that when the time (καιρός) came, the owner of the vineyard sent a slave to the farmers in order to take his share of the grapes. I do not see a specific allegorical reference to "time". It just builds up the plot of the parable, making clear that the owner respected the time necessary to the vines to produce. He did not haste, but wanted his share of the fruits when it was the appropriate time for that.

I agree with Stein and many others that affirm that "The servant represents the OT prophets."[30] I do not think it is possible, however, to identify them further than this general reference to the prophets. This identification has a few arguments in its favor. First, one of the preferred forms Luke identifies Jesus is by using the office of prophet (Luke 4:24; 7:16, 39; 13:33; 24:19; Acts 3:19–23; 7:37).[31] Second, many times the themes of prophets and rejection are intertwined in this gospel (Luke 4:24–30). Third and most important, the OT prophets are presented as having suffered in the hands of the Jewish people (Luke 6:20–26; 11:47–51; 13:34; Acts 7:52). Fourth, those who know

---

28. "Allegorically, the 'long time' has been thought to reflect the delay of the parousia, but the reference, if any, is rather to the long period during and since the sending of the prophets, since there is no reference to the parousia or the final judgment in the parable." Marshall, *The Gospel of Luke: A Commentary on the Greek Text*, 728–29. Also, "This note can hardly refer to the delay of the parousia, for the landlord does not symbolize Jesus." Fitzmyer, *The Gospel According to Luke*, 1283.

29. Kloppenborg, *The Tenants in the Vineyard*, 205.

30. Stein, *Luke*, 492. Geldenhuys has a similar interpretation: "The servants who were sent to fetch of the fruit of the vineyard represent the various prophets and other messengers of God in Old Testament days who from time to time were sent to the Jewish people and were but too often ill-treated and rejected by the Jewish leaders (cf. Jer 7:25, 25:4; Amos 3:7; Zech. 1:6)." Geldenhuys, *Commentary on the Gospel of Luke*, 498. Against Kloppenborg who says that "Luke has done nothing to promote the identification of the slaves with the prophets." Kloppenborg, *The Tenants in the Vineyard*, 208.

31. José Severino Croatto, "Jesus, Prophet like Elijah, and Prophet-Teacher like Moses in Luke-Acts," 451–65.

the history of the Old Testament would acknowledge as a fact the mistreatment that many prophets of old have received (e.g. criticism of Moses in Num 16, Jeremiah being put into the well in Jer 38, Micaiah slapped in the face in 1 Kings 22:23-27; Uriah persecuted and killed in Jer 26:20-23).

In the Lukan version of the parable of the wicked tenants there is a clear progression in the violence from slave one to three. The first slave was beaten and sent away empty-handed. He was expelled from the vineyard without any fruits and was assaulted. Bock comments that "Δέρω (*derō*) can refer either to striking someone on the face or the body (Luke 22:63; John 18:22; 2 Cor 11:20) or to a total physical beating."[32]

The owner sent another (ἕτερον) slave and this one "they also beat (δείραντες) and treated him shamefully (ἀτιμάσαντες), and sent him away empty-handed". The new factor in the mistreatment of this second slave is that the vinedressers somehow "abused" him.[33] Although it is not possible to know exactly what was done with this second slave, the meaning of ἀτιμάσαντες is to "deprive someone of honor or respect, to dishonor/shame". This is "an especially grievous offense in the strongly honor-shame oriented Semitic and Greco-Roman societies".[34] Philo has an interesting discussion about parents and children in which he teaches that he who dishonors the servant dishonors also the master.[35] The action reflected in this verb can refer to saying something dishonoring (John 8:48-49); beating someone (Acts 5:40-41), having homosexual relations (Rom 1:24), not treating someone according to their due honor (Rom 2:23; James 2:6), or denuding someone (LXX of 2 Kings 10:4-5). What is clear is that this servant was beaten and treated in a shameful way and that was a way of declaring war against the owner of the vineyard.

Now the lord of the vineyard sends a third (τρίτον) slave. The Greek text says: οἱ δὲ καὶ τοῦτον τραυματίσαντες ἐξέβαλον. The verb δέρω is changed for the stronger τραυματίζω and the verb ἐξαποστελῶ is substituted by the

---

32. Bock, *Luke 9:51-24:53*, 1598. This word is not specific to the point of being possible to know the quantity, form nor the intensity in which the man was beaten. Sometimes it is used to express whips and sometimes blows or strikes.

33. Johnson, *The Gospel of Luke*, 305.

34. BDAG, 148

35. *The Decalogue*, 119. Philo of Alexandria and Yonge, *The Works of Philo*, 528-29.

stronger ἐκβάλλω.³⁶ The word τραυματίζω has not only the meaning of wounding (cf. BDAG, 1014), but of wounding someone badly. Louw and Nida define it as "to hurt or wound, normally resulting in some mark or permanent scar on the body" (cf. L&N, 230). The only other occurrence in the New Testament is Acts 19:16 in which a demon possessed man leaps, masters and overpowers the sons of Sceva, who fled wounded (τετραυματισμένους). The LXX uses this verb to describe the mortal wound of Saul (1 Kings 31:3); the wounds that the suffering servant received (Isa 53:5), and mortal wounds of war (Ezekiel 28:23; 35:8). Reiling and Swellengrebel says that the word refers probably to "heavy, but non-fatal, bruises or wounds inflicted by some instrument."³⁷

It is clear, therefore, that Luke is showing a progression of violence in the way the vinedressers treated the servants. I do not think this should be interpreted in the sense that Israel augmented the mistreatment of the prophets over time, but it serves to show that the present generation was about to do the worst act of all, i.e., the murder of the son of the vineyard's owner, which, evidently, points to Jesus Christ and to his murder.

The Lukan Jesus created the perfect ethos for the climax of the story and he builds it up by using one of his preferred devices, an inner monologue: τί ποιήσω; πέμψω τὸν υἱόν μου τὸν ἀγαπητόν· ἴσως τοῦτον ἐντραπήσονται. The inner monologue has the functions of "disclosing a person's character, worries or concerns" and "deepen the reader's involvement".³⁸ It creates tension in the reader to know exactly how the character will answer to the troubling circumstance. In the case of this parable, the answer is completely unexpected and builds the tension up even more, because the owner now decides to send his own son to meet the vinedressers. In a clear reference to the person of Jesus Christ, Luke says that this son is the "beloved" son, adjective he has used for Jesus in Luke 3:22 and 9:35, both of them describing God speaking in first person with or about Jesus Christ in the baptism and in the transfiguration respectively. The reader of Luke knows for sure that the beloved son in the parable represents Jesus Christ.

---

36. "force to leave, *drive out, expel*" (BDAG, 299).
37. Reiling and Swellengrebel, *A Handbook on the Gospel of Luke*, 642.
38. Anselm Grün, *Jesus: The Image of Humanity*, 53. Grün goes on saying: "The monologue creates a secret and inner bond between the audience and the character; here the audience is as it were let into the actor's confidence. . . . The inner monologue is meant to move readers to new action, to repentance, so that they take the right course."

It is startling to see that the owner of the vineyard decides to send the son. He has absolutely no guarantees the tenants will respect him and the recent facts point that they will not. This is clear by the use of the Greek word ἴσως, which points to a possibility: "maybe so, maybe not" they will respect my son.[39] The owner expect that the tenants will show deference and respect his son, but due to the way they have dealt with the slaves, he cannot be sure of their curse of action.[40]

Now Luke uses a dialogue. It brings to light the secret conversation the tenants had among themselves when they saw the heir coming. The verb Luke uses is διαλογίζομαι. Johnson makes the point that "Only Luke uses the verb *dialogizomai*, which throughout the narrative describes evil designs and calculations (2:35; 5:21–22; 6:8; 9:46–47; 12:17)."[41] The scene is reminiscent of the patriarchs plotting to kill Joseph (Gen 37:18–20). The reason the tenants decide to kill the heir is so that they might take the inheritance to themselves. The concept of inheritance is very important here because it connects this allegorical parable with an important theme in the history of Israel, since Abraham until the division of land to each family and Israel herself as inheritance of the Lord.

Having decided to take their plans into fruition, the tenants throw the heir outside the vineyard and assassinate him. It is possible that this reference to the son and heir being expelled from the vineyard have as referent the fact that he dies outside Jerusalem (cf. Heb 13:12–14), but one cannot be sure of that.[42]

---

39. "The adverb *isōs* appears only here in the NT; it expresses uncertainty —"maybe so, maybe not." Johnson, *The Gospel of Luke*, 305.

40. "The master still has a final option, and with great patience, reflection, and some uncertainty, he exercises it. This uncertainty in the soliloquy shows how a parable often does not correspond to reality, since God is never said to be hesitant or uncertain about the fate of his Son. What the delay and reflection indicates is that the tenants' behavior has brought a dilemma. The owner figures that perhaps he has not sent someone with sufficient rank, so he decides to send his "beloved son" (τὸν υἱόν μου τὸν ἀγαπητόν, *ton huion mou ton agapēton*). This expression recalls Jesus' baptism (3:22), as well as his transfiguration (9:35; Leaney 1958: 250), and may imply that the man in the parable has only one son." Bock, *Luke 9:51–24:53*, 1599.

41. Johnson, *The Gospel of Luke*, 305. The verb means to think or reason carefully, esp. about the implications of someth., *consider, ponder, reason (BDAG, 232)*. Reiling and Swellengrebel comment on its verbal aspect: "The imperfect is durative and implies that it took some time before they came to the decision expressed in what follows." Reiling and Swellengrebel, *A Handbook on the Gospel of Luke*, 643.

42. Kloppenborg, speaking about this reference of the son being killed outside the vineyard says: "It therefore seems doubtful that in his editing of the parable of the Tenants this distinction held any great significance for Luke." Kloppenborg, *The Tenants in the Vineyard*, 211.

In this verse [13] the Messianic consciousness of Jesus is expressed very clearly. In these words He declares plainly that, while He is a divine Messenger and One who acts on God's authority, He is quite different from all the other divine messengers, as, e.g., the prophets. He is altogether unique—the beloved Son of the Father. In addition, He is the very last One to come to the people, and indeed to the whole world. After His coming no higher revelation and no mightier manifestation of God's love is to be expected. Through His coming to the people they (and especially the leaders) have now their last chance.[43]

Having conducted the readers to this moment, the Lukan Jesus uses another device to engage even more the hearers and the readers. He uses a question: "What then will the owner of the vineyard do to them?" Jesus himself is the one who answers the question in Luke: "He will come and destroy those tenants and give the vineyard to others." It is not easy to determine the identity of these "others" outside the parabolic world. As the context speaks about authority (Luke 20:1–8) and the parable focuses on the tenants hired to develop the vineyard and, thus, point to the leaders of Israel, it is more logical to affirm that these others are the new leaders of Israel, i.e., the twelve apostles. That makes sense in Luke, whose second volume will present exactly how this new leadership preached the gospel throughout the world.

Those hearing Jesus understood the gravity of what he was saying and reacted using one of the most emphatic negation of the Greek language μὴ γένοιτο.[44] Kloppenborg has an interesting discussion about what was the content of Jesus's talk that produced the reaction of the people, the punishment of the vinedressers or the whole story. He concludes correctly, I think, that the second option is better and presents three reasons. First, Luke is distinguishing the people from the leaders in his whole gospel. Second, the verbal construction ἀκούσαντες + finite verb commonly in Luke presents a reaction of the people to a story as a whole. Third, Kloppenborg thinks that the people

---

43. Geldenhuys, *Commentary on the Gospel of Luke*, 498.

44. "*Heaven forbid!* Lit. "may it not be (so)! . . . It expresses a strong reaction or negation, used by Paul generally after a rhetorical question. The phrase is often found in the LXX as a translation of Hebrew *ḥălîlāh lî/lānû*, lit. "an abomination to me/us." Fitzmyer, *The Gospel According to Luke*, 1285. "No way!" Carroll, *Luke: A Commentary*, 393.

at this point did not identify the vinedressers with the leaders of Israel.[45] Although I disagree with this last argument, I concur with Kloppenborg's interpretation that the reaction of the people refers to the whole story and not just to the punition on the vinedressers.

Jesus, then, answers by quoting Psalm 118:22, a text used again by Luke in Acts 4:11, clearly referring to Jesus himself as the stone and to the leaders who oppose Jesus as the builders. Borgman presents a good resume of the metaphor of the stone: "Rejecting me is to invite destruction: mine is the authority. I am the cornerstone of whatever house Israel hopes to have".[46]

Luke still makes clear for the readers that the scribes and chief priests perceived that he had told this parable against them (Luke 20:19). Bock presents a good summary of the teaching present in the parable:

> The parable contains a passion prediction, a messianic claim, and a promise that death will not end God's plan. God will bring in others from whom he will obtain fruit and who will share in blessing. The parable also shows God's patience in withholding judgment, though judgment becomes inevitable now that the Son is rejected (Giblin 1985: 73). The parable is Jesus' response to the leadership's plot to get him (19:47; Tannehill 1986: 192). It also answers the question posed in 20:1–8: Jesus is sent from God; his authority is from heaven.[47]

It is important to remember that what prompted Jesus to tell this parable was a questioning of his authority. Jesus, therefore, expanded the subject but did not change it. He presented the whole history of salvation with the old dispensation of the prophets in the Old Testament, the coming of the son of God, the murder of the Messiah and the new leadership He is providing to his church. The teaching and actions of Jesus have the seal of God himself.[48] Kloppenborg presents two summaries of conclusion for the Lukan version of this parable: "First it illustrates the contrast between the people (λαός), whom Luke has already depicted as favorably disposed to Jesus, and their leaders,

---

45. Kloppenborg, *The Tenants in the Vineyard*, 212.
46. Paul Carlton Borgman, *The Way According to Luke*, 220.
47. Bock, *Luke 9:51–24:53*, 1592.
48. "Moreover, the parable is also the answer to their previous question—He is acting on the authority of the Father who sent Him." Geldenhuys, *Commentary on the Gospel of Luke*.

who are not". And "Second, Luke uses the story to introduce a principle of judgment that one's reaction to Jesus as the Christ will define one's fate, for good or ill."[49]

7.3 Does this Parable Teach about Land?

As it happened with other parables analyzed in this dissertation, the teaching this parable brings about land is not the main reason for it, but it is important when one considers its cultural and economic context and the Lukan overall teaching on this subject. Since Dodd and Jeremias, authors recognize that this parable does not use an impossible situation, but one intimately related to the context of agricultural Galilee.[50] As we have seen, Herzog takes this to another level, when he only pays attention to the economic situation of Jesus's times and strips the parable of any spiritual sense connected to the history of salvation.[51] But one does not need to do that to see agro-economic aspects in this parable.

In the second chapter we have seen a few economic characteristics of the Roman Empire, including the absenteeism of rich landowners who would contract tenants to develop their lands and the fact that while these landowners would commonly accumulate more and more wealth, their tenants would live at subsistence level. That chapter demonstrated also that this kind of situation sometimes caused uprisings among the people and that commonly the land amassed by the wealthy were the very land once owned by the poor. That kind of historical context should be presupposed in the reading of this parable.

Thus, it was common for the rich owner of the vineyard to be an antihero for the people. In the Thomasine version of this parable, the landowner is called a "usurer".[52] Kloppenborg, considering the version of the gospel of Thomas more original than the Synoptic ones, says that it: "serve[s] instead to underscore the folly of the usurer who not only loses his land – the basis of wealth and status in the ancient world – but also his heir, that is, his ability

---

49. Kloppenborg, *The Tenants in the Vineyard*, 218.
50. Dodd, *The Parables of the Kingdom*, 96; Jeremias, *Rediscovering the Parables*, 61.
51. Herzog, *Parables as Subversive Speech*, 102.
52. Kloppenborg, *The Tenants in the Vineyard*, 250; 279.

to perpetuate his name."⁵³ This is also a socially engaged reading divested of theological aspects in the steps of Herzog's interpretation.

I think it is possible, however, to reconcile this socially conscious and engaged interpretation of the parable without stripping its theological meaning from it; meaning which is clearly presented in Luke and the other Synoptics. Kloppenborg shows that owners of vineyards in Judea were commonly rich landholders.⁵⁴ In Israel, the class who would be most similar to such people were the leaders who are presented in the text as opposing Jesus.

What happens in the parable, therefore, is that Jesus reverts the common position enjoyed by "the chief priests and the scribes with the elders" (Luke 20:1) as landholders and depicts them in the position some of the people who were also hearing Jesus commonly had, as tenants and workers for the wealthy. Jesus places God himself, the rightful owner of the land, in the position of the rich and commonly oppressive owner of the vineyard.

Moreover, through this parable, Luke makes it clear again that a very important aspect of the sin of the leaders of Israel was that they wanted to personally benefit from the "inheritance" of Israel, which belonged to God. In Luke's writing, as we have seen, it is not possible to separate the spiritual dimension of life from the economic one. "No servant can serve two masters, for either he will hate the one and love the other, or he will be devoted to the one and despise the other. You cannot serve God and money. The Pharisees, who were lovers of money (φιλάργυροι), heard all these things, and they ridiculed him." (Luke 16:13–14). Luke makes clear throughout his gospel that the Jewish leaders were choosing the second option, serving money.

This preference for money instead of God was evident in the way the leaders of the people dealt with their properties. One of the areas in which this would appear was in the egotistic way they were dealing with their properties. They would promote social banquets which gave them self-affirmation in order to examine if other people were good enough to participate in their distinguished class (Luke 14:1–24). They were also taking widows' houses (Luke 20:46–47) probably by means of deceiving them in order to take possession of

---

53. Kloppenborg, *The Tenants in the Vineyard*, 281. Further on the same page, he says: "By contrast the mission of the son in Thomas is an abject failure and that failure underscores the grave miscalculation of the owner."

54. Kloppenborg, *The Tenants in the Vineyard*, 300–301.

their houses. Thus, behind an appearance of piety, Israel's leaders wanted to benefit from the people and to extract material things from them, including houses and fields, by using their privileged position. Both in the privileged position of respected leaders and in the material aspect, the leaders of Israel were taking possession of the inheritance and the vineyard of the Lord. This is the reason why Jesus depicted the history of salvation by using the figure of the wicked tenants trying to take possession of the vineyard. The chief priests, scribes and elders were promoting social injustice in order to benefit themselves, augmenting their possessions and their land.

Instead of knowing that all land belongs to God and working hard to develop the land in a way to bless most of the people according to a jubilee ethics, the Israelite elite was using the land only for themselves. They were living as if they were the ultimate owners of land and its produce. However, through this parable, Jesus makes clear to them that by systematically and historically ignoring the prophets (who preached social justice and the priority of God) and by resisting the beloved Son, they would need to face the wrath of God.

There is therefore a very important aspect of social justice in this parable. This aspect is not found in comparing the owner of the parable to an abusive landowner, but by placing God as the owner of the vineyard, by depicting the leaders as vinedressers who were forcefully trying to take possession of the vineyard to themselves and by demonstrating the terrible consequences of dealing with God's land without respecting God's will.

CHAPTER 8

Conclusion: Summary and Significance

This thesis aimed to make the case that Luke teaches his readers a jubilee-informed ethics, which has the following central tenets. First, God is the ultimate owner of all land (Lev 25:23). Second, in consequence, every person has the obligation of using the land in a way that is pleasing to God. Third, acting as a faithful "tenant" or "slave" of God in what concerns land results in divine blessings. Fourth and finally, acting as the sole proprietor of land, ignoring its divine ownership, results in curses from God. I am calling these teachings a land-jubilee ethics, which the author of Luke-Acts proposes as an answer to the situation of land injustice and oppression present in the Roman Empire in general and in Israel in particular.

The path used to reach the conclusions referred above was as follows: The first chapter summarized studies in correlate areas to land justice in Luke and reached the conclusion that the subject of the present study was both necessary and absent from the studies of the New Testament and Luke. One finds a few practical writings about land justice and the New Testament, many studies on general possessions and the gospel of Luke, and studies which acknowledge the jubilee as a central theme in Luke-Acts, but despite that, no other study about land in the gospel of Luke was found to this date. After presenting the justification for such a dissertation, chapter 1 presented in a summarized form some of the presuppositions and methodology that guided this research.

The second chapter, firstly, presented a general picture of the economic stratification of the Roman Empire to make clear that Roman society was based in a system for the betterment of those who were already well off. We have seen that 3% of the population owned most of the cultivable land throughout the whole empire. The second part of chapter 2 demonstrated that, historically, this situation generated conflict between the *honestiores* and the *humiliores*, causing the collapse of the Republic and the rise of the Empire. The third part of the third chapter shows that despite the change from Republic to empire, the economic system in this last was such that it propitiated those who were wealthy amassing more and more land while the small holders would commonly lose their lands and become tenants, daily workers or even slaves. There was a spiral upward for a small percentage of the population, while more than 80% would commonly live around the subsistence level or experience a downward spiral. While that was the reality, Roman institutions like patronage, worship of the emperor and a culture of shame and honor would keep the overall status quo.

Still in the second chapter, I have called the Roman Empire a system of oppression. This is justified since the empire became enormous and powerful by means of conquering foreign land and denominating it *ager publicus* and, subsequently establishing systems of taxation that would weigh heavier on the poor who already lived at a subsistence level. This system of oppression also had the participation of the affluent by their constant thirst for accumulating more land (*latifundia*). They would bind the poor in debt, and by slavery. Thus, the second chapter accomplished the goal of demonstrating the context to which Luke was writing his gospel in what concerns land and the consequent need and sensibility of the subject. Since the original readers of the gospel of Luke and Acts were experiencing such a context daily, they would interact differently with some images and histories present in the work. For example, to say in such a context that the God of Israel, not the emperor and not the prosperous, is the rightful owner and ruler of all land is very countercultural. That is what Luke does.

The third chapter continued the subject of land injustice, but focused specifically on the nation of Israel. I demonstrated that since the Second Temple Period, land started to accumulate in the hands of a few leaders of Israel, especially those in sync with the current conqueror of the nation. This pattern continues in the first century, with the religious and political leaders of Israel who have friendly relations with the Roman rulers becoming, together with wealthy foreigners, the owners of the majority of the good land available. The consequence is that while the most rich and powerful were perpetuating their well-being, the majority of the people were ejected into poverty, losing

Conclusion: Summary and Significance

their land and becoming tenants, hired workers or slaves of the elites. As it happened in Rome, in Israel this situation also gave rise to groups of brigands who would use violence in order to try to subvert this situation of injustice. Those in power commonly destroyed these groups.

While chapters 2 and 3 have a historical approach, chapter 4 presents a summarized land theology of the Old Testament. The aim of the chapter is showing the reader that land was always a central theme in the Bible, that one of the most important asseverations the OT does is that God is the owner of the land and the one who has the right to define how humans are supposed to use land. At the same time, the fourth chapter demonstrates that Israel was unfaithful in her dealing with land, practicing injustice against the land and oppression against the poor in order to accumulate land and that was one of the very important reasons for the Babylon captivity. Thus, chapters 2 to 4 deal with the historical and theological contexts of land ethics. Luke keeps most of the theology and ethics of the Old Testament to propose an answer for the situation of land injustice in which he lives.

The central chapter of this dissertation is the fifth. It shows first the centrality of the jubilee for the gospel of Luke. The manner Jesus uses Isaiah 61:1–2 in Luke 4:14–30 demonstrates the central importance of the Jubilee for the Lukan Jesus and that Luke writes his gospel in the light of that statement. Now, since the jubilee is central in the gospel of Luke and land is central to the jubilee, one should expect that land is also very important in Luke-Acts. The rest of the chapter aims to prove that this syllogism is correct. The arguments are four. First, in the gospel, Jesus and God are presented as the ultimate landowners. Second, Jesus teaches throughout the gospel that those who deal with land as if it is their own are subject to punishment and those who use the land in a way pleasing to God receive blessings. Third, Luke presents Jesus as identified with the landless having no place of himself even to rest for one night. The last argument is drawn from Acts. Acts shows that the community that surges after the disciples of Jesus practice the jubilee land ethics that Jesus taught. They did that both by practicing different forms of community of goods and also by Christian hospitality.

The analysis of chapter 5 was broad. Many texts were dealt with in Luke and Acts, but by the nature of the case it was impossible to deal with the texts in a more exegetical and deeper fashion. This is the reason for chapters Six and Seven, to present a more detailed and exegetical treatment of two passages and in order to show that they bear with this land ethics that Luke proposes for those who want to be disciples of Jesus.

Thus, chapter 6 demonstrates that The Parable of the Rich Fool (Luke 12:13–21) teaches the error of considering oneself the ultimate owner of land, when God, who is the rightful owner, can at any time recall the soul he lends to men. The seventh chapter presents an interpretation of The Parable of the Wicked Tenants (Luke 20:9–19). This parable also presents God as the ultimate owner of all land and teaches the stupidity of trying to steal the land that belongs to God.

Luke therefore presents a well-developed and harmonious jubilee land ethics against the land injustice that was common in Israel and in the Roman Empire. The central theological affirmation for this land ethics is that God is the supreme owner of all land and the main consequence of that is that humans are supposed to use land in an altruistic way that is pleasing to God.

The application of the jubilee ethics found in Luke is not an easy matter to discuss. There is no doubt that "The message of the biblical Jubilee is exceedingly rich in insights in terms of socio-economic and moral-spiritual issues and is capable of offering positive solutions to some of the main problems of today's world."[1] The question is if these insights and solutions are to be applied by society in general, by the church or by the individual believer and what role the church should have in this process.

Those who study and apply the jubilee have applied mostly in three ways: (1) political engagement; (2) social engagement by local churches; and (3) individual believers applying the principles of the jubilee.

Fernando Lua is an example of those who affirm that the jubilee legislation implies political engagement by the church. He writes using the Philippine experience of a country plagued by immoral debt. After presenting the economic history and situation of the country and the jubilee legislations, Lua presents a few recommendations for today, including the defense against all forms of marginalization and oppression. He says: "Churches are to be actively involved in these advocacies. The church should not remain silent."[2] Lua also defends the principles of simple living, sharing with the poor, lending to the poor with no interest, and believers organizing cooperatives. More related

---

1. Gunjević, *Jubilee in the Bible*.
2. Fernando C. Lua, "The Year of the Jubilee," 368.

with the present dissertation, the last recommendation of the article is that the church should

> Push for the Philippine government to fully implement land distribution to our poor farmers under the Comprehensive Agrarian Reform Program or Republic Act 6657 signed into law by then President Corazon C. Aquino in 1988. The law has very good intentions toward promoting social justice and giving opportunity to landless farmers to rise out of poverty.[3]

The last line of the article is very telling, since on it the author elevates the jubilee to a condition of a mandate valid for contemporary believers: "There is hope for us as long as we live these kingdom values and follow the Jubilee mandate."[4]

Atula Ao makes a similar proposal writing from a North-East Indian tribal perspective.[5] He contends that a jubilee ethics is to be implemented and that it should have socio-economic, ecological and gender-reconciliation implications. On the land aspect, he says:

> With the message of Jubilee the tribals should recover their original freedom of Promised Land ownership. The implication here will be that the goodness of God for the tribal people is mediated by the goodness and kindness of other persons including the Government. The message of Jubilee propels the tribals to return the land that was grabbed away due to greed, development and privatization.[6]

This way of comprehending the jubilee also generated the initiative called Jubilee 2000, a campaign calling the richest nations to forgive the debt of the most poor and indebted countries.[7]

---

3. Lua, 370.
4. Lua, 372.
5. Ao, "Jubilee and Liberaion," 1–20.
6. Ao, "Jubilee and Liberaion," 8.
7. Nozomi Miura, "Justice in the Bible, Globalization, and Jubilee," 58 et seq. Other proposals that focus on what nations should are presented here. Ilsup Ahn proposes forgiveness for the illegal migrants in the US based on the Jubilee injunctions. "According to the politics of forgiveness, the U.S. government and her citizens should consider to offer political and legal forgiveness to many eligible undocumented migrants by offering them an opportunity to become legitimate members of this society on the basis of the jubilee principle that *no humans*

Another way of applying the jubilee principles is focusing not on the government, but on local churches. That is the focus of Maria Harris in the article "Proclaiming Jubilee Justice".[8] She concludes the article with the following pastoral suggestions for churches and other religious bodies: "Raise questions", "Create a truth and reconciliation committee", "Set up a 'Leviticus 25:23' fund", "Think small", and "Observe a regular Sabbath".[9]

There are scholars who affirm that the Jubilee was valid only at that specific time and place in which the law was given. Thus, they propose that only general principles about God and ethics can be justly extracted from the jubilee and applied by the individual believer. Michael Harbin, for example, defends that the "current idea of the 'Jubilee principle' is not a valid understanding of the OT institution of Jubilee".[10] Speaking about the principles one can correctly extract from the Jubilee, Harbin proposes three main ones. First, "God is sovereign, and as the Creator-God owns the entire cosmos". Second, "God is gracious in that he gives gifts to people who are undeserving". Thirdly, "God is just and righteous and expects mankind to exhibit justice and righteousness in the way they manage the gifts God gives them".[11] This kind of understanding seems to be underlying the document called Towards a Better Distribution of Land, issued by the Roman Catholic Apostolic Church in preparation for "The Great Jubilee of the year 2000" proclaimed by this institution.[12] Although this document deals with agrarian problems related to nations and globalization, its call is for the action of all Christians as individuals. Seemingly pairing with the last position, Willoughby affirms that "Luke himself points the way forward by not dwelling upon Jubilee imagery

---

should be kept under permanent indebted, enslaved, or illegal status." Ahn, "Proclaiming the Jubilee Year for Undocumented Migrants," 66. Lazonby proposes solutions for contemporary socio-political and environmental issues of over-farming, climate change, international debt, modem-day slavery, land expropriation, and wealth accumulation; all based on his reading of the jubilee traditions. Lazonby, "Applying the Jubilee to Contemporary Socio-Economic and Environmental Issues," 30–50.

8. Harris, "Proclaiming Jubilee Justice," 15–24.
9. Harris, 321–23.
10. Harbin, "Jubilee and Social Justice," 698.
11. Harbin, "Jubilee and Social Justice," 698–99.
12. Roger Etchegaray et al., *Towards a Better Distribution of Land* (Vatican, 1997). See also Whelan, "Jesus Is the Jubilee, 204–29. Another jubilee year was proclaimed by Pope Francis in 2015. See Tuohy, "Extraordinary Jubilee and Preachers of Mercy," 2–22.

but by allowing it to be redefined by the content of Jesus' own ministry as he describes it in the pages of his gospel".[13]

Thus, scholars studying the jubilee are applying it to contemporary realities in three main ways. Some call for political engagement, other for church action, and still others for change of individual application of the principles of the jubilee. What kind of practical action does this dissertation call for?

The first call of the jubilee sermon of Jesus is individual. Each person who hears the proclamation Jesus does that he is the one fulfilling Isaiah 61 is faced with the decision of accepting this identification or rejecting it. It is evident that Luke wants his readers to accept the identity of Jesus as the Messiah who brings release from sin and also from suffering and oppression. There is no jubilee without the acknowledgement of Jesus's identity as the Israelite Messiah and Savior of the world.

Put in this way, it becomes clear that any proclamation of jubilee, campaign or proposal that ignores this fact is doomed to fail. There is no common foundation in general society over which the principles of the jubilee can be successfully applied.

Luke presents in Acts there is only one community able to apply the jubilee principles and live its ethics. This community is the church. More than calling the world to change economically, the church should embody the kind of life of land and economic altruism and hospitality, while it announces Jesus as the reason for living this different kind of life. Thus, the center and main motivation for living a jubilee informed ethics is the person of Jesus and only in a personal relationship with him one will be able and willing to live such a life.

---

13. Willoughby, "The Concept of Jubilee and Luke 4:18–30," 55.

Bibliography

Acuña, Mauricio. "'No Había Entre Ellos Ningún Necesitado': La Normatividad de La Comunidad de Bienes En Hechos 2–6." *Kairós* 48 (2011): 35–53.
Adams, Samuel L. *Social and Economic Life in Second Temple Judea*. Louisville: Westminster John Knox Press, 2014.
Ahn, Ilsup. "Proclaiming the Jubilee Year for Undocumented Migrants: Anti-Immigration Biopolitics and a Christian Theopolitical Response." *Polit. Theol.* 18 (2017): 249–68. https://doi.org/10.1179/1462317X15Z.000000000177.
Alexander, Joseph Addison. *Commentary on the Prophecies of Isaiah: Vol II*. New and Re. New York: Scribne, Armstrong & Co., 1878.
———. *The Later Prophecies of Isaiah*. New York: Wiley and Putnam, 1847. https://books.google.com/books?id=WhMXAAAAIAAJ.
Ando, Clifford. *Imperial Ideology and Provincial Loyalty in the Roman Empire*. Berkeley: University of California Press, 2013.
Ao, Atula. "Jubilee and Liberaion: A North-East India Tribal Perspective." Pages 1–20 in *Bangalore Theological Forum*. Edited by united Theological College. Bangalore: Dept. of Research and Post-graduate Studies, 2013.
Aquinas, Thomas. *Catena Aurea: Commentary on the Four Gosels Collected out of the Works of the Fathers by S. Thomas Aquinas*. Oxford: John Henry Parker, 1843.
Aquino, João Paulo Thomaz de. "Atos 6:1–7: A Gênese Do Ofício Diaconal?" *Fides Reformata* 15 (2010): 9–20.
Aschim, Anders. "The Genre of 11QMelchizedek." Pages 17–31 in *Qumran between the Old and New Testaments*. Edited by Thomas L. Thompson Frederick H. Cryer. Sheffield, England: Sheffield Academic Press, 1998.
Atkinson, Kenneth. *An Intertextual Study of the Psalms of Solomon: Pseudepigrapha*. Lewiston: Edwin Mellen Press, 2001.
Aviam, Mordechai. "People, Land, Economy, and Belief in First-Century Galilee and Its Origins: A Comprehensive Archaeological Synthesis." Pages 5–48 in *The Galilean Economy in the Time of Jesus*. Edited by David A. Fiensy and Ralph K. Hawkins. Atlanta: Society of Biblical Literature, 2013.

Babcock, Bryan C. "Year of Jubilee." *The Lexham Bible Dictionary*. Edited by John D. Barry. Bellingham: Lexham Press, 2016.

Baesens, Viviane. "Royal Taxation and Religious Tribute in Hellenistic Palestine." Pages 180–99 in *Ancient Economies Modern Methodologies: Archaeology, Comparative History, Models and Institutions*. Edited by Peter F. Bang, Mamoru Ikeguchi, and Hartrmut G. Ziche. Bari: Edipuglia, 2006.

Bailey, Kenneth E. *Poet & Peasant and Through Peasant Eyes: A Literary -Cultural Approach to the Parables in Luke*. Combined E. Grand Rapid: Eerdmans, 1983.

Bailey, Lloyd R. *Leviticus-Numbers*. Macon: Smyth & Helwys, 2005.

Balentine, Samuel E. *Leviticus*. Louisville: John Knox Press, 2012.

Baloglou, Christos P. "Hellenistic Economic Thought." Pages 105–46 in *Ancient and Medieval Economic Ideas and Concepts of Social Justice*. Edited by S. Todd Lowry and Barry Gordon. Leiden; New York: Brill, 1998.

Bang, Peter Fibiger. "Predation." Pages 197–217 in *The Cambridge Companion to Roman Economy*. Edited by Walter Scheidel. Cambridge: Cambridge University Press, 2012.

Baron, Salo Wittmayer. *A Social and Religious History of the Jews. Vol. 1*. New York: Columbia University Press, 1952.

Bauckham, Richard. *The Bible in the Contemporary World: Hermeneutical Ventures*. Grand Rapids: Eerdmans, 2015.

———. "The Rich Man and Lazarus: The Parable and the Parallels." *New Testam. Stud.* 37 (1991): 225–46.

Berger, Adolf. *Encyclopedic Dictionary of Roman Law: Volume 43*. Philadelphia: The American Philosophical Society, 1953.

Bergsma, John Sietze. *The Jubilee from Leviticus to Qumran: A History of Interpretation*. Leiden: Brill, 2007.

Bevan, Edwyn. *A History of Egypt Under the Ptolemaic Dynasty*. London: Methuen, 1927.

Bickermann, Elias, and Amram Tropper. *Studies in Jewish and Christian History: A New Edition in English Including The God of the Maccabees*. Leiden: Brill, 2007.

Birch, Bruce C., Walter Brueggemann, Terence E. Fretheim, and David L. Petersen. *A Theological Introduction to the Old Testament*. Nashville: Abingdon Press, 2005.

Blake, William O. *The History of Slavery and The Slave Trade, Ancient and Modern: The Forms of Slavery That Prevailed in Ancient Nations, Particularly in Greece and Rome*. Columbus: H. Miller, 1861.

Blenkinsop, Joseph. *Isaiah 56–66*. New York: Doubleday, 2000.

Blomberg, Craig L. *Interpreting the Parables*. Downers Grove: InterVarsity Press, 2012.

Bock, Darrell L. *A Theology of Luke and Acts: God's Promised Program, Realized for All Nations*. Grand Rapids: Zondervan, 2012.

———. *Luke 1:1–9:50*. Grand Rapids: Baker, 1994.

———. *Luke 9:51–24:53*. Grand Rapids: Baker Academic, 1996.

Borgman, Paul Carlton. *The Way According to Luke : Hearing the Whole Story of Luke-Acts*. Grand Rapids: Eerdmans, 2006.

Bovon, François. *Luke 2: A Commentary on the Gospel of Luke 9:51–19:27*. Minneapolis: Fortress Press, 2013.

Bovon, François, and Helmut Koester. *Luke 1 : A Commentary on the Gospel of Luke 1:1–9:50*. Minneapolis.: Fortress Press, 2002.

Bowman, Alan, and Andrew Wilson. *The Roman Agricultural Economy*. Oxford: Oxford University Press, 2016.

Boyce, Richard Nelson. *Leviticus and Numbers*. Louisville: Westminster John Knox Press, 2008.

Bradley, K. R., and Paul Cartledge. *The Cambridge World History of Slavery. Volume 1*. Cambridge: Cambridge University Press, 2011.

Bradley, Keith R. *Slaves and Masters in the Roman Empire : A Study in Social Control*. Oxford: Oxford University Press, 1987.

Brawley, Robert L. "Ethical Borderlines between Rejection and Hope: Interpreting the Jews in Luke-Acts." *Curr. Theol. Mission* 27 (2000): 415–23.

Briggs, Richard S. *Words in Action : Speech Act Theory and Biblical Interpretation*. Edinburgh: T & T Clark, 2004.

Bright, John. *A History of Israel*. 3rd editio. Philadelphia: Westminster Press, 1981.

Brodie, Thomas L. *Genesis as Dialogue: A Literary, Historical, & Theological Commentary*. Oxford: Oxford University Press, 2004.

Bruce, F. F. "The Church of Jerusalem in Acts of the Apostles." *Bull. John Rylands Univ. Libr. Manchester* 67 (1985): 641–61.

Brueggemann, Walter. *A Commentary on Jeremiah: Exile and Homecoming*. Grand Rapids: Eerdmans, 2003.

———. *A Mandate to Be Different: An Invitation to the Contemporary Church*. Louisville: Westminster John Knox Press, 2007.

———. *God, Neighbor, Empire: The Excess of Divine Fidelity and the Command of Common Good*. Waco: Baylor University Press, 2016.

———. *Isaiah: 40–66*. Louisville: Westminster John Knox Press, 1998.

———. *The Land: Place as Gift, Promise, and Challenge in Biblical Faith*. Minneapolis: Fortress Press, 2002.

Bruehler, Bart B. *A Public and Political Christ: The Social-Spatial Characteristics of Luke 18:35–19:48 and the Gospel as a Whole in Its Ancient Context*. Eugene: Pickwick Publications, 2011.

Bruno, C. R. "'Jesus Is Our Jubilee'... But How? The OT Background and Lukan Fulfillment of the Ethics of Jubilee." *JETS* 53 (2010): 81–101.

Bunson, Matthew. *Encyclopedia of the Roman Empire*. New York: Facts on File, 2002.

Burridge, Richard A. *Imitating Jesus: An Inclusive Approach to the New Testament Ethics*. Grand Rapids: Eerdmans, 2007.

———. *What Are the Gospels?: A Comparison with Graeco-Roman Biography*. Grand Rapids; Dearborn: Eerdmans; Dove Booksellers, 2004.

Butler, Trent C. *Luke*. Nashville: Broadman & Holman, 2000.

Byrd, Robert C. *The Senate of the Roman Republic: Addresses on the History of Roman Constitutionalism*. Washington, DC: U.S. Government Printing Office, 1994.

Calvin, John. *Commentary on a Harmony of the Evangelists Matthew, Mark, and Luke*. Bellingham: Logos Bible Software, 2010.

Campbell, Constantine R. *Verbal Aspect, the Indicative Mood, and Narrative: Soundings in the Greek of the New Testament*. New York: Peter Lang, 2007.

Capper, Brian J. "Holy Community of Life and Property amongst the Poor: A Response to Steve Walton." *EQ* 80 (2008): 113–27.

———. "The Interpretation of Acts 5:4." *JSNT*. 19 (1983): 117–31. https://doi.org/10.1177/0142064X8300601908.

———. "The Judaean Cultural Context of Community of Goods in the Early Jesus Movement: Part II." *Qumran Chron.* 26 (2018): (In Press).

———. "The Judaean Cultural Context of Community of Goods in the Early Jesus Movement." *Qumran Chron.* 26 (2016): 29–49.

Carroll, John T. *Luke: A Commentary*. Louisville: Westminster John Knox Press, 2012.

Carroll R., M. Daniel. "La Cita de Isaias 58:6 En Lucas 4:18: Una Nueva Propuesta." *Kairós* 11 (1992): 61–78.

Casson, Lionel. *Everyday Life in Ancient Rome*. Baltimore: The Johns Hopkins University Press, 1998.

Chancey, Mark. A. "Archaeology, ‚Ethnicity and First Centuriy C.E. Galilee: The Limits of Evidence." Pages 205–18 in *A Wandering Galilean: Essays in Honour of Séan Freyne*. Edited by Zuleika Rodgers, Margaret Daly-Denton, and Anne Fitzpatrick McKinley. Leiden: Brill, 2009.

Charles, Robert Henry, ed. *Pseudepigrapha of the Old Testament*. Oxford: Clarendon Press, 1913.

Charpin, Dominique. *Writing, Law, and Kingship in Old Babylonian Mesopotamia*. Chicago: The University of Chicago Press, 2010.

Childs, Brevard S. *Biblical Theology in Crisis*. Philadelphia: Westminster Press, 1974.

———. *Introduction to the Old Testament as Scripture*. Philadelphia: Fortress Press, 1979.

———. *Isaiah*. Louisville: Westminster John Knox Press, 2001.

Collins, John J. *Jewish Wisdom in the Hellenistic Age*. Louisville: Westminster John Knox Press, 1999.

Collins, Raymond F. *Wealth, Wages, and the Wealthy: New Testament Insight for Preachers and Teachers*. Collegeville: Liturgical Press, 2017.
Conzelmann, Hans. *The Theology of St. Luke*. Philadelphia: Fortress Press, 1982.
Coogan, Michael D. *The Oxford History of the Biblical World*. Oxford: Oxford University Press, 1998.
Craddock, Fred B. *Luke*. Louisville: John Knox Press, 1990.
Croatto, José Severino. "Jesus, Prophet like Elijah, and Prophet-Teacher like Moses in Luke-Acts." *JBL* 124 (2005): 451–65.
Croom, Alexandra. *Roman Clothing and Fashion*. Gloucestershire: Amberley, 2000.
Davies, W. D. *The Gospel and the Land*. Berkeley: University of California Press, 1974.
———. *The Territorial Dimension of Judaism*. Berkeley: University of California Press, 1982.
Decker, Rodney J. *Reading Koine Greek: An Introduction and Integrated Workbook*. Grand Rapids: Baker Academic, 2014.
Dennison, James T. Jr. "The Eschatological Jubilee: Luke 4:16–30." *Kerux* 31 (2016): 31–36.
Derfler, Steven L. *The Hasmonean Revolt: Rebellion or Revolution*. Lewiston: Edwin Mellen Press, 1990.
Dinkler, Michal Beth. "'The Thoughts of Many Hearts Shall Be Revealed': Listening in on Lukan Interior Monologues." *JBL* 133 (2015): 373–99.
Dodd, C. H. *The Parables of the Kingdom*. Rev. Ed. New York: Charles Scribner's Sons, 1961.
Donahue, John R. "Tax Collectors and Sinners an Attempt at Identification." *Cathol. Biblic. Q.* 33 (1971): 39–61.
———. "Two Decades of Research on the Rich and the Poor in Luke-Acts." Pages 129–44 in *Justice and the Holy: Essays in Honor of Walter Harrelson*. Edited by Walter J. Harrelson, Douglas A. Knight, and Peter J. Paris. Atlanta: Scholars Press, 1989.
Duncan-Jones, Richard. *Structure and Scale in the Roman Economy*. Cambridge: Cambridge University Press, 2002.
Dunn, James D. G. *Baptism in the Holy Spirit: A Re-Examination of the New Testament Teaching on the Gift of the Spirit in Relation to Pentecostalism Today*. London: SCM Press, 2010.
Van Eck, Ernest. "Do Not Question My Honour: A Social-Scientific Reading of the Parable of the Minas (Lk 19:12b–24, 27)." *HTS Teol. Stud.* 3 (2011). https://doi.org/10.4102/hts.v67i3.977.
Edwards, James R. *The Gospel According to Luke*. Grand Rapids: Eerdmans, 2015.
Ekholm, K., and J. Friedman. "'Capital' Imperialism and Exploitation in Ancient World Systems." Pages 41–58 in *Power and Propaganda: A Symposium on*

Ancient Empires. Edited by Mogens Trolle Larsen. Copenhagen: Akademisk Forlag, 1979.

Elmslie, W. A. L. "Ethics." Pages 275–302 in *Record and Revelation: Essays on the Old Testament By Members of the Society for Old Testament Study*. Oxford: Clarendon Press, 1951.

Esler, Philip Francis. *Community and Gospel in Luke-Acts: The Social and Political Motivations of Lucan Theology*. Cambridge: Cambridge University Press, 1989.

Etchegaray, Roger, François-Xavier Nguyen Van, Thuan, and Diarmuid Martin. *Towards a Better Distribution of Land*. Vatican, 1997. http://www.vatican.va/roman_curia/pontifical_councils/justpeace/documents/rc_pc_justpeace_doc_12011998_distribuzione-terra_en.html.

Fiensy, David A. *Christian Origins and the Ancient Economy*. Eugene: Cascade, 2014.

———. *The Social History of Palestine in the Herodian Period: The Land Is Mine*. Lewiston: Edwin Mellen Press, 1991.

Finger, Reta Halteman. "A Theology of Welcome : The Hospitable Hidden Women of Acts 2 , 4 , and 6" (n.d.).

———. "Cultural Attitudes in Western Christianity Toward the Community of Goods in Acts 2 and 4." *Menonite Q. Rev.* 78 (2004): 235–70.

Finley, M. I. *The Ancient Economy*. Berkley: University of California Press, 1999.

Fitzmyer, Joseph A. *The Gospel According to Luke*. New Haven: Yale University Press, 2006.

Flesher, Paul Virgil McCracken. *Oxen, Women, or Citizens?* Atlanta: Scholars Press, 1987.

Frédéric Louis Godet. *A Commentary on the Gospel of St. Luke*. New York: I. K. Funk & Co., 1881.

Freyne, Seán. *Galilee From Alexander the Great to Hadrian. 323 B.C.E. 135 C.E.: A Study of Second Temple Judaism*. Wilmington: Michael Glazier, 1980.

Fusco, Vittorio. "Luke-Acts and the Future of Israel." *Novum Testam.* 38, no.1 (1996): 1–17.

García Martínez, Florentino, and Eibert J. C. Tigchelaar. *Qumran Origins and Apocalypticism*. Leiden: Brill, 2007.

Garland, David E. *Luke*. Grand Rapids: Zondervan, 2011.

Garnsey, Peter, and Richard P. Saller. *The Roman Empire: Economy, Society and Culture*. Oakland: University of California Press, 2015.

Geldenhuys, Norval. *Commentary on the Gospel of Luke: The English Text with Introduction, Exposition and Notes*. Grand Rapids: Eerdmans, 1952.

Gerstenberger, Erhard S. *Leviticus: A Commentary*. Louisville: Westminster John Knox Press, 1996.

Goddeeris, Anne. *Economy and Society in Northern Babylonia in the Early Old Babylonian Period (ca. 2000–1800 BC)*. Leuven; Hadleigh: Brad, 2003.

Golden, Gregory K. *Crisis Management during the Roman Republic: The Role of Political Institutions in Emergencies*. Cambridge: Cambridge Univesity Press, 2013.

Goodacre, Mark. "The Protoevangelium of James and the Creative Rewriting of Matthew and Luke." Pages 57–76 in *Connecting Gospels: Beyond the Canonical/Non-Canonical Divide*. Edited by Francis Watson; Sarah Parkhouse. Oxford: Oxford University Press, 2018.

Goodacre, Mark S. *Thomas and the Gospels : The Case for Thomas's Familiarity with the Synoptics*. Grand Rapids: Eerdmans, 2012.

Gorman, Frank H. *Divine Presence and Community: A Commentary on the Book of Leviticus*. Grand Rapids; Edinburgh: Eerdmans; Handsel Press, 1998.

Gosse, Bernard. "L' Année de Grâce Du Seigneur Selon Is 61,1–2a et Sa Citation En Lc 4,18–19." *Sci. Esprit* 69 (2017): 91–106.

Grabbe, Lester L. *Judaism From Cyrus to Hadrian. Volume One: The Persian and Greek Periods*. Minneapolis: Fortress Press, 1991.

———. "The Seleucid and Hasmonean Periods and the Apocalyptic Worldview - An Introduction." Pages 11–31 in *The Seleucid and Hasmonean Periods and the Apocalyptic Worldview*. Edited by Lester L. Grabbe, Gabriele Boccacini, and Jason M. Zurawski. London: Bloomsbury, 2012.

———. "Yehud: A History of the Persian Province of Judah." Pages 302–4 in *A History of the Jews and Judaism in the Second Temple Period*. London: T & T Clark International, 2004.

Grant, Michael. *Herod the Great*. New York: American Heritage Press, 1971.

Green, Joel B. *The Gospel of Luke*. Grand Rapids: Eerdmans, 1997.

———. *The Theology of the Gospel of Luke*. Cambridge; New York: Cambridge University Press, 1995.

Greene, Alan. *Permanent States of Emergency and the Rule of Law: Constitutions in an Age of Crisis*. Oxford: Hart Publishing, 2018.

Gregory, Bradley C. "The Postexilic Exile in Third Isaiah: Isaiah 61:1–3 in Light of Second Temple Hermeneutics." *JBL* 126 (2007): 475–96.

Grenfell, B. P., and J. P. Mahaffy, eds. *Revenue Laws of Ptolemy Philadelphus*. Oxford: Clarendon Press, 1896.

Grubbs, Judith Evans. *Women and the Law in the Roman Empire: A Sourcebook on Marriage, Divorce and Widowhood*. London: Routledge, 2002.

Grün, Anselm. *Jesus: The Image of Humanity: Luke's Account*. London: Bloomsbury, 2010.

Gundry, Robert H. *Commentary on Luke*. Grand Rapids: Baker, 2011.

Gunjević, Lidija. *Jubilee in the Bible: Using the Theology of Jürgen Moltmann to Find a New Hermeneutic*. Leiden: Brill, 2018.

Habel, Norman C. *The Land Is Mine: Six Biblical Land Ideologies*. Minneapolis: Fortress Press, 1995.

Hall, Gary Harlan. *Deuteronomy*. Joplin: College Press, 2000.

Hamel, Gildas. "Poverty and Charity." Pages 308–24 in *The Oxford Handbook of Jewish Daily Life in Roman Palestine*. Edited by Catherine Hezser. Oxford: Oxford University Press, 2012.

Hanneken, Todd Russell. "The Subversion of the Apocalypses in the Book of Jubilees." Leiden: Brill, 2012.

Hannum, Hurst. *Autonomy, Sovereignty, and Self-Determination The Accommodation of Conflicting Rights*. Philadelphia: University of Pennsylvania Press, 1996.

Hanson, K. C., and Douglas E. Oakman. *Palestine in the Time of Jesus : Social Structures and Social Conflicts*. Minneapolis: Fortress Press, 2002.

Hanson, Paul. *Isaiah 40-66*. Louisville: John Knox Press, 1995.

Harbin, Michael A. "Jubilee and Social Justice." *JETS* 54 (2011): 685–99.

Harris, Maria. "Proclaiming Jubilee Justice: Moment of Opportunity." *Way* 39 (1999): 315–24.

Harris, R. Laird. "Leviticus." Pages 499–654 in *Genesis - Numbers*. Grand Rapids: Zondervan, 1990.

Hartley, John E. *Leviticus*. Dallas: Word Books, 1992.

Hays, Christopher M. *Luke's Wealth Ethics: A Study in Their Coherence and Character*. Tübingen: Mohr Siebeck, 2010.

———. *Renouncing Everything: Money and Discipleship in Luke*. New York: Paulist Press, 2016.

Hendriksen, William. *Exposition of the Gospel According to Luke*. Grand Rapids: Baker Book House, 1978.

Hertig, P. "The Jubilee Mission of Jesus in the Gospel of Luke : Reversals of Fortunes." *Missiology* 26 (1998): 167–79.

Herzog II, William R. *Prophet and Teacher: An Introduction to the Historical Jesus*. Louisville: Westminster John Knox Press, 2005.

Herzog, William R. *Parables as Subversive Speech: Jesus as Pedagogue of the Oppressed*. Louisville: Westminster/John Knox Press, 1994.

Hezser, Catherine. *Jewish Slavery in Antiquity*. Oxford: Oxford University Press, 2005.

Hiers, Richard H. "Transfer of Property by Inheritance and Bequest in Biblical Law and Tradition." *Journal of Law and Religion* 10 (1993): 121–55.

Hock, Ronald F. "Lazarus and Micyllus: Greco-Roman Backgrounds to Luke 16:19–31." *JBL* 106 (1987): 447–63.

Hoehner, Harold W. *Chronological Aspects of the Life of Christ*. Grand Rapids: Zondervan Publishing House, 1977.

Hofheinz, Marco. "Good News to the Poor: The Message of the Kingdom and Jesus' Announcement of His Ministry According to Luke." *Lexingt. Theol. Q.* 47 (2017): 41–55. http://www.lextheo.edu/category/quarterly/ (View online).

Holden, Stein, Keijiro Otsuka, and Klaus W. Deininger. *Land Tenure Reform in Asia and Africa: Assessing Impacts on Poverty and Natural Resource Management*. Basingstoke: Palgrave Macmillan, 2013.

Holgate, David A. *Prodigality, Liberality and Meanness in the Parable of the Prodigal Son: A Greco-Roman Perspective on Luke 15:11–32*. Sheffield: Sheffield Academic Press, 1999.

Homer, Sidney, and Richard Eugene Sylla. *A History of Interest Rates*. New Brunswick: Rutgers University Press, 1991.

Horsley, Richard A., and John S. Hanson. *Bandits, Prophets and Messiahs: Popular Movements in the Time of Jesus*. Minneapolis: Winston Press, 1985.

Horst, Pieter W. Van Der. "Hellenistic Parallels to the Acts of the Apostles." *JSNT* 25 (1985): 49–60.

How, W. W., and H. D. Leigh. *A History of Rome: To the Death of Caesar*. New York: Longmans, Green and Co., 1907.

Howard-Brook, Wes. *"Come out, My People!": God's Call out of Empire in the Bible and Beyond*. Maryknoll: Orbis Books, 2011.

Huddleston, J. "What Would Elijah and Elisha Do? Internarrativity in Luke's Story of Jesus." *J. Theol. Interpret.* 5 (2011): 265–81.

Huey, F. B. "Jeremiah, Lamentations." Nashville: Broadman Press, 1993.

Hultgren, Arland J. *The Parables of Jesus: A Commentary*. Grand Rapids: Eerdmans, 2000.

Ireland, Dennis J. *Stewardship and the Kingdom of God: An Historical, Exegetical, and Contextual Study of the Parable of the Unjust Steward in Luke 16:1–13*. Leiden: Brill, 1992.

Isaac, Munther. *From Land to Lands, from Eden to the Renewed Earth: A Christ-Centered Biblical Theology of the Promised Land*. Carlisle: Langham Academic, 2015.

Jakonda, Sulaiman Z., and Rural Development Counselors for Christian Churches in Africa. *Your Kingdom Come: A Book on Wholistic Christian Development*. Jos, Nigeria: RURCON, 2001.

Jeffers, James S. *The Greco-Roman World of the New Testament Era: Exploring the Background of Early Christianity*. Downers Grove: InterVarsity Press, 2006.

Jeremias, Joachim. *Jerusalem in the Time of Jesus: An Investigation Into Economic and Social Conditions During the New Testament Period*. Philadelphia: Fortress Press, 1975.

———. *Rediscovering the Parables*. New York: Charles Scribner's Sons, 1966.

Jervell, Jacob. *The Theology of the Acts of the Apostles*. Cambridge: Cambridge University Press, 2006.

Jipp, Joshua W. *Divine Visitations and Hospitality to Strangers in Luke-Acts: An Interpretation of the Malta Episode in Acts 28:1–10*. Leiden: Brill, 2013.

———. *Saved by Faith and Hospitality*. Grand Rapids: Eerdmans, 2017.

Johnson, Luke Timothy. *Prophetic Jesus, Prophetic Church: The Challenge of Luke-Acts to Contemporary Christians.* Grand Rapids: Eerdmans, 2011.

———. *Sharing Possessions: What Faith Demands.* Grand Rapids: Eerdmans, 2011.

———. *The Gospel of Luke.* Collegeville: Liturgical Press, 1991.

Joshel, Sandra R. "Slavery and Roman Literary Culture." *The Ancient Mediterranean World. Vol 1 of the Cambridge World History of Slavery.* Edited by F. W. Walbank, A. E. Astin, M. W. Frederiksen, and R. M. Ogilvie. Cambridge: Cambridge University Press, 2011.

Kay, Philip. *Rome's Economic Revolution.* Oxford: Oxford University Press, 2016.

Kehoe, Dennis P. "Landlords and Tenants." Pages 298–311 in *A Companion to the Roman Empire.* Edited by David S. Potter. Malden: Wiley-Blackwell, 2010.

———. *Law and Rural Economy in the Roman Empire.* Ann Arbor: The University of Michigan Press, 2007.

———. "Law and Social Formation in the Roman Empire." Pages 144–66 in *The Oxford Handbook of Social Relations in the Roman World.* Edited by Michael Peachin. Oxford: Oxford University Press, 2011.

———. "The State and Production in the Roman Agrarian Economy." Pages 33–53 in *The Roman Agricultural Economy.* Edited by Alan Bowman and Andrew Wilson. Oxford: Oxford University Press, 2016.

Keller, Timothy. *Counterfeit Gods: The Empty Promises of Money, Sex, and Power, and the Only Hope That Matters.* New York: Riverhead Books, 2011.

Kim, Kyoung-Jin. "Stewardship and Almsgiving in Luke's Theology." Sheffield: Sheffield Academic Press, 1998.

Kim, Sun-Jong. "Lecture de La Parabole Du Fils Retrouvé À La Lumière Du Jubilé." *Novum Testam.* 53 (2011): 211–21.

Kiuchi, Nobuyoshi. *Leviticus.* Downers Grove: IVP Academic, 2007.

Klausner, J. "The Economy of Judea In the Period of the Second Temple." Pages 179–205 in *The World History of the Jewish People: The Herodian Period.* Edited by Michael Avi-Yonah. New Brunswick: Rutgers University Press, 1975.

Kleinig, John W. *Leviticus.* Saint Louis: Concordia Publ. House, 2003.

Kloppenborg, John S. *The Tenants in the Vineyard.* Tübingen: Mohr Siebeck, 2010.

Kollmann, Bernd. *Joseph Barnabas: His Life and Legacy.* Collegeville: Liturgical Press, 2004.

Koole, Jan L. *Isaiah. Part III. Volume 3: Isaiah Chapters 56–66.* Leuven: Peeters, 1998.

Köstenberger, Andreas J., Benjamin L. Merkle, and Robert L. Plummer. *Going Deeper with New Testament Greek: An Intermediate Study of the Grammar and Syntax of the New Testament.* Nashville: B&H Academic, 2016.

Krautbauer, Anna, Stephen Llewelyn, and Blake Wassell. "A Gift of One Eunuch and Four Slave Boys: P.Cair.Zen I 59076 and Historical Construction."

JSJ 45.3 (2014): 305–25. https://doi.org/10.1163/15700631-12340058, http://booksandjournals.brillonline.com/content/journals/15700631 (Subscriber access).

Kruger, Michael J. *Canon Revisited: Establishing the Origins and Authority of the New Testament.* Wheaton: Crossway, 2012.

———. *The Question of Canon: Challenging the Status Quo in the New Testament Debate.* Nottingham: InterVarsity, 2013.

Kugel, James L. "A Walk through Jubilees: Studies in the Book of Jubilees and the World of Its Creation." Leiden: Brill, 2012.

Kugler, Robert A. *The Testaments of the Twelve Patriarchs.* Sheffield: Sheffield Academic Press, 2001.

Lagrange, Marie-Joseph. *Évangile selon saint Luc.* Paris: J. Gabalda, 1948.

Lange, John Peter. *A Commentary on the Holy Scriptures: Exodus, Leviticus: Critical, Doctrinal and Homiletical, with Special Reference to Ministers and Students.* New York: Scribne, Armstrong & Co., 1870.

Lanier, Gregory R. "Mapping the Vineyard: Main Lines of Investigation Regarding the Parable of the Tenants in the Synoptics and Thomas." *CurrBR.* 15 (2016): 74–122. https://doi.org/10.1177/1476993X15577030.

Lasetso, Razouselie. *The Nazareth Manifesto: The Theology of Jubilee and Its Trajectories in Luke-Acts.* Delhi: ISPCK, 2005.

Lazonby, David. "Applying the Jubilee to Contemporary Socio-Economic and Environmental Issues." *J. Eur. Baptist Stud.* 16 (2016): 30–50.

Lenski, R. C. H. *The Interpretation of St. Luke's Gospel.* Minneapolis: Augsburg Pub. House, 1961.

Levine, Amy-Jill. "Luke and the Jewish Religion." *Interpretation* 68 (2014): 389–402. https://doi.org/10.1177/0020964314540107.

Levine, Amy-Jill, and Ben Witherington. *The Gospel of Luke.* Cambridge: Cambridge University Press, 2018.

Levine, Lee I. *Judaism and Hellenism in Antiquity: Conflict or Confluence.* Peabody: Hendrickson, 1999.

Lilburne, Geoffrey R. *A Sense of Place: A Christian Theology of the Land.* Nashville: Abingdon Press, 1989.

Lincoln, A. T. "Sabbath, Rest, and Eschatology in the New Testament." Pages 197–220 in *From Sabbath to Lord's Day: A Biblical, Historical and Theological Investigation.* Edited by D. A. Carson. Eugene: Wipf & Stock, 1999.

Lindslay, Art. "Does God Require the State to Redistribute Wealth? An Examination of Jubilee and Acts 2–5." Pages 79–93 in *For the Least of These: A Biblical Answer to Poverty.* Edited by Anne Bradley and Art Lindsley. Grand Rapids: Zondervan, 2014.

Lintott, Andrew W. *The Romans in the Age of Augustus.* Malden: Wiley-Blackwell, 2010.

Litwak, Kenneth Duncan. *Echoes of Scripture in Luke-Acts: Telling the History of God's People Intertextually*. London: T & T Clark International, 2005.

Longenecker, Bruce W. "Exposing the Economic Middle: A Revised Economy Scale for the Study of Early Urban Christianity." *JSNT* 31 (2009): 243–78. https://doi.org/10.1177/0142064X08101524.

Longenecker, Richard N. *The Challenge of Jesus' Parables*. Grand Rapids: Eerdmans, 2000.

Longman III, Tremper. *Proverbs*. Grand Rapids: Baker Academic, 2006.

López Rodriguez, Darío. *The Liberating Mission of Jesus: The Message of the Gospel of Luke*. Eugene: Pickwick Publications, 2012.

Louis, Paul. *Ancient Rome at Work : An Economic History of Rome From the Origins to the Empire*. Abingdon: Routledge, 2006.

Lovano, Michael. *All Things Julius Caesar: An Encyclopedia of Caesar's World and Legacy*. Santa Barbara: ABC-CLIO, 2015.

Lua, Fernando C. "The Year of the Jubilee: A Model for Uplifting the Lives of the Poor?" *Jian Dao* 41 (2014): 343–73.

Lundbom, Jack R. *Deuteronomy: Law and Covenant*. Eugene: Cascade Books, 2017.

Malamat, Abraham, H. Tadmor, M. Stein, S. Safrai, H. H. Ben-Sasson, and S. Sttinger. *A History of the Jewish People*. Edited by H. H. Ben-Sasson. Cambridge: Harvard University Press, 1976.

Malherbe, Abraham J. "Christology in Luke-Acts 2." *Restor. Q.* 2 (1958): 115–27.

Malina, Bruce J., and Richard L. Rohrbaugh. *Social-Science Commentary on the Synoptic Gospels*. Minneapolis: Fortress Press, 2003.

Mann, Thomas W. *Deuteronomy*. Louisville: Westminster John Knox Press, 1995.

Manning, J. G. *Land and Power in Ptolemaic Egypt: The Structure of Land Tenure*. Cambridge: Cambridge University Press, 2003.

Manning, Joseph Gilbert. *The Last Pharaohs: Egypt Under the Ptolemies, 305–30 BC*. Princeton: Princeton University Press, 2010.

Mantel, H. D. "The High Priesthood and the Sanhedrim in the Time of the Second Temple." Pages 264–81 in *The World History of the Jewish People: The Herodian Period*. Edited by Michael Avi-Yonah. New Brunswick: Rutgers University Press, 1975.

Marchant, David, Noach Orlowek, and Shlomo Fox-Ashrei. *Understanding Shmittoh: Its Sources and Background & Halochos of Shmittoh*. Jerusalem: Feldheim Publishers, 1993.

Marshall, I. Howard. *Luke: Historian & Theologian*. Downers Grove: InterVarsity Press, 1998.

———. *The Gospel of Luke: A Commentary on the Greek Text*. Grand Rapids: Eerdmans, 1978.

Marzano, Annalisa. *Roman Villas in Central Italy: A Social and Economic History*. Leiden: Brill, 2007.

Matera, Frank J. "Jesus' Journey to Jerusalem (Luke 9:51–19:46): A Conflict with Israel." *JSNT* 51 (1993): 57–77.

Matson, David Lertis. *Household Conversion Narratives in Acts: Pattern and Interpretation*. Sheffield: Sheffield Academic Press, 1996.

Matthews, Victor H., and Don C. Benjamin. *Social World of Ancient Israel 1250–587 BCE*. Peabody: Hendrickson Publishers, 1993.

Mattingly, D. J. *Imperialism, Power, and Identity: Experiencing the Roman Empire*. Princeton; Oxford: Princeton University Press, 2014.

Mattingly, David. "The Imperial Economy." Pages 283–97 in *A Companion to the Roman Empire*. Edited by David S. Potter. Malden: Wiley-Blackwell, 2010.

May, Roy H. *The Poor of the Land: A Christian Case for Land Reform*. Maryknoll: Orbis Books, 1991.

Mayer, Emanuel. *The Ancient Middle Classes: Urban Life and Aesthetics in the Roman Empire, 100 BCE–250CE*. Cambridge: Harvard University Press, 2012.

McGeough, Kevin. *The Romans: New Perspectives*. Santa Barbara: ABC-CLIO, 2004.

McIntosh, Jane. *Ancient Mesopotamia: New Perspectives*. Santa Barbara: ABC-CLIO, 2005.

McKeown, James. *Genesis*. Grand Rapids: Eerdmans, 2008.

Mentan, Tatah. *The State in Africa: An Analysis of Impacts of Historical Trajectories of Global Capitalist Expansion and Domination in the Continent*. Bamenda: Langaa Research & Publishing CIG, 2010.

Metzger, James A. *Consumption and Wealth in Luke's Travel Narrative*. Leiden; Boston: Brill, 2007.

Milgrom, Jacob. *Leviticus 23–27*. New York: Doubleday, 2001.

Miller, Douglas J. *Jesus Goes to Washington: His Progressive Politics for a Sustainable Future*. Eugene: Wipf & Stock, 2013.

Miller, J. Maxwell, and John H. Hayes. *A History of Ancient Israel and Judah*. Philadelphia: The Westminster Press, 1986.

Miller, Patrick D. *Deuteronomy*. Louisville: Westminster John Knox Press, 2012.

Miller, Stephen R. *Daniel*. Nashville: Broadman & Holman, 1994.

Mitchell, Alan C. "The Social Function of Friendship in Acts 2:44–47 and 4:32–37." *JBL* 111 (1992): 255–72.

Miura, Nozomi. "Justice in the Bible, Globalization, and Jubilee." *Journal of Theta Alpha Kappa* 28 (2004): 38–57.

de Moor, Johannes C. "The Targumic Background of Mark 12:1–12: The Parable of the Wicked Tenants." *JSJ* 29 (1998): 63–80.

Morley, Neville. "The Poor in the City of Rome." Pages 21–39 in *Poverty in the Roman World*. Edited by Margaret Atkins and Robin Osborne. Cambridge: Cambridge University Press, 2006.

Motyer, J. Alec. *Isaiah*. Downers Grove: InterVarsity Press, 2009.

Moxnes, Halvor. *The Economy of the Kingdom: Social Conflict and Economic Relations in Luke's Gospel*. Eugene: Wipf & Stock, 1988.

Mugabe, Henry Johannes. "Parable of the Rich Fool: Luke 12:13–21." *Rev. Expo.* 111 (2014): 67–73.

Müller, Mogens. "The Reception of the Old Testament and in Matthew and Luke-Acts: From Interpretation to Proof from Scripture." *Novum Testam.* 43 (2001): 315–30.

Murphy, Catherine M. "Wealth in the Dead Sea Scrolls and in the Qumran Community." Leiden: Brill, 2002.

Neusner, Jacob. *From Politics to Piety the Emergence of Pharisaic Judaism*. Englewood Cliffs: Prentice-Hall, 1972.

———. *Judaism in Late Antiquity: Part Two. Historical Synthesis*. Leiden: Brill, 1995.

———. *Rabbinic Literature & the New Testament: What We Cannot Show, We Do Not Know*. Eugene: Wipf & Stock, 2004.

Newman, Barclay Moon, and Eugene A. Nida. *A Handbook on the Acts of the Apostles*. New York: United Bible Societies, 1972.

Nicolet, Claude. *The World of the Citizen in Republican Rome*. Berkeley: University of California Press, 1988.

Niebuhr, B. G. *Lectures on the History of Rome: From the Earliest Times to the Comencement of the First Punic War*. Edited by M. Isler; Leonhard Schmitz. London: Taylor and Walton, 1848.

Niebuhr, Barthold Georg. *The Roman History, Vol. 2*. London: C. And J. Rivington, 1827.

Noble, Joshua A. "'Rich toward God': Making Sense of Luke 12:21.'" *CBQ* 78 (2016): 302–20.

Nolland, John. *Luke*. Vol 1. Dallas: Word Books, 1989.

North, Gary. *Leviticus: An Economic Commentary*. Tyler: Institute for Christian Economics, 1994.

North, Robert. *Sociology of the Biblical Jubilee*. Rome: Pontifical Biblica Institute, 1954.

O'Toole, Robert F. *Luke's presentation of Jesus: A Christology*. Roma: Pontificio Istituto Biblico, 2004.

Oakman, Douglas E. "Execrating? Or Execrable Peasants!" Pages 139–64 in *The Galilean Economy in the Time of Jesus*. Edited by David A. Fiensy and Ralph K. Hawkins. Atlanta: Society of Biblical Literature, 2013.

———. *Jesus, Debt, and the Lord's Prayer: First-Century Debt and Jesus' Intentions*. Eugene: Cascade Books, 2014.

———. *Jesus and the Economic Questions of His Day*. Lewiston: E. Mellen Press, 1986.

Olmstead, W. G. "Judgement." Pages 458–63 in *Dictionary of Jesus and the Gospels*. Edited by Joel B. Green, Jeannine K. Brown, and Nicholas Perrin. Downers Grove: IVP Academic, 2013.

Osborne, Robin. "Introduction: Roman Poverty in Context." Pages 1–20 in *Poverty in the Roman World*. Edited by Margaret Atkins and Robin Osborne. Cambridge: Cambridge University Press, 2006.

Oswalt, John. *The Book of Isaiah: Chapters 40–66*. Grand Rapids: Eerdmans, 1998.

Pao, David W. *Acts and the Isaianic New Exodus*. Eugene: Wipf & Stock, 2000.

Parsons, Mikeal C. *Luke*. Edited by Baker. Grand Rapids, 2015.

———. "The Place of Jerusalem on the Lukan Landscape: An Exercise in Symbolic Cartography." *Literary Studies in Luke-Acts: Essays in Honor of Joseph B. Tyson*. Edited by Richard P. Thompson; Thomas E. Phillips. Macon: Mercer University Press, 1998.

Pastor, Jack. *Land and Economy in Ancient Palestine*. London: Routledge, 2012.

Paul, Shalom M. *Isaiah 40–66: A Commentary*. Grand Rapids: Eerdmans, 2012.

Pennington, Jonathan T. *Reading the Gospels Wisely: A Narrative and Theological Introduction*. Grand Rapids: Baker Academic, 2012.

Peterson, David. *The Acts of the Apostles*. Grand Rapids: Eerdmans, 2009.

Phillips, Thomas E. "Reading Issues of Wealth and Poverty in Luke-Acts." Lewiston: Edwin Mellen Press, 2000.

Philo of Alexandria, and Charles Duke Yonge. *The Works of Philo: Complete and Unabridged*. Peabody: Hendrickson, 2008.

Premnath, D. N. "Latifundization and Isaiah 5:8–10." Pages 301–12 in *Social-Scientific Old Testament Criticism: A Sheffield Reader*. Sheffield: Sheffield Academic Press, 1997.

Pritchard, James Bennett. *The Ancient Near Eastern Texts Relating to the Old Testament*. Princeton: Princeton University Press, 1969.

Puig i Tàrrech, Armand. *Jesus: An Uncommon Journey: Studies on the Historical Jesus*. Tübingen: Mohr Siebeck, 2010.

Rad, Gerhard von. *Deuteronomy: A Commentary*. London: SCM Press, 1988.

———. *Old Testament Theology: The Theology of Israel's Historical Traditions*. Louisville: Westminster John. Knox Press, 2001.

———. "The Promised Land and Yahweh's Land in the Hexateuch." Pages 79–93 in *The Problem of the Hexateuch and Other Essays*. New York: McGraw-Hill Book Company, 1966.

Rathbone, Dominic. "Poor Peasants and Silent Sherds." Pages 305–32 in *People, Land, and Politics: Demographic Developements and The Transformation of Roman Italy, 300 BC-AD 14*. Edited by Luuk de Ligt and Simon Northwood. Leiden: Brill, 2008.

Read-Heimerdinger, Jenny. "Barnabas in Acts: A Study of His Role in the Text of Codex Bezae." *JSNT* 72 (1998): 23–66.

Reden, Sitta von. *Money in Ptolemaic Egypt: From the Macedonian Conquest to the End of the Third Century BC*. Cambridge: Cambridge University Press, 2007.

Redfield, Robert. *The Little Community and Peasant Society and Culture*. Chicago: University of Chicago Press, 1989.

Reiling, J., and J. L. Swellengrebel. *A Handbook on the Gospel of Luke*. New York: United Bible Societies, 1993.

Richardson, Peter. *Herod: King of the Jews and Friend of the Romans*. Columbia: University of South Carolina Press, 1996.

Riddle, John M. *Tiberius Gracchus: Destroyer or Reformer of the Republic*. Lexington: D. C. Heath and Company, 1970.

Ringe, Sharon H. *Jesus, Liberation, and the Biblical Jubilee: Images for Ethics and Christology*. Philadelphia: Fortress Press, 1985.

Roberts, Keith. *The Origins of Business, Money, and Markets*. New York: Columbia University Press, 2011.

Rocca, Samuel. *Herod's Judaea*. Tübingen: Mohr Siebeck, 2008.

Rooker, Mark F. *Leviticus*. Nashville: Broadman & Holman, 2000.

Rosenberg, Jacob, and Avi Weiss. "Land Concentration, Efficiency, Slavery and the Jubilee." Pages 74–87 in *The Oxford Handbook of Judaism and Economics*. Edited by Aaron Levine. Oxford: Oxford University Press, 2010.

Rosner, Brian S. *Greed as Idolatry: The Origin and Meaning of a Pauline Metaphor*. Grand Rapids: William B. Eerdmans, 2007.

Ruiten, J. van. "Abraham in the Book of Jubilees: The Rewriting of Genesis 11:26–25:10 in the Book of Jubilees 11:14–23:8." Leiden: Brill, 2012.

Runge, Steven E. *Discourse Grammar of the Greek New Testament: A Practical Introduction for Teaching and Exegesis*. Bellingham: Lexham Press, 2010.

Safrai, Ze'ev. *The Economy of Roman Palestine*. London: Routledge, 1994.

Sanders, Jack T. *The Jews in Luke-Acts*. London: SCM Press, 1987.

Sanders, James A. "Sins, Debts, and Jubilee Release." Pages 84–92 in *Luke and Scripture: The Function of Sacred Tradition in Luke-Acts*. Edited by James A. Sanders Craig A. Evans. Eugene: Wipf & Stock, 1993.

———. *The Monotheizing Process: Its Origins and Development*. Eugene: Cascade, 2014.

Schäfer, Peter. *The History of the Jews in the Greco-Roman World: The Jews of Palestine from Alexander the Great to the Arab Conquest*. Abingdon: Taylor & Francis Group, 2002.

———. *The History of the Jews in the Greco-Roman World*. London: Routledge, 2003.

Scheidel, Walter. "Roman Population Size: The Logic of the Debate." Pages 17–70 in *People, Land, and Politics: Demographic Developements and The Transformation of Roman Italy, 300 BC-AD 14*. Edited by Luuk de Ligt and Simon Northwood. Leiden: Brill, 2008.

———. "Stratification, Deprivation and Quality of Life." Pages 40–59 in *Poverty in the Roman World*. Edited by Margaret Atkins and Robin Osborne. Cambridge: Cambridge University Press, 2006.

Scheidel, Walter, and Steven J. Friesen. "The Size of the Economy and the Distribution of Income in the Roman Empire." *J. Rom. Stud.* (2009): 61–91.

Schottroff, Luise. *As Parábolas de Jesus: Uma Nova Hermenêutica*. São Leopoldo: Sinodal, 2007.

Schweizer, Eduard. *The Good News According to Luke*. Atlanta: John Knox Press, 1984.

Scullard, Howard Hayes. *From the Gracchi to Nero: A History of Rome from 133 B.C. to A.D. 68*. London: Routledge, 2003.

Segal, Michael. *The Book of Jubilees: Rewritten Bible, Redaction, Ideology and Theology*. Leiden: Brill, 2007.

Sellew, Philip. "Interior Monologue as a Narrative Device in the Parables of Luke." *JBL*. 111 (992): 239–53.

Sharon H. Ringe. *Luke*. Louisville: Westminster John Knox Press, 1995.

Sharon, Nadav. "Judea under Roman Domination: The First Generation of Statelessness and Its Legacy." Atlanta: Society of Biblical Literature, 2017.

Siker, Jeffrey S. "'First to the Gentiles': A Literary Analysis of Luke 4:16–30." *J. Biblic. Lit.* 111 (1992): 73–90.

Silva, Valmor da. "Direito à Terra, Direito à Vida: Perspectivas Ecológicas a Partir de Levítico 25." *Fragm. Cult.* 26 (2016): 596–606.

Sloan, R. B. "Jubilee." Pages 396–97 in *Dictionary of Jesus and the Gospels*. Edited by Joel B. Green, Scot McKnight, and I. Howard Marshall. Downers Grove: IVP Academic, 1992.

Sloan, Robert Bryan. *The Favorable Year of the Lord: A Study of Jubilary Theology in the Gospel of Luke*. Austin: Scholar Press, 1977.

Smith, David Andrew. "'No Poor Among Them': Sabbath and Jubilee Years in Lukan Social Ethics." *Horizons Biblic. Theol.* 40 (2018): 142–65.

Snodgrass, Kline R. "From Allegorizing to Allegorizing: A History of the Interpretation of the Parables of Jesus." Pages 3–29 in *The Challenge of Jesus' Parables*, 2000.

———. *Stories with Intent: A Comprehensive Guide to the Parables of Jesus*. Grand Rapids: Eerdmans, 2008.

Snodgrass, Klyne. "Recent Research on the Parable of the Wicked Tenants: An Assessment." *Bull. Biblic. Res.* 8 (1998): 187–216.

Southern, Patricia. *Augustus*. London: Routledge, 2014.

Spencer, F. Scott. "To Fear and Not to Fear the Creator God: A Theological and Therapeutic Interpretation of Luke 12:4–34." *J. Theol. Interpret.* 8 (2014): 229–49.

Sri, Edward. "Release from the Debt of Sin: Jesus' Jubilee Mission in the Gospel of Luke." *Nov. Vetera* 9 (2011): 183–94.
Stein, Robert H. *Luke: An Exegetical and Theological Exposition of Holy Scripture*. Nashville: Broadman Press, 1992.
Stephenson, Andrew. *Public Lands and Agrarian Laws of the Roman Republic*. Baltimore: The John Hopkins Press, 1891.
Stern, M. "The Herodian Dinasty and the Province of Judea at the End of the Period of the Second Temple." Pages 124–78 in *The World History of the Jewish People: The Herodian Period*. Edited by Michael Avi-Yonah. New Brunswick: Rutgers University Press, 1975.
———. "The Reign of Herod." Pages 71–123 in *The World History of the Jewish People: The Herodian Period*. Edited by Michael Avi-Yonah. New Brunswick: Rutgers University Press, 1975.
Strieder, Inácio. "A Bíblia E A Fundamentação Ético-Teológica Dos Direitos Humanos." *Symp. Filos.* 1 (1998): 11–17.
Stulman, Louis. *Jeremiah*. Nashville: Abingdon Press, 2005.
Talbert, Charles H. *Reading Acts: A Literary and Theological Commentary on the Acts of the Apostles*. Macon: Smyth & Helwys, 2005.
Tan, Kim. "Pentecost, Jubilee, and Nation Building." *Vision* 15 (2014): 72–80.
Tannehill, Robert C. "Acts of the Apostles and Ethics." *Interpretation* 66 (2012): 270–82. https://doi.org/10.1177/0020964312443193.
———. *Luke*. Nashville: Abingdon Press, 1996.
———. *The Narrative Unity of Luke-Acts. A Literary Interpretation: Volume 1: The Gospel According to Luke*. Minneapolis: Fortress Press, 1994.
———. *The Narrative Unity of Luke-Acts. A Literary Interpretation: Volume 2: The Acts of the Apostles*. Minneapolis: Fortress Press, 1990.
Tannehill, Robert C. "Israel in Luke-Acts: A Tragic Story." *JBL* 104 (1985): 69–85.
Temin, Peter. *The Roman Market Economy*. Princeton: Princeton University Press, 2013.
Thielman, Frank. *Theology of the New Testament: A Canonical and Synthetic Approach*. Grand Rapids: Zondervan, 2005.
Toutain, Jules. *The Economic Life of the Ancient World*. New York: Barnes & Noble, 1968.
Trocmé, André. *Jesus and the Nonviolent Revolution*. Scottdale: Herald Press, 1973.
Tsai, Daisy Yulin. *Human Rights in Deuteronomy: With Special Focus on Slave Laws*. EBook. Berlin; Boston: De Gruyter, 2014.
Tuohy, Seamus. "Extraordinary Jubilee and Preachers of Mercy: Some Light from the Scriptures on Jubilee." *Doctrin. Life*. 66 (2016): 2–22.
Turner, Max. "The Work of the Holy Spirit in Luke-Acts." *Word World* 23 (2003): 146–53.

Ulrich, Dean R. "The Need for More Attention to Jubilee in Daniel 9:24–27." *BullBR*. 26 (2016): 481–500.

Uytanlet, Samson. *Luke-Acts and Jewish Historiography: A Study on the Theology, Literature, and Ideology of Luke-Acts*. Tübingen: Mohr Siebeck, 2014.

VanderKam, James C. *Book of Jubilees*. London: Bloomsbury Publishing, 2001.

———. *The Dead Sea Scrolls and the Bible*. Grand Rapids, Mich: Eerdmans, 2012.

———. "The Origins and Purposes of the Book of Jubilees." *Studies in the Book of Jubilees*. Edited by Matthias Albani, Jörg Frey, and Armin Lange. Tübingen: Mohr Siebeck, 1997.

Vanhoozer, Kevin J. *First Theology: God, Scripture & Hermeneutics*. Leicester: Apollos, 2002.

———. *Is There a Meaning in This Text? : The Bible, the Reader, and the Morality of Literary Knowledge*. Grand Rapids: Zondervan, 2009.

———. *The Drama of Doctrine: A Canonical-Linguistic Approach to Christian Theology*. Louisville: Westminster John Knox Press, 2005.

Vaux, Roland de. *Ancient Israel: Its Life and Institutions*. Grand Rapids: Eerdmans, 1997.

Vengeyi, Obvious. "A Luta Continua Biblical Hermeneutics for Liberation: Interpreting Biblical Texts on Slavery for Liberation of Zimbabwean Underclasses." University of Bamberg Press, 2013.

Via, Dan Otto, Jr. *The Parables: Their Literary and Existential Dimension*. Philadelphia: Fortress Press, 1967.

Vickers, Michael. *The Ancient Romans*. Oxford: Ashmolean Museum, 1992.

Vos, Geerhardus. *Biblical Theology: Old and New Testaments*. Grand Rapids: W.B. Eerdmans, 1948.

Walker, Peter W. L. *Jesus and the Holy City: New Testament Perspectives on Jerusalem*. Grand Rapids: Eerdmans, 1996.

Wallace, Daniel B. *Greek Grammar Beyond the Basics: An Exegetical Syntax of the New Testament*. Zondervan, 1996.

Walter C. Kaiser, Jr. "Leviticus." Pages 983–1191 in *The New Interpreter's Bible: A Commentary in Twelve Volumes. Vol 1*. Nashville: Abingdon Press, 1994.

Waltke, Bruce K. *An Old Testament Theology: An Exegetical, Canonical, and Thematic Approach*. Grand Rapids: Zondervan, 2008.

Walton, Steve. "Primitive Communism in Acts ? Does Acts Present the Community of Goods (Acts 2:44–45; 4:32–35) as Mistaken?" *Evang. Q.* 80 (2008): 99–111.

Watson, Francis. *Gospel Writing: A Canonical Perspective*. Grand Rapids: Eerdmans, 2013.

Watts, John D. *Isaiah 34–66*. Waco: Word Books, 1985.

Weber, Max. *The Agrarian Sociology of Ancient Civilizations*. London: Verso, 2013.

Wenham, Gordon J. *The Book of Leviticus*. Grand Rapids: Eerdmans, 2009.

Westermann, Claus. *Isaiah 40-66: A Commentary*. Philadelphia: The Westminster Press, 1969.

Whelan, Matthew Philipp. "Jesus Is the Jubilee: A Theological Reflection on the Pontifical Council for Justice and Peace's Toward a Better Distribution of Land." *J. Moral Theol.* 6 (2017): 204–29.

Whyte, Robert Orr. *Land and Land Appraisal*. The Hague: Dr. W. Junk B. V. Publishers, 1976.

Wiedemann, Thomas. *Greek and Roman Slavery*. Baltimore: The John Hopkins University Press, 1981.

———. *Slavery*. Oxford: Clarendon Press, 1987.

Willis, Timothy M. *Leviticus*. Nashville: Abingdon, 2009.

Willoughby, Robert. "The Concept of Jubilee and Luke 4:18–30." Pages 41–55 in *Mission and Meaning: Essays Presented to Peter Cotterell*. Edited by Antony Billington, Tony Lane, and Max Turner. Carlisle: Paternoster Press, 1995.

Witherington III, Ben. *Isaiah Old and New: Exegesis, Intertextuality, and Hermeneutics*. Minneapolis: Fortress Press, 2017.

———. *The Acts of the Apostles: A Socio-Rhetorical Commentary*. Grand Rapids: Eerdmans, 2009.

Woolf, Greg. "Imperialism, Empire and the Integration of the Roman Economy." *World Archaeol.* 23 (1992): 283–93.

———. "Writing Poverty in Rome." Pages 83–99 in *Poverty in the Roman World*. Edited by Margaret Atkins and Robin Osborne. Cambridge: Cambridge University Press, 2006.

Wright, Christopher J. H. *God's People in God's Land: Family, Land, and Property in the Old Testament*. Edited by Eerdmans. Grand Rapids, 1990.

———. "Land and Land Reform." Pages 535–37 in *New Dictionary of Christian Ethics & Pastoral Theology*. Edited by David John Atkinson, David Field, Arthur F. Holmes, and Oliver O'Donovan. Downers Grove: IVP Academic, 1995.

Wright, Stephen I. "Parables on Poverty and Riches (Luke 12:13–21; 16:1–13; 16:19–31)." Pages 217–39 in *The Challenge of Jesus' Parables*. Edited by Richard N. Longenecker. Grand Rapid: Eerdmans, 2000.

Xeravits, Géza G. *King, Priest, Prophet: Positive eschatological protagonists of the Qumran library*. Leiden: Brill, 2002.

Yoder, John Howard. *The Politics of Jesus: Vicit Agnus Noster*. Grand Rapids: Eerdmans, 1994.

York, John O. *The Last Shall Be First the Rhetoric of Reversal in Luke*. London: Bloomsbury Academic, 2015.

Young, Edward J. *The Book of Isaiah: The English Text with Introductions, Exposition, and Notes. Volume III. Chapters 40 through 66*. Grand Rapids: Eerdmans, 1965.

———. *The Book of Isaiah: Volume III, Chapters 40 through 66.* Grand Rapids: Eerdmans, 1972.

Younger, William W. Hallo; K. Lawson. *The Context of Scripture, Volume Two: Monumental Inscriptions from the Biblical World.* Leiden: Brill, 2000.

Zimmerman, Kari-Shane Davis. "Neither Social Revolution nor Utopian Ideal: A Fresh Look at Luke's Community of Goods Practice for Christian Economic Reflection in Acts 4:32–35." *Heythrop J.* 53 (2012): 777–86. https://doi.org/10.1111/j.1468-2265.2010.00588.x.

Zimmermann, Reinhard. *The Law of Obligations Roman Foundations of the Civilian Tradition.* Oxford: Oxford University Press, 2007.

Zimmermann, Ruben. *Puzzling the Parables of Jesus: Methods and Interpretation.* Minneapolis: Fortress Press, 2015.

Langham Literature, with its publishing work, is a ministry of Langham Partnership.

Langham Partnership is a global fellowship working in pursuit of the vision God entrusted to its founder John Stott –

> *to facilitate the growth of the church in maturity and Christ-likeness through raising the standards of biblical preaching and teaching.*

Our vision is to see churches in the Majority World equipped for mission and growing to maturity in Christ through the ministry of pastors and leaders who believe, teach and live by the word of God.

Our mission is to strengthen the ministry of the word of God through:
- nurturing national movements for biblical preaching
- fostering the creation and distribution of evangelical literature
- enhancing evangelical theological education

especially in countries where churches are under-resourced.

Our ministry

Langham Preaching partners with national leaders to nurture indigenous biblical preaching movements for pastors and lay preachers all around the world. With the support of a team of trainers from many countries, a multi-level programme of seminars provides practical training, and is followed by a programme for training local facilitators. Local preachers' groups and national and regional networks ensure continuity and ongoing development, seeking to build vigorous movements committed to Bible exposition.

Langham Literature provides Majority World preachers, scholars and seminary libraries with evangelical books and electronic resources through publishing and distribution, grants and discounts. The programme also fosters the creation of indigenous evangelical books in many languages, through writer's grants, strengthening local evangelical publishing houses, and investment in major regional literature projects, such as one volume Bible commentaries like the Africa Bible Commentary and the South Asia Bible Commentary.

Langham Scholars provides financial support for evangelical doctoral students from the Majority World so that, when they return home, they may train pastors and other Christian leaders with sound, biblical and theological teaching. This programme equips those who equip others. Langham Scholars also works in partnership with Majority World seminaries in strengthening evangelical theological education. A growing number of Langham Scholars study in high quality doctoral programmes in the Majority World itself. As well as teaching the next generation of pastors, graduated Langham Scholars exercise significant influence through their writing and leadership.

To learn more about Langham Partnership and the work we do visit langham.org